AVAILABILITY OF CREDIT AND SECURED TRANSACTIONS IN A TIME OF CRISIS

In light of the financial crisis, it has become clear that the globalization of financial markets has not been matched by the globalization of legal certainty relating to financial transactions. The ability to give security influences not only the cost of credit but also, in some cases, whether credit will be available at all. Increasing the availability and lowering the cost of credit can make important contributions to international and domestic economic development. Assessing the international challenges posed by inefficient secured credit laws, this book explores how these can be overcome to facilitate credit through legal reforms. Leading authorities in the field address the key issues surrounding the availability of credit; the role of banks in economic development and financial crises; UNCITRAL's legislative efforts, and international organizations and financial institutions and their involvement in the reform of secured transactions law.

N. Orkun Akseli is Senior Lecturer in Commercial Law at Durham University Law School, where he teaches Company Law, Commercial Law, International Banking Law and International Commercial Dispute Resolution.

AVAILABILITY OF CREDIT AND SECURED TRANSACTIONS IN A TIME OF CRISIS

Edited by

N. ORKUN AKSELI

CAMBRIDGE
UNIVERSITY PRESS

CAMBRIDGE
UNIVERSITY PRESS

University Printing House, Cambridge CB2 8BS, United Kingdom

Published in the United States of America by Cambridge University Press, New York

Cambridge University Press is part of the University of Cambridge.

It furthers the University's mission by disseminating knowledge in the pursuit of education, learning and research at the highest international levels of excellence.

www.cambridge.org
Information on this title: www.cambridge.org/9781107027442

First published 2013

A catalogue record for this publication is available from the British Library

Library of Congress Cataloguing in Publication data
Availability of credit and secured transactions in a time of crisis / edited by N. Orkun Akseli.
pages cm
Includes bibliographical references and index.
ISBN 978-1-107-02744-2 (hardback)
1. Security (Law) 2. Credit – Law and legislation. 3. Financial crises. I. Akseli, N. Orkun (Nazmi Orkun) editor of compilation.
K1100.A97 2013
346.07′4 – dc23 2013017434

ISBN 978-1-107-02744-2 Hardback

This collection is dedicated to my parents and family

CONTENTS

CONTRIBUTORS

N. Orkun Akseli is Senior Lecturer in Commercial Law at Durham University Law School, UK.

Spyridon V. Bazinas is Senior Legal Officer and the Secretary of Working Group VI (Security Interests) at the International Trade Law Division of the Office of Legal Affairs, UNCITRAL Secretariat, Vienna, Austria.

Hugh Beale QC is Professor of Law at the University of Warwick and Visiting Professor at the University of Amsterdam and the University of Oxford.

David Bholat is Visiting Scholar at Newcastle University, UK.

Frederique Dahan is Lead Counsel and Head of the Financial Law Unit in the Legal Transition Team of the European Bank for Reconstruction and Development (EBRD).

Henry Deeb Gabriel is Professor of Law at Elon University Law School, North Carolina and an elected member of the Governing Council of the International Institute for the Unification of Private Law (Unidroit).

Roy Goode QC is Emeritus Professor of Law and Fellow of St John's College, Oxford University and the Director of the Secured Transactions Law Reform Project.

Joanna Gray is Professor of Financial Regulation at Newcastle University Law School, UK.

TERENCE C. HALLIDAY is Co-Director, Center on Law and Globalization, American Bar Foundation and University of Illinois College of Law; Research Professor, American Bar Foundation; Adjunct Professor of Sociology, Northwestern University; Adjunct Professor, School of Regulation, Justice and Diplomacy, Australian National University.

GERARD MCCORMACK is Professor of International Business Law at the University of Leeds, UK.

NOEL MCGRATH is Lecturer at the University College Dublin School of Law.

LOUKAS MISTELIS is Clive M. Schmitthoff Professor of Transnational Commercial Law and Arbitration at Queen Mary University of London Centre for Commercial Law Studies.

ANJANETTE H. RAYMOND is Assistant Professor of Business Law and Ethics at the Kelley School of Business at the University of Indiana in Bloomington.

FOREWORD

ROY GOODE

Many studies conducted by the World Bank over a number of years have demonstrated that developing countries whose laws do not permit non-possessory security in movable property face a serious impediment to economic development. Several organizations, among them the World Bank itself, the European Bank for Reconstruction and Development, the United Nations Commission on International Trade Law (UNCITRAL) and the International Institute for the Unification of Private Law (Unidroit), have sought to encourage the enactment of secured transactions laws which will encourage banks and other financiers to extend credit and thereby promote economic growth.

This collection of essays has as its primary purpose an evaluation of the *Guide on Secured Transactions* published by the United Nations Commission on International Trade Law. UNCITRAL has several important instruments to its credit, including its 1985 Model Law on International Commercial Arbitration and its 1997 Model Law on Cross-Border Insolvency, both of which have been highly influential. Disappointing so far has been the response to its 2001 Convention on the assignment of receivables in international trade, which, after 11 years, has secured only a single ratification. Possible explanations are offered in this volume. The great advantage of the Guide is that it is soft law, available as a tool for countries planning to modernize their personal property security law but requiring no ratification and posing no threat to national laws. The Guide is an impressive work, organized under the direction of Spyridon Bazinas, Senior Legal Officer of UNCITRAL, and deserves close examination. In these essays it has been criticized as heavily influenced by Article 9 of the American Uniform Commercial Code and defended on the ground that if this is the case, it may be because the ideas embodied in Article 9 represent the best approach to secured transactions law. Whatever view one has on this debate, it is undoubtedly the case that American lawyers take their commercial law seriously, mould it to produce solutions to practical issues and invest a huge amount of time and resources to produce the instruments required. One also should not overlook the fact that Article 9 and equivalent Personal Property Security Acts have now been enacted in well over seventy States in several different countries, two at least of which are outside the US hegemony. It would therefore be surprising if the ideas embodied in Article 9 did not feature significantly in the Guide. On the other hand, as was demonstrated in work leading to the Cape Town Convention on International Interests in Mobile Equipment and its associated Protocols, civil law and other systems have much to bring to the table, including intellectual rigour, the elegance of civil code drafting and an awareness of the need to provide due safeguards for debtors and certain other restrictions on freedom of contract in the broader interest of society.

This collection of essays, skilfully edited and introduced by Orkun Akseli, brings together a number of leading experts from different countries and in different fields to examine the role of credit generally and secured lending in particular, as well as the role of international organizations in setting and promoting international standards in this field. The view that bank credit is an unqualified good is rightly subjected to critical scrutiny. Moreover, as many commentators have pointed out, the reform of security law to open up access to credit, though a necessary condition of economic growth, will not be effective unless underpinned by adequate bank regulation and an independent and efficient judicial system. Other contributors have noted the value of plurality of legal approaches and the importance of offering legal regimes which have due regard to a country's culture, traditions and state of development. This volume provides new insights into what is a complex and controversial field of law and policy at both national and at international level. It is to be warmly welcomed.

Roy Goode
Oxford
14 March 2013

ACKNOWLEDGEMENTS

This collection, and the conference from which it emanates, would not have been possible without the generous support it has received from the World Bank and the *Modern Law Review* Seminar Funds. I am grateful to both of these institutions for their financial support. I am indebted to all those who held papers, chaired sessions and made contributions to the conference and to this volume, who have shown great patience with the project as it has progressed, in particular, to Spyridon V. Bazinas (UNCITRAL), Professor Hugh Beale QC (Warwick), Dr. David Bholat (Newcastle), Dr. Frederique Dahan (EBRD), Professor Henry Gabriel (Elon), Professor Sir Roy Goode QC (Oxford), Professor Joanna Gray (Newcastle), Professor Terence C. Halliday (American Bar Foundation), Professor Gerard McCormack (Leeds), Dr. Noel McGrath (Dublin), Professor Loukas Mistelis (CCLS, Queen Mary London), Professor Riz Mokal (the World Bank), Anjanette H. Raymond (Indiana) and Harry Sigman (California). Cambridge University Press staff has provided crucial support. I would like particularly to thank Kim Hughes, Richard Woodham, Samantha Richter and Fleur Jones for their patience, ongoing support and efficient management of the production process.

Introduction

N. ORKUN AKSELI

This collection of essays emanates from a conference – *International Legal Standards on Secured Transactions, Facilitation of Credit and Financial Crisis* – sponsored by the World Bank, funded by the *Modern Law Review* Seminar Funds and hosted by Newcastle University Law School in May 2010. That conference addressed the challenges posed by inefficient secured credit laws and explored the avenues to overcome these difficulties by examining the international legal standards set by international financial institutions and international legislative bodies.[1]

This collection, along the same lines, assesses the challenges posed by inefficient secured credit laws by looking at how challenges can be overcome to facilitate credit through legal reforms based on international standards set by international legislative bodies and financial institutions in the light of the financial crisis. The collection focuses particularly on the legislative texts prepared by the United Nations Commission on International Trade (UNCITRAL), and harmonization and modernization initiatives by the World Bank and the European Bank for Reconstruction and Development (EBRD). The collection deals with key issues such as the availability of credit, international financial institutions and their involvement in secured transactions law reform, utility and efficacy of the UNCITRAL's legislative efforts, and the extent to which these international standards set by international standard-setting bodies and financial institutions may be used to help reform the law of credit and security.

Since the early 1970s, an increasing variety of international conventions and instruments on secured transactions law have been produced by international legislative and financial organizations. The general aim of these instruments has been to modernize the law of secured credit with

[1] In particular, the UN Convention on the Assignment of Receivables in International Trade; UNCITRAL *Legislative Guide on Secured Transactions.*

the assumption that harmonized modernization of the law of secured credit lowers the cost of credit. In that context, these instruments aim to assist both developing and developed economies in reforming their laws. The law of secured transactions has remained within the boundaries of domestic law with close links to the law of property, contracts and insolvency, where the law represents cultural stance and public policy preferences that vary among States. These factors are coupled with different economic or political expectations, competition among legal systems, the tensions inherent in international law making[2] and the scepticism of legal practitioners towards new rules and adapting to them. For years, all of these factors have prevented a meaningful secured transactions law reform that could have successfully accompanied the globalization of financial markets. In terms of international instruments on secured transactions law, certain arguments have been put forward that some of these instruments have been influenced by a particular legal system.[3] While this argument may have some theoretical support, it is clear that many of the principles of international instruments on secured transactions have been implemented in national laws and derive from these laws and not from a particular system. This has been done in two ways. First, States directly implemented principles of the international texts in their domestic law; and second, States that have implemented a secured transactions law that is consistent with the recommendations of, for example, the UNCITRAL Secured Transactions Legislative Guide, have essentially implemented the principles of the Receivables Convention in their domestic law.[4]

It needs to be understood that law is 'a vehicle for social change'.[5] At a time when a country's social fabric, economic and financial strength are changing due to the global financial crisis and ensuing credit crunch, it is crucial to modernize the law of secured credit and respond to the needs of businesses. That can be achieved either by taking international

[2] *See* R. Goode, 'Rule, Practice, and Pragmatism in Transnational Commercial Law' 54 *ICLQ* 539 (2005).

[3] *See e.g.* G. McCormack, *Secured Credit and the Harmonisation of Law: The UNCITRAL Experience* (Cheltenham: Edward Elgar, 2011).

[4] For more discussion on this matter *see below* G. McCormack 'Secured Transactions Law Reform, UNCITRAL, and the export of foreign legal models'; S.V. Bazinas 'The utility and efficacy of the UNCITRAL Legislative Guide on Secured Transactions' and N.O. Akseli 'The utility and efficacy of the UN Convention on the Assignment of Receivables and the Facilitation of Credit', Chapters 2, 8 and 9, respectively, below.

[5] R. Wacks, *Philosophy of Law: A Very Short Introduction* (Oxford University Press, 2006), p. xii.

instruments as an example, adapting their rules according to the needs of domestic law and legal tradition, or looking at other comparator jurisdictions and taking example from their experiences. This is obviously not something that can be done overnight. It can only be achieved with a clear remit, inclusion of all interested parties and on an incremental basis. If the law responds to the needs of businesses, this will not only be significant for the economic growth of a country, but also indicative of the fact that the country's law is regarded as an influential example or suitable for exportability to overseas law reform activities.[6]

The ability to give security influences not only the cost of credit but also, in some cases, whether credit will be available at all. The difficulties posed by inefficient secured credit laws are felt acutely in both advanced and emerging economies as a result of financial crisis. Businesses have expectations from the law[7] and the State has a responsibility to establish a financial and legal framework which understands the barriers to access to finance, and either addresses those barriers or enables businesses to negotiate them. In emerging or developing markets, unpredictable and poor secured credit laws deter international financial organizations and banks from extending credit and investing in those countries. In developed markets, inefficient secured transactions laws hinder further economic growth. Arguably, increasing the availability of credit and lowering its cost contributes to international and domestic economic development. It is believed that international instruments on secured transactions law aim to provide predictability and modernized rules which will have a positive impact on the availability and cost of credit and can be influential and taken as helpful examples in the domestic law reform activities. International standards set by international legislative bodies and financial organizations have the necessary merit to achieve this.

The collection encompasses essays from a broad range of perspectives in order to contextualize the availability of credit and secured transactions law reform: from the role of banks in economic development and financial crises (Bholat); from the facilitation of credit and political and policy

[6] For similar lines of argument, *see* R. Goode, 'Insularity or Leadership? The Role of the United Kingdom in the Harmonization of Commercial Law' 50 *ICLQ* 751 (2001).

[7] *See* 'Secured Transactions Law: The Case for Reform' available at http://securedtransactionsproject.wordpress.com/case-for-reform/ (last accessed 12 January 2013). It is submitted that the Secured Transactions Law Reform Project is an excellent platform to discuss the inefficiencies of secured transactions law and unpick the shortcomings of the current secured transactions law in England, and a basis to reform the law incrementally in a way that responds to the needs of businesses in the twenty-first century.

perspectives (McCormack); from the position of international financial institutions (Bazinas and Dahan); from the involvement of international organizations and the impact of this on the law and the market (Halliday); from UNCITRAL's legislative texts (Bazinas and Akseli); and from the domestic perspective of the secured transactions law reform in England (Raymond). The volume's conclusions present a clear view of the efficacy and utility of international legal standards and their impact on making the credit available and secured transactions law reform in a time of crisis (Beale). The comments under each part (Gray, Mistelis, Gabriel and McGrath) reflect critical perspectives.

Part I of the collection focuses on the availability of credit, challenges in access to credit, and the problems in harmonizing and reforming the law by adopting a specific model. Taking the role of banks in economic development and financial crises with particular reference to their loan portfolio in Britain in the period leading up to and following the Great Recession as the starting point for his analysis, David Bholat, in his chapter 'Money, bank debt, and business cycles: between economic development and financial crises', looks at the role conventionally attributed to banks in economic theory and history. Bholat focuses particularly on Joseph Schumpeter, who draws a distinction between economic growth and economic development on the basis of the presence or absence of banking. He then presents a more sceptical story based on Friedrich Hayek's theory, which tends to depict banks as uniquely problematic institutions in the making of financial crises. Finally, Bholat offers some UK data on the behaviour of banks leading up to and following the current crisis. In particular, the relative growth in net lending secured on real estate, among other evidence, casts doubt on their role in economic development, indicating instead their centrality to what has been described as 'financialization'. In his chapter, 'Secured transactions law reform, UNCITRAL and the export of foreign legal models', Gerard McCormack, develops his earlier argument that modernization does not equal a liberalization agenda and subjects it to greater scrutiny. In this novel treatment, McCormack analyses the effects of recognizing security rights. He criticizes the harmonization of the law of secured credit, particularly in the 'liberal' American-nuanced way that the UNCITRAL Guide seeks to do. He then considers why 'liberal' secured credit regimes are considered to be beneficial. Moreover, McCormack addresses in greater detail critical perspectives on the international harmonization and modernization agenda. He concludes against the secured transactions reform in the American-oriented manner that the Guide seeks to effect. Joanna Gray, in her contribution in

Part I of the collection, stresses the interplay between the ability to create security, increased financialization and the banking crisis of 2008.

Part II of the collection considers the role and interest of international financial institutions and international organizations in setting standards on secured transactions for robust financial systems in emerging economies and credit facilitation. In his chapter, 'International organizations as global lawmakers: seven shifts in practice for secured transactions law and beyond', Terence Halliday undertakes an in-depth analysis of the impact of law on the market by questioning why international organizations produce standards. Halliday analyses four theories (professional, ecological, realist and idealist) in responding to why international organizations and financial institutions develop standards. He then develops his argument into how and whether they should produce standards and suggests seven shifts in international organizations' orientation and practices. These include comparing private international financial institution lawmaking to public international organizations' lawmaking, naive developmentalism to contingent developmentalism, unexamined theories to tested theories, arbitrary exemplars to alternative models, narrow disciplinarity to broad inter-disciplinarity, globalized localisms to normative options, static norms to recursivity. In his initial chapter, 'The creation of international commercial law standards by international financial institutions: why they do it and whether they should', Spyridon Bazinas discusses the examples of overlap between international legislative bodies and the international financial institutions in producing international legal standards on secured transactions law. Bazinas suggests that international financial institutions should coordinate their efforts with international legislative bodies to continue their economic development mandate and could focus on the economic analysis of law to achieve an efficient law reform. Frederique Dahan, in her chapter, 'The power of secured transactions law and the challenge of its reform', analyses the philosophy that the EBRD, as an international financial institution, has applied in its work in the field of secured transactions reform. Dahan states that this philosophy is based on two important elements in secured transactions law and law reform: the facilitative objective of the secured transactions law should be made legally efficient, and secured transactions law is versatile and the law reform should embrace that versatility. She maps out the EBRD's work in reducing the credit risk in a legally efficient manner by analysing the Core Principles for secured transactions law. The chapter then progresses to the EBRD's recognition of secured transactions' versatility. Dahan concludes that the secured transactions law reform will continue, and that in this process the EBRD's legal efficiency criteria in law reform will be a useful device. In his chapter, 'Commentary on the involvement of international financial institutions in secured transactions law reform', for effective law reform, Loukas Mistelis suggests a stronger cooperation between international financial institutions and international legislative bodies.

Part III of the collection considers the UNCITRAL *Legislative Guide on Secured Transactions* and the UN Convention on the Assignment of Receivables in International Trade. These two texts and their general principles provide a valuable tool for legislators in their law reform efforts. Spyridon Bazinas in his chapter, 'The utility and efficacy of the UNCITRAL *Legislative Guide on Secured Transactions*', analyses, in great depth, the effectiveness of the UNCITRAL *Legislative Guide on Secured Transactions* ('the Guide') in reducing the cost of credit. The chapter systematically looks at the key policy issues of the Guide in addition to the soft law approach adopted by it. Bazinas concludes by responding in detail to the critique of the Guide. In his chapter, 'The utility and efficacy of the UN Convention on the Assignment of Receivables and the Facilitation of Credit', Orkun Akseli discusses the general principles of the UN Convention on the Assignment of Receivables. Akseli's argument is that modern rules that efficiently endorse receivables financing are critical in reducing the cost of credit and have the potential to increase cash flow and further investment in the face of financial crisis. These rules may be used as a starting point in domestic law reform activities. Henry Gabriel, in his chapter, focuses on the soft law nature of the Guide and on the factors that make the Receivables Convention less successful than expected.

Part IV of the collection focuses on whether and the extent to which international standards set by international standard-setting bodies and financial organizations may be used to help reform the law of credit and security. The particular significance of this theme is that with the collapse and quasi-nationalization of banks in the UK, apart from a reform in banking regulation, it is necessary to achieve the reform of the law of credit and security to facilitate access to credit. In her chapter, 'How may international standards assist law reform in England?', Anjanette Raymond provides an analysis as to why there is a need for reform in secured transactions law in England. She considers law reform efforts in England and the ultimate failure of the reforming initiative. Her chapter finally suggests modernization of English personal property security law. Noel McGrath, in his chapter, 'Commentary on the international standards and the reform of English personal property securities law', provides a different perspective in terms of domestic law reform. McGrath comments that law reform in secured transactions law may be achieved by incremental changes.

Hugh Beale, in his concluding chapter, 'The UNCITRAL *Legislative Guide on Secured Transactions* as a model for law reform: some conclusions', presents the case for a secured transactions law system that could work more efficiently.

PART I

Availability of credit

1

Money, bank debt and business cycles: between economic development and financial crises

DAVID BHOLAT

Mistakes happen. These include errors in undertaking economic enterprise. In an advanced market economy, the space and time between the input of factors of production and the consumption of outputs is wide. Thus, commerce in the present unfolds over hazardous and high stakes horizons, reflecting the fact that future wants cannot be known with certainty. To some extent, the capriciousness of consumer demand is the by-product of advanced advertisement techniques which constantly create new needs.[1] But more fundamentally, the dynamic nature of consumption reflects the non-linear development of the self as such – changes over the course of life in what individuals want and need – which we ourselves are not always able to anticipate until it is encountered or revised by 'stimulus and suggestion'.[2] Given the time inconsistency of even our self, any enterprise in an advanced market economy carries uncertainty that prospective profits have been miscalculated, such that expenditures end up exceeding revenue.[3] The eternal economizing dilemma – what to produce and when, given scarce resources and budget constraints – is therefore rooted in the still more fundamental existential question 'What is to be done? How ought we to live?' we continually refine, but never resolve.[4] Given these realities, financial loss for some firms and the families they support are intractable outcomes in a dynamic commercial economy.

However, when market miscalculations are clustered in space and time, suspicion rightly arises that this correlation may have a common cause. When, in addition, these clusters are cyclical, their repeated experience elicits the need for theory to explain them. While cycles are common in

[1] T. Veblen, *Theory of the Modern Business Enterprise* (New York: Camino Classics, 2005).

[2] F. Knight, *Ethics of Competition* (Piscataway, NJ: Transaction Publishers, 1997), p. 42.

[3] F. Knight, *Risk, Uncertainty, and Profit* (Charleston, SC: Nabu Press, 2010).

[4] L. Tolstoy, *What Is To Be Done?* (Rockville, MD: Wildside Press, 2007).

nature, they are cause for despair in human history. This is so because cycles signify not simply repetition, but regression.[5] The more times human history repeats itself – mistakes assuming cyclical form – the more intractable and ossified problems become. Hence 'cycles', full stop, are not explanations for economic crises, but rather, indicate a problem requiring further intellectual investigation.

Although each business cycle is unique and has diverse sources, we should suspect that the main culprit in amplifying economic errors is an institution whose scale and scope is as broad and as deep as the miscalculations themselves. In modern economies, the institution that best fits this description is money. Money functions as the unit of account according to which the price of goods and services are reckoned, the standard by which profits and losses are measured, and the medium of exchange which activates production and enables consumption. Intuitively then, a general theory of economic errors should make reference to money and, by extension, institutions such as the banking system whose debts help constitute it. Indeed, a financial crisis might be best defined as an episode which casts doubt on the monetary system, thus threatening the means of payment which the market economy presupposes in order to function at all.[6]

Yet the simple proposition that money matters is more controversial than might be suspected. Neither New Keynesianism nor neo-Classical economics – the orthodox paradigms in economics from the mid-1980s up until the present – attributed much significance to measures of money before the current crisis.[7] As ex-Federal Reserve Governor Larry Meyer has pointed out, 'money plays no explicit role in today's consensus macro model, and it plays virtually no role in the conduct of monetary policy'.[8]

A conversation I had with a finance academic at Oxford University in 2006 is indicative. When I voiced alarm that the Federal Reserve had

5 G. Hegel, *The Philosophy of History*, John Silbree (trans.) (Mineola, NY: Dover Publications, 2004), p. 54.

6 F. Capie, October 2011, 'British Financial Crises in the Nineteenth and Twentieth Centuries', paper presented at Oxford University; L. Telser, 'Securing the Means of Payment: The Ultimate Requisite of a Modern Economy', *The Economists' Voice* 5.3 (2008); K. Hart, 'The Financial Crisis and the End of All Purpose Money,' *Economic Sociology European Electronic Newsletter* 12.2 (2011), pp. 4–10.

7 T. Congdon, *Money in a Free Society: Keynes, Friedman, and the New Crisis in Capitalism* (New York: Encounter Books, 2011), pp. xxiii–xxviii.

8 C. Goodhart, February 2007, 'Whatever Became of the Monetary Aggregates?', *LSE Financial Markets Group Paper Series Special Paper* 172, pp. 2–3.

ceased publication of the M3 monetary aggregate at a time when broad money was expanding relative to Gross Domestic Product (GDP), my concerns were dismissed by the counterargument that monetary growth was a sign of economic prosperity akin to an expansion in the volume of commodities produced by the real economy.

Note that the contemporary neglect of the special economic significance of money is a stark alteration in theoretical fashions from the 1970s and 1980s, when Milton Friedman and Monetarism dominated the discipline. Monetarism's conceptual calling card was a sophisticated version of the quantity theory of money, in which changes in the money stock were interpreted as leading indicators of nominal income, price inflation and overall economic activity.[9] But by the mid-1980s, Monetarism had lost currency, so to speak. Monetarists lacked clear consensus about which monetary aggregates to target because of the vulnerability of such aggregates to institutional innovations (in the 1980s, for instance, the spread of instantly cashable 'savings accounts'). Moreover, critics noted the poor correlation between monetary growth and short-term economic fluctuations because the velocity of money – the speed at which £1 circulates in the economy – muddles a one-to-one relation between the quantity of money and price. In addition, critics expressed concerns about reverse causality, since independent increases in aggregate demand and prices might stimulate bank lending and thus monetary growth.[10] Taken together, the cumulative consequence of these critiques was to shift macroeconomics away from analysis of the volume and velocity of monetary aggregates to interest rates and output gaps as the key intermediate operational targets for monetary policy.[11]

Although the proximate factor for the relative neglect of money by many modern macroeconomists stems from the perceived failures of Monetarism in the early 1980s, economic incredulity towards the real economic significance of money goes back much further. In fact, such scepticism is found at the very origins of economics, when the field in its modern form appeared in opposition to the Mercantilist conflation of metallic money with wealth. Hence, Adam Smith pejoratively referred to money as 'dead stock', in contrast to fixed capital investments, which

[9] M. Friedman, *Money Mischief: Episodes in Monetary History* (Orlando, FL: Mariners Books, 1994).

[10] W. Greider, *Secrets of the Temple: How the Federal Reserve Runs the Country* (New York: Touchstone, 1989); N. Kaldor, 'How Monetarism Failed', *Challenge* 28.2 (1985).

[11] Congdon, *Money in a Free Society.*

he viewed as the source of 'real wealth'.[12] In some respects, assumptions built into the models used by current economists embody their founding fathers' attitude about the properly subordinate role money should play in the economy. Yet this normative commitment, when not understood as such, can blind analysts to the powerful role of wealth effects and monetary illusions in the real world. However much we may sympathize with Hume's postulate that 'money is not, properly speaking one of the subjects of commerce but only the instrument which men have agreed upon to facilitate the exchange of one commodity for another', such a perspective is anachronistic in a world where money is itself the most heavily traded commodity via foreign exchange (forex) markets.[13]

The minor role for money in modern macroeconomics explains why the predominant focus of the field is on pathways from real economic instability to banking crises, rather than the reverse.[14] Although details vary, the sequence in most models starts from the proposition that worsening economic conditions impair the net worth of borrowers and/or the worth of their collateral, causing banks to make fewer loans and/or lend at higher rates, which in turn causes contractions in demand and still worse economic conditions.[15] Note, however, that the adverse shocks starting this sequence are presupposed rather than explained. Moreover, they are implicitly exogenous of the financial sector. While banks and other financial institutions are positioned in these models as amplifying business cycles, they are not identified as their primary cause.[16]

The premise of this chapter is that this perspective on the relationship between the real economy and money is inadequate for explaining recent events. For example, in spite of concerns about rising loan-to-value and loan-to-income ratios in the housing market, the number of mortgage arrears as a percentage of all loans, and their financial value, is smaller in

12 A. Smith, *An Inquiry into the Nature and Causes of the Wealth of Nations*, 2 vols. (University of Chicago Press, 1976), vol. 1, p. 309.

13 D. Hume, 'Of Money', *Writings on Economics*, Eugene Rotwein (ed.) (University of Wisconsin Press, 1970), p. 33.

14 A recent exception is M. Schularick and A. Taylor, 'Credit Booms Gone Bust: Monetary Policy, Leverage, Cycles and Financial Crises, 1870–2008', *Centre for Economic Policy Research Discussion Paper Series* 7570 (July 2011).

15 B. Bernanke and M. Gertler, 'Agency costs, net worth, and business fluctuations', *American Economic Review* 79.1 14–31 (1989).

16 A recent survey of the literature on the links between the real economy and the financial sector is Basel Committee on Banking Supervision, 'The Transmission Channels between the Financial and Real Sectors: A Critical Survey of the Literature', *BIS Working Paper* 18 (February 2011).

the UK today than comparative figures during the 1990s recession. Thus, the recent economic crisis in the UK does not appear to have been caused by domestic insolvency shocks external to the banking sector. Rather, the crisis in the UK appears to have started with liquidity disturbances internal to the global banking system, which then spilled over into the real economy, with subsequent negative impacts on employment, output and the credit rating of sovereign bonds. Recent events, therefore, call for recovery and renewal of an older economic tradition which treated money and banks as fundamental to the explanation of business cycles.[17] Although crises, like consumers, are adaptive and dynamic, major global downturns are not stochastic 'black swan' shocks, but patterned events correlated with banking crises, with the sector featuring prominently in both the Great Depression and the ongoing Great Recession.[18] While economic errors may not always and everywhere be a monetary phenomenon, the role of money and banks warrants more scrutiny than they have been given in recent years by macroeconomists.

The remit of this chapter is therefore to critically review other, older frameworks for understanding the relationship between the availability of bank credit, and economic development and crises. In the process of re-presenting these frameworks, the chapter also clarifies key conceptual terms presumed by this edited volume, such as 'money', 'banking', and 'economic development'. Observe that I forsake any claim that this chapter's explanation of these concepts corresponds to how other contributors use and understand these terms. Indeed, my premise is that because these terms are now so pervasive and plural, they have lost their precision. Given current economic conditions, a more systematic reflection on them seems in order.

The chapter unfolds as follows. It first considers what distinguishes banking from other financial institutions. The key point made is that banks gain their socio-structural significance in the UK economic system because their liabilities (namely, sight deposits) function as money.[19] In elaborating this point, I return to the insights of Joseph Schumpeter, who

17 A good survey of this literature is offered by J. Toporowski, *Theories of Financial Disturbances: An Examination of Critical Theories of Finance from Adam Smith to the Present Day* (Cheltenham: Edward Elgar Press, 2005).

18 S. Keen, *Debunking Economics: The Naked Emperor Dethroned?* (London: Zed Books, 2011), p. xi.

19 *cf.* J. Tobin, 'Commercial banks as creators of "money" ', in *Banking and Monetary Studies*, D. Carson (ed.) (Homewood, Ill.: Richard Irwin Incorporated, 1963); C. Goodhart, *The Evolution of Central Books* (Cambridge, MA: MIT Press, 1988).

is among the most famous economists to have argued that the banking system's money-making capacity makes them more important than capital markets in generating economic growth. At the same time, this capacity renders banks structurally brittle, with leverage threatening their solvency, and the peculiar legal liability of sight deposits making them ripe for runs.

The precarious funding structure of banks poses risks not only for themselves, but also potentially to the economic system as a whole. The third section of this chapter then explores the possible systemic risk banks can pose, by returning to Friedrich Hayek's argument that the practice of maturity transformation, i.e. 'borrowing short and lending long', can induce investment incompatible with consumer preferences. Hayek's argument is particularly insightful because it encourages us to think about the effects of money not only on general price inflation, but also on the specific kinds of commodities produced by the real economy and the distributional consequences of asymmetric access to additional purchasing power enabled by banks' debt issuing.

Thus, Schumpeter and Hayek have been chosen for comparison not simply because they were coincidentally both Austrian, but more justifiably because they give different emphasis to the benefits and costs of banks in modern market economies. The chapter is preliminary. It does not seek to take sides. Instead it aims to critically assess both positions, and to do so in light of recent events. Finally, the chapter concludes by speculating on the future to which the present is leading. Although a short-term contraction in the quantity of available credit is the most obvious consequence of recent events, a qualitative expansion in the same period of objects posted to secure lending demonstrates the resilience of capitalism rather than its crisis.

I. Lending on leverage

The trouble much economics has with incorporating money into models is illustrated by the difficulty it has with offering an adequate explanation for its existence. Most models begin by positing a 'cash-in-advance constraint', portraying money as a useful media of exchange developed to solve coordination problems caused by the absence of a double coincidence of wants, which allegedly hampers barter economies.[20] In other words, much economics takes a transaction cost approach to

[20] G. Ingham, *The Nature of Money* (Cambridge: Polity Press, 2004), p. 17; *cf.* N. Kiyotaki and R. Wright, 'On Money as a Medium of Exchange', *Journal of Political Economy* 97 (1989), 927–54.

explaining money, seeking to ground its origins in the past on the basis of the present benefits it confers. However, the problem with this functionalist explanation is that it does not correspond to historical facts. As anthropologist Caroline Humphrey has pointed out, 'No example of a barter economy, pure and simple, has ever been described let alone the emergence from it of money'.[21] Instead, most objects which later developed into mediums of exchange emerged outside of the market, as artefacts in religious ceremonies or recompense initially pertaining to legal proceedings.[22]

The transaction cost approach for explaining the existence of banking is similarly unsatisfying. According to this approach, banks reduce search costs by substituting ad hoc arrangements with a permanent channel to connect savers and borrowers; lower bargaining costs because they make use of standardized agreements; and reduce enforcement costs by acquiring specialized expertise in monitoring loans, collecting information which allows them to distinguish good from bad borrowers with greater acuity than non-experts.[23] Note that the transaction cost advantages ascribed to banks can be attributed to financial intermediaries more generally.[24] Categorical commensuration has been catalyzed by institutional developments propitious to it, namely, the advent of the universal banking model in Britain. Since trading profits and financial advisory fees now constitute the primary source of operating income for the sector, the specific practice of banking – accepting deposits and making loans – might seem of secondary importance. Indeed, before the financial crisis, many academics emphasized capital markets at the expense of banking, because of the growing significance of securities over loans as direct sources of external finance for large firms.[25] Indeed, one often detects a tacit teleology in the economic literature that banks are financial organizations specially suited to 'backward' countries, which give way to capital markets in more 'advanced' ones.[26]

21 Quoted in D. Graeber, *Debt: The First 5,000 Years* (Brooklyn, NY: Melville House, 2011), p. 29.

22 P. Grierson, 'The Origins of Money', *Research in Economic Anthropology* 1 1–35 (1978).

23 F. Mishkin, 'Assymetric Information and Financial Crises: A Historical Perspective', in *Financial Markets and Financial Crises*, R. Glenn Hubbard (ed.) (University of Chicago Press, 1991), pp. 69–108, pp. 73–4.

24 F. Mishkin, *The Economics of Money, Banking, and Financial Markets* (8th edn.) (New York: Columbia University Press, 2008), pp. 35–9.

25 S. Sassen, *The Global City: New York, London, Tokyo* (Princeton University Press, 2001), p. 7.

26 A. Gerschenkron, *Economic Backwardness in Historical Perspective* (Cambridge, MA: Harvard University Press, 1962).

Yet it is salient to consider that bank assets as a percentage of GDP have risen in most developed countries over the last thirty years, refuting the view that the economic importance of banks has diminished over time.[27] For example, British banks today hold assets of five-times GDP, compared to the nineteenth century, when they were equal to around 5 per cent.[28] Nevertheless, arguments supporting the intuition that banks are special types of financial institutions need not rest on empirical evidence subject to circumstantial changes, such as whether bank representatives exercise control over directors in corporate boardrooms.[29] Rather, as will be developed, an analytical position which accords primacy to banks can be defended on the structural fact that banks' debt acts as money. Consequently, while equities and bonds intermediate an existing stock of money between borrowers and lenders, the banking system can make new money by issuing debt over and above existing savings.[30] The dynamic, money-making function of the banking system is completely obscured by transaction cost approaches which analogize banks to other forms of finance and foster a reductionist view that bank debt, bonds and equity are simply substitutes for each other.[31]

In order to appreciate this point, it is helpful to have a clear definition of money and banks. Money may be defined as a special form of credit which conventionally acts as a means of final payment. Viewed from the other side of the ledger, money could also be described as a special form of debt, a liability 'not against any specific person but against the entire community, one that is unconditional as to where, when, against what, or whom it may be exercised'.[32] One form of debt which has historically functioned as money in England is sovereign debt, such as tally sticks issued by the Treasury until 1826 as a record of tax liabilities owed to the government or, more recently, paper notes issued by the government's

27 S. Heffernan, *Modern Banking* (Chichester: Wiley and Company), pp. 75–6.

28 Bank of England, 'The Bank of England and Prudential Regulatory Authority: Our Approach to Banking Supervision' (May 2011), available at www.bankofengland.co.uk/publications/other/financialstability/uk_reg_framework/pra_approach.pdf (last accessed 10 January 2013).

29 *See* R. Hilferding, *Finance Capital: A Study of the Latest Phase of Capitalist Development*, Morris Watnick and Sam Gordon (trans.) (London: Routledge, 1981).

30 B. Bossone, 'What Makes Banks Special? A Study of Banking, Finance, and Economic Development', *World Bank Policy Research Paper* 2408 (1999).

31 E. Fama, 'Banking in the Theory of Finance', *Journal of Monetary Economics* 6 39–57 (1980).

32 M. Moini, 'Toward a General Theory of Credit and Money', *Review of Austrian Economics* 14.4 267–317, 301–4 (2001).

bank, the Bank of England, which represented its bona fide debt to pay domestic bearers precious metal until 1914.[33] But sovereign debt is not the only kind of debt which can circulate as a means of payments, i.e. as money. In theory, any debt might become money so long as a community accepts it as such.

In fact, the dominant form of money in the UK today is bank debt. By most estimates, private bank debts constitutes over 97 per cent of the monetary media, conventionally labelled M-4, while government-issued notes and coin account for less than 3 per cent.[34] What has historically enabled bank debt to function as a cash substitute is a unique type of bank liability referred to as sight deposits. Sight deposits are liabilities legally payable to the account holder on demand, at par, without penalty. Banks are therefore special kinds of financial institutions by virtue of the fact that their liabilities act as money. So defined, 'banks' encompass other businesses in the UK such as building societies and credit unions, although, given the relative asset size of nominal banks, the term 'bank' in this chapter refers primarily to this sub-group.[35]

The instantly exercisable option the public holds on sight deposits makes banks vulnerable to liquidity crises, since deposit debt greatly exceeds the physical cash it represents. For instance, at year end 2010, British banks held only around 0.1 per cent of their total assets in cash and coin. The British banking system is therefore more precisely termed a 'fractional-reserve' banking system, because banks hold only a fraction of cash and coin against deposit liabilities, in contrast to 'full reserve' banking systems, where banks act as depositories and fully back them with legal tender.[36] Although banks employ intricate management techniques to deal with liquidity demands, their efficacy may be weakest when needed most, as liquidity crises are characterized by the fact that ordinarily

[33] J. Ryan-Collins, T. Greenham, R. Werner and A. Jackson, *Where does Money come from? A Guide to the UK Monetary and Banking System* (London: New Economics Foundation, 2011).

[34] F. Hutchinson, M. Mellor and W. Olsen, *The Politics of Money: Toward Sustainability and Economic Democracy* (London: Pluto Press, 2002).

[35] The chapter thus excludes so-called Constant Net Asset Value Funds not officially backed by government deposit insurance, but which also offer sight deposits redeemable on par without penalty. P. Tucker, 21 January 2010, 'Shadow Banking, Financial Markets and Financial Stability,' speech to BGC Partner Seminar, London, available at www.bankofengland.co.uk/publications/speeches/2010/speech420.pdf, p. 4 (last accessed 10 January 2013).

[36] R. Phillips, *The Chicago Plan and New Deal Banking Reform* (Armonk, NY: M.E. Sharpe, 1995).

marketable assets are no longer so. In sum, a fundamental structural challenge posed by the existing monetary system is that its dominant currency consists of the nominally fixed liabilities of banks backed by assets that fluctuate in value over time.[37] The fact that most money today is private bank debt means that occasional proposals to 'denationalize money' overlook the reality that this has in part been achieved already.[38] As Joseph Schumpeter once quipped, to claim that money today is 'the creature of the state is as true and as false as to say that the institution of marriage is a creature of law'.[39]

Indeed, Schumpeter remains a treasure trove of insights on the special role played by banks in developed market economies, an issue he discusses at length in his *Theory of Economic Development*. Schumpeter's ambition in that book is to explain why productivity improvements in the modern world 'recur'[40] at rates above rises in population so as to constitute a distinctive growth path he termed 'economic development' – an economy which not only increases its quantitative output, but also perpetually changes the qualitative composition of commodities. As is well known, Schumpeter cast entrepreneurs in the starring role, because their innovative techniques raise productivity, cut costs and lead to the more efficient and differentiated production of commodities. However, less known is the equal emphasis Schumpeter placed on banks in the process of economic development. The significance Schumpeter ascribed to banks can be gleaned from his comment that 'capitalism' is distinguished from other economic systems by 'the additional phenomenon of credit creation – by the practice of financing enterprise by bank credit'.[41] According to Schumpeter, the banker 'makes possible the carrying out of new combinations, authorizes people, in the name of society as it were to form them' because the banker is 'not so much primarily a middleman in the commodity "purchasing power" as a *producer* of this commodity', and for this reason the banker is the very 'ephor of the exchange economy'.[42]

[37] C. Goodhart, *The Central Bank and the Financial System* (London: Macmillan Press, 1995), p. 4.

[38] *See* F. Hayek, *Denationalization of Money* (London: Institute of Economic Affairs, 1978).

[39] J. Schumpeter, *A History of Economic Analysis* (Oxford University Press, 1996), p. 1090.

[40] E.L. Jones, *Growth Recurring: Economic Change in World History* (Ann Arbor: University of Michigan Press, 1988).

[41] J. Schumpeter, *Capitalism, Socialism, Democracy* (New York: Harper Press, 1976), p. 167.

[42] J. Schumpeter, *The Theory of Economic Development: An Inquiry into Profits, Capital, Credit, Interest, and the Business Cycle* (Piscataway, NJ: Transaction Publishers, 1982), p. 74. Emphasis in original.

The spirit of Schumpeter's comments is best appreciated by recalling that when banks make loans and thus create deposits, the bank has increased the availability of credit to the loan recipient without diminishing the 'purchasing power' of other creditors (depositors), who are still able to use their bank deposits as a means of payment. Thus, when a bank extends credit through a loan (a bank asset), it can then open a deposit account for the loan recipient (a bank liability) which inverts the taken-for-granted temporal sequence that savings must precede investment.[43] As Schumpeter appreciated, 'Banks . . . no longer . . . "lend their deposits" or "other people's money" but . . . "create deposits" . . . what the banker does with money cannot be done with any other commodity'.[44]

On the basis of such considerations, Schumpeter argued for an elective affinity between banking and economic development. Since banks multiply the amount of money in circulation, they greatly increase the purchasing power available to budding entrepreneurs, who otherwise would need to finance themselves from a smaller pool of savings. While the immediate impact of bank lending may be price inflation, as entrepreneurs use new 'purchasing power' to bid up factors of production (land and labour), Schumpeter argued that the long-run effect of banks is deflationary. As factors of production are redeployed in more efficient enterprises through the mediation of banks, the quality and quantity of commodities increase, costs and prices fall, and loans are repaid.[45]

The actual historical evidence with respect to the role played by banks in economic development is mixed.[46] For example, economic growth during the British Industrial Revolution was primarily financed from firms' retained earnings rather than bank lending.[47] In the nineteenth century,

[43] V. Chick, 'The Evolution of the Banking System and the Theory of Saving, Investment and Interest', *Money, Method, and Keynes: Selected Essays of Victoria Chick*, P. Arestis and S. Dow (eds.) (London: Macmillan, 2009), pp. 79–92.

[44] Schumpeter, *History of Economic Analysis*, p. 320.

[45] Schumpeter, *Theory of Economic Development*, p. 245.

[46] For an excellent overview of the debate, *see* M. Collins, *Banks and Industrial Finance in Britain, 1800–1939* (Cambridge University Press, 1991).

[47] G. Herrigel, 'Corporate Governance', *The Oxford Handbook of Business History*, G. Jones and J. Zeitlin (eds.) (Oxford University Press, 2009), pp. 470–500; A. Chandler, *Scale and Scope: Dynamics of Industrial Capitalism* (Cambridge, MA: Harvard University Press, 1990), especially pp. 235–392. Particularly during the nineteenth century, banks often allocated funds on non-price criteria such as family connections and status. For an excellent regional study exploring this topic, *see* M. Phillips, *A History of Banks, Bankers, & Banking in Northumberland, Durham, and North Yorkshire illustrating the commercial development of the North of England, From 1755 to 1894* (London: Effingham, Wilson, & Company, 1894).

most assets held by the largest British banks were short-dated, foreign bills of exchange, rather than long-term loans to domestic industry.[48] Therefore, while Schumpeter's view of banks as handmaidens of industrial enterprise possessed plausibility within the Continental European context in which he was writing, it appears over-generalized if taken as a necessary feature of banking as such.[49] Indeed, the deflationary view of banks Schumpeter championed is compromised if the main borrowers of 'purchasing power' are buying and consuming existing assets rather than creating new ones. Under these conditions, a tension may develop between two incompatible incentives: a conflict between the public good in having stable monetary growth and price stability, on the one hand, and the profit incentive of private banks to increase the availability of credit, on the other.[50] The recent spread of securitization arguably exacerbated this tension, enabling banks to increase their origination volume without full regard to credit risks, since loans could be sold off-balance sheet to other investors.[51]

In theory, the same capital structure which makes debt important on both sides of bank balance sheets also acts as a limit to its over-issue. Banks are more 'leveraged' than other types of businesses, meaning they finance operations predominantly through debt rather than equity. A high debt-to-equity ratio means banks are particularly prone to insolvency. In 2006, for example, median bank leverage, defined as the ratio between assets and equity, was approximately twenty-five.[52] This meant that only a 4 per cent financial loss could make most British banks insolvent. The recent implementation of mark-to-market accounting should have made banks even more sensitive to possible bankruptcy, since equity capital is

[48] P.L. Cottrell, 'Domestic finance, 1860–1914', *The Cambridge Economic History of Modern Britain Volume II: Economic Maturity, 1860–1939* (Cambridge University Press, 2004).

[49] T. Guinnane, 'Delegated Monitors, Large and Small: Germany's Banking System, 1800–1914', *Journal of Economic Literature* 40.1 73–124 (March 2002); *cf.* C. Fohlin, 'Universal Banking in Pre-World War I Germany: Model or Myth?' *Explorations in Economic History* 36 305–43 (1999).

[50] New Economics Foundation, *Evidence to the Independent Commission on Banking* (2011), p. 3, available at http://bankingcommission.independent.gov.uk/?page_id=11 (last accessed 10 January 2013).

[51] Although, as more acute analyses have revealed, the banking sector remained heavily exposed to securitized products through the holding of their own or other banks' securities, as well as through credit guarantees to special purpose investment vehicles. G. Gorton, 'The Subprime Panic', *National Bureau of Economic Research Working Paper 14398* (2008), pp. 28–9.

[52] Bank of England, *Financial Stability Report* 25 (2009), p. 21.

jeopardized not only by the writing of bad loans, but also sudden and unexpected falls in the market price of trading book assets.[53]

However, in spite of the spectre of insolvency, British banks vastly increased their leverage in the late twentieth century, with particular sharpness in the new millennium. In recent years, leverage in the banking sector was five-times the magnitude of what it was at the close of the nineteenth century.[54] A recent, often-cited factor for the increasing leverage of British banks is that the UK tax code allows corporations to deduct interest paid on debt from bank profits, but does not confer equal treatment for dividends paid on stock.[55] In this vein, it is sometimes noted that recent changes in accounting regimes make it more difficult for banks adequately to make provision against financial losses. Whereas in the past, banks could make general, undefined provisions, adoption of the International and Financial Reporting Standards (IFRS) in 2006 means banks are encouraged to make provisions only according to particular, well-defined asset classes, making financial preparation for 'known unknowns' more difficult.[56] Perhaps as a consequence, provisions as a percentage of total assets declined in the sector during the build-up to the 2007 crisis.

But while the role of tax and accounting rules contributed to increasing leverage, a more central factor seems to have been the 'shareholder value' paradigm which recently dominated managerial conceptions of best practice.[57] One outcome of the predominance of the 'shareholder value' paradigm has been that return on equity (ROE) – the ratio of net income to common equity – has arguably become the most important metric used by investors and management to appraise the performance of banks. Suffice it to recall that at the start of 2007, soon-to-be-doomed Northern Rock was both the most highly leveraged bank and highest

[53] F. Allen and E. Carletti, 'Mark-to-market accounting and liquidity pricing', *Journal of Accounting and Economics* 45 358–78 (2008).

[54] Capie, 'British financial crises in the nineteenth and twentieth centuries'.

[55] D. Shoemaker, 'Removing tax advantages of debt is vital', *Financial Times*, 30 December 2010, available at www.ft.co./cms/s/0/0ab3e042-11eo-814c-00144feabdc0.html #axzz2aGOyjwFs (last accessed 10 January 2013).

[56] ENB Consulting, 'Overview of the Banking Sector', unpublished presentation (4 February 2009).

[57] Bank leverage has also been subsidized by deposit insurance and other State guarantees. Although the exact value of these subsidies is not known, the Independent Commission on Banking believes they exceed £10 billion per year: Independent Commission on Banking, *Final Report* (2011), p. 130.

rated stock in Europe.[58] Set against a legal background of limited liability, where equity holders are fully rewarded for risk but partially insulated from losses,[59] leverage allowed banks to increase their ROE through larger net income earned on a thinning layer of equity.

However, the argument for making shareholders the primary beneficiaries of bank boards' fiduciary duties is debatable, given that only a fraction of bank funding comes from equity.[60] Moreover, the downside to the 'shareholder value' paradigm manifested itself during the financial crisis, when some banks required additional share capital, but refrained from issuing it, for fear of diluting their equity holders' financial interests, which, in any case, aligned with their own, given that bank executives receive a sizable share of their compensation in the form of stock options.[61] Rather than reduce leverage by issuing new equity or by reducing payments to their staff and shareholders, British banks appear to have instead deleveraged by contracting lending. Consequently, although the size of the sector's Central Bank reserves has increased exponentially since 2009, bank lending in the same period has been volatile and sometimes negative, meaning repayments are exceeding new loan flows.

A fundamental interpretive decision is whether to view this contraction in bank lending as an independent or dependent variable. Viewed as an independent variable, banks determine (cause) the credit supply according to profit targets, constrained by internal risk models, regulation, and, above all, the willingness of Central Banks and banks as a sector to lend to each other. Alternatively, viewed as a dependent variable, bank credit creation or lack thereof is an effect of the loan demand expressed by the non-bank public. In reality, both views contain truth, and the relative strength of either interpretation changes with context.

Whatever the case, the current crisis is misunderstood if conceived as a recession caused, first and foremost, by under-consumption and a credit crunch. Rather, the seeds for the bust were sown by an earlier, unsustainable boom in Britain caused by over-consumption and negative savings.

[58] M. Onado, 'Northern Rock: Just the Tip of the Iceberg', *The Failure of Northern Rock: A Multi-Dimensional Case Study*, F. Bruni and D. Llewellyn (eds.) (Vienna: SUERF-The European Money and Finance Forum, 2009), p. 104.

[59] P. Ireland, 'Property and contract in contemporary corporate theory', *Legal Studies* 23(3) 453–509 (2003).

[60] J. Macey and M. O'Hara, 'The Corporate Governance of Banks', *Federal Reserve Bank of New York Economic Policy Review* 9.1 91–107, 93 (April 2003).

[61] K. French et al., *The Squam Lake Report* (Princeton University Press, 2010), p. 70.

In recent years UK household debt, defined as household liabilities as a percentage of nominal disposable income, exceeded 150 per cent, a level of indebtedness which, figured as a proportion of GDP, exceeds rates in the United States and the European Union.[62] Once the fabled land of Protestant parsimony, high levels of debt have become a common fact in Britain within a generation.[63]

The larger volume of consumer credit and corresponding household debt in the years leading up to the crisis is sometimes explained as the result of a 'global savings glut'.[64] According to this hypothesis, large amounts of savings in Asian economies were recycled through banks accessing global wholesale markets, which then lowered interest rates and increased financial investment in recipient countries such as Britain. Whatever the merits of this thesis, its implications for domestic policy are less clear assuming a commitment to capital liberalization, since current account imbalances reflect structural differences in labour regulation and productivity between Europe and East Asia. Instead, it is helpful to clarify how banking by its very nature might keep interest rates lower than in an economy without a banking system, even in the absence of international flows and factors.

II. Fractional-reserve-banking and financialization

In order to flesh out the potential relation between banking, lowered interest rates, and misdirected productions, it is helpful to return to the monetary theory of the business cycle proposed by Friedrich Hayek, who extended the insights of his mentor, Ludwig von Mises, and other predecessors working in the so-called Austrian School tradition of economics. For this reason, this section draws both from the writings of Hayek and subsequent Austrian School commentators in order to summarize what Mises called the circulation credit theory of the business cycle (CCT).

62 Financial Services Authority, *The Turner Review: A Regulatory Response to the Global Banking Crisis* (2009), p. 13.

63 *Cf.* M. Weber, *The Protestant Ethic and the Spirit of Capitalism*, Talcott Parsons (trans.) (Mineola, NY: Dover Press, 2003).

64 B. Bernanke, 'The Global Saving Glut and the US Current Account Deficit', speech to Virginia Association of Economists, Richmond, Virginia, 10 March, 2005, available at www.federalreserve.gov/boarddocs/speeches/2005/200503102/default.htm (last accessed 10 January 2013).

Although CCT is more commonly known as Austrian Business Cycle Theory (ABC), it builds on a theoretical edifice first constructed by the Swedish economist Knut Wicksell. Wicksell invoked the concept of the natural rate of interest as a heuristic for describing the price of money (the interest rate) in an economy with an inelastic currency. In this imaginary economy, the theoretical or 'natural' rate of interest is determined principally by the supply of savings. In the real world, however, Wicksell observed that banks are able to extend credit in excess of savings, thereby lowering the market rate of interest below the 'natural' rate. According to Wicksell, such an artificially low interest rate will stimulate demand for bank loans, eventually inflating and distorting market prices. Writing at the turn of the twentieth century, Wicksell looked to the constraints of the gold standard to check such outcomes. According to Wicksell, this would occur because rising prices would increase the non-banking public's demand to convert their bank liabilities (deposits) into cash (gold). When this occurred, reserves would decrease and banks would be forced to raise interest rates to a level corresponding to the natural rate in order to stem outflows of gold.[65]

In the early twentieth century, Mises extended Wicksell's insights on the consequence of banks' lending lowering market interest rates below the rate that would otherwise prevail if investment was funded only from the savings of an inelastic currency.[66] Hayek then refined the theoretical framework. The distinctive feature of Mises–Hayek business cycle theory is the claim that artificially lowered interest rates do not impact the price level uniformly, but do so through changes in the relative prices of commodities produced by different sectors. In effect, bank lending subsidizes investments which otherwise would not have taken place if the natural rate of interest prevailed. Like all subsidies, bank debt (loans) thus influences the specific pattern of economic development by increasing the purchasing power of the particular industries to which it is extended.[67]

[65] On Wicksell, *see* D. Laidler, *Fabricating the Keynesian Revolution: Studies of the Inter-war Literature on Money, the Cycle, and Unemployment* (Cambridge University Press, 1999), p. 28.

[66] Some Austrians argue that the banking system has a distorting effect on interest rates only in a fiat money system with a Central Bank, but not under a free banking system based on a metallic standard. G. Selgin, *Free Banking in Britain: Theory, Experience, and Debate, 1800–1845* (London: Institute of Economic Affairs, 1984); G. Selgin and L.H. White, 'In Defence of Fiduciary Media – or, We are Not Devo(lutionists), We are Misesians!' *Review of Austrian Economics* 9.2 83–107 (1996).

[67] While explaining the monetary sources of business cycles, Hayek did not offer any easy resolution for them. 'So long as we make use of bank credit as a means of furthering

In some respects, Hayek's version of ABC theory is a more formal statement of the common knowledge that banking involves maturity transformation. In other words, banks do not temporally match assets and liabilities, but 'borrow short and lend long'. The conventional wisdom is that maturity transformation produces interest rates more favourable to fixed capital investments than otherwise would be the case if long-term funding was exclusively determined by savers, because of the general propensity of the non-bank public to hold higher cash balances than banks.[68] However, the benefits of banking for economic growth come with the potential cost that the inter-temporal allocation of real resources via market prices may be distorted in the process.

In order to understand why this may happen, recall that the interest rate may be defined as the price of money. Like all prices in a market economy, the interest rate may be interpreted as communicating consumer preferences. For instance, when the supply of savings increases, this indicates the public is willing to sacrifice present for future consumption. An increase in savings increases the funds available for investment and lowers the interest rate. Assuming, as Hayek did, that the expected rate of profit exceeds the interest rate – an assumption not without critics and particularly dubious during a depression[69] – demand for loans will increase, as the prospective net present value of investments improves when discounted by a lower interest rate. According to Hayek, since investment in the production of capital goods, that is, intermediate goods such as machines and tools used to produce other goods, are especially interest rate sensitive, an increase in the supply of savings will stimulate investment in this sector of the economy since outputs will come to fruition in the future which is when consumers will use their savings for

economic development we shall have to put up with the resulting trade cycles. They are, in a sense, the price we pay for a speed of development exceeding that which people would voluntarily make possible through their savings, and which therefore has to be extorted from them.' Nevertheless, Hayek did draw the following policy conclusion. 'As soon as it is realised that, owing to the existence of banks the equilibrating forces of the economic system cannot bring about the automatic adjustment of all its branches to the actual situation, which is described by classical economics theory, it is justifiable even from a liberal point of view that the banks should be subjected to degrees of publicity as to the state of their business which is not necessary in the case of other undertakings; and this would by no means imply a violation of the principle of business secrecy . . . ' FA Hayek, *Monetary Theory and the Trade Cycle*, N. Koldor and H. M. Croone (trans.) (New York: Sentry Press, 1933), pp. 189, 190, 239.

68 Financial Services Authority, *Turner Review*, p. 68.

69 M. Lavoie, *Introduction to Post-Keynesian Economics* (London: Palgrave Macmillan, 2006), pp. 54–82.

expenditure.[70] In this way, consumer time preference is reflected in the productive structure of the economy.

However, the harmony between the price of money and productive structure of the economy is broken if the supply of bank credit exceeds actual savings. Although new investment in capital goods will occur if the expected rate of profit exceeds the cost of borrowing, an artificially lowered rate of interest causes the savings rate to fall. In other words, the non-bank public may bring forward their consumption, causing the price of final consumer goods to rise relative to capital goods. As this happens, according to Hayek investment projects in the capital goods sector will be abandoned, once it becomes apparent that they were stimulated by credit expansion rather than actual consumer demand.[71] The mispricing of money thus propagates a temporal mismatch between the structure of production and consumer preferences, turning boom into bust.[72] In his mature writings, Hayek suggests that the tipping point occurs when banks reduce the rate of growth in new credit extended because of concerns with rising leverage of their counterparties and the threat this poses to the banks' own solvency if counterparties default.[73] A contraction in bank lending causes the price level to fall, and the subsequent slow reallocation of resources from incomplete investment projects to other uses results in a period of declining economic output and unemployment; in other words, a recession or even depression.

Despite many merits, a key problem with Hayek's monetary theory of the business cycle is its rigid determinism, specifically the claim that the capital goods sector is necessarily the primary site of over-expansion and malinvestment. The argument that 'the demand for money' is 'in the last resort a demand for capital goods' is a conclusion

[70] *cf.* F. Hayek, 'Monetary Policy in the United States after the Recovery of 1920', *The Collected Works of F. A. Hayek Volume 5: Good Money: The New World Part I*, S. Kresge (ed.) (University of Chicago Press, 1999), pp. 105–6, fn. 28. Hayek's argument is that low interest rates offer the greatest advantage to long-term investments because it lowers interest payments over a longer stretch of time.

[71] P. Bagus, 'Monetary Reform and Deflation – A Critique of Mises, Rothbard, Huerta de Soto and Sennholz', *New Perspectives on Political Economy* 4.2 131–57, 139 (2008).

[72] These two paragraphs sum up key points made by R. Garrison, 'Austrian Business Cycle Theory', *Business Cycles and Depressions: An Encyclopedia*, D. Glasner (ed.), (London: Routledge, 1997), pp. 23–6; J. H. De Soto, *Money, Bank Credit, and Economic Cycles*, Melinda Stroup (trans.) (Auburn, AL: Ludwig von Mises Institute, 2006).

[73] Thus the tipping point is endogenous to the model since rising leverage is itself a function of bank lending. F. Hayek, 'Three Elucidations of the Ricardo Effect', 77 *Journal of Political Economy* 274–85 (1969).

that does not follow from the premise.[74] This determinism is at odds with the broader belief expressed by Hayek that entrepreneurial activity is dynamic and unpredictable. This presumably applies to banks *qua* entrepreneurs. Therefore, what is needed is the elaboration of a position 'more faithful to Hayek than Hayek is to himself', to borrow a turn of phrase from German philosopher Schleiermacher. This involves relaxing Hayek's *a priori* assumption as to in which sector bank credit flows by empirically examining the statistical data at a particular period in history.

In fact, doing so reveals that net lending to the financial, insurance, and real estate sector (FIRE) has greatly exceeded bank lending to non-financial private corporations in recent years, with particular sharpness after 1980. Between 1998 and 2008, for example, sterling loans from British banks to financial companies grew by over 200 per cent relative to GDP, compared to 50 and 60 per cent for the household and private non-financial sectors, respectively.[75] Hayek's perspective on the distributional impact of differential bank lending is helpful for interpreting these facts. According to Hayek, those sectors which initially acquire new purchasing power gain a strategic advantage over other sectors because such funds allow them to outbid competitors for real resources.[76] This increases the income of persons in the relatively privileged sector, next increasing the prices of commodities which they buy in increased quantity, which then increases the incomes of the sellers of these commodities, and so on.[77] However, those persons who receive funds last as they are spent into circulation, or never receive them at all, are relatively disadvantaged, because prices will have adjusted upward in response to the increased availability of credit.[78]

74 *See* L. von Mises, *The Theory of Money and Credit* (Indianapolis, Ind.: Liberty Fund, 1981), p. 241.

75 Independent Commission on Banking, *Final Report*, p. 50.

76 De Soto, *Money, Bank Credit, and Economic Cycles*, p. 533.

77 F. Hayek, *Prices and Production* (New York: Augustus M. Kelly, 1935), p. 9.

78 M. Rothbard, *The Mystery of Banking*, 2nd edn. (Auburn: Ludwig von Mises Institute, 2008), p. 101. As Hayek nicely puts it, 'The effect we are discussing is rather similar to that which appears when we pour viscous liquid, such as honey, into a vessel. There will, of course, be a tendency for it to spread to an even surface. But if the stream hits the surface at one point, a little mound will form there from which the additional matter will slowly spread outward. Even after we have stopped pouring in more, it will take some time until the even surface will be fully restored . . . But as long as we pour at a constant rate, the mound will preserve its height relative to the surrounding pool . . . ' Hayek, 'Three Elucidations of the Ricardo Effect', 281.

Thus, in the years prior to the crisis, when the flow of UK bank lending to the financial sector exceeded lending to other sectors, these eventualities could be interpreted as the financial sector disproportionately benefiting from the additional purchasing power granted by banks. This fact might partly explain why, in spite of increasing competition within the FIRE sector, financial profits remained high, contrary to the expectations of neo-classical theory.[79] Such evidence is also broadly consistent with the thesis of 'financialization' – the idea that the financial sector has accumulated claims and clout relative to other sectors of the economy over the last thirty years – suggesting a possible mechanism for why this may have occurred.[80] Although more research needs to be conducted on this topic, the path-breaking scholarship of Friedrich Hayek and Joseph Schumpeter indicate the need to critically reconsider the relationship of money and banks to the business cycle.

III. Conclusion

The aim of this chapter has been to briefly arm readers with some initial intellectual equipment to understand why increasing the availability of bank credit is an ambiguous goal whose pursuit may foster either economic development or crisis.[81] In particular, whether bank credit plays a progressive or destabilising role in the real economy is contingent on the form new money assumes, the sectors into which it is lent, and spare capacity in the economy. In recent years, when as much as two-thirds of balance sheets represented further lending to the financial sector, British banks may not have been giving credit where credit was due, so to speak.[82] Although securing lending with collateral may theoretically have reduced credit risk for individual banks, it may also have contributed to systemic risk in the sector as a whole. Bank lending to the FIRE sector increased the price of financial assets, which were then used to secure further bank

79 J. Crotty, 'If Financial Market Competition is so Intense, Why are Financial Firm Profits so High? Reflections on the Current "Golden Age" of Finance,' *Political Economy Research Institute Working Papers* 134.

80 G. Krippner, 'The Financialization of the American Economy', *Socio-economic Review* 3 173–208 (2005); E. Engelen, 'The Case for Financialization', *Competition & Change* 12.2 111–19 (June 2008).

81 *See* McCormack, Chapter 2 this volume.

82 P. Gai, A. Haldane and S. Kapadia, 1 August 2011, 'Complexity, Concentration, and Contagion', available at www.bankofengland.co.uk/publications/speeches/2011/speech512paper.pdf, p. 2 (last accessed 10 January 2013).

loans, with self-perpetuating circularity.[83] When the crisis struck, collateral failed to do the work creditors wanted it to do. Creditors had recourse to assets whose market value was depressed and whose sale would have placed further downward pressure on prices and balance sheets.[84] The availability of secured credit should therefore always be viewed cautiously and holistically as an equal and opposite accounting entry. Thus the irony that what had been praised in recent years as the 'democratization of credit' is now widely criticised as forced imposition to service debts.

Yet, rather than diminish demand for debt finance, recent events have actually encouraged an expansion in the objects used to collateralize them. This striking enlargement in the scale and substance of secured transactions has occurred across markets. At the highest levels of haute finance, the crisis witnessed government lending upon a suite of securities beyond those conventionally classified as Central Bank eligible, and through relatively novel channels such as long-term reverse repos.[85] At the same time, on the high street, pawnbrokers are proliferating because of the slowdown in consumer credit offered by banks, accepting as pledges cars, fine wine, 'anything really that has got a high value', states one pawnbroker manager.[86] While the constellation of these trends is particular to the present, they are logical conclusions of financial culture, by which I mean that worldview which fabricates the existence of a uniform monetary substance existing behind sensuously diverse things, rendering them commensurate and capable of being leveraged.[87]

In sum, our present evinces a complicated interplay of continuity and change, at a crossroads between economic development and financial crisis.[88] The immediate result of recent events has been the unleashing

83 G. Soros, *The Alchemy of Finance* (Hoboken, NJ: Wiley, 2003), p. 86.

84 I. Fisher, 'The Debt-Deflation Theory of Great Depressions', *Econometrica* 1.1 337–57 (1933).

85 A sale and repurchase agreement (repo) is a financial transaction involving the sale of securities with commitment to repurchase the same or similar securities at a later date. A reverse repo is this financial transaction viewed from the perspective of the cash lender who takes temporary possession of the security.

86 Quoted in W. Smale, 16 August 2010, '*New Age of Pawnbrokers?' BBC News*, www.bbc.co.uk/news/business-10974721 (last accessed 10 January 2013).

87 H. de Soto, *The Mystery of Capital: Why Capitalism Triumphs in the West and Fails Everywhere Else* (New York: Basic Books, 2003).

88 M. Postone, 'Theorizing the Contemporary World: Robert Brenner, Giovanni Arrighi, David Harvey,' *Political Economy and Global Capitalism: The 21st Century, Present and Future*, R. Albritton, B. Jessop, and R. Westra (eds.) (London: Anthem Press, 2010), pp. 7–24.

of widespread, if inchoate, dissatisfaction with capitalism that places its specific configuration in flux. But the longer term legacy of our historical moment may well be the strengthening of financial culture, as evidenced by the further expansion in objects imagined as assets adequate to secure lending during the crisis.

2

Secured transactions law reform, UNCITRAL and the export of foreign legal models

GERARD McCORMACK*

I. Introduction

UNCITRAL, the United Nations Commission on International Trade Law, has produced a Legislative Guide on secured transactions, or secured credit law, as it is variously called.[1] The Guide follows the broad contours of Article 9 of the United States Uniform Commercial Code, though it is not an exact copy. It aims to harmonize and modernize the law of secured credit across the globe.[2] In UNCITRAL's view, the Legislative Guide will aid the growth of individual businesses and also general economic prosperity. Harmonization and 'modernization' are assumed to equal 'liberal' security regimes and the facilitation of secured credit. In this chapter,

* The author would like to thank Terry Halliday and Peter Vincent-Jones for their input on earlier drafts of this chapter, but, of course, the the usual disclaimer applies.

[1] The Guide went through the UN General Assembly approval process in December 2008 – UN General Assembly Resolution 63/121 – though the editorial revisions were only completed in 2009 and an intellectual property annex was 'pre-released' on 15 July 2010. For the content of the Legislative Guide, see the UNCITRAL website, www.uncitral.org/, and for background, see B. Foex, L. Thevenoz and S. Bazinas (eds.), *Reforming Secured Transactions: The UNCITRAL Legislative Guide as an Inspiration* (Geneva: Schulthess, 2007); H. Buxbaum, 'Unification of the Law Governing Secured Transactions: Progress and Prospects for Reform' 8 *Uniform Law Review* 321 (2003).

[2] UNCITRAL describes its mission as follows: 'The core legal body of the United Nations system in the field of international trade law. A legal body with universal membership specializing in commercial law reform worldwide for over 40 years. UNCITRAL's business is the modernization and harmonization of rules on international business' (www.uncitral.org/). This may represent mission creep from the UN resolution establishing UNCITRAL – Resolution 2205 (XXI) – which spoke of 'progressive harmonization and unification'. The focus now on 'modernization and harmonization' sees UNCITRAL in a more proactive light actively striving for the reform of global commercial law; *see* S. Block-Lieb and T. Halliday, 'Harmonization and Modernization in UNCITRAL's Legislative Guide on Insolvency Law' 42 *Texas International Law Journal* 475 (2007).

the modernization equals liberalization agenda is subjected to greater scrutiny.

UNCITRAL is not the only international organization working on the design of an 'efficient' legal regime for secured transactions. For example, the European Bank for Reconstruction and Development (EBRD) in 1994[3] and the Organization of American States (OAS) in 2002[4] have both produced Model Laws and done follow-up work of greater or lesser intensity. The World Bank has formulated principles for 'Effective Insolvency and Creditors Rights System' (revised in 2005)[5] and has also produced a series of reports designed to evaluate the ease of doing business across the globe. As part of the evaluation process, the *Doing Business* reports have made use of a ten-point template measuring the degree to which secured credit and bankruptcy laws in particular jurisdictions 'protect the rights of borrowers and lenders' and thus facilitate secured lending.[6]

So UNCITRAL is not alone in its efforts, but its work gains added credibility and legitimacy from its perceived representatives and its institutional aura as a United Nations (UN) organ.[7] UNCITRAL was established as a UN offshoot in 1966 on the basis that a UN-related law reform body would provide more inclusive representation of the world's legal and economic systems and accordingly better coordination among other international actors.[8] There has been considerable controversy recently over UNCITRAL's working methods and the extent to which its outputs reflect

[3] *See* its website: www.ebrd.com/pages/homepage.shtml and for some of the later work done by its 'secured transactions' team, *see* EBRD, *Publicity of Security Rights: Guiding Principles for the Development of a Charges Registry* (London: EBRD, 2004) and *Publicity of Security Rights: Setting Standards* (London: EBRD, 2005) and *see generally*, J.-H. Rover, *Secured Lending in Eastern Europe: Comparative Law of Secured Transactions and the EBRD Model Law* (Oxford University Press, 2007).

[4] *See* its website: www.oas.org/en/default.asp and for later work, *see* OAS, *Adoption of the Model Registry Regulations under the Model Inter-American Law on Secured Transactions*, OEA/Ser.K/XXI.7 CIDIP-VII/RES.1/09 rev. 2, 16 October 2009. *See also* the work of the Asian Development Bank (www.adb.org/), which has produced a *Guide to Movables Registries* (2002).

[5] *See* www.worldbank.org/, and the principles are also available as Annex 5 to *Secured Transactions Systems and Collateral Registries* (Washington DC: International Finance Corporation, 2010).

[6] The template is available as Annex 3 to *Secured Transactions Systems and Collateral Registries*, 2010.

[7] *See* T. Halliday, 'Legitimacy, Technology and Leverage: The Building Blocks of Insolvency Architecture in the Decades Past and Decades Ahead' 32 *Brooklyn Journal of International Law* 1081 (2007).

[8] The Schmitthoff Report (UN Doc. A/6396) reprinted in 1 *UNCITRAL Yearbook* 2 (1966) and available online at www.uncitral.org/ and associated links.

a neo-liberal American agenda.[9] This chapter does not engage directly with this controversy, but it does consider the closeness in approach between the UNCITRAL Secured Transactions Guide and the American Article 9 and the extent to which this proximity may inhibit the prospects of the UNCITRAL Guide achieving widespread international acceptance. A key argument in the chapter is that the avowed aim of the Guide to reform the law worldwide along 'neo-liberal' American lines is fraught with difficulty, not least by overlooking the regulatory and cultural plurality of the countries on which it seeks to have an impact.

The chapter begins by asking, what is the effect of recognizing security rights? In short, what do security rights do for you? The second part of the chapter asks, why harmonize the law of secured credit particularly in the 'liberal' American-nuanced way that the UNCITRAL Guide seeks to do? The third part considers why 'liberal' secured credit regimes are considered to be beneficial. The fourth part addresses in greater detail critical perspectives on the international harmonization and modernization agenda. The final part concludes and summarizes the discussion, counselling against the 'silver bullet' of secured transactions reform, especially in the American-oriented manner that the Guide seeks to effect.

II. Security rights

While there is probably no universally recognized definition of security rights, it is generally taken as meaning a right over property to ensure the payment of money or the performance of some other obligation. The property over which security is taken is referred to as 'secured' or 'collateralized'. The security taker has a superior claim to payment of the debt out of the secured property than the generality of the debtor's creditors and

[9] For a discussion of UNCITRAL working methods referring to earlier controversies, *see* 'UNCITRAL rules of procedure and methods of work: Note by the Secretariat' A/CN.9/676 (2009) and A/CN.9/697 (2010). Note, too, UN General Assembly Official Records Sixty-fifth session, Supplement No. 17 (A/65/17) Annex 111. The controversies covered the role and status of non-State actors, primarily US-based organizations, in UNCITRAL deliberations. On the dangers of 'interest group capture', *see* R. Cranston, 'Theorizing Transnational Commercial Law' 42 *Texas International Law Journal* 597, nn. 49–55 (2007). For analogies with the American Article 9 drafting process, *see* A. Schwartz and R. Scott, 'The Political Economy of Private Legislatures' 143 *University of Pennsylvania Law Review* 595 (1995); E. Janger 'Predicting When the Uniform Law Process Will Fail: Article 9, Capture, and the Race to the Bottom' 83 *Iowa Law Review* 569 (1998). More generally, *see* G. McCormack, *Secured Credit and the Harmonisation of Law* (Cheltenham: Edward Elgar, 2011).

will generally have access to speedier enforcement mechanisms. In the event that the secured debt is not repaid, the security taker will normally have a right of sale over the secured assets, whether unilaterally or by seeking the intervention of an administrative mechanism or court. The secured creditor therefore has greater leverage than unsecured creditors. The debtor may also be more likely to pay a secured debt – failure to pay can result in the loss of a crucial asset for the debtor's business – thereby giving the secured creditor a stronger hand in debt restructuring negotiations. Security also opens up the possibility of the creditor availing itself of self-help remedies, though self-help is a controversial concept in many jurisdictions, not least because it is seen to be possibly inconsistent with constitutional guarantees safeguarding peaceful possession of property.

Economists suggest that security addresses the problems of adverse selection, moral hazard and uninsurable risk in lending decisions.[10] Security aligns the incentives of creditors and borrowers and adds a credible commitment to the relationship. Security performs a disciplinary function and is a cornerstone of the theory of control rights and incomplete contracts that has been developed by Oliver Hart and others.[11]

Adverse selection refers to the fact that some borrowers may turn out to be unreliable or untrustworthy. A lender cannot simply raise interest rates to screen out these borrowers, because honest borrowers with sound projects will drop out of the picture as well. The potential pay-off from the project may not be enough to meet the borrowing costs. Where security is taken, however, adverse selection problems are addressed more powerfully. The lender can back up its assessment of the character of the borrower and the soundness of the business plan with information on the value of the collateral. As well as the revenues generated from the project, the lender can look to the collateral for repayment. Moral hazard refers to the possibility that a borrower may abscond with the loan. The larger the loan, the greater the moral hazard; but if the borrower provides security, the lower are the lender's costs in monitoring moral hazard. The borrower has given the lender a hostage against flight risk in the shape of security. The insurance risk arises from the fact that the borrower may not be able to repay due to certain events that are not easily insurable,

[10] *See generally*, J. Stiglitz and A. Weiss, 'Credit Rationing in Markets with Imperfect Information' 71 *American Economic Review* 393 (1981). *See also* G. Akerlof 'The Market for "Lemons": Qualitative Uncertainty and the Market Mechanism' 84 *Quarterly Journal of Economics* 488 (1970).

[11] *See generally*, O. Hart and J. Moore, 'Default and Renegotiation: A Dynamic Model of Debt' 113 *Quarterly Journal of Economics* 1 (1998).

or insurable at all. Uninsurable risk may be reduced in unsecured lending through making smallish loans to a large number of borrowers, i.e. spreading. Security allows more concentrated lending and also reduces uninsurable risk, since the security serves as an alternative repayment mechanism.[12]

By way of summary, security rights provide the creditor with property rights which strengthen the creditor's contractual claims against the debtor in various ways. Firstly, the security taker should have priority over other creditors in the event of the debtor becoming insolvent. Secondly, the security taker should have a measure of control over the secured assets, or at least share control with the debtor, thereby strengthening the debtor's hands in restructuring negotiations. Thirdly, the security taker should have easier enforcement mechanisms available to it than the generality of creditors, including a power of sale over the secured assets. Fourthly, the easier debt enforcement opportunities may include self-help measures such as sale of the secured assets through unilateral action by the creditor, without having to seek the permission of a court or administrative agency. But not all these features are present in every jurisdiction. Not all jurisdictions, for instance, recognize the full priority of secured claims. A proportion of secured asset realizations may be carved out, or set aside, for the benefit of unsecured creditors. There may also be restrictions on the enforcement of security rights and in particular limitations, or indeed, wholesale prohibition, on self-help enforcement. However, the overall effect of recognizing security rights is to improve a creditor's hand in dealing with adverse selection, moral hazard and uninsurable risk issues.

III. Why harmonize the law of secured credit?

In short, UNCITRAL has advocated harmonization of the law of secured credit to make the law more liberal and facilitative of security and this, in turn, is seen as producing more economic growth. It has suggested the removal of restrictions on the taking of security and increasing the range of assets that can be used as security. It has also suggested the introduction of mechanisms for the registration of security rights, thereby

[12] *See* H. Fleisig, 'The Economics of Collateral and Collateral Reform' in F. Dahan and J. Simpson (eds.), *Secured Transactions Reform and Access to Credit* (Cheltenham: Edward Elgar, 2008), p. 81.

enhancing the available information about such rights. In the UNCITRAL view:[13]

> The key to the effectiveness of secured credit is that it allows borrowers to use the value inherent in their assets as a means of reducing credit risk for the creditor. Risk is mitigated because loans secured by the property of a borrower give lenders recourse to the property in the event of non-payment. Studies have shown that as the risk of non-payment is reduced, the availability of credit increases and the cost of credit falls. Studies have also shown that in States where lenders perceive the risks associated with transactions to be high, the cost of credit increases as lenders require increased compensation to evaluate and assume the increased risk.

There is a suggestion that too many countries have too many restrictions on the taking of security and that countries with 'inadequate' secured transactions regimes have suffered significant losses in gross domestic product (GDP) in consequence. These studies suggest that gaps or weaknesses in collateral-based credit systems hinder financial and economic development.[14] Simply stated, banks and other financial institutions will not engage in large-scale lending activities if their position as secured creditors in the liquidation of their borrowers is not sufficiently certain, or that sufficient means for the enforcement of security are not available. More controversially, it has also been suggested that businesses in less developed financial systems and civil law countries substitute less efficient forms of external finance, trade credit and other sources of funds, for bank loans and equity.[15]

There are also sector-specific studies that purport to demonstrate the value of particular types of collateral, and the economic impact of a stable legal environment for security creation and enforcement. One such study concerns the 2001 Cape Town Convention on International Interests in Mobile Equipment and the Protocol on Matters Specific to Aircraft

[13] 'Draft legislative guide on secured transactions – Report of the Secretary General' A/CN 9/WG VI/WP 2 (2002) Addendum 1 at para. 4 and *see also*, the report from the World Bank Group, *Secured Transactions Systems and Collateral Registries*, 2010, pp. 6–13.

[14] *See generally*, H. Fleisig, 'Economic Functions of Security in a Market Economy', in J. Norton and M. Andenas (eds.), *Emerging Financial Markets and Secured Transactions* (London: Kluwer, 1998), p. 15. *See also* D. Arner, C. Booth, P. Lejot and B. Hsu, 'Property Rights, Collateral, Creditor Rights and Insolvency in East Asia' 42 *Texas International Law Journal* 515 (2007).

[15] *See* the series of studies carried out by the so-called 'law matters' or 'legal origins' thesis – R. La Porta, F. Lopez de Silanes, A. Shleifer and R. Vishny. Their work includes 'Legal Determinants of External Finance' 52 *Journal of Finance* 1131 (1997) and 'Law and Finance' 106 *Journal of Political Economy* 1113 (1998).

Equipment.[16] It was estimated that savings to the aircraft industry from the creation of a sound international legal framework governing aircraft financing amounted to $4 billion a year in borrowing costs. Moreover, since 2003 the Export-Import Bank of the United States 'has offered a one-third reduction of its exposure fee on . . . financings of new U.S.-manufactured large commercial aircraft for buyers in countries that ratify . . . and implement the Cape Town [Convention]'.[17]

There is a consensus among international financial institutions that a 'liberal' secured credit regime is a general social and economic good. Two examples serve to highlight that consensus. The first comes from the late 1990s upheavals in the 'Tiger' economies of East Asia. In the aftermath, an influential G22 report highlighted the importance of debtor/creditor regimes and also set out the features that, in its view, should be contained in such regimes:[18]

> The law should permit . . . all economically important assets to serve as collateral for a loan: and security interests in tangible property . . . and in intangible property . . . to be created. All economically important agents should be able to act as lenders and as borrowers in secured transactions and all economically important secured transactions should be permitted. The creation of security interests should be inexpensive relative to the amounts lent.

Secondly, when the former socialist economies in Central and Eastern Europe were undergoing the transition to a more free market-oriented system, the task of reforming credit laws assumed a high priority on the legislative agenda.[19] Organizations like the EBRD considered that such laws impacted in a crucial way on the pace of private sector investment

[16] The Cape Town Treaty consists of a main convention that sets out the general governing rules, and a series of supplemental protocols that set out specific rules for particular types of collateral (e.g. aircraft). *See generally*, R. Goode, 'Transcending the Boundaries of Earth and Space: The Preliminary Draft UNIDROIT Convention on International Interests in Mobile Equipment' 3 *Uniform Law Review* 52 (1998); I. Davies, 'The New Lex Mercatoria: International Interests in Mobile Equipment' 52 *ICLQ* 151 (2003).

[17] News Release, 'Cape Town Treaty on Cross-Border Financing of Aircraft, Helicopters and Aircraft Engines, Takes Effect Today (March 1)' (February 28, 2006), www.exim.gov/pressrelease/ and *see generally*, R. Goode, H. Kronke and E. McKendrick, *Transnational Commercial Law* (Oxford University Press, 2007), p. 441: 'the international regime established by the Convention could reduce borrowing costs by several US $billion a year'.

[18] Report of the Working Group on International Financial Crises (Washington DC: IMF, 1988), p. 47 and available on the IMF website: www.imf.org/external/index.htm (last accessed 10 January 2013.)

[19] *See generally*, Rover, *Secured Lending in Eastern Europe Comparative Law.*

activity and were essential in fostering market-based decision-making.[20] Consequently, the EBRD produced a Model Law on Secured Transactions to guide States in their reform efforts.[21]

But the UNCITRAL Guide goes much further than the EBRD Model Law. In the context of secured credit law, it is typical to draw a distinction between common law and civil law jurisdictions.[22] Common law jurisdictions – generally sympathetic to the concepts of party autonomy and self-help – have a liberal attitude towards security, allowing security interests to be taken with a minimum of formality over both present and future assets to secure existing and future indebtedness. '[T]hey allow universal security rather than require specific security.'[23] By contrast, civil law jurisdictions have been more cautious in their approach to non-possessory security and typically have imposed restrictions on the taking of security.

The EBRD Model Law attempts to accommodate features from both civil law and common law traditions, whereas the UNCITRAL Guide is firmly in the common law mould. Moreover, it goes far beyond the English common law, appropriating the main features of Article 9 of the American Uniform Commercial Code. For instance, the UNCITRAL Guide rejects the idea of carving out a proportion of collateral realizations for the benefit of unsecured creditors – an idea that finds recognition in the UK Insolvency Act[24] but is dismissed in the United States.[25] Likewise, the UNCITRAL Guide adopts a functional approach towards

[20] *See also*, D. Berkowitz, K. Pistor and J.-F. Richard, 'The Transplant Effect' 51 *AJCL* 163, 164 (2003): 'newly designed model laws for secured transactions marketed the value of Western law to their counterparts in the East, backing their campaign to transplant their home legal system with financial aid promises and/or the prospect of joining the European Union'.

[21] EBRD, *Model Law on Secured Transactions* (London: EBRD, 1994); on which, *see* Rover, *Secured Lending in Eastern Europe Comparative Law.*

[22] *See* S. van Erp, 'Civil and Common Property Law: Caveat Comparator – The Value of Legal Historical-Comparative Analysis' 11 *European Review of Private Law* 394 (2003) and more generally, R. Cuming, 'The Internationalization of Secured Financing Law: The Spreading Influence of the Concepts of UCC, Article 9 and its Progeny' in R. Cranston (ed.), *Making Commercial Law: Essays in Honour of Roy Goode* (Oxford: Clarendon Press, 1997), p. 499.

[23] R. Goode, 'Security in Cross Border Transactions' 33 *Texas Journal of International Law* 47, 48 (1998).

[24] Section 176A, and *see also* Insolvency Act 1986 (Prescribed Part) Order 2003.

[25] S.L. Harris and C.W. Mooney, 'Measuring the Social Costs and Benefits and Identifying the Victims of Subordinating Security Interests in Bankruptcy' 82 *Cornell L. Rev.* 1349 (1997).

the creation and registration of security rights, effectively recharacterizing certain transactions as security rights although they were not ostensibly designed as such. Again, this conforms with the approach evidenced in the US Article 9, but is one that is at variance with the English common law. In addition, in the details of the filing system suggested for security interests, the UNCITRAL Guide maps on to the American rather than the English system.

Filing systems are designed to address information asymmetries in credit markets.[26] Lenders depend on information about borrowers to perform an initial screening function as well as monitoring and controlling the actions of borrowers during the lifetime of the loan. Information sharing facilities may allow lenders to allocate credit more efficiently and to increase overall lending volumes. Such facilities may also improve the behaviour of borrowers, since there is less of an opportunity, or incentive, to over-borrow from several banks simultaneously without any of them knowing. The UNCITRAL Guide, however, follows the Article 9 notice filing system under which the security agreement itself is not filed, but instead a so-called 'financing statement' providing limited information. Notice filing is party specific rather than transaction specific. The information filed is an invitation to further inquiry rather than a synopsis of the transaction. The filed notice merely indicates that a person may have a security interest in the collateral concerned, but further inquiry by a searcher from the potential creditor and/or debtor will be necessary to ascertain the facts. A degree of scepticism about the merits of notice filing seems appropriate.[27] Divorcing registration from particular individual transactions opens up the possibility that the register may become less reliable as a source of information, since a searcher cannot be sure whether a particular entry relates to an actual transaction or to a transaction that was contemplated but never in fact materialized.[28]

[26] *See* F. Lopez de Silanes, 'Turning the Key to Credit: Credit Access and Credit Institutions' in F. Dahan and J. Simpson (eds.), *Secured Transactions Reform and Access to Credit* (Cheltenham: Edward Elgar, 2008), p. 6.

[27] J. White, 'Reforming Article 9 Priorities in Light of Old Ignorance and New Filing Rules' 79 *Minnesota Law Review* 529, 530 (1995); U. Drobnig, 'Present and Future of Real and Personal Security' *European Review of Private Law* 623, 660 (2003). According to the Scottish Law Commission, the only civil law jurisdictions to have introduced notice filing are Quebec and Louisiana; *see* Discussion Paper, *Registration of Rights in Security by Companies* (Edinburgh, October 2002), para. 1.28.

[28] For a far fuller discussion of the technical and other merits of the UNCITRAL Secured Transactions Guide versus other secured transactions model laws and instruments, *see*

IV. Why 'liberal' security regimes are considered to be beneficial

In short, liberal security regimes are considered to be beneficial because they are seen to promote economic growth. This is for two general reasons. Firstly, there is the contract/property rights argument, which goes along the lines that the secured creditor has bargained for rights of a proprietary nature. The law should respect this contractual bargain and the property rights acquired by the secured creditor in the debtor's assets. Recognition of property rights is good, so the argument goes, for economic growth. Secondly, security is a risk-reduction device and therefore increases the availability and lowers the cost of credit. The effect of minimizing risk is to encourage lenders to make loans that they would not otherwise make and also to reduce the risk premium that a lender might otherwise input into the interest rate calculations. The overall effect is to facilitate economic activity.

The general value of property rights argument is supported by the new institutional economics school, led by Douglass North, who argue that financial systems require certain legal and institutional elements to be in place to function effectively.[29] These include the recognition of property rights and the use of property to secure loans. This 'property rights including security rights will produce economic growth' argument has been reinforced by the 'legal origins' or 'law matters' thesis advanced by La Porta, Lopez de Silanes, Shleifer and Vishny.[30] It is also supported by an indirect offspring of La Porta – the *Doing Business* Reports commissioned by the World Bank.[31] The thesis was first developed in the area of investor protection, but it also encompasses creditor rights and legal institutions more generally. The thesis says that 'law matters' in that legal institutions impact on economic growth.[32] But more

G. McCormack, 'American Private Law Writ Large?: The UNCITRAL Secured Transactions Guide' 60 *ICLQ* 597 (2011).

29 North's theories are developed in *Institutions, Institutional Change and Economic Development* (New York: Cambridge University Press, 1990). *See also* C. Goodhart, 'Economics and the Law: Too Much One-Way Traffic?' 60 *MLR* 1, 5 (1997) (referring to Mancur Olson).

30 *See* La Porta, Lopez de Silanes, Shleifer and Vishny, 'Legal Determinants of External Finance' and by the same authors, 'Law and Finance'. The first three named authors refine the 'legal origins' thesis and defend it against criticisms in 'The Economic Consequences of Legal Origins' 46 *Journal of Economic Literature* 285 (2008).

31 The *Doing Business* reports are available at www.doingbusiness.org/ (last accessed 10 January 2013).

32 But *see* M. Roe, 'Legal Origin and Modern Stock Markets' 120 *Harvard Law Review* 460 (2006), who argues that politics is a more relevant causal factor. In 'The Economic

controversially, the thesis also asserts that countries that adopted the common law perform better than those with a civil law origin. Legal families are evaluated on the basis of their economic performance, and generally the common law comes out as superior. The alleged superiority of the common law is founded on two propositions. The first is that judges have greater independence in common law than in civil law systems, so that the government has less influence on market developments. The second is that the common law, being based on case law rather than on legislative codes, is more responsive to the changing conditions and requirements of society.

The legal origins literature has, however, been criticized for a US-centric approach.[33] The thesis suggests that US law is the benchmark, the goal of legal convergence, the end of (legal) history. The thesis has also been criticized as the work of a small group of economists whose knowledge of legal differences and cross-cultural legal comparisons displays deficiencies.[34] The civil/common law distinction is fundamental to the thesis, with membership of a legal family seen as a cause for past and present economic development. But the way in which legal systems are assigned by proponents of the thesis to one or other legal family is crude. For example, France is assigned to the same legal family as Lithuania, but their economies (and their laws) are like apples and oranges in many other respects. All legal systems are mixed to a degree and the civil law/common law divide seems especially irrelevant for the sphere of economic law covered by the legal origins literature. Other aspects of a society, such as politics, culture or religion and geographical position, are much more likely to influence economic development than membership of a particular legal family.[35]

Consequences of Legal Origins', La Porta et al. use 'legal origins' as a sort of proxy for politics. They 'adopt a broad conception of legal origin as a style of social control of economic life (and maybe of other aspects of life as well) . . . [They] argue that common law stands for the strategy of social control that seeks to support private market outcomes, whereas civil law seeks to replace such outcomes with state-desired allocations.'

33 *See generally*, R. Michaels, 'Comparative Law by Numbers? Legal Origins Thesis, Doing Business Reports and the Silence of Traditional Comparative Law' 57 *American Journal of Comparative Law* 765 (2009) and the literature referred to therein. There is also a symposium on the legal origins thesis in the 2009 *Brigham Young University Law Review*.

34 *See* U. Braendle, 'Shareholder Protection in the USA and Germany: "Law and Finance" Revisited' 7 *German Law Journal* 257 (2006).

35 *See* M. Siems, 'Legal Origins: Reconciling Law & Finance and Comparative Law' 52 *McGill Law Journal* 55 (2007). *See also* on legal origins, P. Wood, *Law and Practice of International Finance* (London: Sweet & Maxwell, 2008), Chapter 3.

Despite the criticism, the legal origins literature has heavily influenced the *Doing Business* reports issued by the International Finance Corporation (IFC), a member of the World Bank Group. These reports purport to measure and compare the 'ease of doing business' in more than 130 countries worldwide.[36] Indeed, the lead author of the earlier *Doing Business* reports is a frequent co-author with the originators of the 'legal origins' thesis.[37] While the reports purport to assess attractiveness for investors rather than economic performance per se, there are obvious linkages between the two. The reports have tended to show that credit bureaus, stronger creditor rights and simpler civil procedure rules have a significant impact on access to credit.[38] It is argued that strong creditor protection should lead to deeper credit markets and better financing for firms and individuals. The *Doing Business* reports have identified many laws, rules and institutions, in four basic categories that constitute the basis for private credit – (1) mechanisms for the registration of property; (2) information sharing arrangements or credit bureaus; (3) collateral rules and creditor rights; and (4) contract enforcement. The reports conclude that the wealth of a particular country is an important indicator of the effectiveness of institutions in that country that guarantee access to credit.[39] In the main, richer countries are said to have more expeditious procedures to register ownership of property; a higher presence of private credit bureaus; greater coverage and quality in terms of the information collected by information sharing institutions; more extensive creditor rights and security rights, as well as better measures of contract enforcement.

The *Doing Business* reports have major resonance with national governments, which have often taken conscious steps to improve a country's rankings. This may not be a positive move, however, not least because countries may be more inclined to improve their rankings by 'gaming' the system rather than taking the politically more problematic step of addressing problems highlighted in the reports.[40] Otherwise the *Doing Business* reports may be subjected to similar criticism as the legal origins

36 *See* www.doingbusiness.org (last accessed 21 December 2012).

37 The reference is to Simeon Djankov, now Finance Minister and Deputy Prime Minister of Bulgaria, and for co-authored publications, *see* S. Djankov, R. La Porta, F. López de Silanes and A. Shleifer, 'The Regulation of Entry' 117 *Quarterly Journal of Economics* 1 (2002); 'Courts' 118 *Quarterly Journal of Economics* 453 (2003) and also, with J. Botero, 'The Regulation of Labor' 119 *Quarterly Journal of Economics* 1339 (2004).

38 *See* Lopez de Silanes, 'Turning the Key to Credit' in *Secured Transactions Reform and Access to Credit*.

39 Ibid., p. 20.

40 R. Michaels, 'Comparative Law by Numbers? Legal Origins Thesis, Doing Business Reports and the Silence of Traditional Comparative Law' 57 *American Journal of Comparative Law*

thesis; namely, faulty research, insufficient attention to detail, a common law bias (actual or perceived) and a preference for free market solutions and deregulation over other values such as solidarity and justice and the preservation of separate legal cultures.[41]

The deregulatory and free market agenda was quite explicit in the first *Doing Business* report in 2004, which purported to show that a 'heavy' regulatory regime produced the worst results in terms of economic outcomes because it was usually associated with inefficiency within public institutions, long delays in reaching decisions, high costs of administrative formalities, lengthy judicial proceedings, higher unemployment and more corruption, less productivity and lower investment.[42] The report also said 'Common law countries regulate the least. Countries in the French civil law tradition the most. However, heritage is not destiny.' The overall conclusion was a stark one that 'One Size Can Fit All' in respect of the legal regulation of business. There have, however, been criticisms of the *Doing Business* reports from the Independent Evaluation Group within the World Bank. In a 2008 critique, the Group recommended greater transparency and some modifications to the 'Doing Business' methodology.[43] The critique also suggests that the focus on regulatory costs and burdens should only be one dimension of any overall reform of the investment climate in a particular country. Essentially, the *Doing Business* reports use a creditor-centred approach with the highest grading given to countries that emphasize private contractual solutions rather than court-based ones. This approach appears one-dimensional and overly simplistic. It also ignores the recent economic success of countries such as China, where many of the desiderata considered necessary by international financial institutions, such as strong property rights, are absent.[44]

765, 772 (2009); B. Arrunada, 'Pitfalls to Avoid when Measuring Institutions: Is Doing Business Damaging Business?' 35 *Journal of Comparative Economics* 729 (2007).

41 *See generally*, G. Sarfaty, 'Why Culture Matters in International Institutions: The Marginality of Human Rights at the World Bank' 103 *American Journal of International Law* 647 (2009).

42 *See* the 2004 *Doing Business* Report, p. 83: 'Heavier regulation of business activities generally brings bad outcomes, while clearly defined and well-protected property rights enhance prosperity.'

43 World Bank Independent Evaluation Group, *Doing Business: An Independent Evaluation, Taking the Measure of the World Bank-IFC Doing Business Indicators* (Washington DC: World Bank, 2008).

44 C. Paulus, 'Global Insolvency Law and the Role of Multinational Institutions' 32 *Brooklyn International Law Journal* 755, 762 (2007). For somewhat varying views on the Chinese example, see *Secured Transactions Systems and Collateral Registries*, pp. 67, 104.

In recent times, a popular exponent of the linkage between property rights and economic development has been Hernando De Soto, in writings such as *The Mystery of Capital: Why Capitalism Triumphs in the West and Fails Everywhere Else.*[45] De Soto argues that people in developing countries lack an integrated formal property system and he contrasts this with the US where, in his view, a clear system of property rights was created from early on. De Soto suggests that the absence of such a system makes it impossible for the poor to leverage informal ownership into collateral for the extension of credit. In De Soto's view, the combined effect of bureaucracy and outdated legal systems is to drive economic activities underground in developing countries and to stifle investment activity. But property systems in the wealthy West allow assets, through ownership documentation, to lead an 'invisible, parallel life alongside their material existence'.[46] In developing countries, comparable means of documentation are lacking, thereby creating 'dead capital'.

Formal property systems are said to produce six effects that facilitate the generation of capital. The first is fixing the economic potential of assets. De Soto uses the analogy of generating electric power from a lake in the mountains, suggesting that the potential value locked up in an asset can be revealed, transformed and energized in the same way.[47] The second effect is the integration of dispersed information into one system. The third is making people accountable – incorporation into a more integrated legal system facilitates individual accountability. The fourth effect is to put assets into a more accessible condition so that they can do additional work. Assets become 'fungible' and can be fashioned to suit practically any transaction. Fifthly, increased fungibility in turn helps to network people and convert citizens into individually identifiable and accountable business agents. Increased information and integrated law makes risk more manageable, not least by facilitating the pooling of assets to secure debts. The final effect is the protection of transactions. To sum up, a documented system of ownership can 'provide a link to the owner's credit history, an accountable address for the collection of debts and

[45] H. De Soto, *The Mystery of Capital* (London: Black Swan, 2008). *See also*, G. Hardin, 'The Tragedy of the Commons' 162 *Science* 1243 (1968), but for refinement and criticism of Hardin's work, see *Governing the Commons: The Evolution of Institutions for Collective Action* (New York: Cambridge University Press, 1990) by the winner of the 2009 Nobel Prize for Economics, Elinor Ostrom. For a much more nuanced analysis, *see* R. Ellickson, 'Property in Land' 102 *Yale LJ* 1315 (1992), and in particular the conclusion at 1397.

[46] De Soto, *The Mystery of Capital*, 2008, p. 7.

[47] Ibid., pp. 47–61.

taxes, the basis for creation of reliable public utilities, and a foundation for the creation of securities (like mortgage backed bonds) that can be rediscounted and sold in secondary markets'.[48]

De Soto's work has been lavishly praised, with Bill Clinton, for example, calling him the 'world's greatest living economist',[49] but the work has also attracted criticism on a number of grounds. Some have questioned the statistical validity of the claims about the size of the informal economy.[50] Others would argue that it is excessively narrow in its approach to economic development – basically a 'single bullet' approach. It is suggested that there should be a greater emphasis on culture and the local social context, and how local conditions affect people's perceptions of their opportunities.[51] There are further empirical studies that take issue with the link between property registration mechanisms and the increase in credit to the poor.[52] Also, many micro businesses operate in the informal sector beneath the radar screen of the authorities.[53] They may not see the merit in availing of a reformed law if this meant appearing on the official radar. Moreover, they may not possess much in the way of conventional collateral, and reforming collateral law is unlikely to change that situation. In many countries, improved access to credit has only come about through the willingness of alternative financial institutions to look at cash flows rather than assets. Highlighting secured lending and collateral may put 'undue attention on an issue that the pioneer microfinance organizations and practitioners have worked very hard to reduce to a lower status'.[54]

48 Ibid., p. 7.

49 *See* University of North Carolina at Chapel Hill News Release of October 19, 2004 available at www.unc.edu/news/archives/oct04/fpg_desoto101904.html (last accessed 16 July 2013).

50 *See* the review of De Soto's other famous book, *El Otro Sendero* (*The Other Path*), by R. Rossini and J. Thomas 18 *World Development* 125 (1990).

51 *See* R. Samuelson, 'The Spirit of Capitalism' 80 (Jan/Feb) *Foreign Affairs* 205 (2001): 'Unfortunately, de Soto strains too much. He wants to make property rights – or their absence – the center of everything.'

52 *See* S. Galliani and E. Schargrodsky, 'Property Rights for the Poor: Effects of Land Titling' *Ronald Coase Institute Working Paper* (January 2009), who conclude: 'Our results suggest that land titling can be an important tool for poverty reduction, albeit not through the shortcut of credit access, but through the slow channel of increased physical and human capital investment, which should help to reduce poverty in the future generations.'

53 M. Holtmann, 'Use of Security in Challenging Environments: The Microfinance Perspective' in Dahan and Simpson (eds.), *Secured Transactions Reform and Access to Credit*, p. 159.

54 Ibid., p. 167.

There is also the experience in De Soto's native Peru which suggests that property registration, of itself, is unlikely to have much effect. To bring about concrete reform, it may have to be followed by more politically challenging steps such as improving the norms and efficiency of the judicial system as well as rewriting bankruptcy codes, and restructuring financial market regulation. Reforms of this nature may entail much more challenging choices for policymakers.[55] Radical critiques suggest that one must look more to the current distribution of property rights rather than the formalization of such rights. Mattei, for instance, argues that the 'formalization' movement uses an illusory economic theory to justify the freezing and naturalization of the status quo.[56]

Whatever the validity of the ideological criticism, certainly De Soto's rhetoric is overblown. 'Trifling details' such as significant differences between legal systems and property registration systems in developed countries simply do not concern him. According to De Soto,[57] in the West 'all the property records (titles, deeds, securities and contracts that describe the economically significant aspects of assets) are continually tracked and protected as they travel through time and space'. Regimes of personal property without registration thrive, however, in many parts of the developed world. It is almost as if De Soto is carried away by his own rhetoric and forgets the need for qualification, asserting that 'citizens in advanced nations can obtain descriptions of the economic and social qualities of any available asset without having to see the asset itself'.[58] As a bald, general statement, this is simply not true and casts doubt on the accuracy of De Soto's own research and his overall thesis about the role of registration of assets as a necessary concomitant of economic development.[59] De Soto also ignores the fact that Latin American countries, including Peru, have Civil Codes modelled on the Napoleonic

[55] *See* review of *The Mystery of Capital* by C. Woodruff in 39 *Journal of Economic Literature* 1215 (2001).

[56] *See* U. Mattei, 'The Peruvian Civil Code: Property and Plunder' 6 *Global Jurist Topics* nn. 18, 19 (2005) and *see also*, U. Mattei and L. Nader, *Plunder: When the Rule of Law is Illegal* (Oxford: Wiley-Blackwell, 2008).

[57] De Soto, *The Mystery of Capital*, p. 60.

[58] Ibid., p. 53.

[59] *See* B. Kozolchyk, 'A Road Map to Economic Development through Law: Third Parties and Comparative Legal Culture' 23 *Arizona Journal of International and Comparative Law* 1, 2–3 (2005): 'a merchant's inventory is nowhere represented by a "property document" . . . The preceding objections are not intended as quibbles; they go to the heart of de Soto's argument.'

Codes of France and Spain.[60] These Codes may not be the most 'efficient' and comprehensive in terms of protecting property rights, including the position of secured creditors, but they may not necessarily be any better or worse than the Codes in some modern European civilian jurisdictions. In short, De Soto, and others' theses, which suggest that the development of the West is explicable on the basis of a better formal structure of property rights that Western economies possess and developing countries lack, seems much too pat, as well as being belied by the facts.

V. Improving credit cost and availability

Studies by various international financial institutions have suggested a correlation between enhanced security rights on the one hand, and greater access to, and cheaper credit on the other.[61] This correlation has been borne out in an empirical study by Haselmann and Pistor examining the effect of legal change in respect of collateral rights on the lending behaviour of banks in twelve transition economies.[62] The study concludes that banks increase the supply of credit subsequent to legal change and that the ability to 'collateralize' or use assets as security, seems to be an important determinant of credit supplied in the economy. It also finds that foreign-owned banks respond more strongly to legal change than incumbents. This is consistent with the proposition that especially in emerging and transition economies, information asymmetries are of greater concern compared to developed markets. Collateral rights tend to reduce information gaps between lenders and borrowers; to even the playing field between foreign and domestic lenders and to open up the credit market to new participants.

Where asset collateralization is legally possible, it is argued that all but the largest borrowers should get better terms on a secured rather than an unsecured loan. Better terms can take the form of lower interest rates, larger loans relative to income and also more generous repayment periods. A more prosaic example has been cited in the case of a

60 *See* Mattei, 'The Peruvian Civil Code': 'Latin American private law derives in large measure from Spanish and Portuguese law.'

61 *Secured Transactions Systems and Collateral Registries*, pp. 7–13.

62 *See* R. Haselmann and K. Pistor, 'How the Law affects Lending' 23 *Review of Financial Studies* 549 (2009).

credit union for International Monetary Fund (IMF) and World Bank employees:[63]

> When the borrowers offer collateral for a loan instead of only a signature, the credit union offers better terms: it will, lend at interest rates that are about half as high, make loans that are five to ten times larger relative to income and give the borrower as much as five times longer to repay.

In other cases, however, there may not be simple trade-off between interest rates and the cost of credit. For instance, sub-prime borrowers may be charged high interest rates and also required to provide security. With blue-chip borrowers, on the other hand, capacity to service the loan is not considered to be an issue. Security does not enter into the reckoning and the competition among lenders for a valuable source of business keeps interest rates low. Moreover, there are greater costs incurred in secured as distinct from unsecured lending.[64] Secured loans are more expensive to set up, since the expenses involved in arranging and documenting the transaction are higher. For this reason, it is not just loans to blue-chip borrowers, but sometimes small loans, or loans to buyers with strong repayment records, that may be offered on an unsecured basis. While evidence suggests that 60–65 per cent of loans to businesses in the US are secured, the precise effect of security on credit cost and availability is very difficult, if not impossible, to verify empirically.[65]

VI. Critical perspectives on the harmonization and modernization of secured credit law

This section addresses three critical perspectives on UNCITRAL's harmonization and modernization agenda. The first considers general issues of fairness and, in particular, fairness to unsecured creditors, from enhanced recognition of security rights. The second perspective looks at secured credit law reform as part of a neo-liberal economic agenda pushed by international organizations that also includes privatization and marketization of key sectors of a national economy. The third perspective

[63] *See* Fleisig, 'The Economics of Collateral and Collateral Reform' in *Secured Transactions Reform and Access to Credit*, pp. 81, 85.

[64] *See generally*, R. Mann, 'Explaining the Pattern of Secured Credit' 110 *Harvard Law Review* 626 (1997).

[65] *See* Lopez de Silanes, 'Turning the Key to Credit' in *Secured Transactions Reform and Access to Credit*, p. 10.

considers secured credit reform as a possible instrument of American foreign policy and American economic interests.

1. *Security and fairness*

The concept of security runs counter to instinctive conceptions of fairness, in that it may involve one creditor being paid whereas other creditors remain unpaid.[66] In short, the idea of proportionate satisfaction of creditor claims, i.e. pari passu distribution, is disturbed. This concern can be met in various ways. For instance, one might argue that the general instrumentalist justifications for security override individual conceptions of fairness. In other words, increased credit creation and lower cost credit will help to stimulate economic activity and lead to better economic conditions for all. Moreover, to the extent that security is seen as a fair exchange for the credit, the secured creditor has bargained for security and priority, whereas other creditors have not. Consequently, it does not seem unfair to privilege the secured creditor over other creditors who could equally have contracted for security but chose not to do so. On the other hand, there may be involuntary creditors, i.e. creditors not in a contractual relationship with the debtor, who are not in a position to bargain for security. Also, there are other non-adjusting creditors, or poorly adjusting creditors, where it is unrealistic to suppose that they could bargain for security or where the transaction costs of doing so are too great. These creditors in a weak bargaining position are perhaps most likely to be the ones that will be hardest hit by the debtor's insolvency. The insolvency may impact disproportionately on them, in that they are not very capable of sharing or passing on the costs of the loss. Large financial institutions most likely to take security are in a much better position to pass on losses.

Employees and small trade creditors are typically non-adjusting, or poorly-adjusting, creditors. Different jurisdictions may have different ways of protecting such creditors, whether through social safety nets, insurance schemes, or the like. Other possible approaches would be to impose restrictions on the taking of security, thereby leaving a margin of unsecured assets that are available for payment of unsecured debts, or else to set aside a proportion of secured realizations for the benefit of unsecured creditors. The UNCITRAL Guide, however, follows the thread

[66] For a strong critique of pari passu, *see generally*, R. Mokal, 'Priority as Pathology: The Pari Passu Myth' 60 *CLJ* 581 (2001).

of Article 9 of the American Uniform Commercial Code and counsels against this, recognizing the 'full' priority of security rights.

2. Secured credit and 'neo-liberal' economic reforms

Secured credit law reform is generally promoted on the basis that it will foster market-based decision making on credit issues. Reform is often seen as part of an overall economic agenda – the so-called Washington consensus – that includes privatization and marketization.[67] They may be viewed as interlinked ingredients in an overall growth and development strategy. In the early 1990s, international financial institutions pushed the advantage of a rapid privatization process but, in many instances, this led to a massive transfer of State resources into the hands of privileged insiders, or the economically powerful. There is a growing recognition that rapid privatization is not the best prescription for reform.[68] The Chinese experience indicates that a slower, more gradual process is more conducive to long-term economic stability.[69] A gradual process of privatization allows the restructuring of large firms to take place before their move, in whole or in part, into the private sector.

One of the presumptions underpinning the Washington consensus is that markets will intrinsically lead to efficient outcomes, but, the recent global financial crisis has instead highlighted the possibility of desirable government intervention that can guide economic growth and make everyone better off. Commentators, such as Joseph Stiglitz, have also criticized the focus of the Washington consensus on GDP, which is seen as the be-all and end-all of development. He argues that:[70]

> because GDP is relatively easy to measure, it has become a fixation of economists. The trouble with this is that we measure what we strive for. Sometimes, increases in GDP are associated with poverty reduction, as was the case in East Asia. But that was not an accident: governments designed

[67] *See* J. Stiglitz, *Globalisation and its Discontents* (London: Penguin, 2002), pp. 16, 53–4.

[68] *See* ibid., p. 6: 'countries were told by the West that the new economic system would bring them unprecedented prosperity. Instead, it brought unprecedented poverty . . . The contrast between Russia's transition, as engineered by the international economic institutions, and that of China, designed by itself, could not be greater'.

[69] *See* J. Ohnesorge, 'Developing Development Theory: Law and Development Orthodoxies and the North East Asian Experience' 28 *University of Pennsylvania Journal of International Economic Law* 219 (2007) and *see also*, J. Ohnesorge, 'The Rule of Law, Economic Development, and the Developmental States of Northeast Asia' in C. Antons (ed.), *Law and Development in East and South East Asia* (London: RoutledgeCurzon, 2003).

[70] *See* J. Stiglitz, *Making Globalization Work* (London: Penguin, 2006), p. 45.

> policies to make sure that the poor shared in the benefits. Elsewhere, growth has often been accompanied by increased poverty and sometimes even lower income levels for individuals in the middle.

It is submitted that this is a valuable insight and that the merits of secured credit reform should be disaggregated from wider notions about the alleged efficacy of market-based decision making, and the implementation of a privatization agenda.

3. The UNCITRAL Guide as an instrument of American economic power

There have been many analyses of the role of transplants in the legal modernization and harmonization process.[71] It is the case that a variety of factors drive countries to adopt legal transplants from other jurisdictions and models of greater, or lesser, sophistication have been used to explain the typology of transplants.[72] Professor Alan Watson, for example, has acknowledged that reception and transplants come in all shapes and sizes, speaking of an imposed reception, solicited imposition, penetration, infiltration, crypto-reception, inoculation and so on.[73] Another approach is to propound a straightforward distinction between coercive transplants and voluntary receptions. The notion of 'coercive' transplants can be used to explain the relationship between a colonial power and its dependencies whereby the law of the mother country is imposed on its 'foreign' possessions and territories as part of the project of imperial governance. The concept of 'voluntary' reception explains situations where the aura, or prestige, of a particular jurisdiction persuades other countries to adopt its laws.[74]

71 *See generally*, W. Twining, 'Social Science and Diffusion of Law' 32 *Journal of Law and Society* 203 (2005), 205; 'Diffusion of Law: A Global Perspective' 49 *Journal of Legal Pluralism* 1 (2004). *See also*, F. Schauer, 'The Politics and Incentives of Legal Transplantation' (2000) *Centre for International Development at Harvard Working Paper No. 44*; T. Waelde and J. Gunderson, 'Legislative Reform in Transition Economies: Western Transplants – A Shortcut to Social Market Economy Status' 43 *ICLQ* 347 (1994).

72 But for a somewhat different perspective, *see* O. Kahn-Freund, 'On Uses and Misuses of Comparative Law' 37 *MLR* 1 (1974) and for a response, *see* A. Watson, 'Legal Transplants and Law Reform' 92 *LQR* 79 (1976). *See also*, W. Ewald, 'Comparative Jurisprudence (11): The Logic of Legal Transplants' 43 *AJCL* 489 (1995).

73 A. Watson, *Legal Transplants: An Approach to Comparative Law* (Edinburgh: Scottish Academic Press, 1974), p. 30.

74 *See* U. Mattei, 'A Theory of Imperial Law: A Study on U.S. Hegemony and the Latin Resistance' 10 *Indiana Journal of Global Legal Studies* 383, 385 (2002).

The sufficiency of this basic taxonomy has been challenged. In particular, the distinction between coercive and voluntary transplants could be seen as a matter only of degree, and not of kind. There is not a straightforward dichotomy between 'free' or 'coercive' transplants of a foreign model – law is a detailed and complex machinery of social control that cannot effectively function without some cooperation from local officials, usually consisting of a professional elite, possibly created by the imperial power. This elite provides the degree of consent to the reception of foreign legal ideas that is necessary for any transplant to occur.[75] In this connection, one might also make use of the notion of reflexive law, thereby acknowledging that the influence exerted by exporting or 'hegemonic' jurisdictions is most likely to be effective when it seeks to achieve its ends not by direct prescription, but by inducing second-order effects on the part of social actors in the receiving State.[76] One may also tie in the concept of path dependency.[77] The law, and lawyers, tend to absorb change by digging deeper into existing soil, rather than branching out into new fields. Political and other influences may trigger legal development and cause the law to produce certain outcomes, but the form that represents these outcomes is determined by the legal doctrine prevailing in the jurisdiction concerned.[78] In short, the law develops in a path-dependent fashion.

Another commentator, Professor Ugo Mattei, has sought to explain transplants on the basis of prestige or efficiency.[79] While acknowledging

[75] *See* Berkowitz, Pistor and Richard, 'The Transplant Effect', who suggest that indigenous lawmaking operates as a kind of focal point for cooperative lawmaking behaviour, which then serves as the focal point for cooperative economic behaviour. *See also*, G. Teubner, 'Legal Irritants: Good Faith in British Law, or How Unifying Law Ends Up in New Divergences' 61 *MLR* 11 (1998).

[76] *See generally*, G. Teubner, 'Substantive and Reflexive Elements in Modern Law' 17 *Law and Society Review* 239 (1983).

[77] L. Bebchuk and M. Roe, 'A Theory of Path Dependence in Corporate Ownership and Governance' 52 *Stanford Law Review* 127 (1999).

[78] *See generally*, E. Micheler, *Property in Securities: A Comparative Study* (Cambridge University Press, 2007), Chapter 15 'Legal Development as a Path-dependent Process', and see the statement at p. 228: 'Legal doctrine causes the law to develop path-dependently'. *See also*, H. Spamann, 'Contemporary Legal Transplants – Legal Families and the Diffusion of (Corporate) Law' *Brigham Young University Law Review* 1813 [2009]; J. Armour, S. Deakin, P. Lele and M. Siems, 'How Do Legal Rules Evolve? Evidence from a Cross-Country Comparison of Shareholder, Creditor, and Worker Protection' 57 *American Journal of Comparative Law* 579 (2009).

[79] U. Mattei, 'Efficiency in Legal Transplants: An Essay in Comparative Law and Economics' 14 *International Review of Law and Economics* 3 (1994). *See also*, A. Ogus, 'Competition Between National Legal Systems: A Contribution of Economic Analysis to Comparative

that each single legal transplant has its own peculiarities that make it different from every other, Mattei deploys economic analysis to explain the perceived convergence of modern legal systems as a movement towards efficiency, despite the large variety of institutional backgrounds. A synergy is also said to exist between 'efficiency' and 'prestige', with the most efficient models being seen as the more prestigious. The 'efficiency' notion links up with concepts of regulatory competition. This implies convergence around a single, efficient system which wins out through the competitive process. But the evidence about regulatory competition suggests that it may produce rules that are far from optimal from the viewpoint of economic theory.[80] There is also the risk of 'social dumping'[81] and a so-called race to the bottom.[82] Proponents of the 'efficiency' thesis then have to fall back on arguments about the long-term benefits of market solutions. In some cases, the idea of co-evolution may better explain the process whereby countries observe and emulate practices in jurisdictions to which they are closely related by trade and institutional connections. The co-evolution concept assumes that a variety of diverse systems may exist side-by-side, with each one retaining its viability. More fundamentally, a recent empirical study of private credit in more than 100 countries over twenty-five years has amassed evidence contradicting the hypothesis that legal institutions converge toward the more successful ones over time.[83] In addition, the study suggests that since credit institutions vary so much across countries and legal origins, the evidence is also inconsistent with the 'functional convergence' hypothesis that institutions in different countries, while distinct on the surface, functionally converge to accomplish the same goals.

Evidence of a lack of a convergence, however, is not necessarily inconsistent with the proposition that certain legal systems may hold an appeal on prestige or other grounds. John Braithwaite and Peter Drahos, in their

Law' 48 *ICLQ* 405 (1999) and *see generally*, F. von Hayek, 'Competition as a Discovery Procedure' 5 *Quarterly Journal of Austrian Economics* 3, 9 (2002).

80 *See* D. Esty and D. Geradin (eds.), *Regulatory Competition and Economic Integration: Comparative Perspectives* (Oxford University Press, 2001).

81 In the context of EC employment law, the ECJ made specific reference to social dumping in *Laval un Partneri Ptd* v. *Svenska* (341/05) [2007] ECR I-5751, para. 103.

82 *See generally*, C. Barnard, 'Social Dumping and Race to the Bottom: Some Lessons for the EU from Delaware?' 25 *EL Rev* 57 (2000); L. Enriques and M. Gelter, 'Regulatory Competition in European Company Law and Creditor Protection' 7 *European Business Organization Law Review* 417 (2006).

83 *See* S. Djankov, C. McLiesh and A. Shleifer, 'Private Credit in 129 Countries' 84 *Journal of Financial Economics* 299 (2007).

seminal book on *Global Business Regulation*,[84] have spoken of how models are adopted 'when they appeal to identities that we hold dear. An identity that is particularly crucial in this regard is that of being successful, modern, civilised, advanced. The periphery models the centre in the world system because of this pursuit of modernity in identity (or postmodernity, for the truly avant-garde).' The French economist Michel Albert has spoken of the irresistible force of US legal expansionism.[85] US legal paradigms gain a competitive advantage from the political and ideological sway exercised by the US. Alternative approaches are overwhelmed by American political and cultural influences. Albert explains the spread of American influences using notions of seductiveness and appeal. In his view, the intrinsic characteristics of the neo-American model exalt the success of risk-taking, gambling and 'glittery' behaviour. In the same vein, another commentator has talked about how the European Community method of rational planning, bureaucratic solutions, suppression of political passion and a steady incrementalism, is incapable of igniting the popular emotions in a way that would allow Europe to mount a true global challenge to the US.[86]

Mattei has now moved away from his earlier reliance on 'prestige' or 'efficiency' to propound a theory of 'imperial law':[87]

> Imperial law is produced, in the interest of international capital, by a variety of both public and private institutions, all sharing a gap in legitimacy. . . . Imperial law is shaped by a spectacular process of exaggeration, aimed at building consent for the purpose of hegemonic domination. Imperial law subordinates local legal arrangements world-wide. . . . Predatory economic globalization is the vehicle, the all-mighty ally, and the beneficiary of imperial law.

In the realm of literary and cultural discourse, notions of imperialism and American hegemony have been advanced by Edward Said.[88] He talks about American culture's phenomenally incorporative capacity and a system of pressures and constraints which induces other States to follow the

[84] J. Braithwaite and P. Drahos, *Global Business Regulation* (Cambridge University Press, 2000), p. 591.

[85] M. Albert, *Capitalism Against Capitalism: How America's Obsession with Individual Achievement and Short-term Profit has Led it to the Brink of Economic Collapse* (London: Whurr, 1993).

[86] *See* S. Dillon, 'Looking for the Progressive Empire: Where is the European Union's Foreign Policy?' 19 *Connecticut Journal of International Law* 275, 278 (2004).

[87] *See* Mattei, 'A Theory of Imperial Law'. *See also*, J. Gardner, *Legal Imperialism, American Lawyers and Foreign Aid in Latin America* (Madison: University of Wisconsin Press, 1980).

[88] E. Said, *Culture and Imperialism* (London: Chatto & Windus, 1993). *See also*, M. Hardt and A. Negri, *Empire* (Cambridge, MA.: Harvard University Press, 2000).

essentially imperial identity and direction of US norms.[89] In his view, the pressures are subtle, and generally indirect.[90] Said makes the point that[91] 'American attitudes to American greatness, to hierarchies of race, to the perils of other revolutions . . . have remained constant, have dictated, have obscured the realities of empire, while apologists for overseas American interests have insisted on American innocence, doing good, fighting for freedom.' Said also links his theory of imperialism with a lawmaking creed that suggests it is the goal of US foreign policy to bring about a world increasingly subject to the rule of law, as defined in US terms.

In the sphere of secured credit, the UNCITRAL Guide can be considered as an instrument by which the norms set out in Article 9 of the American Commercial Code are writ large across the globe. The Guide reproduces the key features of Article 9, emphasizing the removal of restrictions on the taking of security, all-assets security, notice filing of security interests on American lines, and the full priority of security rights. US private and public interests combined and collaborated in the formulation and development of the Guide. It is hardly surprising that agencies of the US government, as well as US private interests, should act to defend what they consider to be US business interests. Leading economies, including the US, 'have a collective interest in promoting generalized dependency and reverence from the periphery'.[92] But as one US commentator remarks, 'efforts to export U.S. legal models are more likely to succeed if they eschew detailed, distinctively U.S.-derived prescriptions in favour of presenting advise or exemplars in terms of more "general" standards, "international" norms, "universal" principles . . . '[93] The work of bodies such as UNCITRAL is considered to represent best international practice.[94] The US, by virtue of its economic power, and the associated prestige of its economic and legal models, heavily influences the work of such bodies

89 Said, *Culture and Imperialism*, p. 392. 90 Ibid., p. 401. 91 Ibid., p. 7.

92 *See* the following statement by the Commercial Finance Association (CFA), General Counsel – (UN Press Release ECO/56 L/3061–29/03/2010): 'CFA members, which include large United States banks but also smaller lenders, often make loans to companies located in other countries supported by collateral. The guide will help countries to modernize their laws, so that lenders who are interested in making loans in other countries will know with certainty and predictability what their rights and obligations are.'

93 *See* J. deLisle, 'Lex Americana? United States Legal Assistance, American Legal Models and Legal Change in the Post-Communist World and Beyond' 20 *University of Pennsylvania Journal of International Economic Law* 179, 269 (1999), and *see also* his comment at p. 202 about the US government promoting the indirect export of US models through multilateral organizations that shape international standards.

94 *See generally*, K. Pistor, 'The Standardization of Law and Its Effect on Developing Economies' 50 *AJCL* 97 (2002).

and, putting the point simply, what is considered to be good for the US is also considered to be good for the world.[95] But there are many who disagree with the assessment of what is good not only for the world but also for the US.

VII. Conclusion

Security rights give the credit provider property rights, normally in the debtor's assets. The whole harmonization and modernization agenda appears to be driven largely by a desire to remove restrictions on the taking of security. This is because of a widespread belief that a 'liberal' secured transactions regime promotes economic growth. In many World Bank and other studies, the availability of credit has been identified as one of the key factors driving economic growth. Lack of access to credit, and in particular low-cost credit, is seen as a major constraint on economic development. While economic and other factors may hamper access to credit, legal, regulatory and institutional frameworks are also seen significantly to contribute to this problem. In many jurisdictions, the laws relating to secured transactions are fragmented and antiquated. Businesses may be unable to utilize the full value of their assets or, if they try to do so, they are straitjacketed down a particular and restrictive path. Unlocking the value of collateral to serve as security is seen as a highly important task.

But the harmonization and modernization agenda also has its critics. The law of secured finance is often perceived to embody cultural attitudes and public policy choices that vary greatly among States. In this area of commercial law, sovereignty issues remain central since many of the rules governing enforcement of security rights reflect policy interests that are external to the credit relationship itself. An agreement between debtor and creditor cannot regulate completely the operation of the resulting security right against third parties. In the event of debtor insolvency, there is an additional layer of policy issues to be considered. The rules governing the distribution of the debtor's assets may reflect local social goals. There are dangers in terms of detrimental social consequences if theoretically free markets are left to enjoy full rein.

Changes to law and legal doctrine in a particular jurisdiction often mirror, to a greater or lesser extent, changes that have taken place in other jurisdictions. The desire for change may stem from societal developments

[95] *See* Braithwaite and Drahos, *Global Business Regulation*, p. 587.

or from a desire to promote the social and economic infrastructure of a particular country. Turkey exemplifies a country that set out on a path of modernity as a result of top-down political leadership and then consciously borrowed laws and legal institutions from other jurisdictions that were considered to offer a superior product.[96] Changes may also to a greater extent be coerced. In decades and centuries past, the UK exported the common law to its overseas territories and possessions, and generally these former colonies persisted with the common law as they gained political independence. The French Napoleonic Code found its way to Spain as a result of military conquest and from there it passed to the Hispanic world of Central and South America. In recent times, coercion has come in more subtle forms, perhaps through conditions attached to international loans to developing countries from the World Bank and IMF.

The US strongly influences, if not entirely controls, the workings of these international financial institutions, in particular, the IMF. World Bank and IMF conditionality may require economic austerity measures, and also changes to the economic structures of the country concerned, including privatization and restructuring of State-owned enterprises and strengthening the role of the private sector. The conditions may also require changes to corporate law, as well as the enactment of measures to enhance the availability of credit by means of a modern secured transactions regime. Prescriptions in this regard are most unlikely to be expressed as crudely as 'Enact Article 9 of the American Uniform Commercial Code'. Instead, they are more likely to call for progress and advancement in line with best international practice.[97] Best international practice is considered to be represented by the work of organizations such as UNCITRAL. The US, through economic power and the associated prestige of its economic and legal models, heavily influences the work of UNCITRAL and analogous bodies. Certainly the UNCITRAL Secured Transactions

[96] *See* E. Orucu, 'Turkey: Change under Pressure' in E. Orucu, S. Attwool and S. Coyle, *Studies in Legal Systems: Mixed and Mixing* (London: Kluwer, 1996), p. 89. *See also*, E. Orucu, *Critical Comparative Law: Considering Paradoxes for Legal Systems in Transition* (Deventer: Kluwer, 1999), p. 81: 'No single legal system served as the model. The choice was driven in some cases by the perceived prestige of the model, in some by efficiency and in others by chance. Choosing a number of different models may have given the borrowings "cultural legitimacy" as the desire to modernise and westernise was not beholden to any one dominant culture.'

[97] *See* Pistor, 'The Standardization of Law', 108, on how the influence of a foreign law can be obscured by the use of an international instrument.

Guide reproduces the key features of Article 9 of the American Uniform Commercial Code in apparent preference to alternative models from other jurisdictions.

While some of the rhetoric about the economic efficacy of property rights, including security rights, is certainly overblown, there is nevertheless some empirical evidence that enhanced and more widely available security rights may open the door to greater economic growth. On the other hand, there is little evidence that following a detailed blueprint such as the American Article 9 writ large in the UNCITRAL Secured Transactions Guide will necessarily give a further boost to growth prospects. Indeed, it may even harm them. A study based on the Eastern European experience demonstrates various potential inefficiencies when law is transplanted into an 'alien' implementing or enforcing environment.[98] The study sees indigenous norms and institutions functioning better than transplanted ones, and while the possibility of borrowing from other countries is not precluded, the 'fit' of foreign with domestic law is enhanced by meaningful adaptation of imported laws to local conditions.[99] There are no magical elixirs that bring about a happy ending to the quest for growth.[100] In short, there is no Holy Grail, and the UNCITRAL Secured Transactions Guide, if and to the extent that it implies otherwise, is a false god.

[98] *See* Berkowitz, Pistor and Richard, 'The Transplant Effect'.

[99] Referring to Cass Sunstein – 'the meaning of legal statements is a function of social norms, not of the speaker's intentions' – in 'On the Expressive Function of Law' 144 *University of Pennsylvania Law Review* 2021, 2050 (1996), and *see also*, C. Sunstein, 'Social Norms and Social Roles' 96 *Columbia Law Review* 903, 925 (1996).

[100] *See* W. Easterly, *The Elusive Quest for Growth: Economists' Adventures and Misadventures in the Tropics* (Cambridge, MA: MIT Press, 2001), p. 289.

3

Commentary on the availability of credit

JOANNA GRAY

McCormack's critique of the UNCITRAL *Legislative Guide on Secured Transactions* at the May 2010 conference was most certainly one of the more provocative and controversial of the day, to judge from the participant comments at the time, in particular with respect to the claims made in the fourth part as to the extent to which US hegemony might lie behind the international harmonization and modernization agenda. In reflecting on the revised paper some time on from the seminar, at a time when economic growth seems ever more elusive, then any recipe that law reform can provide to promote it, is worthy of re-examination. McCormack's discussion of the orthodoxy that drives World Bank and UNCITRAL efforts in this area, deriving its intellectual force from the work of La Porta et al., provides a useful reminder of the faith in strong private property rights, including the ability to grant enforceable security interests therein, as being a key driver of access to credit on the most efficient terms for firms and households, the engines of growth, and that increasing the supply of credit is in itself a public good. The point might also have been made here that, in light of the role of excess leverage in contributing to the build-up of systemic risk in the banking sector that led to the financial crisis of 2008 that any claim to offer cheap and widely available credit as a public good is open to attack. Albeit the ability to create security interests in property was in itself by no means a central villain of the piece in the banking crisis of 2008, with many other factors such as the tax privileging of debt, weak and wrongly targeted regulation and the explosive growth of securitization instruments and markets playing their part, an 'underwater' homeowner facing foreclosure on her home from a lender and whose consumption and investment decisions are, in consequence, the antithesis of growth promoting, may feel somewhat differently about the virtues of strong form, lender protective and easily enforceable security interests. Especially when many of those very same lenders have seen the benefit of bail-outs, assistance and forbearance that their borrowers can only dream of. Such is the gist of Robert Shiller's recent analysis,[1] which finds resonance in McCormack's use of Mattei's work to critique what he sees as De Soto's somewhat gung-ho readiness to accept and formalize through law reform the status quo in terms of distribution of property rights and economic power. McCormack's discussion of security and fairness in the context of who benefits most from taking security finds a friend in Shiller's plea to democratize and humanize financial capitalism.

Even if one accepts the central thesis of the legal origins literature and hence the virtues of the UNCITRAL law reform, McCormack counsels as to the need to consider the efficacy of the proposed reform in terms of its own stated objectives. The persistent effects of extra-legal factors such as politics, culture, religion and geography can operate as a drag and, indeed, even subvert the best-intentioned and planned issue-specific and 'law only' reform initiatives. The recently reported[2] tasking of De Soto himself by the new Muslim Brotherhood-dominated Egyptian government to tame, document and formalize Egypt's vast informal economy provides a real example of just what factors beyond the reforms of contract and property law, effective registration systems and judicial enforcement may need to be addressed before these reforms reach their desired consequences.

Turning to Bholat's thought-provoking contribution to this collection in which he reflects on the nature of money – the way in which it is created by fractional reserve banking and how it feeds in to credit cycles/systemic disturbances etc. – it needs to be said that those readers of this volume, most of whom will be lawyers, even if they are reasonably conversant with economic modes of thought, will need to concentrate hard and persevere to understand the essential argument made herein. However, such perseverance will pay off, since the chapter is clearly written and packed with ideas.

The general theme of this volume appears originally to have been conceived as exploring the received truth that clarifying and harmonizing the legal basis for the taking of security increases the ability of banks to lend/lowers cost of credit and promotes economic development. Just as McCormack has taken issue with this thesis from a law reform perspective, Bholat rehearses some of the economic arguments which might mount

[1] R. Shiller, *Finance and the Good Society* (Princeton University Press, 2012).

[2] G. Tett, 'Comment', *Financial Times*, 28 April 2012.

the same challenge. He cautions against buying into that premise at face value and shows us that the use of the technique of taking security on a grant of credit has led to an increase in financialization and connectedness within the financial sector itself (his illustrated use of reverse repos serves as an example) and this can be systemically disturbing. This is the essential message of Bholat's analysis, and he leads the reader back to it in conclusion after some fascinating material on the nature and origins of money. No lawyer has yet produced an analysis equal to the late Francis Mann's seminal work, *The Legal Aspect of Money*, but reading Bholat's piece one realizes such an attempt is overdue, especially at a time when other disciplines such as cultural anthropology are producing such interesting scholarship on the nature and origins of money and debt, as Bholat highlights.

His conclusion on the resilience of capitalist culture through the expansion of its core (and use of pawnbroking as an example) is a very interesting one, although some may find the idea in his final sentence really quite depressing. For if more leverage through new conduits of lending (and consequent continued enslavement of the self through use of a greater range of physical objects to secure the means to supply wants) is a consequence of the crisis in confidence in banks, then it seems that Tolstoy's question highlighted at the start of Bholat's chapter is not being asked loudly enough at the individual or social level. If objects pledged in a shadow banking system are becoming new types of money and the fetishism of commodities is increasing, then it seems timely to remind us of the origins of money as religious artefacts and ask if sources of value in society have not moved on from the golden calf, etc., or are they really turning back to that? It is to be hoped not and, instead that as we strive to rethink the financial system, more imaginative and inclusive solutions can be found.

PART II

Involvement of international financial institutions in secured transactions law reform

4

International organizations as global lawmakers: seven shifts in practice for secured transactions law and beyond

TERENCE C. HALLIDAY

I. Introduction

The global management of markets in the past twenty-five years has been punctuated by one geopolitical crisis and two massive financial crises. Together they have precipitated an unprecedented burst of law-making activity by international financial institutions (IFIs) and development banks, international professional associations, entities of the United Nations, the European Union, and powerful States determined to shape the world in their own image. These frenetic endeavours have proceeded not independently but in mutual awareness, sometimes competitively and sometimes cooperatively. The net effect, however, has been greatly to amplify the role of international organizations (IOs) as global lawmakers, as architects of transnational legal orders and, indeed, of States.[1]

The availability of credit, in general, and the salience of secured transactions law, in particular, have been integral components of each crisis. Following the collapse of the Soviet Union and the emancipation of its Soviet bloc satellite countries, IOs embarked upon projects of sweeping legal infrastructure building, not least, of secured transaction regimes. The European Bank for Reconstruction and Development (EBRD) developed a Model Law on Secured Transactions and followed it with higher level principles that might readily be adopted by States. On a parallel track, the EBRD created a diagnostic instrument for appraisal of secured

[1] T. C. Halliday, 'Architects of the State: International Financial Institutions and the Reconstruction of States in East Asia' 37(2) *Law & Social Inquiry* 265–96 (2011); T.C. Halliday and G. Shaffer, 'Transnational Legal Orders: A Theoretical Framework', in *Transnational Legal Orders* (Montego Bay, Jamaica 2012); G. Shaffer, 'Transnational Legal Process and State Change: Opportunities and Constraints' 37 *Law & Social Inquiry* 229 (2012).

transaction laws and regimes in all its member countries, diagnoses that were displayed in public report cards that compared nations to each other and over time – all of which was intended to impel countries to create or reform secured transactions law and to build organizations, such as public registries, which would open up sources of credit for transitional and developing economies.[2]

Even before the onset of the Asian Financial Crisis in late 1997, the Asian Development Bank (ADB) had initiated projects across eleven Asian nations that sought to integrate insolvency with secured transactions law.[3] The threat to the global economy of the Asian Financial Crisis precipitated the International Monetary Fund (IMF, the Fund) and World Bank into vigorous lawmaking efforts. The World Bank, in particular, embarked on a six-year programme to create global principles for creditors' rights and insolvency systems,[4] which guided both the Bank and the Fund in their design of a comprehensive diagnostic instrument on insolvency regimes – Report on the Observance of Standards and Codes – that included diagnostic questions on protection of creditors.

Not to be left out of this flurry of regional and global norm-making activity, the United Nations entity responsible for the development of trade law also entered the norm-making lists. UNCITRAL (UN Commission on International Trade Law), a small entity based in Vienna, had a forty-year history of producing sometimes widely adopted conventions (e.g. Convention on Sales of Goods), model laws and legislative guides. UNCITRAL had brought together States and leading IOs, industry and professional organizations in the 1990s, to produce a receivables convention. Buoyed by its success, determined not to lose momentum, and alert to potential competition from UNIDROIT, UNCITRAL boldly launched a seven-year-long endeavour to produce a *Legislative Guide on Secured Transactions* (UNCITRAL Legislative Guide) in 2009,[5] a success it has followed with subsequent products.

And Europe, too, was not to be left behind. Coterminous with the UNCITRAL Legislative Guide, a small group of distinguished scholars,

[2] European Bank for Reconstruction and Development (EBRD), *Transition Report 1999*: 'Ten Years of Transition' (London: EBRD, 1999).

[3] *Law and Development at the Asian Development Bank* (Manila: Asian Development Bank, 1999).

[4] World Bank, *Principles and Guidelines for Effective Insolvency and Creditor Rights Systems* (Washington DC: World Bank, 1999); World Bank, *Principles for Effective Insolvency and Creditor Rights Systems* (Washington DC: World Bank, 2005).

[5] United Nations Commission on International Trade Law (UNCITRAL) 2009.

led by an eminent German academic, Professor Ulrich Drobnig, at the Max Planck Institute for Comparative and International Private Law, began the ambitious project of reformulating the European civil and common law of secured transactions into a single unified document.[6]

For social scientists, these instances of lawmaking responses to crises and aspirations to enhance the vitality of markets raise some basic questions. Why do IOs engage in this kind of lawmaking? How do they go about producing rules for the world? And if they are going to make a difference, and achieve the goals they set themselves, what *modus operandi* are likely to produce more successful outcomes?

This chapter draws upon on extensive research project on IO lawmaking since the Asian Financial Crisis[7] to answer two of those questions. First, the chapter reviews four theories that might explain why IOs produce standards in response to major crises. Second, the chapter offers seven ways in which IO lawmaking will increase the probability that there will be a closer fit between norms propagated by IOs and actual behaviour those norms seek to alter. In the course of answering both questions I will argue more briefly that the process of global lawmaking has major consequences for its pragmatic outcomes.

[6] R. Macdonald, 'Transnational Secured Transactions Reform: Book IX of the Draft Common Frame of Reference in Perspective' 17 *Zeitschrift fur Europäisches Privatrecht* 745 (2009).

[7] This research has relied upon participant observation in global lawmaking forums, including UNCITRAL's Working Group on Insolvency, since 2000; extensive interviews with international civil servants at the ADB, EBRD, IMF, World Bank and UNCITRAL; participation in regional forums conducted by the OECD; extensive interviews with private lawmaking bodies, such as professional associations; detailed analysis of IFI draft and final documents; interviews of UNCITRAL's Secretariat and meetings with delegates and analysis and delegations to Working Groups on secured transactions, insolvency and transport law; fieldwork in Indonesia, Korea and China from 1999 to 2008 on the adoption of global standards after the Asian financial crisis. Research on insolvency reforms is brought together in T.C. Halliday and B.G. Carruthers, *Bankrupt: Global Lawmaking and Systemic Financial Crisis* (Palo Alto: Stanford University Press, 2009). Research on UNCITRAL's lawmaking initiatives on secured transactions, insolvency and maritime law is forthcoming in a volume entitled *Global Legislators: The Making of International Trade Law,* by S. Block-Lieb and T.C. Halliday (Chicago: American Bar Foundation, 2013); S. Block-Lieb and T.C. Halliday, 'Legitimacy and Global Lawmaking' *Fordham Law Legal Studies Research Paper No. 952492* (2006); S. Block-Lieb and T.C. Halliday 'Incrementalisms in Global Lawmaking' *Brooklyn Journal of International Law* XXXII 851–903, 2011; T.C. Halliday and B.G. Carruthers, 'Epistemological Conflicts and Institutional Impediments: The Rocky Road to Corporate Bankruptcy Reforms In Korea' in *Korean Law Reform,* T. Ginsburg (ed.) (London: Routledge Press, 2004), pp. 114–33; T.C. Halliday and B.G. Carruthers, 'Institutional Lessons from Insolvency Reforms in East Asia' in *Forum on Asian Insolvency Law Reform (FAIR), Insolvency and Risk Management in Asia* (Delhi, India: World Bank and Asian Development Bank, 2004).

It must be emphasized that this chapter reflects a theoretical aspiration to explain the conditions under which law has an impact on economies and an empirical aspiration to find evidence that supports or rejects theories of IO impact on credit and other markets. The chapter does not intend to be normative, since I have no disciplinary competency to appraise the actions of IOs by policy or ethical standards.

II. Why IOs produce standards: four theories

Why IOs produce standards may seem self-evident, but that is not so. Empirical research on IOs reveals that there are at least four theories[8] of IO action, each of which has some measure of evidence to support it.

1. Idealist theory

For want of a better term, we might style idealist theory as acceptance of the statements that IOs themselves advance about why they are producing what they are producing. Either in the mandates of the organizations themselves, or in their presentation of their collective selves to the world on websites or in annual reports, or in the prolegomena to specific law-making products, we discover discursive justifications for respective IO enterprises.

UNCITRAL, for instance, has construed its mission in three broad rhetorical declarations since its inception in 1966.[9] This UN entity was created originally to provide a private law alternative to the public law-creating bodies of the UN, such as the International Law Commission. UNCITRAL's founding advocates proposed a dual mandate for its

[8] There are other theories, including those of private legislatures, public choice, international political economy and constructivism, among others. I offer these four since they provide an illustrative sampling of alternatives on which we have much evidence. For other theories or summaries of theories, *see* E.S. Cohen, 'Constructing Power through Law: Private Law Pluralism and Harmonization in the Global Political Economy' 15 *Review of International Political Economy* 770–99 (2008); L. Martin and B. Simmons, 'International Organisations and Institutions', in *Handbook of International Relations*, W. Carlsnaes, T. Risse, and B. Simmons (eds.) (London: Sage, 2012); P.B. Stephan, 'Accountability and International Lawmaking: Rules, Rents and Legitimacy' 17 *Northwestern Journal of International Law and Business* 681–735 (1996).

[9] S. Block-Lieb and T.C. Halliday, 'Harmonization and Modernization in UNCITRAL's Global Legislative Guide on Insolvency Law', 42 *Texas International Law Journal* 481–514 (2007).

activities. On the one hand, it would unify trade law across the world in order to facilitate international commerce; and on the other hand, it would harmonize the laws of nations to reduce differences in laws across countries on the premise that less variation lowered barriers to trade. More recently, however, UNCITRAL has become expansive in its ambitions and now it champions the 'modernization' of law, a mandate that permits any kind of reform that can rhetorically be construed as 'modern'. Sometimes this takes the form of 'out-with-the-old,' i.e. replacing extant law, and/or 'in-with-the-new', where there might or might not already have been prior law on the books.

In the linked areas of secured transactions and insolvency law, UNCITRAL offers more specific justifications for its years of expensive and time-consuming deliberations. Put bluntly, its logic for secured transactions reforms is that better secured transactions laws will attract more credit to markets, which in turn will stimulate the economy, produce economic growth, and facilitate global trade.[10] Its logic for its insolvency enterprise is that orderly and efficient handling of companies in financial distress will lessen the numbers of corporate failures, increase the capacity to turn companies around that need temporary protection from creditors, reduce the likelihood that an aggregation of corporate failures will threaten national and international credit systems, and thereby protect the financial stability that was threatened in national and international debt crises.

The World Bank's justification for its creditors' rights/insolvency principles is very similar, although that goal is in service of the Bank's highest order aspiration to alleviate world poverty. Hence the Bank's reform programmes proceed on the premises that better secured transactions law will stimulate markets and induce economic growth ultimately to lift nations and their populations out of poverty. Given the charge of the IMF to protect the stability of the global financial system, its goals with its insolvency norms,[11] and its joint diagnostic endeavour with the Bank on secured transaction Reports on the Observance of Standards and Codes (ROSCs), are to preserve financial stability within and across nations. Hence the erection of secured transaction and insolvency regimes within national legal systems are building blocks to increase the robustness of a

[10] *See* Bazinas, Chapter 5, this volume.

[11] International Monetary Fund (IMF), *Orderly and Effective Insolvency Procedures: Key Issues* (Washington DC: International Monetary Fund, 1999).

global financial architecture.[12] In its turn, the IMF justified its 1999 text of policy alternatives for corporate insolvency regimes on grounds that a better regime ultimately would produce greater financial stability, a prime mandate for the IMF.[13]

The point here is not to be critical of these justifications, but rather, to acknowledge that the intentions of an IO might not be taken at face value. Other theories, however, complicate this assumption because they propose, at best, that intentions are more complex and that the orientations and legal products of IOs must be scrutinized with a searching and discriminating eye.

2. Realist theory

Perhaps the most sceptical theory of IOs is well entrenched in scholarship on international relations (IR).[14] Realist theory insists that States are the dominant actors on the international stage. IOs most often are ciphers for powerful States or blocs of States. Of course, a blatant cooptation of an IO by a powerful State is likely to delegitimate the IO so State dominance of IOs needs to be less visible, rather veiled, and very much muted.

With respect to international trade law the vulgar version of realist theory, which indeed is refracted through some scholarship on international political economy, would argue something like the following. The dominant stockholder and only veto player in the IMF is the United States (US). As a result, the US and the Treasury Department will strive to use the IMF as an instrument for US financial and trade policy. Hence we could expect that promulgations of legal standards by the IMF either will conform fairly closely to US law or practice, or IMF officials will be attuned to minimal thresholds for norm development that are acceptable to the US. A similar argument is not infrequently made for the Bank.

Realists would turn a sceptical eye even on IOs that strive to be representative and mitigate the influence of powerful States with advanced economies. In UNCITRAL's Working Group on Secured Transactions, for instance, numbers of delegates believed that the US delegation, together with the Canadians, and two professional associations, dominated the development of the Legislative Guide, both in its form and substance.

12 G22, 'Summary of Reports on the International Financial Architecture' (Washington DC: G22, 1998).

13 *See* IMF, *Orderly and Effective Insolvency Procedures.*

14 Martin and Simmons, 'International Organisations and Institutions'.

The strongest critics alleged that UNCITRAL had effectively adopted Article 9 of the US Uniform Commercial Code.[15] Whether this is true is vigorously contested by US and Canadian delegates and some others, but there is no denying the perception among some of a realist move by the US.

In the Working Group on Secured Transactions a conflict between States – another aspect of realist international relations – can best be observed by the strong exchanges during deliberations between the German and US delegations. On the registration of security charges and retention of title the German delegation had a very different view than the US delegation, grounded, some said, in a difference of economic interests over whose banking system would have the advantage in Central and Eastern Europe. Towards the end of deliberations, a compromise was crafted by an academic expert who was a member of the Canadian delegation. At that point emergence of a transnational solution threw a veil over conflicting State interests.

In UNCITRAL's Working Group on Insolvency, a close analysis of the most frequent delegates, delegations and speakers shows that a tiny handful of about ten delegates, almost all from advanced economies, and numerically most often from the US, were the core actors in development of the *Legislative Guide on Insolvency Law*.[16]

For realists, powerful States will prefer to work through IOs because it is a way of laundering their otherwise nakedly apparent influence. Particularistic national interests are converted into universal global standards. The dominance of the Global North is disguised by the appearance of global representation and the numerical dominance – at least on paper – of the Global South.

3. Professional theory

In this view, IOs are multilateral vehicles for the creation and implementation of professional norms and practices. This might be construed as a 'realist' theory not of States, but of competing occupations. There are

[15] *See* McCormack, Chapter 2, this volume; G. McCormack, 'American Private Law Writ Large? The UNCITRAL Secured Transactions Guide' 60 *ICLQ* 597–625 (2011); G. McCormack, *Secured Credit and the Harmonisation of Law: The UNCITRAL Experience* (Cheltenham: Edward Elgar, 2011).

[16] T.C. Halliday, J. Pacewicz and S. Block-Lieb. 'Who Governs? Delegations in Global Trade Lawmaking' 7 *Regulation and Governance* 279–98 (2013).

several threads to professional theory. The first, from international relations scholarship, has observed that much of what was usually transacted among diplomats in the affairs of nations has now passed to lawyers.[17] International relations have been 'legalized'. A second thread is extrapolated from the theory of professional competition inside States. For any given problem, there is the potential for different occupations or professions to compete over which has 'jurisdiction' or a monopoly over the solution of the problem. If the issue is a failing company, should that be the province of accountants, as in Britain, or of lawyers, as in the US?[18] A third thread relates to the rise of deference to experts and technical authority. In something so complicated as secured loans, in all their bewildering varieties, the only persons who have competency turn out to be either lawyers or finance specialists.

The implications for IOs and their products are twofold. On the one hand, global and regional lawmaking may reflect a competition among different professions (accountants v. lawyers) or different schools of thought within the same profession (civil v. common lawyers) for dominance over the form and substance of norms. On the other hand, the form of the norms may reflect the imprint of whatever profession had ascendancy in the lawmaking. A product crafted by lawyers is likely to look like a legal document. Some critics of UNCITRAL's Convention on the Carriage of Goods by Sea (Rotterdam Rules) charge that its enormous complexity most benefits lawyers and judges, since it will take years for the meaning and interpretations of this legalistic document to settle.

If realist theory posits that IOs act at the behest of powerful States, professional theory would hypothesize that IOs are influential institutions that can be captured to benefit a particular professional epistemology and monopolistic claim over an area of work. Hence we should inspect the output of IOs to examine which profession's interests seem to dominate and how that domination expresses itself in the form and content of the norms. Furthermore, does the domination of a particular profession give competitive advantage to particular States in global trade competition?

[17] J.H.H. Weiler, 'The Rule of Lawyers and the Ethos of Diplomats: Reflections on the Internal and External Legitimacy of WTO Dispute Settlement', 35 *Journal of World Trade* 191–207 (2001).

[18] B.G. Carruthers and T.C. Halliday, *Rescuing Business: The Making of Corporate Bankruptcy Law in England and the United States* (Oxford University Press, 1998).

4. *Ecological theory*

In contrast to realists, ecological theory takes seriously the autonomy and distinctiveness of IOs.[19] Extrapolating from studies of communities or of competition among business firms and other organizations within a given territory,[20] an ecological approach observes that a population of IOs exists in a given niche of international relations and those IOs face fundamental challenges of survival which affect their relations with each other. Each IO has to obtain sufficient resources from its 'niche' to be established and survive. IOs inside a given ecology, such as the international trade law ecology, potentially compete with each other, at one extreme, for sufficient resources to maintain their organizational mandate, or at the other extreme, for primacy in regional or global lawmaking. This struggle for competitive advantage leads to the production of norms that concomitantly maintain the flow of resources necessary for norm production and distinguish one IO from another.

It follows that IOs can cooperate or compete with each other in given ecology. Their products have the effect or express the intention of differentiating one IO from another. Whereas the World Bank has produced principles for a creditors' rights regime, UNCITRAL has produced a legislative guide, the EBRD a model law, and the EBRD and IMF/World Bank their respective diagnostic instruments. The geographic scope of the transnational norms may differ (EBRD, Europe and Central Asia; von Baer project, Europe; World Bank and UNCITRAL, the world) and so, too, the substantive content of the norms (UNIDROIT has its Cape Town Convention on Aircraft Leasing; the Hague Conference on Private International Law its conventions on intermediated securities; UNCITRAL its legislative guide).

[19] Ecology theory, to my knowledge, has not yet been extended to IOs. Block-Lieb and I will argue in *Global Legislators* that ecological analysis offers a fresh and powerful perspective to explain why given IOs enter or leave arenas of lawmaking, how they sustain themselves in those arenas, and how they negotiate relationships with each other to permit their coexistence in those arenas: S. Block-Lieb and T.C. Halliday 'Social Ecology, Recursivity and Temporality: A Sociology of Global Law-Making', in Paper presented at *American Sociological Association Annual Meeting*, Las Vegas (2011).

[20] J.H. Freeman and P.G. Audia 'Community Ecology and the Sociology of Organizations' 32 *Annual Review of Sociology* 145–69 (2006); M.T. Hannan, 'Ecologies of Organizations: Diversity and Identity' *Journal of Economic Perspectives* 19 51–70 (2005); P.A. Popielarz and Z.P. Neal, 'The Niche as a Theoretical Tool' 33 *Annual Review of Sociology* 65–84 (2007).

Put another way, IOs produce transnational norms and laws not merely to perform their mandated function, but the norms themselves provide the means for IOs to function at all. Hence we can expect that any effort at regional or global lawmaking by an IO is as much an effort for the IO to maintain its competitiveness and status in an ecology as it is to solve the substantive problem that lawmaking appears to have engendered.

The juxtaposition of these four theories invites us to ask not only to look upon IO lawmaking with a critical eye, but also whether lawmaking by IOs might be done differently so as to avoid the loss of legitimacy or biases or loss of influence that might otherwise result if, indeed, IOs are shown to be acting for reasons other than their stated claims.

III. How IOs should produce legal norms: seven shifts in orientation and practices

This analysis rests upon the following premises. First, IOs are going to create and advocate transnational legal norms for one or another reason, including those reviewed in the previous section. Second, IOs prefer that the norms they craft will be enacted by States and implemented in practice. Therefore, *if* IOs are to promulgate legal norms, and *if* they want to ensure enactment of the norms (law-on-the-books), and *if* they want actual implementation (law-in-action), *then*, third, to minimize the potential implementation gap between the norms and practice they will need to make seven shifts in orientation and practice. Again, it must be emphasized that this is not a normative analysis about what is ethically desirable but, rather, a pragmatic analysis about what research indicates are the contingent conditions for legally induced changes in practice.

IV. *From* invisible IFI lawmaking *to* visible IO lawmaking

A technocratic instinct permeates many IFIs. Heavy reliance on technical specialists, often law professors, leading lawyers, or national lawyer-reformers, assures IFIs that their products will meet minimum standards of technical proficiency and be located near the leading edge of current academic thinking or progressive national law reform movements. Usually these specialists are from advanced economies whose nations frequently are exemplars for regions or the world, and often from elite institutions, whether notable universities or renowned law or accounting firms. This approach to IO lawmaking is brokered by IFI staff who use consultancies to produce efficient outcomes that do not require endless bargaining or broader political settlements. Most often such lawmaking is done invisibly, far from the public eye and removed even from specialists, firms and other interested parties who also have expertise or economic power.

Attraction to this kind of lawmaking appeals to IFIs because at best it is relatively cheap, seems efficient, moves swiftly, satisfies technical standards, and multiplies the output of products. However, it confronts major dangers that ultimately may subvert intended outcomes. Choice of expert advisers rests with IFI staff who may be more or less tendentious in their views. Biases towards advanced economies or particular legal systems can easily appear. A deficit of representativeness and lack of transparency compounds suspicion of closed-door proceedings with inherent resistance by potential adopting nations to norms which they had no hand in developing. To facilitate enactment and implementation of transnational legal norms, cross-national research indicates three conditions must be satisfied.

Firstly, global lawmaking, like global IOs, must be legitimate.[21] Legitimation requires representation. Hence, development of global legal norms must take place in international forums or IOs where several kinds of representation are manifestly apparent: (a) representation of all nations to which the norms may be directed; and (b) representation of technical experts.[22] Such representation goes a long way both to legitimate the lawmaking process and to increase the probability that participants will adopt the product.

More pointedly, and secondly, global lawmaking must involve potential 'veto players'. These are actors who have the power to nullify the far-reaching impact of proposed reforms. When the US and other major trading nations refused to adopt UNCITRAL's Hamburg Rules for the carriage of goods by sea, this virtually guaranteed the Rules would not be adopted universally. When the dominant corporate groups in Indonesia decided they had been marginalized in corporate bankruptcy lawmaking, they successfully subverted entirely the implementation of the law for all businesses. If the former condition requires involvement of all nations and interests, this condition suggests that some means of accommodating 'veto players' must be satisfied.

21 I. Hurd, 'Legitimacy and Authority in International Politics' 53 *International Organization* 379–408 (1999).

22 S. Block-Lieb and T.C. Halliday, 'Legitimacy and Global Lawmaking', *Fordham Law Legal Studies Research Paper No. 952492* (2006).

Third, the process of deliberation itself must be seen to be fair.[23] If the criteria of representation and inclusion of 'veto players' are satisfied, but actual lawmaking itself is captured by one or a handful of dominant interests, then the probability of implementation of even the most pristine lawmaking product sharply declines.

V. *From* naive developmentalism *to* contingent developmentalism

'Developmentalisms' of one sort or another stalk State-building and market-making. We are quite familiar with theories that all national politics inexorably are headed towards the nirvana of democracy *or* all forms of economy will invariably converge on a certain form of liberal capitalism *or* a State with an independent judiciary or central bank is a *sine qua non* of modernity and thus more or less inevitable.

Less obvious are implicit developmentalisms that underlie global lawmaking for international and national trade. A clear subtext, sometimes made explicit in preambles to global normative texts, postulates that we know what legal paths lead to economic development, what legal steps will release more credit, what legal institutions will prevent financial crises in developing or developed countries. For instance, it is widely supposed in lawmaking on secured transactions that public registries of secured credit will stimulate the availability of credit in developing countries. The fact that this developmental assumption flies in the face of evidence from advanced economies (Germany) or developing economies (China) seems not to have slowed the stride for insistence on the value of registries among key IOs. It is also accepted as an article of faith that development of a stable market economy requires sophisticated corporate rehabilitation regimes. It is a plausible argument on its face, but neither booming China nor India has had such a regime, whereas the casualties of 2008 and the Euro-crisis – US, Ireland and Spain – have created such regimes, a disjunction that might give IO lawmakers pause.

Rather than proceed with naive linear models of one-size-fits-all law and economic development, it is necessary for IOs and global lawmakers to recognize that there may be multiple paths to financial stability, economic growth, extension of credit, development of markets, and alleviation of poverty. Surprisingly little work has been done even by regional

[23] I. Hurd, *After Anarchy: Legitimacy and Power in the United Nations Security Council* (Princeton University Press, 2007); I. Hurd, 'Breaking and Making Norms: American Revisionism and Crises of Legitimacy' 44 *International Politics* 194–213 (2007).

IFIs to identify some of those clusters of nations that reveal one path versus another. The rule-of-thumb shorthand of supposing a universal developmentalism aids huge IFIs to manage the vastness of diversity they confront with radically simplified models.

This pragmatic tendency to fit all nations into a developmental straitjacket derives in part from the fallacy of false extrapolations. That falsity of logic frequently accompanies the selection of one great global economy, for example, the US, as an exemplar of an 'advanced' ideal of law and economic development to the exclusion of other equally successful economies (e.g. Germany, France, Scandinavian nations, Singapore, Hong Kong, among others of the OECD countries) which have gone about their economic development rather differently. The fact that the US creates security in certain ways may be suggestive or constructive or creative, but should hardly suggest that Article 9, or a variation on its theme, is the only or best, or even paradigmatic, way to secure credit or release credit.

Political economists show us that there are at least two varieties of capitalism in Europe and the US,[24] and quite probably others elsewhere and others that are emerging. Economic history and common sense should lead IOs to expect that a variety of laws, legal institutions and developmental paths are likely to lead to varieties of market economies. If global norms fail to reflect these historical and comparative realities, they are likely to fall short of their optimistic aspirations.

VI. *From* unexamined theories *to* tested theories

An immense amount of global lawmaking proceeds on the basis of plausible, persuasive and portable theories. On their face they seem obvious, not least because some examples can be adduced to give the verisimilitude of evidentiary support. The adoption of the Washington Consensus swept the world, often propelled by IFIs,[25] until institutional economists pointed out that markets actually need institutions to make them work,[26] and another wave of lawmaking occurred under the banner of the New Washington Consensus. Several weak pieces of research in the 1990s (e.g. Schleifer et al.), coupled with plausible writings by a persuasive

[24] P.A. Hall and D. Soskice (eds.), *Varieties of Capitalism: The Institutional Foundations of Comparative Advantage* (New York: Oxford University Press, 2001).

[25] J. Stiglitz, *Globalization and Its Discontents* (New York: Norton, 2002).

[26] D.C. North, *Institutions, Institutional Change and Economic Performance* (Cambridge, New York: Cambridge University Press, 1990).

popular author,[27] among other writings, convinced many IOs that certain sorts of property rights regimes, especially those proximate to common law legal systems, were fundamental to economic development. The fact that many, perhaps most, of the world's most successful economies did not have common law foundations, or that the fastest sustained burst of economic growth in a major country occurred despite the almost complete absence of secure property rights connections (i.e. China), seemed not to phase global lawmakers.

Unexamined or empirically unverified theories come much closer to home. Convincing empirical support for the claims that a more developed secured transactions regime, or at least a contractually based private regime of security, has a powerful effect on economic development or increased flows of credit within countries or to countries with such laws has been difficult to find. It appears that we simply do not know if a certain kind of secured transactions regime produces any of the outcomes – from economic development to foreign investment to increased credit to cheaper credit – sought by IO reformers.[28] Even an eminent drafter of Canadian and IO standards, Professor Roderick Macdonald, opines on a narrower but fundamental point[29] that:

> despite heroic efforts by the IMF, the World Bank, and a brace of international norm entrepreneurs to prove this theorem,[30] the evidence is far from conclusive. Indeed, borrowing the language of a former U.S. President, one might say that the proselytizers for modernizing secured transactions law belong to the 'faith-based constituency' as opposed to the 'evidence based constituency'.[31]

[27] H. De Soto, *The Mysterty of Capital: Why Capitalism Triumphs in the West and Fails Everywhere Else* (New York: Basic Books, 2000).

[28] It would be of immense value if IFIs and IOs would publish their empirical foundations for such assertions, as: 'The *Guide* is based on the premise that sound secured transactions laws can have significant economic benefits for States that adopt them, including attracting credit from domestic and foreign lenders and other credit providers, promoting the development and growth of domestic business (in particular small and medium-sized enterprises) and generally increasing trade.' Or: 'It is well established, through studies conducted by such organizations as the International Bank for Reconstruction and Development, the International Monetary Fund, the Asian Development Bank and the European Bank for Reconstruction and Development that one of the most effective means of providing working capital to commercial enterprises is through secured credit', *Legislative Guide on Secured Transactions*, pp. 1–2.

[29] That 'maximizing the scope of application of consensual security rights while minimizing transactions costs for all credit providers is the optimal configuration of a secured transactions regime', Macdonald, 'Transnational Secured Transactions Reform'.

[30] *See* ibid. [31] Ibid.

Of course, global or national public policy cannot always wait for rigorous research to catch up with demands for action. But if this is the case, at least some immediate or intermediate steps can be taken. First, well-resourced IFIs would lessen their vulnerability to fads, or plausibility theories, if they would devote some resources to research and research broadly conceived – by economic and legal historians, comparative political scientists and sociologists of markets, institutional economists who actually study institutions, comparative lawyers who study law-on-the-books and law-in-action. Very quickly it would be possible to get a reality check on whether the face validity of a theory comports with different types of evidence already in hand. Parenthetically, the quality of such work should be tested in the rigorous market of academic scientific publications and their practices of peer review.

Second, IOs must ask when certain types of reforms will work and not work. When does State-led economic development, in the relative absence of private law, produce major shifts from developing to developed nations? When can privatization work and when will it fail? What kinds of institutions or legal regimes can be built in developing and transitional economies and at what stages of development, in what regions, under what sorts of governments? Almost certainly it will be the case that a secured transaction registry will work magnificently in some settings and fail completely to achieve its goal in others. A contingent analysis that escapes the temptation of one-size-fits-all must test theories of legally induced development. Much material for such tests already exists. IOs that lead the way in retrieving such evidence will be much less likely to promulgate instruments fated to fail.

VII. *From* arbitrary exemplars *to* alternative models

Although this pathology of IO practice has already been anticipated above, it bears repeating explicitly. Current initiatives by IFIs or IOs too often proceed as if there is either one model of institutions or one country that truly represents the universal global ideal.

One way that IOs not infrequently proceed is to discover some institutions they see in countries that they believe to be paradigmatic, and seek to replicate those institutions elsewhere. The list is long: strong and independent courts; well-developed debt collection systems; a multifaceted corporate bankruptcy regime; an independent central bank; specialized judges; cultures of deference to law; security on moveables or intangibles – the list varies depending on which aspect of markets IO lawmakers seek to regulate. But for almost any of these single institutions two questions must be asked: where are examples of thriving markets and trade regimes where these institutions did *not* exist? and what kind of soil is necessary for any of these to be planted and thrive?

A second type of arbitrary exemplar brings us back to the handful of States, and too often one State in particular, that are thought to embody the best of what law can contribute to markets and trade. How seldom does one ever hear in the deliberative chambers of IOs or in corridor talk of lawmaking institutions or IFI seminars that a national exemplar of economic growth might be the Netherlands or Chile or Hong Kong or Bahrain or South Korea? How often one hears about the US? But arguably, the US is a quite peculiar exemplar. Whereas many European nations share cultural and legal, political and economic factors in common, the US has a singular history (a country of immigrants, strong local political authority, slavery and civil war within the past 150 years, a legacy of racism), a distinctive culture (strong Protestant heritage, high contemporary religiosity and religious diversity, linguistic impoverishment), repressive and punitive elements to its legal system (capital punishment, huge prison populations), distinctive attributes to its version of common law (heavy reliance on law to regulate its disparate, mobile populations; the sacralization of rights discourse; the high status and power of judges; a high ratio of lawyers to population), business distinctives (a proportional dearth of family conglomerates at the top of the business pyramid; constant infusion of migrant labour; distinctive forms of corporate control; enormous inventive capacities), and a sophisticated elite system of higher education (great law schools, research universities, etc.). Those who have lived, worked and studied in several countries, including the US, seldom doubt that American exceptionalism is real. Why, then, do IOs and IFIs persist in elevating this peculiar country to paradigmatic status?

There are correctives in this tendency to 'globalize the local' or to generalize from the particular. The first is for IOs to mobilize their tacit knowledge that there are several varieties of successful law and markets. To make reforms meaningful, these varieties must be identified, labelled, and offered as alternative exemplars of what markets and trade might approximate.

The second is to discern in each case the degree to which law features very strongly in some of them and not so strongly in others. Each variety of paradigmatic markets, each type of capitalism or credit markets, differs in its configuration of the substance of commercial law, the form of commercial law, the form of regulatory institutions, the patterns of informal trade practices, the characteristic forms of dominant economic organization. Rather than an effort to fit all countries into the same mould, this approach recognizes what comparative scholars and practitioners intuitively understand to be true, namely, that the world offers different moulds and law features in a variety of ways across those moulds.

The implication for lawmaking IOs and IFIs is clear. If law-induced economic development and stability is to have an impact in practice, then global norms will achieve more success when their high level points of convergence nevertheless permit variations on the themes of compliance by varieties of law and markets. One-size-fits-all norms, a lack of alternative ways of conforming to high level norms, the attempted imposition of bright-line detailed rules on all countries – all these increase the probability of avoidance or rejection by nations or their interest groups.

VIII. *From* narrow disciplinarity *to* broad interdisciplinarity

IOs and IFIs rely substantially on the expertise of university faculty or specialists with the highest qualifications that universities can grant. That reliance varies from the IO adoption of general theories that emerge from universities (e.g. better protection of property rights stimulates economic growth) or specific consultations aimed at drafting a particular set of norms. Yet, close examination of the publications of lawmaking IOs, or attendance at IO seminars, or informal mixing with IO lawmakers leads the observer to wonder if universities only have two faculties: law, of course, and also economics.

There is a double problem here. On the one hand, no matter how sophisticated the legal training of the lawyers or law professors, that training seldom includes the very task they undertake in lawmaking IOs, i.e. designing the legal architecture of national markets and international trade. About substantive or procedural law they are exceedingly sophisticated. About law's institutions or practices, about institution-building or market-making, they are much less well-equipped. On the other hand, reliance on only two epistemologies about how social institutions work, i.e. legal and economic thought, essentially denies the salience that most universities of the world have given to other human sciences, all of which are thought to have distinctive insights and orientations on the very issues that involve global lawmaking.

The results are manifest. One may be to rely on very limited theories of human motivation, such as 'incentives' or 'rational action'. The academy fights vigorously over the limits and scope of such theories, but IOs often proceed tacitly or manifestly on this mono-motivational premise. When such theories penetrate the law, as in the schools of law and economics variously pioneered by Richard Posner and Douglass North, among others, they simultaneously 'colonize' legal thought and severely constrain legal imagination that can be applied to global lawmaking, enactment and implementation.

There are two correctives to this narrow epistemological frame. The first is for IOs to reach into the entire university and to recognize explicitly the varieties of disciplinary theory and research on (legal) change. To caricature these varieties of behavioural theories, one can imagine the following orientations to IO-led efforts at global or regional legal change: a lawyers' prescription might 'implant law'; an economic prescription will be to 'change incentives'; a sociologist's orientation may be to build institutions and occupations; an anthropologist's plea will be to acknowledge cultural singularity and beliefs; a psychologist's approach will include a gauging of expectations, such as fairness; a comparative politics analysis would invariably look at distributions of power inside and outside the State.

A second corrective is to recognize the power of inter-disciplinary research. In their cross-disciplinary research scholars forge correctives to disciplinary myopia. Much socio-legal research deliberately endeavours to connect historians with finance specialists, psychologists with lawyers, comparative lawyers with institutional sociologists, international law experts with anthropologists – and much of this work is focused precisely on the problem confronted by IOs engaged in global lawmaking. Except for seminars such as the one which produced this book, it is rare for the lawmaking arms of IOs and IFIs to reach beyond lawyers and/or lawyer/economists. As a result, many of their initiatives are destined to fail even before they leave Washington or London or Vienna or Manila.

If IOs are to have an impact on legal systems across the world, they will need to bring the full power of the social sciences and history to problems of constructing markets, building institutions, melding cultures, changing mentalities and altering practices in the widely varying circumstances that are represented by the heterogeneity of the world's nations and peoples.

IX. *From* globalized localisms *to* normative options

This chapter has argued that one-size-fits-all in the guise of 'best practices' or 'global standards' continues to confound effective legal change, just as reliance on exemplars of legal regimes that themselves are peculiar or exceptional. Santos has aptly warned against the seduction of 'globalizing localisms', that is, taking one country's national practice and laundering it through IOs so that it now appears as a set of universal, neutral norms.[32]

But there is a related and vexing problem for IOs. In what form should global norms be cast for effective adoption and implementation by States and in practice? In the Working Group on Secured Transactions at UNCITRAL a long discussion continues today on whether the *Legislative Guide on Secured Transactions*, during its development and since its development, should be 'hardened' into a model law. The current *Guide* already has a bright-line rule quality to it, as if it were a model law that could be dropped onto a country's statute books. Reactions to the World Bank Principles by some IO reformers took the opposite view – that they were so general that legislators without strong local technical experts would have little guidance and great difficulty in drawing them into national law.

This problem is partly compounded by the diagnostic instruments used by the IMF/World Bank and some other IFIs. For various reasons there is a tendency for those instruments, such as ROSCs,[33] to ask quite specific questions about particular laws, regulations, organizations, reports, and the like. It is more difficult, perhaps, both for IFI or IO lawyers and country officials to assess answers to broadly construed questions about how certain functions are managed or goals attained than to provide checklists through which officials can methodically proceed.

While the forms of global norms are too difficult to arbitrate here, two shifts would mitigate the two contrary tendencies of IOs (to offer broad principles which provide insufficient guidance; or to offer bright-line rules that offer insufficient adaptability).

First, sets of IO legal norms might be produced in a hierarchy of abstraction, from greater abstractness to greater specificity. In other words, a set of norms would be organized in pyramidal fashion with high level goals or aspirational norms at the top of the hierarchy to achieve certain

[32] J. Jensen and B. De Sousa Santos (eds.), *Globalizing Institutions: Case Studies in Renovation and Innovation* (Aldershot, Burlington: Ashgate, 2000); De Sousa Santos, 'Law and Democracy: (Mis)trusting the Global Reform of Courts' in ibid., pp. 252–81.

[33] These are 12 instruments used by the IMF and World Bank to assess the regulatory institutions that are thought to enhance financial stability. *See* www.worldbank.org/ifa/rosc.html (last accessed August 2012).

functional outcomes and lower orders of specificity to assist legal drafting, institutional construction, and the like. Since there are varieties of law and markets, it should also be the case that commentary or recommendations provide options. In the UNCITRAL *Legislative Guide on Insolvency*, for instance, there is (a) a hierarchy of nine key objectives, (b) chapters that might parallel a statute with commentary about alternative ways of meeting objectives, and (c) recommendations, often in the form of statutory language, which frequently give options.[34] When combined with the World Bank *Principles*, these two sets of norms offer a hierarchy of options that respect national sovereignty and the ability of national legislators to adapt their local laws, sometimes following exactly particular recommendations, if they fit the local situation, and sometimes finding an alternative way to meet the high level objectives. The *Legislative Guide on Secured Transactions* has many more bright-line rules that appear to give national legislators less room to move, but a careful reading of the commentary suggests that alternative ways might be found to satisfy the principal functions the UNCITRAL hopes to be implemented.

A second shift would require a more fundamental change of mentality by IFI legal departments and trade lawmaking IOs. It would begin by acknowledging explicitly and adapting creatively to what the lawyer-legislators of IOs already know, namely, that States vary greatly in their regulatory capacities, sophistication of professions, autonomy of courts and organization of markets. Given this variation, IFIs might begin the admittedly hard work of providing broad alternatives to countries. For countries with limited resources, legal cultures inimical to a heavy carrying capacity, underdeveloped economies and fragile States, the IOs might offer a simple and robust set of options that can be enacted, that would make a real difference if implemented, even if they fall far short of the sophisticated gold-plated models familiar to the lawyer-legislators in IOs. For countries that do have sophisticated markets, highly developed regulatory systems and strong State capacity, elaborate models might well fit appropriately.

In short, both moves would require a tectonic shift in IO lawmaking. Hierarchies of functions and norms would be clustered in two or more alternative configurations to be offered to states with qualitatively different capacities and histories. Put starkly, a simple and robust model would provide an alternative to a complex and sophisticated model.

[34] Block-Lieb and Halliday, 'Legitimacy and Global Lawmaking'.

X. *From* static norms *to* recursive dynamics

Comparative research on national lawmaking in global contexts shows that it invariably proceeds through cycles of successive attempts to reconcile law-on-the-books and law-in-action until some settling occurs.[35] This recursivity of law is manifestly obvious in national lawmaking. After the Asian financial crisis, Indonesia went through one iteration after another of presidential decrees, regulations, court cases, out-of-court dispute settlement, professional reconstruction and statutory amendment until a corporate bankruptcy regime settled, ultimately, far below the level of change anticipated by the IMF or World Bank. After the 1997 crisis in Korea, likewise the National Assembly and Ministry of Finance and Economy and Supreme Court produced waves of statutory amendments, administration interventions and court rulings, until the National Assembly enacted a massive, integrated corporate bankruptcy statute in 2006, in Korea's case, a piece of law that conformed rather closely to global norms.

National lawmaking in a globalizing world almost always occurs within a regional or global context of transnational norm-making. However, global lawmaking tends to be much less flexible and much less capable of revision than its national counterpart. UNCITRAL rarely circles back to revise its model laws or legislative guides in the light of experience. It has taken decades to do so for its arbitration rules, for instance. IFIs may have more flexibility, and perhaps they do so under the surface, but these do not amount readily to new versions of previously promulgated norms. The result of this inertia or fixity of norms will invariably be to widen inexorably the gap between the norms and the exigencies of economic and other changes which influence national lawmaking. Or, perversely, nations may ostensibly adopt global norms but cynically act differently in practice – the apparent outcome of China's corporate bankruptcy reforms.

There are two shifts that would integrate the recursivity of law into IO lawmaking practices. First, IOs and IFIs would find ways and devote resources to hearing and listening to State lawmakers, industry interests, professionals and academics, among others, across the diverse spectrum of countries for which they have a lawmaking mandate. Of course, this, too, can easily be distorted so that IOs end up listening only to people in their own networks (e.g. major law firms that represent IFIs in their aid or monitoring activities) and only those who are easy to reach. In the development of its insolvency principles, the World Bank did conduct

[35] Halliday and Carruthers, *Bankrupt*.

forums across the world and there is evidence that, indeed, the Bank did 'listen'. A perceptible shift can be discerned over time away from a US-centric bankruptcy system. Moreover, such feedback would mitigate some of the pathologies mentioned above and permit adaptations in the forms of norms (e.g. mixes of principles and rules), ways to satisfy functional objectives for norms, and test theories of behaviour and institutional transformation.

Second, a learning orientation built on feedback from interested actors should produce successive versions or amendments of global norms. For instance, there might be a place for suitably adapted analogs to the Bank's earlier forums some three to five years after norms have been promulgated, and a subsequent adaptation of those norms in a Version 2.0. Similarly, UNCITRAL struggles to remain contemporaneous in tracking how its norms are implemented, what case law and regulatory apparatuses are constructed around them, and what variations on the UNCITRAL themes ultimately result in practice. This would result in UNCITRAL dynamism easily being lost as the memory and momentum of norm production begins to fade.

A move in both these directions would have effects that ultimately would increase the probability of changes in practice. A shift towards recursive or cyclical rounds of engagement between IOs and their audiences would ensure that IO norms are relevant to rapidly changing market behaviour, trade patterns and financial situations. Such a shift would tangibly increase the legitimacy of IOs and IFIs, especially among the 150 or more nations that are not part of the OECD. If invited to give their views, and if those views perceptibly are incorporated into subsequent versions of UNCITRAL, IMF or World Bank norms, then the probability of alignment between global and local norms increases substantially.[36]

XI. Conclusion

If IOs are to be effective global lawmakers, then it is necessary both to understand why they are engaging in global lawmaking and to adjust their practices to reflect empirical research on what makes global lawmakers effective.

[36] T.C. Halliday and G. Shaffer, 'Transnational Legal Orders: A Theoretical Framework', Working Paper, American Bar Foundation, 2013. S. Block-Lieb and T. Halliday, 'Settling in Transnational Legal Orders: Corporate Bankruptcy Law and International Trade by Sea', Working Paper, American Bar Foundation, 2013.

With respect to the former, the four theories of why IOs act as they do help both IO officials and their collaborators, observers and critics recognize that IOs themselves confront difficult conundrums. They have high ideals, but powerful countries may seek to reduce them to puppets. They need expertise, but key professions may want to place their imprint on their products. They want to make an impact, but they require adequate resources and appropriate settlements with potential rivals. In short, IOs and IFIs must survive and adapt in often fractious and uncertain circumstances, pushed and pulled by interests that would rob them of autonomy and legitimacy. Expecting more of IOs and IFIs than they can reasonably deliver ultimately will drain them of the value they offer to the world community.

With respect to the latter, some significant shifts in the ways IOs approach lawmaking will go far to strengthen their viability, legitimacy and relevance. These in turn will affect their impact. By reinventing their *modus operandi* in the field of trade lawmaking, the salience and vitality of global lawmakers will be magnified. Ideals have a greater probability of becoming real. Transnational law-on-the-books significantly improves its chances for becoming local law-in-action.

5

The creation of international commercial law standards by international financial institutions: why they do it and whether they should

SPYRIDON V. BAZINAS*

I. Introduction

International financial institutions (IFIs) are becoming increasingly active in the preparation of international commercial law standards. This activity creates an overlap with the activities of international legislative bodies and the potential for confusion and conflict. The purpose of this chapter is to discuss briefly some examples of overlap and make the points that: (a) to avoid confusion and conflict, any international commercial law standards prepared by IFIs should be coordinated and be consistent with international commercial law standards prepared by the properly mandated international legislative bodies; (b) to give comprehensive and consistent guidance, increased coordination efforts are also required by international legislative bodies (not IFIs).

II. International commercial law standards by international legislative bodies

International commercial law standards are usually prepared by international legislative bodies, such as the United Nations Commission on International Trade Law (UNCITRAL),[1] the International Institute for

* The views expressed in this article are the personal views of the author and do not reflect the views of the United Nations or UNCITRAL. The chapter is based on a presentation made at the World Bank and the *Modern Law Review* Conference on 'International Legal Standards on Secured Transactions, Facilitation of Credit and Financial Crisis', held on Friday, 14 May 2010, at the University of Newcastle and during which the author was asked to briefly respond to the specific questions set out in this chapter. A first shorter version of this chapter was published in 7 *JIBFL* 427 [2010] (July/August edition).

1 www.uncitral.org/uncitral/en/about_us.html (last accessed 21 December 2012).

the Unification of Private Law (Unidroit)[2] and the Hague Conference on Private International Law (the Hague Conference).[3]

For example, UNCITRAL was established by the United Nations General Assembly in 1966 with the general mandate to promote the progressive harmonization and unification of the law of international trade (which may be private or public, material law or procedural law, substantive law or private international law). UNCITRAL has since become the core legal body of the United Nations system in the field of international trade law.[4] As to the reasons justifying the establishment of UNCITRAL, GA Resolution 2205 (XXI) of 16 December 1966 notes, *inter alia*, that: (a) 'international trade co-operation among States is an important factor in the promotion of friendly relations and, consequently, in the maintenance of peace and security'; (b) 'the interests of all peoples, and particularly those of developing countries, demand the betterment of conditions favouring the extensive development of international trade'; (c) 'divergences arising from the laws of different States in matters relating to international trade constitute one of the obstacles to the development of world trade'; and (d) it is 'desirable that the process of harmonization and unification of the law of international trade should be substantially co-ordinated, systematized and accelerated and that a broader participation should be secured in furthering progress in this area'.[5]

To better understand the purpose of UNCITRAL's work, it is also useful to note the preamble to one of its most successful texts, the United Nations Convention on Contracts for the International Sale of Goods (CISG), which in explaining the objective of the CISG, notes, *inter alia*, that: (a) 'the development of international trade on the basis of equality and mutual benefit is an important element in promoting friendly relations among States'; and (b) 'the adoption of uniform rules which govern contracts for the international sale of goods and take into account the different social, economic and legal systems would contribute to the removal of legal barriers in international trade and promote the development of international trade'.[6]

[2] www.unidroit.org/dynasite.cfm?dsmid=103284 (last accessed 21 December 2012).

[3] www.hcch.net/index_en.php?act=text.display&tid=26 (last accessed 21 December 2012).

[4] www.uncitral.org/uncitral/en/about/origin.html (last accessed 21 December 2012).

[5] www.jus.uio.no/lm/uncitral.2205-xxi/doc.html (last accessed 21 December 2012).

[6] www.uncitral.org/pdf/english/texts/sales/cisg/V1056997-CISG-e-book.pdf (last accessed 21 December 2012).

This text explains the purpose of many of the uniform law texts that UNCITRAL has prepared. For example, the preamble to the United Nations Convention on the Assignment of Receivables in International Trade refers to: (a) international trade on the basis of equality and mutual benefit as an important element in the promotion of friendly relations among States; (b) the fact that problems created by uncertainties as to the content and choice of legal regime applicable to the assignment of receivables constitute an obstacle to international trade; (c) the objective of establishing principles and rules relating to the assignment of receivables that would create certainty and transparency and promote the modernization of the law relating to assignments of receivables; and (d) the adequate protection of the interests of debtors in assignments of receivables.[7] Similarly, the preamble to the UNCITRAL *Legislative Guide on Secured Transactions* refers to the promotion of low-cost credit by enhancing the availability of secured credit, but also to the need for balancing the interests of all persons affected by a secured transaction.[8]

In its 45 years of existence, UNCITRAL has worked in the fields of international commercial arbitration and conciliation, international sale of goods and related transactions, security interests, insolvency, international payments, international transport of goods, electronic commerce, procurement and infrastructure development.[9] Major international commercial law standards prepared by UNCITRAL include conventions (e.g. the United Nations Convention on Contracts for the International Sale of Goods), model laws (e.g. the UNCITRAL Model Law on International Commercial Arbitration), contractual rules (e.g. the UNCITRAL Arbitration Rules), legislative guides (e.g. the UNCITRAL *Legislative Guide on Secured Transactions*) and contractual guides (e.g. the UNCITRAL *Legal Guide on Drawing Up International Contracts for the Construction of Industrial Works*).[10]

The success of UNCITRAL is evident in the acceptability of its texts by States with different legal traditions and at different levels of economic development (even at the time of the Cold War, if one sees the States that adopted, for example, the CISG). This acceptability is more easily measured in the case of conventions and with more difficulty in the case

[7] www.uncitral.org/pdf/english/texts/payments/receivables/ctc-assignment-convention-e.pdf (last accessed 21 December 2012).

[8] www.uncitral.org/pdf/english/texts/security-lg/e/09–82670_Ebook-Guide_09–04–10English.pdf (last accessed 21 December 2012).

[9] www.uncitral.org/uncitral/en/uncitral_texts.html (last accessed 21 December 2012).

[10] www.uncitral.org/uncitral/en/uncitral_texts.html (last accessed 21 December 2012).

of model laws and legislative guides, which by definition allow the legislator a larger degree of flexibility and the enactment of which becomes known only to the extent that the legislation is translated into one of the working languages of the United Nations or is discussed in international bibliography. But even in the case of conventions, their acceptability may be measured not only by the number of ratifications or accessions, but also by the extent to which they have influenced domestic law or discussion among members of the judiciary, the bar and the academic community. For example, the United Nations Convention on the Assignment of Receivables in International Trade has been ratified by only one State, but has influenced the domestic assignment law and the relevant bibliography in a number of States, and its principles are reproduced in the UNCITRAL *Legislative Guide on Secured Transactions.*[11]

It is important to note that the legitimacy of the work of an international legislative body such as UNCITRAL emanates from decisions made by each sovereign State. More concretely, the legislative mandate of UNCITRAL emanates from resolutions agreed upon by States in the General Assembly of the United Nations. States members decide on what topics UNCITRAL should work and States adopt the result of UNCITRAL's work, first at the level of UNCITRAL and thereafter at the level of the General Assembly. Then the executive branch of each government takes the initiative to enact the result of UNCITRAL's work and the legislative branch of government is required to approve it. The extent of expert participation depends on decisions made by States when they form their delegations, but also when they agree that certain expert non-governmental organizations should be invited to the work of UNCITRAL and its working groups.[12] International inter-governmental organizations, such as Unidroit, The Hague Conference, the World Intellectual Property Organization and IFIs, are regularly invited to UNCITRAL meetings.

It should also be noted that the life-cycle of projects in UNCITRAL has decreased in recent years to an average 2–3 years. The response of UNCITRAL to any criticism that this might be too long is that it always endeavours to follow a middle road between time and quality, and, if it has to err, it prefers to err in favour of the quality, the balance and thus

[11] www.uncitral.org/uncitral/publications/bibliography_consolidated.html (last accessed 21 December 2012).

[12] For UNCITRAL's work methods, the Commission, the six working groups of UNCITRAL and the secretariat, *see* www.uncitral.org/uncitral/en/about/methods.html (last accessed 21 December 2012).

the acceptability of its texts (which promotes the efficiency of the process much more than a fast-track approach that leads to texts that may not be generally acceptable). As UNCITRAL tends to 'get it right', it is in the not unpleasant position of using taxpayer money to review and revise its texts every other year. For example, the UNCITRAL Arbitration Rules, prepared in 1976, were revised only in 2010. This may change to the extent that modern developments make it necessary for UNCITRAL to review the implementation of its texts by States and their application by courts and arbitral tribunals, in particular with respect to texts that may be affected by technological developments (for example, e-commerce or e-procurement).

III. International commercial law standards by IFIs

It is a fact of life that IFIs, such as, for example, the International Bank for Reconstruction and Development and the International Financial Corporation (the World Bank Group), the European Bank for Reconstruction and Development (EBRD) and the Asian Development Bank (ADB), prepare international commercial law standards.

For example, the World Bank Group prepared the *Principles and Guidelines for Effective Insolvency and Creditor Rights Systems*[13] and the Toolkit on Secured Transactions Systems and Collateral Registries.[14] Similarly, the EBRD prepared the EBRD Model Law on Secured Transactions[15] and the Core Principles for a secured transactions law,[16] and the ADB prepared the ADB Guide to Movables Registries.[17]

IV. Why do IFIs prepare international commercial law standards?

With respect to the *Principles and Guidelines for Effective Insolvency and Creditor Rights Systems*, it is noted that 'insolvency and creditor rights (ICR) constitutes one of the twelve areas in which the joint World Bank

13 http://siteresources.worldbank.org/GILD/Resources/FINAL-ICRPrinciples-March2009.pdf (last accessed 21 December 2012).

14 www.wbginvestmentclimate.org/uploads/SecuredTransactionsSystems.pdf (last accessed 21 December 2012).

15 www.ebrd.com/pubs/legal/secured.htm (last accessed 21 December 2012).

16 www.ebrd.com/country/sector/law/st/core/model/core.htm (last accessed 21 December 2012).

17 www.adb.org/documents/reports/movables_registries/default.asp (last accessed 21 December 2012).

and International Monetary Fund (IMF) Initiative on Standards and Codes undertakes assessments. In order to carry out these assessments, the World Bank uses the World Bank Principles for Effective Insolvency and Creditor Rights Systems (Principles) and the UNCITRAL *Legislative Guide on Insolvency Law* (Legislative Guide). These two complementary texts represent the international consensus on best practices and set forth a unified standard for ICR systems. In addition, these texts serve as reference points for evaluating and strengthening countries' ICR systems.[18]

With respect to its main objective, the Toolkit notes that it 'is to provide technical advice and guidance to World Bank Group staff, donor institutions, government officials and other practitioners on the implementation of secure transactions law and institutional reforms in emerging market countries'.[19] With respect to the work of the EBRD, it should be noted that

> since the publication of the EBRD Model Law in 1994 there has been a continuing programme of reform of security laws in the Bank's countries of operation. During country specific work of the Bank's Legal Transition Team it became evident that the Model Law is an important and helpful instrument for local reformers. However, it became clear that a more general formulation of the goals and principles of successful reform to foster economic development would be useful. This has led to the EBRD defining a set of ten core principles for modern secured transactions legislation. These principles form the basis for assessing a country's secured transactions law and for identifying the need for reform.[20]

Finally, with respect to the ADB Guide to Movables Registries, it should be noted that

> modern movables registries are attracting increasing interest from ADB's member countries. Such movables registries hold the promise of improved access to credit for debtors due to efficient, transparent registration of a debtor's movable property as collateral for credit. This publication provides a guide to these movables registries. . . . The publication highlights the opportunities for leapfrogging to state-of-the-art electronic movables registries, while recognising the need for pragmatic policy choices to accommodate the special challenges of developing countries. The main

[18] web.worldbank.org/WBSITE/EXTERNAL/TOPICS/LAWANDJUSTICE/GILD/0,,contentMDK:20196839~menuPK:146205~pagePK:64065425~piPK:162156~theSitePK:215006,00.html (last accessed 21 December 2012).

[19] *See* first paragraph of the Introduction of the Toolkit.

[20] www.ebrd.com/country/sector/law/st/core/model/core.htm (last accessed 21 December 2012).

> audience of the publication will be legislators, policy makers, designers, creditors, and other potential users of movables registries. It will also be of interest to those who wish to understand the nature of movables registries arising from a marriage of innovative information technology and a modern secured transactions law.[21]

Thus, based on their own understanding, IFIs prepare international commercial law standards because their Member States ask them to do it to promote economic development and protect their investment.

V. Should IFIs prepare international commercial law standards?

It is common knowledge that IFIs are not as qualified as international legislative bodies to prepare such international commercial law standards. Most people would agree with the view that compared with international legislative bodies, such as UNCITRAL, Unidroit or the Hague Conference, IFIs lack the necessary international legislative mandate, experience and expertise.

However, IFIs could assist States as prescribed in the relevant IFI treaties. Such assistance could include law reform assistance, an assessment of the needs of a State, as well as assistance with capacity- and institution-building. In addition, IFIs could assist States with an activity for which they are best qualified and for which international legislative bodies are not sufficiently qualified, that is, the economic analysis of the law, which is a necessary condition for efficient law reform. Any commercial law standards used in that regard, however, should be coordinated and be consistent with international standards developed by the properly mandated international legislative bodies.

It seems that this is the case with the World Bank Principles and *Guidelines for Effective Insolvency and Creditor Rights Systems* and the World Bank Group Toolkit on Secured Transactions Systems and Collateral Registries which are consistent with the UNCITRAL *Legislative Guide on Insolvency Law*[22] and the UNCITRAL *Legislative Guide on Secured Transactions.*[23] There are efforts under way to develop World Bank Principles on secured transactions that would incorporate the UNCITRAL

21 www.adb.org/documents/reports/movables_registries/default.asp (last accessed 21 December 2012).

22 www.uncitral.org/uncitral/en/uncitral_texts/insolvency/2004Guide.html (last accessed 21 December 2012).

23 www.uncitral.org/uncitral/en/uncitral_texts/payments/Guide_securedtrans.html (last accessed 21 December 2012).

Legislative Guide on Secured Transactions and form a unified standard and reference tool for assessments of national legislation.

With respect to the EBRD Model Law, the EBRD Core Principles on Secured Transactions and the ADB Guide to Movables Registries, it should be noted that UNCITRAL took them into account in preparing the Secured Transactions Guide.[24] It can only be hoped that the EBRD and the ADB will try to ensure that they take the Secured Transactions Guide into account in the law reform assistance efforts.

The question arises, however, as to the relationship and the possible overlap among texts prepared by the various international legislative bodies on the same topic.[25] Overlap among the texts prepared by various international legislative organizations in itself does not create any problem, as long as there is sufficient coordination. A good example of such coordination is the joint effort of UNCITRAL, the Hague Conference and Unidroit in the field of secured transactions. As indicated in a joint publication by the three organizations, States may adopt all their texts on secured transactions without creating any conflict.[26] The publication explains, for example, that the United Nations Convention on the Assignment of Receivables in International Trade (Receivables Convention) (New York, 2001)[27] supersedes the UNIDROIT Convention on International Factoring (Ottawa, 1988), with which it overlaps.[28] In addition, it also explains that the Receivables Convention gives way to the Convention on International Interests in Mobile Equipment (Cape Town, 2001) with respect to receivables arising from the sale or lease of aircraft.[29] Moreover, it explains that the Receivables Convention does not overlap with the Convention on the Law Applicable to Certain Rights in

24 Introduction to the *Guide*, para. 12.

25 The hierarchy between an international uniform law text (convention, model law, legislative guide) and domestic law is a matter of domestic law. Typically, a convention prevails over domestic law; and the relationship of a domestic law implementing a model law or legislative guide and another domestic law is a matter for the national legislator.

26 *See* Document A/CN.9/720, 'Comparison and analysis of major features of international instruments relating to secured transactions' www.uncitral.org/uncitral/commission/sessions/44th.html (last accessed 21 December 2012).

27 www.uncitral.org/uncitral/en/uncitral_texts/payments/2001Convention_receivables.html (last accessed 21 December 2012).

28 www.unidroit.org/english/conventions/1988factoring/main.htm (last accessed 21 December 2012).

29 www.unidroit.org/english/conventions/mobile-equipment/main.htm (last accessed 21 December 2012).

Respect of Securities held with an Intermediary (The Hague, 2006), as it excludes receivables arising from securities.[30]

VI. Conclusions

To the extent that IFIs prepare international commercial law standards in order to carry out their mandate of promoting economic development, they should continue coordinating with international legislative bodies. Such coordination should ensure that comprehensive and balanced guidance is offered to States. This result is consistent with the mandate of IFIs to promote economic development, and international legislative bodies to modernize and harmonize the law with a view to removing legal obstacles to international trade. In addition, IFIs could focus more on the economic analysis of the law that is a necessary prerequisite of efficient law reform.

30 www.hcch.net/index_en.php?act=conventions.text&cid=72 (last accessed 21 December 2012).

6

The power of secured transactions law and the challenge of its reform

FREDERIQUE DAHAN

I. Introduction

In the world of law and development, the reform of secured transactions has fairly recently been 'discovered' or, rather, emphasized. Perhaps the best known example is provided by the World Bank Report, *Doing Business*,[1] which devotes one of its ten chapters to 'Getting Credit'. Such chapter is built around two indices, one of them being the ability of a lender to be granted security over movable property. This may have taken lawyers by surprise: secured transactions law is a rather obscure subject, which is barely taught at law schools, and very rarely on its own. It is not at the core of socio-economic debates that rage on other subjects, such as corporate governance or capital markets development. Yet, secured transaction law is now spearheaded by many key development organizations as a key ingredient for unleashing access to credit.

The European Bank for Reconstruction and Development (EBRD, or the Bank) has recognized the importance of secured transactions reform from its very outset. The EBRD was established in 1991 when communism was crumbling in Central and Eastern Europe and ex-Soviet countries needed support to nurture a new private sector in a democratic environment. Today the EBRD is the largest single investor in the region and, notwithstanding its public sector shareholders, invests mainly in private enterprises, whilst using its close relationship with governments in the region to promote policies that will bolster the business environment. In 2011, the EBRD started a process to expand its activities to the south-eastern Mediterranean region (including Egypt, Jordan, Morocco and Tunisia), entrusted with the same mission of supporting private sector investment.

[1] www.doingbusiness.org/ (last accessed 21 December 2012).

The objective of the Bank is to encourage countries to modernize their secured transactions laws,[2] and it offers assistance at all stages of the reform process to achieve an effective legal framework for secured transactions, building a consensus for those reforms and then assisting in the preparation of necessary legislation and its implementation. The EBRD was fortunate enough to be able to work in partnership with a number of governments in the region where it operates and to assist in the reform of secured transactions law. As an international financial institution operating primarily in the private sector, it had experienced first-hand the difficulty of lending without a proper security package which lenders are accustomed to receive. The EBRD thus embarked on the preparation of the Model Law for Secured Transactions, which was published in 1994; other standard-setting documents followed, perhaps a little less well-known than the Model Law. Other Model Laws and key documents were developed thereafter. Noteworthy were the Organization of American States' Model Inter-American Law on Secured Transactions (2002);[3] the Uniform Law on Secured Transactions developed within the OHADA (*l'Organisation pour l'Harmonisation en Afrique du Droit des Affaires*), adopted in 1997 (and revised in 2010);[4] the World Bank *Principles for Effective Insolvency and Creditor Rights Systems* (2005);[5] and the UNCITRAL *Legislative Guide in Secured Transactions* (2007).[6]

When the EBRD *Secured Transactions Regional Survey* was published in 1999,[7] most countries in the region had undertaken reform on this part of their legal framework. By 2004, all of the countries had done so, thereby providing the legal basis for the taking of security over movable property. Yet the assessment of these regimes is not consistently positive. In some cases, despite what seems to have been considerable efforts, users

[2] In this chapter we use the term 'secured transactions' to embrace all transactions such as pledge and mortgage where the principal aim is to give security, not in the more limited sense (as given in the US under Article 9, Uniform Commercial Code – Secured Transactions) relating only to security over movables.

[3] www.oas.org/dil/Model_Law_on_Secured_Transactions.pdf (last accessed 21 December 2012).

[4] www.ohada.com/actes-uniformes-revises.html (last accessed 21 December 2012).

[5] www.worldbank.org/ifa/IPG%20-%20Revised%20Pples%20FINAL%20%5B21%20Dec%202005%5D.pdf (last accessed 21 December 2012).

[6] www.uncitral.org/uncitral/en/uncitral_texts/payments/Guide_securedtrans.html (last accessed 21 December 2012).

[7] *See* in particular, EBRD, 'Special Focus on Secured Transactions', *Law in Transition* – Autumn 2000, www.ebrd.com/pubs/legal/lit002.htm (last accessed 21 December 2012).

are still denouncing restrictions or problems in the legal and institutional framework.

Interestingly, the wave of secured transactions law reforms did not limit itself to Eastern Europe – in fact, a number of Western jurisdictions considered the reform of secured transactions law, too, most notably New Zealand (1999), France (2006) and Australia (2009); the Law Commission of England and Wales between 2000 and 2003 prepared an extensive reform proposal, which to date has only partially been translated into legislation. The rest of the world has also been receptive to the need for facilitating access to credit by means of secured transactions. Latin America (Mexico), Africa (Ghana) and even China (although the reform was somewhat limited) have all reformed their secured transactions legal frameworks.

In this chapter, we would like to present the philosophy that the EBRD has applied to its work in the field of secured transactions. Such philosophy rests on two key pillars:

- The first is that the objective of the secured transactions law is primarily facilitative and should be made legally efficient. The work of the EBRD has been to emphasize this approach, both when providing direct technical assistance to a country, as well as while assessing and surveying the different legal frameworks in the countries where it operates.[8]
- The second pillar is to embrace secured transactions law in all of its versatility, and to encourage legal reform accordingly. Secured transactions are at the core of many commercial transactions and the legal structure of security remains fairly similar, although there are distinctive features that must be recognized. To put it differently, taking security in the form of an enterprise charge is not conceptually different from using a warehouse receipt where stored commodity is stored and can be used as collateral, or affecting some bonds or equities as security in guarantee of inter-bank borrowing (financial collateral). The EBRD believes that failing to grasp properly the versatility of secured transactions (i) does a disservice to the economy that any reform of secured transactions is meant to serve; (ii) makes further reforms in this area perhaps more difficult; and (iii) unnecessarily creates legal 'silos', making the coherence of the legal framework perhaps harder to achieve.

[8] For more detail, *see* www.ebrd.com/pages/sector/legal/secured.shtml (last accessed 21 December 2012).

Table 6.1. *Ten Core Principles for secured transactions law*

1. **Reduce risk of credit**
   Security should reduce the risk of giving credit, leading to an increased availability of credit on improved terms.
2. **Non-possessory security, easy and cheap to create**
   The law should enable the quick, cheap and simple creation of a proprietary security right, without depriving the person giving the security of the use of his assets.
3. **Satisfaction through realization in case of default**
   If the secured debt is not paid, the holder of security should be able to have the charged assets realized and to have the proceeds applied towards satisfaction of his claim, prior to other creditors.
4. **Effective enforcement**
   Enforcement procedures should enable prompt realization at market value of the assets given as security.
5. **Effective in insolvency**
   The security right should continue to be effective and enforceable after the bankruptcy or insolvency of the person who has given it.
6. **Low cost**
   The cost of taking, maintaining and enforcing security should be low.
7. **All types of assets / debts / persons**
   Security should be available
   - over all types of assets,
   - to secure all types of debts, and
   - between all types of persons.
8. **Publicity**
   There should be an effective means of publicizing the existence of security rights.
9. **Priority**
   The law should establish rules governing competing rights of persons holding security and other person claiming rights in the assets given as security.
10. **Commercial flexibility**
    As far as possible the parties should be able to adapt security to the needs of their particular transaction.

1. Reducing credit risk in a legally efficient manner

In the course of its work, the Bank has formulated ten Core Principles for secured transactions law, which provide broad directions for reform. These principles are set out in Table 6.1.

The Bank formulated the Core Principles after it completed work on its Model Law on Secured Transactions (1994). During the country-specific work of the Bank's Legal Transition Team, it became evident that the Model Law was an important and helpful instrument for local reformers. However, it also became clear that *a more general formulation* of the goals and principles of successful reform was needed to help foster economic development. To some extent, the Core Principles serve to remind lawmakers that they would make a mistake in taking the Model Law as immediately available material that they can simply 'cut and paste' into their own legal system. Merely translating the Model Law into the local language cannot provide the country with an up-and-running new pledge law. There is simply no substitute for the long and painstaking process of legal reform, which implies designing a law that really suits the local circumstances and interfaces efficiently with existing laws. These Core Principles are drawn on the assumption that the role of a secured transactions law is economic, and do not seek to impose any particular solution on a country as there may be many ways of arriving at a particular result. The Core Principles do, however, seek to indicate the result that should be achieved. In order to assess whether the particular route chosen by the country has achieved its objectives, the EBRD focuses on the concept of legal efficiency, that is to say, the extent to which a law and the way it is used provide the benefits that it was intended to achieve.

As mentioned before, the prime purpose of a secured transactions law is economic, since the secured credit market has an essentially economic function (whilst recognizing that it may also have important social functions and consequences); and it is essentially facilitative, since a secured credit market is not a necessity, it being theoretically possible for any jurisdiction to function without it. We work on the premise that the basic legal framework should be *conducive* to a flexible market for secured credit. There are also social issues, for example, relating to consumer credit, and economic issues, such as risk management, but the driving force behind the introduction of a law on secured transactions is the benefits that such law is expected to bring to the economy.

A relatively simple indicator of the success of a secured transactions law reform (or primary motive for undertaking the secured transactions law reform) would be the subsequent increase in the *volume* of secured lending. This is a crude and narrow indicator, inadequate by itself. The intended function of the secured credit market may be more than just to boost the amount of credit granted against security. It may also include, for example, opening up credit to new sectors of society, encouraging

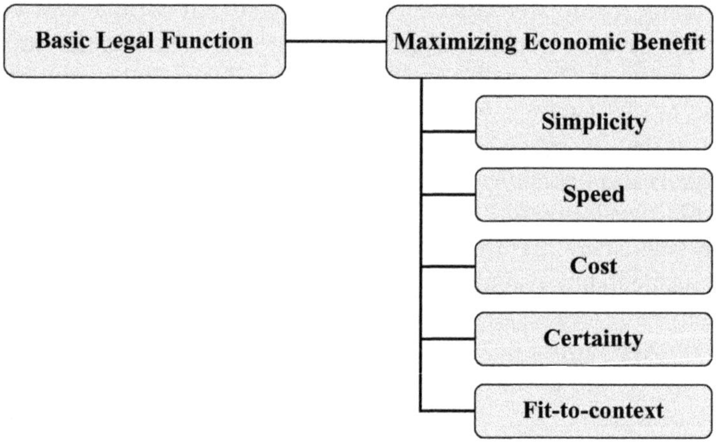

Fig. 6.1 Criteria for legal efficiency of secured transactions law.

new housing construction, or allowing privately-funded infrastructure projects.

The intended function of a law has to be looked at in the context within which it is to operate. Its ramifications have to be considered not just in economic terms, but in social and cultural terms as well. Thus, an appropriate balance has to be found between fulfilling the law's economic purpose and ensuring that the effects of the law are acceptable in context. In this chapter, we analyse legal efficiency by looking at the degree to which the legal framework enables secured transactions:

(a) first, to achieve their basic legal function (on which see below) and
(b) second, to operate in a way which maximizes economic benefit.

And, as shown in Figure 6.1, we break the second criterion into five separate headings: simplicity, speed, cost, certainty and fit-to-context.

The basic legal function of a secured transactions law is to allow the creation of a security right over assets which, in the case of non-payment of a debt, entitles the creditor to have the assets realized and the proceeds applied towards satisfaction of his claim prior to claims of unsecured creditors, based on a predictable prority order among secured creditors. If a secured transactions law only gives the creditor a personal right against the debtor, but no right in the assets, or if there is no right to enforcement, or no priority vis-à-vis other creditors, the law fails to achieve its basic legal function. An absolute priority for taxes and other State claims ahead of the secured creditor, or the right in insolvency of ordinary creditors to share in a portion of the proceeds of secured assets, are more than inefficiencies in the secured transactions law: they are defects which prevent it from fully achieving its basic function. They may be intentional (a super-priority of the State usually is) but they reflect a compromise between two laws with conflicting purposes. Any such compromise inevitably inhibits the effective operation of the secured transactions law and introduces uncertainty into the minds of lenders.

If the legal framework for secured transactions is to operate in a way which ***maximizes economic benefit***, the system for creation and enforcement of pledges or mortgages should be simple, fast and inexpensive, there should be certainty as to what the law is and how it is applied, and it should function in a manner which fits the local context.

Simplicity: Simple does not mean simplistic: it is necessary to strike a balance between simplicity and the sophistication required by the market. Part of simplicity comes from the lack of restrictions and barriers. If the law is to facilitate the use of secured credit it needs to provide a base which offers the necessary flexibility to adapt with the trends of the market. In many countries complexities have developed and become entrenched over time, as laws have been adapted to new circumstances. Such complexities have arisen from the inherent limitation of adapting existing, sometimes long-established, legal systems to deal with new circumstances, rather than the sophistication of those circumstances per se. There exists in transition countries a huge opportunity to focus on the essential elements and to introduce laws which are directly adapted to modern market requirements.

Speed: For most aspects of the legal process, the less time it takes, the more efficient it is. There are exceptions: a notice period or a cooling-off period has to be of appropriate length, but for registration of a pledge or mortgage, for example, there can only be benefits if it takes a few minutes rather than a month. A lender who knows that enforcement of the pledge or mortgage is likely to take several years will derive less comfort from his security.

Cost: Legal costs, almost inevitably have an adverse impact on the economic benefit of a transaction. Delay, complexity and uncertainty all tend to add to costs, so there is a close relation with the other aspects of legal efficiency. Some costs are, at least to an extent, within the control of the parties. Before taking legal advice on structuring a transaction, the parties can assess the value of doing so. The cost of legal advice on a complicated transaction may be outweighed by the benefits; however, the cost of legal advice incurred because of defects in the legal framework always represents a reduction in legal efficiency, as do high fixed costs (for example, registration, notary or court fees).

One does not have to be an economist to understand that if the legal procedures for creating and enforcing a pledge or mortgage are slow, expensive and complex, the cost of secured credit will be higher and the economic benefits of using pledges or mortgages reduced. There are, however, two other elements that need to be taken into account when assessing legal efficiency: certainty and fit-to-context. These elements are sometimes overlooked by economists because they are more difficult to translate into quantifiable indicators, and yet they are critical to the success of a legal system.

Certainty: Certainty is a critical element of any sound legal system. A grain of uncertainty in the legal position can have a pervasive and disproportionate effect. Once a banker hears that there is some doubt in the legal robustness of a transaction, he may quickly become hesitant in pursuing the transaction. The difficulty is one of measurement. If the legal uncertainty relating to a pledge or mortgage could be stated, for example, as a five per cent chance of proceeds on enforcement being reduced, with the amount of the reduction being on average 20 per cent, the risk would be quantified, and it would become easier to manage, as there would be relative certainty. In reality, legal opinions on enforcement cannot be expressed in that way and the natural reaction to unquantifiable uncertainty is extreme caution. Transparency can often strengthen certainty: for instance, easy access for all to information in the land register allows potential mortgage lenders to find out about the property and any other mortgages that may exist.

Fit-to-context: The 'fit-to-context' criterion is the most elusive but nonetheless important, since it covers a number of facets. Simplicity, cost, speed and certainty are all concepts which are relatively easy to understand and to relate to economic benefit. The 'fit-to-context' concept, however, merits more explanation. It is not enough to adopt a law which establishes clearly and unambiguously a simple, fast and inexpensive regime for pledge or mortgage security. The efficient functioning of the law will also depend on whether it is adapted to the economic, social and legal context within which it is required to operate. A secured transaction law, for example, needs:

(a) To respond to the economic need: markets are constantly changing, and the law has to be able to adapt to new products as, for example, when loans are proposed with flexible interest rates.

(b) To fit in the broader financial context within which the law operates: for example, the rules applicable to transfers and pledges of secured loans should not hamper the use of mortgage-backed securities and covered bonds and the secured transactions law should take into account the way in which a pledge is used for securitization transactions involving unsecured loans and other assets.
(c) To fit with existing market practice: whereas much can be learned from other markets, a law has to be compatible with existing market and legal practice and to give confidence to those who rely on it.
(d) To achieve an appropriate balance between fulfilling the economic purpose of taking security and ensuring that its effects are acceptable in the wider social context: the rights of consumers and occupiers of property to appropriate protection cannot be eliminated to suit the economic needs of the secured transactions law, rather, they have to be framed in a way which enables borrowers and lenders to derive the benefits afforded by a flourishing secured credit market, while at the same time ensuring the necessary protections for persons in a vulnerable position.
(e) To achieve any particular objective: for example, the law may aim to extend secured lending activity to a wide range of banks as opposed to creating a lending cartel, or to reduce constraints on the types of pledge and mortgage product that can be offered.

2. *Recognizing secured transactions versatility*

What makes the EBRD approach to secured transactions perhaps unique is the fact that it has recognized and emphasized the power of collateral in a number of different transactional contexts. As an international financial institution which lends primarily to the private sector, the Bank has developed a variety of investment products (or has supported local financial institutions which in turn use these products), and many of which rely on collateral. This has been fed into the advisory arm of the EBRD, in particular the Legal Transition Programme, and has thus positively affected the way secured transactions law reform has been shaped. Here we will take a number of examples, ranging from residential and commercial mortgages to financial collateral.

2.1 Mortgage law

At the start of the transition process, most of the countries of Central and Eastern Europe provided for the possibility of taking security over immovable property, usually on the basis of laws which had their origins in the pre-communist era. The reform priority at that time was to enable movable property to be used as collateral. Not only was there an absence of rules governing security over movables, but many borrowers did not have suitable real estate to offer as security. However, the EBRD approach has always been to treat mortgages as an integral part of secured transactions and to apply the same legal principles to this form of security that is given by contract[9] over real property. The context for pledge law reform has been different, yet, economically speaking, pledge and mortgage fulfil the same purpose and it is illogical that the reform of the legal framework for each should be conducted in isolation.

Mortgage financing has always been a favourite form of financing for banks. The primary credit risk is supported by solid security which does not move and which normally maintains its value. The incentive to avoid default is high, especially for residential property, because a borrower will make every effort to avoid losing his home. Furthermore, in the last few decades, financial markets have designed new techniques to address the fundamental difficulty that banks have in extending mortgages loans: that of managing long-term assets (mortgage loans, of which tenure is typically 20 years+) with short-term liabilities (deposits). The techniques for financing the providers of mortgage loans have also changed, with an increasing interest in using the mortgage loans themselves as collateral, whether for secured borrowing (with the mortgage lender issuing covered bonds), or as a means of divesting the mortgage loan portfolio through securitization (with the acquirer issuing mortgage-backed securities).

Mortgage law reform[10] is not necessarily high on the agenda of many transition countries, because giving security by mortgage is not a new concept. Yet the rules for mortgage have not always developed in the most rational and legally efficient way, and this may be particularly visible in developed economies where a variety of different systems, mostly shaped in a different era, have been more or less adapted over the years to accommodate market changes.[11] One of the opportunities that transition countries represent is precisely the ability to avoid the kind of

[9] This work does not deal with rights given by law to the providers of funds for the purchase of property.

[10] The term 'mortgage law' is used to refer to the law governing mortgage as security and does not extend to the laws governing loans that may be secured by mortgage.

[11] *See* www.ebrd.com/pubs/legal/mit.htm (last accessed 21 December 2012).

obsolete elements in the law which often hinder development in advanced economies.

As seen above, the EBRD Core Principles for a secured transactions law have been widely used in the countries of Central and Eastern Europe as a starting point for reform of laws on security. They apply to mortgage as much as to any other proprietary security.

This is in sharp contrast to other reference materials, such as the UNCITRAL *Legislative Guide on Secured Transactions*, or indeed, the IFC Toolkit on Secured Transactions and Collateral Registries, published in 2010,[12] which both specifically exclude security of immovable property from their scope. The danger of such an approach is to draw an artificial barrier between the two types of security, thus often leading to a different stand on matters where logically there should be no inherent difference. For example, if it is possible to describe the secured debt generally and for the secured debt to fluctuate during the duration of the obligation, it should not matter whatsoever whether the assets given as collateral are movable or immovable. Similarly, if the law has allowed enforcement of the pledge over movable property to take place out of court, enforcement of the mortgage over immovable property should also be allowed out of court. The principal aim of enforcement is to realize the mortgaged property promptly at market value. The mortgagor and the mortgage creditor should share a similar interest that the mortgaged property be realized at the best price. The prerequisites to enforcement and the process by which it is achieved from the formalities of commencement to the distribution of proceeds should be legally efficient. If they are not, costs arising through delay and complexity are likely to reduce the net proceeds, and inefficiency may give the mortgagor opportunities to obstruct the process.

Possible differences in approach could arise from the identity of the borrower – consumers, for instance, may require additional protection as they may lack bargaining power or financial awareness. However, all too often one finds differences drawn between regimes applicable to mortgages and pledges, which are simply borne out of legal conservatism rather than economic rationale.

[12] www1.ifc.org/wps/wcm/connect/industry_ext_content/ifc_external_corporate_site/industries/financial±markets/publications/toolkits/secured±transactions±systems±_±collateral±registries±toolkit (last accessed 21 December 2012).

2.2 Mortgage securities

The relevance of secured transactions law and its versatility is particularly striking as far as mortgage securities are concerned. Mortgage securities[13] have had bad press in the context of the sub-prime mortgage crisis that began in the US in 2007. Yet one should not overlook the valuable role they play in securing funding for mortgage markets, and generally boosting local capital markets, because they create a legal link between the mortgage loans and the source of funding.

In the US model, banks originated mortgage loans, but they were not kept on the banks' balance sheets: they were packaged and sold to specialist government-sponsored entities (such as Fannie Mae, Freddie Mac and Ginnie Mae). These entities in turn financed their portfolios through the issue of mortgage-backed securities (MBS), which were given a high credit rating not only because of the underlying mortgage loan portfolio, but also based on either an implicit or an explicit government guarantee. By contrast, under the German model of *Pfandbriefe*, mortgage loans were retained on the balance sheet of the lending bank, but used as security for bonds issued by the bank to finance its mortgage lending business. The bonds issued, known as covered bonds (CBs)[14] are a means of secured borrowing, and often the legal framework for them is set out in special legislation. To date, CBs have been more prevalent in the transition countries (in particular, the Czech Republic, Hungary, Latvia, Lithuania, Poland and the Slovak Republic), although the total amount issued remains comparatively small. They are a relatively straightforward and regulated way of improving the terms on which banks can obtain funding and they have been well tested in a number of Western European jurisdictions.

It is often overlooked that secured transactions law will play an important role in the feasibility of both covered bonds and mortgage-backed securities. In covered bond transactions, the rights of bondholders to the mortgage loans in the cover pool will often be given by way of pledge.

[13] In this chapter, we define mortgage securities as tradable obligations where the payment obligations are secured, or otherwise supported, by a pool of mortgage loans. This includes both mortgage-backed securities and covered bonds. Generally, 'bond' is used when referring to covered bonds and 'note' when referring to mortgage-backed securities.

[14] Covered bonds are debt securities issued by credit institutions and covered by certain types of assets, usually mortgage loans, but it can also be public sector debt or ship loans; however, in the context of this chapter, only bonds covered by mortgage loans (sometimes referred to as mortgage bonds) are contemplated.

In MBS transactions, the Special Purpose Vehicle (SPV) will often give a pledge of the mortgage loans in favour of the noteholders. The issues that typically arise, then, are those for a covered bond and mortgage-backed securities transaction:

- It should not be necessary to obtain consent from the mortgagor (obligor) for the pledge, and notice to the mortgagor should not be needed as a condition of the validity of the pledge, but merely to make it contentious to third parties.
- It should not be necessary to enter the rights of the bondholders or noteholders as pledgeholder in the mortgage register. Registration of the pledge in the pledge register may be required, but this should be a simple formality requiring a single registration covering all the mortgage loans.[15]
- Because the cover pool for CBs may well be dynamic and fluctuating, it will be necessary in the pledge to describe the collateral (i.e. the mortgage loans) generally, including future loans, so as to avoid any requirement to renew the pledge registration each time the cover pool is amended.

Generally, the ability to easily and effectively give security by way of pledge can greatly facilitate the contractual arrangements to mitigate risks in mortgage securities transactions, which are all resting on contractual arrangements over the cash flows. Pledge over cash, bank accounts and accounts receivable are all necessary building blocks of mortgage securities.

Countries that have a modern framework for secured transactions, enabling the giving of an enforceable, first-ranking pledge right that remains effective on the insolvency of the pledgor (be it the issuer or the originator), will have a great advantage. It thus needs to be well understood by transition countries that failing to tackle their pledge law provisions would have direct consequences on the abilities of investors to structure transactions.

2.3 Warehouse receipts

Food security and warehouse receipts systems are a key objective for the EBRD, especially as the region in which the EBRD operates has such a

[15] *See* EBRD, *Guiding Principles for the Development of a Charge Register* at www.ebrd.com/country/sector/law/st/core/pubsec.pdf (last accessed 10 January 2013).

considerable potential in primary agriculture.[16] In the late nineteenth and early twentieth century, warehouse receipt finance played a major role in enabling the development of US agriculture. Warehouse receipts (WHR) systems constitute an alternative solution for commodity producers, processors and traders to access short-term financing for operations, take advantage of price fluctuations, and secure the storage of their produce. Broadly speaking, the system is based on storage of commodities into a warehouse where the warehouse operator issues a receipt upon delivery of the commodity. The receipt can then be used as collateral – typically, the receipt would be issued in two parts, one part evidencing the commodity ownership, the other part, the right of pledge created against the commodity in the benefit of the holder of that part. There are different approaches in the development of legislative frameworks. In some cases, legislators build upon existing laws, but usually the effort begins with new legislation. Lenders are more likely to feel comfortable when there exists strong legislation in place protecting the rights and interests of depositors in public warehouses; a legal basis for the recognition, perfection and enforcement of the collateral; the negotiability of the receipts; strong safeguards over the integrity of the system; and clear procedures in case of bankruptcy and default of the warehouse. The primary legislation (laws) needs to be simple and clear and provide the structural framework. The secondary legislation (ordinances and regulations) needs to be detailed and comprehensive and deal with the technical specifics of the system and the commodity.[17]

There are clearly themes that are reminiscent of secured transactions, in particular regarding the enforcement over the commodities. The condition for the system of WHR to be used for financing purposes depends to a very large extent on the enforcement system it will provide to the financier, should the borrower default. Since the financier has extended credit comforted by the availability of grain stored in a regulated warehouse, it is essential that, should the borrower/debtor default on the credit, the creditor is able to sell such grain to repay the debt. Enforcement mechanisms should be quick, reliable/certain, simple and adapted to the local context, with its specific risks and perception of risks. This is very important, as commodities are easily moved and highly liquid.

[16] www.ebrd.com/pages/sector/agribusiness.shtml (last accessed 10 January 2013).

[17] For more detail, *see* EBRD-FAO, *The Use of Warehouse Receipt Finance in Agriculture in Transition Countries*, 2009, www.eastagri.org/publications/detail.asp?id=33 (last accessed 10 January 2013).

In legal terms, the means of enforcement will depend on the legal instrument that the creditor holds in the receipt – and thus, the legal right such instrument gives him on the grain. There are typically two options:

- a security right – the WHR is used to provide the lender with a pledge over the grain;
- an ownership right – the WHR is used to transfer ownership of the grain to the lender (the transfer should not have tax or accounting implications, however).

In both options, the issues are similar but differently structured and lead us to draw the following conclusions:

- The law should provide (or cross-refer to) a definition of default which allows the creditor to commence the enforcement of the security.
- The definition should not include a statutory grace period, or a subjective assessment by the court, for instance, of the seriousness of the default.
- The creditor should give notice (contents to be defined) to the debtor/borrower of the commencement of enforcement. It is open to question whether or not the law provides a period (five to ten working days) during which the creditor cannot enforce. This allows the borrower time (i) to challenge the enforcement procedure if he deems that enforcement is unwarranted, and (ii) to redeem himself by curing the default.
- The creditor should register the commencement of enforcement in the electronic Register of WHR (see below) – this gives a certain solemnity to the commencement, so is likely to discourage abusive or frivolous commencement of enforcement.
- The creditor should give notice to the warehouse on the commencement of enforcement – this will be a separate notice if the warehouse and the borrower are not the same person.
- The effect of this notice(s) should be (i) to freeze the grain in the warehouse; (ii) to prevent the sale, transfer, pledge or any other actions over the grain by the debtor and the warehouse. Some systems may have considered the legal option to give the notice the effect of transforming the right of the creditor over the grain to that of ownership, if the right of the creditor until then was that of a security holder.
- Realization should be led by the creditor if the parties have so agreed. There is no need to file a court action if out-of-court enforcement had been contractually agreed.

- The sale of grain can be done directly (private sale) or by auction organized by the creditor, as long as the grain is sold at or close to market price. The creditor should be entitled to transfer ownership of the grain to the purchaser (whether because the law made him the owner of the grain or on the behalf of the borrower).
- There should be a clear ranking order for allocation of the sale proceeds, which should preferably be (1) any unpaid costs to the warehouse and storage fees that may be due; (2) payment to the creditor of outstanding secured debt, plus interest, penalties and enforcement expenses; (3) any surplus paid to the debtor.
- The creditor should have the ability to call for bailiff support to take possession of the grain and transfer it to the purchaser, should the warehouse refuse to cooperate.

However, WHR reform presents specificities, which calls for a differentiated approach.

First, the WHR system must focus on structural components, which include licensing and inspection of public warehouses and insurance and indemnity funds. Ideally, one would want to see a strong system of *licensed and supervised public warehouses.* In the absence of such a system, the financial institution is exposed to the risks related to the warehouse operation, such as improper handling, damage or loss of the collateral, or fraud. These operating risks could be mitigated through a highly selective choice of warehouses and close monitoring by specialist collateral managers (where a third party is liable for the continued presence of the commodities in the warehouse). This means that, in practice, a good deal of effort in this reform will be spent on building a robust and credible licensing and supervising system which, of course, is totally absent from a 'classic' secured transactions reform.

Secondly, it is questionable whether it would be apposite to include the registration of the right of pledge over the grain (via the second part of the WHR used as collateral) into a pledge register. There is no question that the management of WHR finance is much improved if an electronic WHR system is adopted, but the system is not geared primarily for the pledging aspects of the system; it is also to be used for receipt issuance – bringing a significant level of protection against fraud by preventing the double use of warehouse receipts to obtain finance from two different banks, the transfer of previously pledged receipts, or attempts to take delivery with a fake receipt when the real receipt has already been sold or pledged. Banks would use it for financing against the security of pledged commodities, primarily because of the fact that the issuance of a receipt establishes with certainty the existence of the commodity as described in the receipt. This is in sharp contrast with the notice-filing approach of a pledge register, where title of the assets offered as collateral is not evidenced by the registration/filing of the security right. Finally, the electronic system could be used for its trading functionalities of the receipts (legally qualified as securities), offering users possibilities to invest and trade in existing commodities through a safe and easily acceptable electronic system.[18]

So whereas there are strong benefits in incorporating some of the key features of secured transactions reform in the reform of WHR, such as enforcement, it is important to understand the specific features that this reform entails and to keep aspect such as registration clearly separate in order to reap all economic benefits of commodity financing.

2.4 Financial collateral

Financial collateral, as the term suggests, is financial assets provided by a borrower (the collateral provider) to a lender (the collateral taker) to minimize the risk of financial loss to the lender in the event of the borrower defaulting on its financial obligations. Collateral is increasingly used in all types of transactions, including capital markets, bank treasury and funding, payment and clearing systems and general bank lending. The concept of financial collateral has not necessarily come high on the agenda of secured transactions law reformers because in many jurisdictions, the transactions are structured as title finance. *Title transfers* (including repurchase agreements – 'repos') occur where ownership of the collateral passes to the collateral taker, on terms that it or equivalent assets will be transferred back when the obligations are discharged. *Security arrangements* occur where the collateral taker obtains a security interest in the collateral, coupled with physical possession or control, but does not become the owner.

Title transfer arrangements typically take place in the context of:

(i) Securities lending, used to cover short-selling by which the borrower of the securities must get title over the securities in order to sell to

[18] 'They may be a good first step (pending integration into a full-fledged regional exchange network) for countries that are too small for a comprehensive commodity exchange, or where local investors are unable to pay the costs of such a system', in EBRD-FAO, *ibid.*

the third party. When the borrower of the securities must re-deliver them or their equivalent to the lender of the securities, the borrower must purchase those securities in the market.

(ii) Repos, according to which a firm sells securities to a financier and agrees to buy them back at a defined time and at the same sale price plus an amount equivalent to interest. This is a very common practice to support the raising of cash (e.g. overnight finance for banks) supported by collateral.[19]

One of the reasons for using title finance as opposed to security rights was to allow the buyer to have the right to use the securities transferred to him. However, the development of the EU Financial Collateral Directive in 2002 (as amended in 2009[20]) has made the distinction irrelevant when it applies. The types of assets covered by the Directive are:

- cash;
- financial instruments (e.g. shares, bonds, securities); and
- credit claims.[21]

The Directive applies to the collateral taker and the collateral provider provided that both are or belong to one of the following categories:

- public authorities;
- public sector bodies;
- a central bank;
- a financial institution subject to prudential supervision; and
- a legal entity (not a physical person), as long as the counterpart in the transaction belong to one of the above categories.

The Directive has created a set of substantive rules which will apply to all EU Member States. But these are mostly permissive rules, and they leave undisturbed the core mechanisms as to creation/attachment, priority and enforcement principles which exist in each jurisdiction. Precisely, the Directive's objective has been to recognize the arrangements entered into by the parties, regardless of whether these arrangements are made

[19] *See* Philip R. Wood, *Comparative Law of Security Interests and Title Finance* (London: Sweet and Maxwell, 2nd edn., 2007), p. 28.

[20] Directive 2009/44/EC of the European Parliament and of the Council of 6 May amending Directive 98/26/EC on settlement finality in payments and securities settlement systems and Directive 2002/47/EC on financial collateral arrangements as regards linked systems and credit claims, OJ L146, 10.06.2009, p. 37.

[21] Credit claims concept has been introduced by Directive 2009/44/EC.

in the form of a title transfer or a pledge over the collateral. There is some effect on perfection to the extent that formalities are eliminated (i.e. no registration of the pledge should be required). The Directive also prescribes that the right for the collateral taker to use financial collateral or to appropriate financial collateral has to be given effect.

The aim of the Directive is also to provide for rapid and non-formalistic enforcement procedures designed in part to limit contagion effects in the event of default by one of the parties to the arrangement. Thus, Member States are required by the Directive to ensure that the collateral taker is able to realize financial collateral in one of the following manners:

- for financial instruments, by sale or appropriation and by setting off their value against, or applying their value in discharge of, the relevant financial obligations;
- for cash, by setting off the amount against or applying it in discharge of the relevant financial obligations;
- for a credit claim, by sale or appropriation (if so agreed between the parties) or by setting off their value against or applying their value in discharge of, the relevant financial obligations.

Moreover, Member States must recognize the applicable close-out netting provisions, even if the collateral taker or provider is already subject to insolvency proceedings, and specifically disapply insolvency law provisions which would impede the realization of such collateral e.g. any moratorium on enforcement.

However, it must be well understood that even in countries where the Directive applies, the intersection with, or indeed the full application of, secured transactions law will be unavoidable. In the US, for instance, security over financial collateral falls within the scheme created by Article 9 of the Uniform Commercial Code, along with many other types of collateral, although special rules will apply. This is because US Article 9 has adopted the so-called functional approach to secured transactions, which subjects all transactions to the same regime of which the function is to provide security, regardless of the form (security right or transfer of title, etc.) used by the parties' agreement. However, in Europe, the majority of financial collateral arrangements in the European market are done on the basis of title transfers.

One problem which has arisen in England concerns the impact of the Directive (and its implementing provisions contained in the Financial Collateral Arrangements (No. 2) Regulations 2003) over floating charges. Indeed, since the Directive prevents Member States from requiring the performance of a formal act for perfection of a financial collateral arrangement (i.e. registration), the Regulations have thus disapplied section 860 of the Companies Act 2006, which requires (among other types of security) floating charges to be registered at Companies House, as long as they fulfil the other requirements of the Directive of 'possession or control' over the financial collateral. This is quite tricky, because the distinction between fixed and floating charges, under English law, although subject to much uncertainty, rests to a large extent on the control that the chargeholder may or may not have over the property.[22] Since it is indeed possible to take a floating charge over investment property that will permit the chargeholder to deal with the property, there is a need to determine whether or not such floating charge falls under the jurisdiction of the Financial Collateral Arrangements (No. 2) Regulations (in which case, no registration at Companies House will be necessary) or not (in which case, if the floating charge was not registered as prescribed, it would be void against the liquidator and other creditors).

These questions may well be seen to be rather esoteric and mainly driven by the complexity of English law vis-à-vis floating charges. Nevertheless, they illustrate the need to pay attention to the relevant local secured transactions legal framework when looking at financial collateral issues to ensure that provisions are as much as possible coordinated and to leave parties in no uncertainty as to the validity of their arrangements.

2.5 Microfinance and SME lending

Finally, a consideration of secured transaction law would not be complete without mention of its interaction with micro- and small and medium enterprise (SME) finance. Microfinance is a well-established, widely admired framework for bringing credit access to the most neglected segment of borrowers. In the EBRD region, developing microfinance has been challenging, not only because micro-credit represented a completely new product that was considered by the existing commercial bank sector, but also because of the culture heritage associated with credit (credit as a mandated transfer from surplus to deficit units) and the fact that microfinance worked against the new culture of connected lending.[23]

[22] H. Beale, M. Bridge, L. Gullifer and E. Lomnicka, *The Law of Security and Title-Based Financing* (Oxford University Press, 2nd edn., 2012), pp. 35 and 58.

[23] *See* M. Holtmann, 'Use of security in challenging environments: the microfinance perspective', in *Secured Transactions Reform and Access to Credit*, F. Dahan and J. Simpson (eds.) (Cheltenham: Edward Elgar, Elgar Financial Series, 2008), p. 159.

For micro and small entrepreneurs and their creditors, giving and taking collateral can be highly challenging due to poor institutions or inadequate or non-existent legal provisions. Experts working in the field bring shocking stories, such as that of the highway police department in a town in Russia, which was opened for only two hours a week for the registration of pledges on vehicles (this amounted to a capacity of five registrations per week); or that of Russian rules which prevented real estate from being sold as long as anybody possessed a '*propiska*', the right of residence, in the dwelling. The owner had the right to grant *propiska* to people even if the real estate had already been mortgaged to a lender.

In fact, part of the innovation of microfinance, through a variety of mechanisms and cash-flow based lending practices, has consisted of lending *unsecured*. Collateral is only required for loans that are above a threshold amount, where the credit risk but also the transactions costs make the exercise of taking security worthwhile. Collateral can take the form of real estate, machinery and equipment, vehicles, etc., and here, of course, secured transactions law reform will be an important development. However, extension of micro-credit depends much more on the ability of lenders to access credit information and overcome inherent information asymmetries about their potential borrowers' ability to pay. In other words, an information system around credit history of prospective clients is key. Credit information reporting systems have been addressed in a number of important documents, including the IFC *Credit Bureau Knowledge Guide* (2006), and the World Bank/BIS, *General Principles for Credit Reporting*, Consultative Report (2011).[24]

In recent years, the EBRD has also increasingly focused its policy dialogue on the ability of lenders to access credit information on borrowers. The effectiveness of these credit information reporting institutions can be limited by a lack of an appropriate legal framework and proper institutional structure and processes. Here, again, the EBRD has focused on the 'legal efficiency' of the credit information reporting systems, to allow for the sharing of accurate and sufficient credit information to support credit providers in assessing the creditworthiness of a potential borrower/debtor, while respecting the sensitive and confidential nature of such information, whilst maximizing the economic benefits that the system should offer in terms of simplicity, costs, etc. This may indeed take some of the focus away from secured transactions law reform. But if the objectives of

[24] siteresources.worldbank.org/FINANCIALSECTOR/Resources/GeneralPrinciplesforCreditReporting(final).pdf (last accessed 21 December 2012).

the policymakers are indeed to support the development of microfinance and very small entrepreneurs who are likely to operate their business without a legal structure, and often using their personal assets, would it not be more rational to boost credit reporting systems to ensure that the borrower can build a positive credit history which will reassure the lender of its creditworthiness? Surely, a collateral register should never be seen as fulfilling such a role, and it would be a fallacy to pretend that it can.

II. Conclusions

Secured transaction law reform shows no sign of losing momentum. In the region of Central and Eastern Europe where the EBRD has traditionally operated, we believe that the momentum for reform is due to the versatility of the subject matter; secured transaction law potentially has such a broad range of applications, yet it requires specific rules for certain transactions or subject matter. It will be very interesting to see how the experience in Central and Eastern Europe is or is not able to inspire reform in the new region of North Africa and the Middle East where the EBRD is soon to start operating, and whether some of the useful lessons learned in Central and Eastern Europe may be of assistance to North Africa and the Middle East in developing their secured transaction legal frameworks.

Overall, in most transition countries, the basic reforms of the legal regimes for pledge and mortgage are well advanced, but there remains much work to do to assess those regimes and to fine-tune them to ensure that secured credit markets are supported by laws that are appropriate and conducive to the operation of such markets for the mutual benefit of both lenders and borrowers. We believe that the failure to define both the general as well as the detailed objectives of legal reform and subsequently to measure what has been achieved against a stated set of objectives currently often prevents emerging markets from realizing the advantages they should derive from legal reform programmes. In this respect the use of legal efficiency criteria, such as has been developed by the EBRD in the field of secured transactions, provides a basis for bridging the gap between economic analysis and legal reasoning.

7

Commentary on the involvement of international financial institutions in secured transactions law reform

LOUKAS MISTELIS

In this particular topic we have a fascinating junction: it is the crossroads of harmonization,[1] often seen as a value in itself and an area of law which is diverse worldwide but critical for the well-functioning of an economy: in classical jargon, credit and security or, in modern parlance, secured transactions. Because of this critical crossroads, almost everything is arguable and plenty of debate has been waged of what is right, efficient or appropriate. And the debate is pervasive, with quieter periods conditioned on certain impasses and realization of the fact that harmonization of secured transactions laws pertains to some extent to harmonization of bankruptcy laws and touches upon a number of public law issues.

Secured transactions law reform has attracted the attention of formulating agencies, with variable levels of intensity (and success) from the early 1970s. The (then) European Economic Community, UNCITRAL, Unidroit and other supra-national or international organizations entrusted directly or indirectly with lawmaking or standard-setting identified this area as one of particular interest and practical (and legal) harmonizing necessity. It is essential that credit is available at a reasonably

1 M. Andenas and C. B. Andersen (eds.), *Theory and Practice of Harmonisation* (Cheltenham: Edward Elgar, 2012) and, in particular, O. Akseli, 'International Harmonisation of Credit and Security Laws: The Way Forward', in Andenas and Andersen, ibid., pp. 551–71; O. Akseli, 'On the Methods of International Harmonisation of Secured Transactions Law', in C. B. Andersen and U. G. Schroeter (eds.), *Sharing International Commercial Law across National Boundaries: Festschrift for Albert H. Kritzer on the Occasion of his Eightieth Birthday* (London: Wildy, Simmonds & Hill, 2008), pp. 1–12. On harmonization generally, *see also* L. Mistelis, 'Is Harmonisation a Necessary Evil? The Future of Harmonisation and New Sources of Law', in I. Fletcher, L. Mistelis, and M. Cremona (eds.), *Foundations and Perspectives of International Trade Law* (London: Sweet and Maxwell, 2001), pp. 5–27.

low cost and that creditors receive adequate legal protection for funds they have released or credit they have made available.

In addition to the traditional intergovernmental lawmaking organizations which have an appropriate mandate (and 'legitimacy') to draft laws or rules of law and make them available for adoption by States, international financial institutions (IFI) have started formulating rules of law, standards or guidelines for adoption or implementation by States. All of these efforts are made under the guise of harmonization and for the objective of law reform. Moreover, IFIs often have availability of ways of persuading States to adopt the rules of law or standards they have promulgated, while such ways may not be available to traditional intergovernmental lawmaking organizations. To the extent that coordination amongst formulating agencies, to put it mildly, is haphazard or erratic, this results in promulgation of not necessarily conflicting, but often incompatible systems or rules. This is also a process that is both frustrating and uneconomical, let alone confusing and counter-productive. We have before us a real issue and some coordinated action is required to achieve better (compatible and efficient) uniform rule and/or standards capable of international convergence or even harmonization. This does not necessarily imply that IFIs will slow down or reduce their *quasi*-lawmaking activity: mutual and beneficial coexistence is the result of exchange of information and coordination.

Bazinas in Chapter 5 above discusses examples of overlap and suggests that in order to avoid conflicts and confusion there must be coordination and compatibility with international commercial law standards promulgated by intergovernmental lawmaking organizations with appropriate mandates. The burden of compliance lies with IFIs, which must ensure that their own standard-setting or rule-making is consistent with the work of 'legitimate' international lawmaking bodies. At the same time, it is also essential that there is 'internal' coordination amongst the 'legitimate' international lawmaking agencies, not only because they have to lead by example, but also because they have to use their resources effectively.

It is important to reiterate the point that 'the legitimacy of an international legislative body such as UNCITRAL emanates from decisions made by each sovereign State'.[2] In this respect it is important also to point out that this confirmation or approval of legitimacy is at least double

[2] Bazinas, Chapter 5 above, at p. 92.

and also two-dimensional. It is two-dimensional because States give their approval both to the creation and mandate of the international legislative organization (before it starts operating). It is double because the States enable the authorization of each legislative drafting project and confirm the outcome of legislative outcome by consensus or majority, signature (and ratification) as necessary.

There is no doubt that in the last ten to twelve years there has been more coordination than in the past and international lawmaking organizations invite IFIs to their meetings and vice versa, and that the legislative agenda. This is the result of a more structured, though still largely voluntary and informal, but also intensified coordination which seems to have started around 2000.[3] This appears to be a major improvement to the situation in the 1990s, where one could observe a regulatory competition manifested by a law reform race conducted by national or regional technical assistance projects and IFIs and attempts to export legal transplants.[4] Therefore, the current situation gives cause for optimism, as coordination and concordance appear to be prevailing on the agenda of both IFIs and the main formulating agencies.

In addition, as part of lawmaking there is a genuine debate about a cost–benefit analysis: formulating agencies need to 'get it right', but projects which are long in gestation suffer from protracted negotiation and occasionally unpalatable compromises which often have the consequence of harmonizing too little too late and killing the project on the way. Having said that, it is important to know (and reassuring to read in Bazinas) that organizations like UNCITRAL are prepared to err in favour of quality in order to enhance acceptability and wider approval of texts. This process also ensures the longevity of instruments produced and their enduring value.

3 *See* the conference and its published proceedings in book format, Part One: 'The Future of Harmonisation and the Formulating Agencies', in I. Fletcher, L. Mistelis, and M. Cremona (eds.) *Foundations and Perspectives of International Trade Law* (London: Sweet and Maxwell, 2001). The conference brought together experts and/or representatives from UNCITRAL (Herrmann, pp. 28–36), Unidroit (Kronke, pp. 59–66), the ICC (Livanos Cattaui, pp. 37–42), the European Community (Weatherill, pp. 43–58) and the Hague Conference (van Loon, pp. 67–72), while other agencies (e.g. WTO, IMF and WIPO) attended as well. The general theme is also addressed by other contributors, including Bonell, Garro and Kessedjian.

4 *See* L. Mistelis, 'Regulatory Aspects: Globalization, Harmonization, Legal Transplants and Law Reform – Some Fundamental Observations', 34(3) *The International Lawyer* 1055–69 (2000).

It is also important to appreciate that IFIs have for some time embarked on drafting projects, either the promulgation of model laws[5] or the creation and setting of standards.[6] What IFIs may lack in legitimacy they certainly make up for in terms of efficiency and ability to implement, partly through a technical assistance or law reform project. IFIs in their drafting projects do not have to involve all their Member States; they often delegate the drafting to a smaller and more efficient group of experts which is typically more capable of reaching consensus and also agreeing on the major issues and solutions.

One could engage with the question as to why IFIs draft legislative or *quasi*-legislative (standard setting) texts. In my view, this question is rather obsolete. They do engage in this process and to a large extent they have good reasons to do so. Even if one would deny them the legitimacy formally to engage with formal lawmaking, there is certainly scope for them to 'translate' law and widely accepted standards into guidelines, principles and/or standards which can form the basis of domestic legislation. In this way they can provide useful technical assistance and contribute to law reform. Ideally, in this process they can 'popularize' or simplify the work of international legislative agencies and assist with capacity and institution building.[7] Increasingly, instruments of the World Bank are fully compatible with instruments promulgated by UNCITRAL: one such example of such compatibility and consistency, as Bazinas[8] clearly points out, can be found in the World Bank Toolkit on Secured Transactions Systems and Collateral Registries[9] and the UNCITRAL *Legislative Guide on Insolvency Law*[10] and its *Legislative Guide on Secured Transactions.*[11]

[5] *See*, for example, the EBRD Model Law on Secured Transactions published originally in 1994, www.ebrd.com/pubs/legal/secured.htm (last accessed 10 January 2013) and the Core Principles for a secured transactions law, www.ebrd.com/country/sector/law/st/core/model/core.htm (last accessed 10 January 2013).

[6] *See*, for example, the World Bank Principles and Guidelines for Effective Insolvency and Creditor Rights Systems, http://siteresources.worldbank.org/GILD/Resources/FINAL-ICRPrinciples-March2009.pdf (last accessed 10 January 2013) and the Toolkit on Secured Transactions Systems and Collateral Registries, https://wbinvestmentclimate.org/uploads/SecuredTransactionsSystems.pdf (last accessed 10 January 2013).

[7] *See* Bazinas, Chapter 5 above.

[8] Ibid.

[9] www.wbginvestmentclimate.org/uploads/SecuredTransactionsSystems.pdf (last accessed 10 January 2013). This is an impressive piece of work, bringing together the expertise of many eminent lawyers.

[10] *See* www.uncitral.org/pdf/english/texts/insolven/05–80722_Ebook.pdf (for parts one and two) and www.uncitral.org/pdf/english/texts/insolven/Leg-Guide-Insol-Part3-ebook-E.pdf (for part three) (last accessed 10 January 2013).

[11] *See* www.uncitral.org/pdf/english/texts/security-lg/e/09-82670_Ebook-Guide_09–04–10English.pdf (last accessed 10 January 2013).

On other occasions, the international intergovernmental lawmaking agency (in this case, UNCITRAL) followed, or at least took into account, the work of an IFI (in this case, the European Bank for Reconstruction and Development (EBRD)'s Model Law on Secured Transactions[12] and the Asian Development Bank (ADB)'s Guide to Movables Registries[13]) when working on a similar document (UNCITRAL *Secured Transactions Guide*).[14] Accordingly, the lack of 'legitimacy' of IFIs to legislate or to set standards is offset by the cooperation and cross-fertilization with international legislative bodies.

The EBRD provides an excellent example of an IFI which assumed a role in setting standards for secured transactions and movables registration with a view to supporting private sector development and enhancement of a free market in the countries of Central and Eastern Europe and the former Soviet Union. As of 2011, it also expanded its activities in the South-Eastern Mediterranean region, supporting private sector investment. It was because of necessity that in the countries of its operation[15] an appropriate legal regime existed or was being created that would facilitate movement of credit and security provided for it.

The momentum it has been creating with the reform *élan* in this particular area of law has had a significant impact. Not only did countries that appeared to be needy of it reform their law (such as the countries in Central and Eastern Europe and the former Soviet Union, Mexico and Ghana) but also, countries with established legal systems identified their weakness and undertook successful law reform projects. In the latter group one would include Australia (2009), France (2006) and New Zealand (1999). The UK did not follow the proposals of the Law Commission for extensive reform[16] and implemented only part of its suggestions.

Dahan in Chapter 6 above discusses the role and contribution the EBRD has made in the area of secured transactions and aptly identifies the two pillars on which the EBRD work was based: (a) secured transactions law is merely facilitative (or, the other way it could be put is: enabling) and has to be transposed into a law which is efficient; and (b) secured transactions law

[12] *See* www.ebrd.com/pages/research/publications/guides/model.shtml (last accessed 10 January 2013). *See also*, L. Mistelis, 'The EBRD Model Law on Secured Transactions and its impact on collateral law reform in Central and Eastern Europe and the former Soviet Union' 5(4) *Parker School Journal of East European Law* 455–86 (1998).

[13] *See* www2.adb.org/documents/reports/movables_registries/default.asp (last accessed 10 January 2013).

[14] *Supra* n. 11.

[15] www.ebrd.org (last accessed 10 January 2013).

[16] *See* http://lawcommission.justice.gov.uk/areas/company-security-interests.htm (last accessed 10 January 2013) with links to all relevant proposals.

is versatile and adaptable.[17] In this respect, Dahan presents the Ten Core Principles of secured transactions law which were broadly formulated in 1994[18] and also presents more contemporary criteria for legal efficiency of secured transactions law, in particular, functionality and maximization of economic benefit through simplicity, speed, cost efficiency, certainty and adaptability ('fit-to-context').[19] She particularly makes the point that the reason for the success of the EBRD project can be found in the fact that it recognized the need for secured transactions versatility and putting at the centre the concept and power of collateral in different transactions, from residential and commercial mortgage to financial collateral. Dahan's chapter is insightful, doctrinal and informative and presents the range and depth of the work the EBRD has done in this area.

Halliday in Chapter 4 above, sets as his starting point the two massive financial crises and one geo-political crisis which also mandated the increase of lawmaking activity by IFIs. He points out that the real consequence of these crises is the increased role of international organizations 'as architects of transnational legal orders'.[20]

This is a rather controversial statement, given that international lawyers are regularly expressing concerns about fragmentation and lack of multilateralism. Most certainly many efforts are happening within regional contexts. In Europe, for example, we have the work of the EBRD (with an Eastern European and Eurasian focus), Draft Common Framework of Reference and efforts within the EU, as well as work of multilateral (global) agencies such as Unidroit. In Asia we have the work of the ADB, as well as technical assistance provided by the World Bank and the International Monetary Fund (IMF). In Latin America we have major activity by the World Bank and other organizations.

Most importantly, Halliday discusses four different theories (idealist, realist, professional and ecological) which may explain the reasons why international organizations are involved in lawmaking and standard-setting.[21] In his discussion he does not distinguish between international legislative agencies, such as UNCITRAL or Unidroit, and IFIs, such as the World Bank, EBRD etc. This distinction is only occasionally made in the second part of the chapter. He also makes the point that increased legislative and *quasi*-legislative activity will bring about a convergence

17 Dahan, Chapter 6 above.

18 *See* www.ebrd.com/pages/sector/legal/secured/core/coreprinciples.shtml (last accessed 10 January 2013) and ibid.

19 Ibid. 20 Halliday, Chapter 4 above. 21 Ibid.

of the rules of law and acceptable international standards on secured transactions.[22] He presents seven shifts in orientation and practices of international organizations and in this respect specific attention is paid to IFIs; IFIs are now involved in formal (visible) lawmaking and he also notes that development is now contingent. Actually the most convincing shift is the last one: from globalized localisms to normative options; it reflects on the interaction of UNCITRAL with IFIs and creation of global norms emerging from locally harmonized principles.

It is undisputed that IFIs will continue to play an important role in lawmaking and standard-setting in the area of secured transactions. This is because it is necessary for their interaction with States and private parties and because appropriate standards of secured transactions will activate the release of higher amounts of credit. IFIs often have the capacity for effective lawmaking, are not always confined by intergovernmental negotiations and inevitable compromises, and may draw upon the expertise of international and domestic experts as well as the experience of international legislative agencies. It goes without saying that any legislative or quasi-legislative amendment (i.e. standards, principles, guidelines or toolkits) will have to be reality tested and checked against empirical evidence.

Increased cooperation and concordance between IFIs and intergovernmental legislative agencies will most likely produce better results and will be vested with authority and legitimacy, all of which are necessary for any normative product to be met with approval.

[22] Ibid.

PART III

The availability of credit and the utility and efficacy of UNCITRAL's legislative efforts

8

The utility and efficacy of the *UNCITRAL Legislative Guide on Secured Transactions*

SPYRIDON V. BAZINAS*

I. Introduction

At its fortieth session, in December 2007, the United Nations Commission on International Trade Law (UNCITRAL)[1] finalized and adopted the UNCITRAL *Legislative Guide on Secured Transactions* ('Guide')[2]. The Guide deals with the full range of issues that need to be addressed in legislation on proprietary security rights in movable property.

* The views expressed in this chapter are the personal views of the author and do not necessarily reflect the views of the United Nations or UNCITRAL. The chapter is based on a presentation made at the World Bank and the Modern Law Review Conference on 'International Legal Standards on Secured Transactions, Facilitation of Credit and Financial Crisis', which was held on Friday, 14 May 2010, at the University of Newcastle. The author wishes to thank (in alphabetical order) Prof. Michael Bridge, London School of Economics, Department of Law, Prof. Dr. Ulrich Drobnig, Professor Emeritus, Max Planck Institute for Foreign and Private International Law, Hamburg, Prof. Sir Roy Goode, Professor Emeritus, University of Oxford and Prof. Catherine Walsh, McGill University, Faculty of Law, for their comments. Responsibility for any remaining errors or omissions is the author's alone.

1 For a brief description of UNCITRAL and its work, *see* www.uncitral.org/en-index.htm. Professionals both in the private and the public sector who are not familiar with UNCITRAL and its work often find it strange that a UN body, a subsidiary of the UN General Assembly, is involved in the unification and harmonization of the law of international trade. The explanation is simple. Economic development is the other side of peace and stability (presumably, the main mission of the UN), and unification, harmonization or modernization of the law of international trade is a cornerstone (a necessary, but not sufficient condition) of economic development. One should also keep in mind that the law of international trade is broadly understood to include national and international law, civil and commercial law, both substantive and private international law and even public law to the extent that it covers arbitration (which is part of civil procedure law) and public procurement of goods and services. With this mandate, UNCITRAL plays a key role in the efforts of the UN to promote the rule of law (see G.A. Resolution 62/70 of 6 December 2007 on the rule of law at the national and international levels).

2 www.uncitral.org/uncitral/en/uncitral_texts/payments/Guide_securedtrans.html (last accessed 10 January 2013).

The overall objective of the Guide is to promote low-cost credit by enhancing the availability of secured credit.[3] The Guide starts from the premise that trade is an important part of economic development and that trade needs credit to grow, in particular secured credit.[4] To achieve this objective, the Guide includes commentary and legislative recommendations on security rights in tangible and intangible movable assets, including receivables, bank accounts, letters of credit and intellectual property. The recommendations provide the certainty needed for a law on secured transactions. The commentary provides the analysis and flexibility that is inherent in a guide as compared to a model law or a convention.

The purpose of this chapter is to discuss the utility and efficacy of the general (not the asset-specific) commentary and recommendations of the Guide (with the exception of security rights in intellectual property that are discussed briefly in section 10). Section 2 clarifies the concept of a guide as a soft law approach. Section 3 discusses a key policy approach of the Guide, the functional approach. Section 4 deals with the creation of a security right, section 5 with its third-party effectiveness and registration, and section 6 with its priority and enforcement. Section 7 discusses security rights created to secure the purchase price of an asset (acquisition financing). Section 8 deals with the law applicable to the creation, third-party effectiveness, priority and enforcement of a security right. Section 9 discusses the enforcement of a security right in the case of the grantor's insolvency.[5] Section 10 deals with the Supplement on Security rights in Intellectual Property (the 'Supplement'). Section 11 responds to criticism against the Guide and section 12 sets out some conclusions about the utility and efficacy of the Guide.

II. Flexibility and certainty combined: the concept of the Guide

At its thirty-fourth session, in 2001, in view of '*the beneficial economic impact of secured credit law*', UNCITRAL decided to establish a working

[3] Recommendation 1, subpara. (a). For an analysis of the economic impact of secured financing law, *see* Chapter 9 below by Orkun Akseli.

[4] For a discussion of the key objectives and fundamental policies of the Guide, *see* S.V. Bazinas, 'The UNCITRAL Legislative Guide on Secured Transactions – Key Objectives and Fundamental Policies', in *The Reform of UK Property Law, Comparative Perspectives*, J. De Lacy (ed.) (London, New York: Routledge-Cavendish, 2010), p. 456 (hereinafter referred to as 'Bazinas, Key Objectives').

[5] The term 'grantor' means the person granting a security right. The grantor may be the debtor owing payment of the secured obligation or a third party who has a relationship with the debtor (see Introduction to the Guide, B. Terminology and Interpretation).

group with the mandate to develop an efficient legal regime for security rights in goods involved in commercial activity and requested that an international colloquium be held with a view to obtaining the views of experts.[6] At the colloquium, the prevailing view was that a flexible work product would be preferable. The main reason for this approach is that there is no one-size-fits-all law on secured transactions, in particular if all types of asset are to be covered. Property law goes to the foundation of a legal system and at least some aspects of it may not lend themselves to unification.[7] Consistent with these considerations, at its thirty-fifth session in 2002, the Commission 'noted the suggestions made for a set of principles with a legislative guide'.[8] Accordingly, at that session the Commission confirmed 'the mandate given to the Working Group' and that 'the mandate should be interpreted widely to ensure an appropriately flexible work product, which should take the form of a legislative guide'.[9] Thus, the Guide is addressed to the legislator and sets out all the policy issues that need to be addressed in a modern secured transactions law and the possible workable approaches to those issues, with a discussion of their comparative advantages and disadvantages, and a final recommendation to the legislator on each policy issue.[10]

As a result, the Guide combines the flexibility of the commentary with the certainty of legislative recommendations. For example, the Guide draws a distinction between the effectiveness[11] of a security right as

[6] *See* Official Records of the General Assembly, Fifty-Sixth Session, Supplement No. 17 (A/56/17), paras. 351, 358 and 359 (www.uncitral.org/uncitral/en/commission/sessions/34th.html) (last accessed 10 January 2013).

[7] R.A. Macdonald, 'A Model Law on Secured Transactions' 15 *Uniform Law Review* 419 (2010). In the same journal (at 325), Neil B. Cohen, discusses the arguments in favour of and against a model law and concludes that the arguments against a model law are somewhat stronger, but accepts that the matter should be reconsidered in due course. Also in the same journal (at 507), J.H. Röver compares the EBRD Model Law on Secured Transactions and concludes that a model law would be both desirable and feasible.

[8] Official Records of the General Assembly, Fifty-Seventh Session, Supplement No. 17 (A/56/17), para. 200.

[9] Ibid., para. 204.

[10] For a discussion of the methods of international harmonization of secured transactions law, *see* N.O. Akseli, 'On the Methods of Harmonisation of Secured Transactions Law' in C.B. Andersen & U.G. Schroeter (eds.), *Sharing International Commercial Law across National Boundaries: Festschrift for Albert H. Kritzer* (London: Wildy, Simmonds & Hill Publishing, 2008), p. 1.

[11] Reference is made to effectiveness to denote that reference is made to property effects rather than to contractual effects for which reference should be made to '*the validity of a security right*'.

between the person granting the security right and its effectiveness as against third parties.[12] It follows this approach so as to implement two key objectives of any efficient and effective secured transactions law, that is: (a) to allow parties to create a security right in a simple and efficient manner, avoiding unnecessary formalities; and (b) to enhance certainty and transparency of security rights by providing for notice registration as the main method of establishing third-party effectiveness and determining priority among competing claimants.[13]

If the creation of a security right was not distinguished from its third-party effectiveness and the two legal consequences required the same acts (that is, agreement between the parties and registration of a notice), it would not be possible for the law to have a broad scope and apply to retention-of-title sales and financial leases (transactions that typically are form-free or, in any case, are not subject to registration, at least, for creation purposes). As a result, the recommendations of the Guide would not be efficient in addressing one of the main problems of current secured transactions law in many countries (developed and developing, of the common law or the civil law tradition),[14] namely, the fragmentation of secured transactions law that creates gaps and inconsistencies that in turn undermine the certainty, predictability and efficiency of the law in producing (together with other factors, such as an efficient insolvency law, efficient court infrastructure, workable market conditions, etc.) the positive economic results of a secured transactions law.[15] Such beneficial results of an effective and efficient secured transactions law may include

[12] In substance, the same basic distinction is to be found in Book IX of the Principles, Definitions and Model Rules of European Private Law, Draft Common Frame of Reference, which also distinguishes between 'creation' of a security right as between the parties (ch. 2) and effectiveness as against third parties (ch. 3).

[13] Recommendation 1, subparas. (c) and (f). *See also* O. Akseli, *International Secured Transactions Law* (London, New York: Routledge, 2011), pp. 128–32 and 168–72 (hereinafter referred to as 'Akseli International ST Law'). The term 'competing claimant' includes another secured creditor, a buyer of the encumbered asset, a judgment creditor and the mass of creditors or the administrator in the grantor's insolvency (see Introduction to the Guide, B. Terminology and Interpretation).

[14] For an analysis of secured transactions laws of several jurisdictions, *see* H.C. Sigman and E.-M. Kieninger (eds.), *Cross-Border Security over Tangibles* (Munich: Sellier, 2007).

[15] For a full discussion of English secured transactions law, *see* R. Goode, *Commercial Law*, E. McKendrick (ed.) (Oxford University Press, 4th edn., 2010), pp. 619–737. *See also Goode on Legal Problems of Credit and Security*, L. Gullifer (ed.) (London: Sweet & Maxwell, 4th edn., 2008) and H. Beale, M. Bridge, L. Gullifer and E. Lomnicka, *The Law of Security and Title-Based Finance* (Oxford University Press, 2nd edn., 2012).

higher amounts of credit extended at better credit terms, such as lower interest rates and longer repayment periods.

However, to accommodate legal systems in which the relative effectiveness of a security right as between the parties to the relevant security agreement is not incorporated (as a security right, like any other property interest, has by definition, effects against all – *erga omnes*), the commentary of the Guide discusses a different approach. According to this approach, a State may implement the Guide, providing that a security right created by agreement may only be effective upon its creation as against all parties except other secured creditors (as a result, priority among secured creditors has to be determined mainly on the basis of the order of registration or other method of third-party effectiveness).[16] Again, without such an approach, and in particular if registration were made a condition of the effectiveness of a security right against all, the key objective of any effective and efficient secured transactions law of permitting the creation of a security right in a simple and efficient manner could not be achieved; and the law could not be comprehensive in scope, a result that would undermine its efficiency and reproduce the gaps and inconsistencies existing in many currently existing secured transactions laws around the world.

Another example of the fact that flexibility and certainty are combined in the Guide in a harmonious way is that the Guide, commentary and recommendations, is divided into a general part that applies to all types of encumbered asset and an asset-specific part that modifies the general part with respect to certain types of asset, such as bank accounts, letters of credit, negotiable instruments, negotiable documents and intellectual property. Again, there are two levels of flexibility allowed in the Guide in this regard. First, some States may implement the Guide as a whole, while others may implement those parts of the Guide that they may need; and second, with respect to certain types of asset, such as high-value mobile equipment (e.g. ships and aircraft) and intellectual property, the Guide defers to the relevant asset-specific law.[17]

[16] Guide, chapter II, para. 4 and chapter III, para. 8.

[17] Recommendation 2, subparas. (a) and (b). The Guide excludes altogether securities and financial contracts (see recommendation 4, subparas. (c)–(e)). The main reasons for this approach are that securities raise a set of different issues and that they were the subject of work by Unidroit and the Hague Conference. However, the Geneva Securities Convention and the Hague Securities Convention finally dealt only with intermediated securities. As a result, at its 43rd session in 2010, the Commission decided to place the issue of security

Yet another example is the fact that the Guide, following the approach of the United Nations Convention on the Assignment of Receivables in International Trade (the Receivables Convention),[18] neither fully upholds[19] nor fully invalidates[20] anti-assignment clauses. The Guide instead upholds an anti-assignment clause without, however, interfering with other law, under which an assignee may be liable for breach of contract.[21] Further examples of this balanced combination of certainty and flexibility in the Guide are set out below, in particular in the sections on acquisition financing, insolvency and conflict of laws.

In view of the above, the Guide has already become the main reference tool for the modernization and harmonization of secured transactions legislation around the world. First, Book IX on proprietary security in movable assets of the *Principles, Definitions and Model Rules of European Private Law, Draft Common Frame of Reference*, vol. 6 (DCFR), draws heavily on the Guide.[22] Second, the Secured Transactions Systems Collateral Registries publication of the Investment Climate Advisory Services of the World Bank Group is fully consistent with the Guide.[23] This publication is used as a toolkit for World Bank staff involved in secured transactions law reform all over the world. Third, the World Bank is preparing with the UNCITRAL secretariat a set of principles on secured transactions that will incorporate the Guide in the same way that the World Bank *Principles*

rights in non-intermediated securities on its future work agenda (see A/65/17, paras. 264 and 267–8).

18 Article 9. For an analysis of the key features of the Convention, *see* S.V. Bazinas, R.M. Kohn and L.F. del Duca, 'Facilitating a Cost-Free Path to Economic Recovery-Implementing a Global Uniform International Receivables Financing Law' 44(3) *UCC Law Journal* 277 (July 2012).

19 For a comparative law discussion of anti-assignment clauses, *see* C. Rudolph, *Einheitsrecht für internationale Forderungsabtretungen* (Tübingen: Mohr Siebeck, 2005), p. 263.

20 UCC § 9–406.

21 However, in the interest of the economy as a whole, the debtor may not avoid the contract on the sole ground of the assignment, and the assignee is not liable to the debtor on the sole ground that it had knowledge of the anti-assignment clause. Consumer and sovereign debtors may be excluded from this rule. See recommendation 24 and chapter II, paras. 106–10, of the Guide. As to the application of this rule to licence royalties, see Supplement, paras. 102–5.

22 Prepared by the Study Group on a European Civil Code and the Research Group on EC Private Law (Acquis Group), C. von Bar and E. Clive (eds.) (Munich: Sellier, 2009) (http://ec.europa.eu/justice/contract/files/european-private-law_en.pdf) (last accessed 10 January 2013).

23 For the 2010 IFC toolkit, which is being implemented in countries from China to Ghana, *see* www.ifc.org/ifcext/globalfm.nsf/Content/Secured±Transactions±Systems±&±Collateral±Registries±Toolkit (last accessed 10 January 2013).

and Guidelines for Effective Insolvency and Creditor Rights Systems incorporate the UNCITRAL *Legislative Guide on Insolvency Law* (UNCITRAL Insolvency Guide).[24] Fourth, the new Personal Property Security Act of Australia draws heavily on the Personal Property Security Act (PPSA) of New Zealand and the Guide[25] so do laws of several countries implementing the OAS Model Law on Secured Transactions and the OAS Registry Regulations.[26]

It is worth noting in this regard that the Guide is also generally consistent and coordinated with security interests texts prepared by The Hague Conference of Private International Law (the Hague Conference) and the International Institute for the Unification of Private Law (Unidroit). The coordination of the work of the three organizations in the area of secured transactions over the last fifteen years is a testament to their excellent work and shows the path forward.[27]

III. Modernization and harmonization: the functional approach

The Guide follows a modern approach to secured transactions that can be described as an integrated and functional approach, relying on a notice-based public registry for third-party and priority effects, and is reflected in several national and international texts on security rights in movable property.[28] In line with this approach, the Guide uses a unitary and functional notion of 'security right' that encompasses all types of right

[24] Official Records of the General Assembly, Sixty-sixth session, Supplement No. 17 (A/66/17), para. 228.

[25] S. Fischer, 'Personal Property Security Law Reform in Australia', in *The Reform of UK Property Law, Comparative Perspectives*, J. De Lacy (ed.), (London, New York: Routledge-Cavendish, 2010), p. 366. The main draftsman of the Australian PPSA was a delegate to UNCITRAL at the time it was preparing the Guide. For the Australian PPSA, *see* www.ag.gov.au/pps/Pages/default.aspx (last accessed 10 January 2013). For a discussion of the new PPSA of Australia and the UNCITRAL influence, *see* R. Patch, 'Personal Property Securities Reform in Australia' 15 *Uniform Law Review* 459 (2010).

[26] For an analysis of the relationship between the OAS texts and the Guide, *see* M. Dubovec, 'A Guide to a Successful Adoption and Implementation of the OAS Model Law on Secured Transactions and Registry Regulations in Honduras – The National Law Centre Experience' 43 *UCC Law Journal* 825 (October 2011).

[27] UNCITRAL, Hague Conference and Unidroit, *Texts on Security Interests: Comparison and analysis of major features of international instruments relating to secured transactions* (United Nations, Hague Conference and Unidroit, 2011). Happily enough, there is a substantial degree of coordination between these texts and the DCFR, Book IX.

[28] Such texts include UCC Article 9, the Canadian Personal Property Security Acts (PPSA), New Zealand's PPSA www.med.govt.nz/templates/StandardSummary_15299.aspx (last accessed 10 January 2013), the UNIDROIT Convention on International Factoring

in movable property created by agreement to secure payment or other performance of an obligation, regardless of the form of the transaction or the terminology used by the parties, and thus includes transfers of title in goods for security purposes, assignments of receivables for security purposes, retention-of-title rights and financial lease rights. Under the regime recommended in the Guide, security rights may secure all types of obligation, present or future, determined or determinable, including fluctuating obligations and obligations described in a generic way. They may encumber specific assets or all of the assets of a grantor, present and future, including a changing pool of assets. Security rights may be created or acquired by any legal or natural person, including a consumer. However, rights of consumers under consumer protection law cannot be affected.[29]

Thus, the Guide deals in a comprehensive and coordinated way with all devices serving security purposes (including retention-of-title sales and financial leases), and addresses applicable law issues, as well as the

www.unidroit.org/english/conventions/1988factoring/main.htm (last accessed 10 January 2013), the United Nations Convention on the Assignment of Receivables in International Trade www.uncitral.org/uncitral/en/uncitral_texts/payments/2001Convention_receivables.html (last accessed 10 January 2013), the Cape Town Convention on International Interests in Mobile Equipment and the relevant Protocols, www.unidroit.org/english/conventions/mobile-equipment/main.htm (last accessed 10 January 2013), the Hague Convention on the Law Applicable to Certain Rights in Respect of Securities held with an Intermediary, http://hcch.e-vision.nl/index_en.php?act=conventions.text&cid=72 (last accessed 10 January 2013), UNIDROIT Convention on Substantive Rules for Intermediated Securities www.unidroit.org/english/conventions/2009intermediatedsecurities/main.htm (last accessed 10 January 2013), the EBRD Model Law on Secured Transactions, www.ebrd.com/pubs/legal/secured.htm (last accessed 10 January 2013), the Model Inter-American Law on Secured Transactions, www.oas.org/DIL/CIDIP-VI-securedtransactions_Eng.htm (last accessed 10 January 2013), the ADB Guide on Movables Registries, www2.adb.org/documents/reports/movables_registries/default.asp, the *UNCITRAL Legislative Guide on Insolvency Law*, www.uncitral.org/uncitral/en/uncitral_texts/insolvency/2004Guide.html (last accessed 10 January 2013), and the report of the English Law Reform Commission on Company Security Interests, http://lawcommission.justice.gov.uk/areas/company-security-interests.htm (last accessed 10 January 2013); *see also* Bazinas, Key Objectives, 128 and 129.

[29] Recommendation 2. It is true that the application of this rule may create an unequal situation, depending on the particular provisions of consumer protection law in each jurisdiction. The commentary of the Guide draws this matter to the attention of the national legislator and suggests that a State might take a different approach (see Guide, chapter I, para. 11). Compare the approach in the DCFR, Book IX, which excludes from its scope security rights for micro-credits (1:105 (1)) and provides special protection to other consumers (2:107).

treatment of security rights in the case of insolvency consistent with the UNCITRAL Insolvency Guide.[30] Following the approach of the Receivables Convention,[31] to ensure comprehensive and consistent coverage of all possible priority conflicts, the Guide to some extent even addresses issues relating to outright transfers of receivables, without, however, re-characterizing them as secured transactions, as re-characterization would harm transactions that are based on the notion of an outright transfer, such as factoring or securitization of receivables.[32]

This approach is not dictated by ideological considerations or preferences for one or the other national legal system. It is a practical response to the main problem of secured transactions laws around the world, that is, the fragmentation of secured transactions law into multiple laws dealing differently with the transactions that fulfil the same security functions. The result of this fragmentation is the creation of gaps and inconsistencies. For example, in many States, non-possessory security rights are introduced by special laws that apply only to specific types of asset; in other States, the main device that performs the function of a non-possessory security right is . . . the retention of title sale! In many of those States, such non-possessory security rights in the form of retention of title sales are hidden from potential third-party financiers in the sense that they are not subject to any form of publicity.[33]

Markets deal with these problems, but they do so at a cost, which is typically borne by the weaker party in a secured transaction, that is, the debtor (the grantor of the security right may be the debtor or a third party that has a relationship with the debtor). For example, to cover themselves from the risk that there may be a supplier of goods on credit

[30] www.uncitral.org/uncitral/en/uncitral_texts/insolvency/2004Guide.html (last accessed 10 January 2013).

[31] The treatment of receivables in the Guide is consistent with the United Nations Convention on the Assignment of Receivables in International Trade (New York, 2001). For a discussion of the Convention, *see* S.V. Bazinas, 'International Receivables', in *Secured Finance Transactions: Key Assets and Emerging Markets*, P. U. Ali (consulting ed.) (London: Globe Business Publishing Ltd., 2007), p. 83. For a comparison of the Convention, the Unidroit Convention on International Factoring (Ottawa, 1988), the Principles of European Contract Law and the Unidroit Principles of International Commercial Contracts, *see* Rudolph, *Einheitsrecht*. For a comparative law discussion of the issue of the third-party effectiveness of an assignment of receivables, *see* S. Bode, *Die Wirksamkeit einer Forderungsübertragung gegenüber Dritten* (Frankfurt am Main: Peter Lang, 2007).

[32] Recommendation 4 and Guide, chapter I, paras. 25–31.

[33] J. Rakob, in Sigman and Kieninger (eds), *Cross-border Security over Tangibles* at 68–9.

that may have priority, secured lenders increase the interest rate, reduce the repayment period or decrease the amount of credit, whether there is a retention of title in a particular case or not. This cost is unnecessary. A State may deal with various types of secured transactions in one and the same law by way of priority rules, even if some types of security right are given super-priority, that is, priority based on the type of the security right rather than the time of registration. For example, under the Guide, a retention-of-title right is given priority even over an earlier registered security right, as long as a notice is registered in the general security right registry within a short period of time after delivery of the goods.[34]

The functional approach is the approach typically followed in modern secured transactions legislation.[35] It makes possible the comprehensive coverage of all devices that perform security functions, including retention-of-title sales and financial leases. It is also the approach that facilitates harmonization of the laws of various States, as it deals in a comprehensive and similar way with all types of security right.

The functional approach does not mean that devices such as retention-of-title sales and financial leases need to be re-characterized as secured transactions for all purposes. It is sufficient to subject them to secured transactions law for its limited purposes. In particular, with respect to those devices, as already mentioned, the Guide provides that the functional approach may be implemented in a unitary or a non-unitary way (depending on the terminology used), and offers to the national legislator a multiplicity of options.[36]

IV. Simplicity and efficiency: the creation of a security right

One of the key objectives of an effective secured transactions law is 'to enable parties to obtain security rights in a simple and efficient manner'.[37] So the Guide recommends that a security agreement be sufficient for the creation of a security right, although in the case of assets in which the grantor acquires rights or the power to encumber after the time of the conclusion of the security agreement ('future assets'), the security right may be created at that later time.[38] The Guide also recommends that the security agreement must indicate the intent of the parties,

[34] Recommendation 192, alternative B. [35] *Supra* n. 28.

[36] Recommendation 9 and section 7 below. [37] Recommendation 1, subpara. (c).

[38] Recommendation 13. *See also* Akseli, International ST Law, at pp. 132–9.

identify them, and describe the secured obligation and the encumbered assets.[39]

Most importantly, the recommendation of the Guide as to what is a sufficient description of the encumbered assets is a very flexible one. The assets must be described 'in a manner that reasonably allows their identification'.[40] What is a reasonable identification of the assets may differ according to the circumstances and the type of asset involved. For example, in the case of inventory, a generic description, such as 'all my inventory' or 'all my inventory of pcs' or 'all my inventory of pcs in warehouse X', may be enough. However, in the case of intellectual property, a specific description, such as 'my patent X', may be necessary (the same rule applies to the description of the encumbered assets in the notice to be registered).[41]

Similarly flexible is the recommendation of the Guide with respect to the form of a security agreement. A security agreement need be in writing only if it is not accompanied by delivery of the encumbered assets to the secured creditor.[42] This approach combines flexibility (no need for written agreement) with the protection of the legitimate interests of the secured creditor (written agreement only if the secured creditor is not in possession of the assets). The flexibility goes even further.[43] First, it is enough if the agreement is concluded or, at least, evidenced in writing. Second, the writing need only indicate the grantor's intent to create a security right, that is, the secured creditor's signature is not required. Third, the writing may lead to that result by itself or in conjunction with the course of conduct of the parties, that is, an order, shipment, delivery and acceptance of the goods may be enough. And fourth, writing includes an electronic communication and signature includes an electronic signature.[44]

To facilitate financing practices, such as revolving credit arrangements, the Guide recommends that it should be possible for a security right to secure any type of obligation, including future, conditional or fluctuating obligations.[45] Also, to reduce risks and ensure better credit terms for borrowers, the Guide recommends that it should be possible to create a security right in future assets, that is, assets created or acquired by the grantor after the creation of a security right, including all assets of a grantor, present and future.[46] In order to facilitate consideration of the

39 Recommendation 14. 40 Ibid., subpara. (d). 41 Recommendation 63.
42 Recommendation 15. 43 Ibid. 44 Recommendations 11 and 12.
45 Recommendation 16. 46 Recommendation 17.

matter by the national legislator, the commentary discusses the various approaches taken in different legal systems in this regard to ensure that grantors are not over-committed.[47]

In order to simplify the creation of security rights in all assets of an enterprise, the Guide recommends that all-asset security rights (floating charges or enterprise mortgages) be permitted. Characteristic elements of such transactions are two: a security right may be created in all assets of a grantor with a single agreement, and the grantor has the right to dispose of certain of its assets (e.g. inventory) in the ordinary course of its business.[48] The Guide discusses over-collateralization, suggesting ways in which it could be addressed, but makes no recommendation, as the appropriate response may vary widely from State to State.[49]

In any case, recognizing the need to protect certain parties or exclude certain types of asset from the scope of secured transactions law, the Guide defers to consumer protection legislation.[50] In addition, the Guide defers to legislation according to which certain types of asset (e.g. employment benefits or household goods) may not be transferred or encumbered.[51]

A key recommendation of the Guide is the recommendation that deals with proceeds.[52] As the Guide is intended to facilitate non-possessory security rights, to protect the secured creditor from unauthorized transfers or transfers in the ordinary course of business (or in good faith) by the grantor, it recommends that the security right extend to the proceeds from the disposition of the assets by the grantor.[53] Even in cases in which the security right follows the assets in the hands of the transferee, it makes sense for the security right to extend to the proceeds (where, for example, the proceeds may be of higher value than used assets). This approach ensures that the secured creditor is sufficiently secured and thus is more likely to offer better credit terms to the borrower. However, it does not mean that the secured creditor will ever obtain more than it is owed.[54]

47 Guide, chapter II, paras. 51–5. 48 Ibid., para. 63.

49 Ibid., para. 69. The DCFR, Book IX, intentionally does not allow enterprise charges, since experience in Scandinavian countries has shown that such charges are often used by banks to monopolize financing of an enterprise.

50 Recommendation 2, subpara. (b).

51 Recommendation 18 and Guide, chapter II, paras. 49 and 50.

52 Recommendation 19.

53 The term 'proceeds' is defined to mean '*whatever is received in respect of encumbered assets*' and includes proceeds of proceeds (*see* Introduction to the Guide, B. Terminology and Interpretation).

54 Guide, chapter II, paras. 72–89.

V. Certainty and transparency: third-party effectiveness and registration

1. *Third-party effectiveness*

As already mentioned, the Guide distinguishes between effectiveness as between the grantor and the secured creditor, on the one hand, and as against third parties (such as other secured creditors, buyers of the encumbered assets, judgment creditors and the mass of creditors or the insolvency administrator in the grantor's insolvency), on the other. In this way, the Guide avoids imposing unnecessary formalities on the creation of a security right (registration is not necessary for the creation of a security right).[55]

This approach also makes it possible to encompass all devices serving security purposes, including acquisition financing devices, such as retention-of-title sales and financial leases, and thus to deal with the uncertainty and inconsistency created by a piecemeal approach to secured transactions. This approach does not undo title devices, though, as it essentially results in submitting them to registration of a notice and to ordering them in a reasonable priority context in a way that promotes supplier financing.[56]

It is true that this approach may create some concern in legal systems in which a security right by nature has effects *erga omnes*. In view of this reality, the commentary of the Guide discusses a different approach which provides that upon its creation a security right is effective against all except other secured creditors (in other words, the priority against other secured creditors is based on the order of priority in registration or other method of third-party effectiveness).[57] This approach is based on the assumption that, once a security right is effective against the grantor, it should be effective against the grantor's creditors (unsecured creditors, buyers of the encumbered assets, judgment creditors and the mass of creditors or the administrator in the grantor's insolvency), while the registration of a notice should be the basis of the relationship of a secured creditor with a third-party creditor.

In addition, by providing that the general method for achieving the effectiveness of a security right against third parties is the registration of a notice of the security right in a publicly available registry, the Guide

55 Recommendation 34.

56 *See* below. The DCFR, Book IX follows the same general approach (3:101).

57 Guide, chapter II, para. 4 and chapter III, para. 8.

creates the basis for transparency with regard to security rights.[58] This means that a third-party financier can find enough information in the registry that suggests that a security right may exist in the assets that may be offered to it as collateral for credit. The third-party financier can then discover whether a security agreement still exists and, if so, whether there is any outstanding amount of credit, or whether there is no longer any security agreement or any outstanding balance. This approach balances the needs of third-party financiers for information with the need of the parties to the security agreement for confidentiality and for an easy, simple and inexpensive registration system. And what makes this balance possible is the type and the legal consequence of registration, that is, notice registration and third-party effectiveness. If the legal consequence was the creation of a security right, the document of the transaction would need to be registered, and the registrar would have to check the document and issue a certificate. Such a result would upset the balance between publicly available information and confidentiality of the transaction and would be the end of a simple, inexpensive, quick and easy registration.[59]

Moreover, the Guide takes a flexible approach to the extent that it does not undo effective practices in which third-party effectiveness of a security right is achieved by a way other than registration. For example, the Guide recognizes practices in which possession of the encumbered asset is transferred to the secured creditor,[60] a document or notice regarding a security right is registered in a specialized registry, such as a ship, aircraft, patent or trade mark registry,[61] third-party effectiveness is achieved automatically with respect to proceeds or attachments,[62] third-party effectiveness of a security right in a bank account or letter of credit is achieved by control,[63] and third-party effectiveness of a security right in a negotiable instrument may be achieved by transfer of possession of the instrument.[64]

2. *Registration*

With respect to registration, the Guide combines efficiency with flexibility by recommending a notice-based registration system. As the commentary to the Guide points out, 'registries based on a notice-registration concept exist in an increasing number of States and have also attracted

[58] Recommendation 33. [59] For a discussion of registration, *see* section V.2. below.
[60] Recommendation 37. [61] Recommendation 38.
[62] Recommendations 39–41. [63] Recommendation 49 and 50.
[64] Recommendations 51–3.

considerable international support'.[65] It is worth noting that notice-based registration has been so successful that it has been adopted even in the context of specialized (including asset-based) registration systems, such as the registration systems for the types of high-value mobile equipment covered by the Cape Town Convention on International Interests in Mobile Equipment and its Protocols,[66] and patent and trade mark registries.[67] For the same reason, notice-based registration is even advocated for immovable property registries.[68]

In such a notice-based registration system, quick and easy registration is ensured by requiring registration of a notice that contains a limited yet sufficient amount of data, that is, the identifier and address of the grantor and the secured creditor or its representative, a description of the encumbered assets and, if permitted by the law, a selection of the period of effectiveness of the registration and, if a State chooses the option offered, the maximum amount for which the security right may be enforced.[69] First, this information is sufficient for the searcher to determine whether some assets of the grantor may be encumbered by a security right, in the sense that it provides a warning. Second, it does more than that, and points the searcher to the source of information about the transaction to which the notice may relate, that is, the secured creditor identified in the notice.

Document registration is also discussed in the commentary, but is not recommended. The reason is that a notice-registration system is inherently more efficient. It simplifies the registration process, minimizes the administrative burden, delays and costs, reduces the risk of error and liability and is sufficient in view of the legal consequences of registration, that is, third-party effectiveness.[70] A national legislator may adopt the

65 Guide, chapter IV, para. 14.

66 These are asset-based rather than debtor-based registries. Briefly, asset-based registration has the disadvantage that it is necessary to have a unique identification and it cannot accommodate a generic description or after-acquired property, but it has the advantage that it shows all registrable interests, not merely those created by the debtor. *See* article 31 of the Convention and section 5 of the Aircraft Registry Regulations and Official Commentary (Revised Edition) by Sir Roy Goode (Rome: Unidroit, 2008), 122. The Aircraft Registry is a particularly successful example of such a registry (*see* www.internationalregistry.aero/irWeb/Controller.jpf). *See also* DCFR, Book IX, chapter 3, section 3.

67 Supplement, paras. 132–4.

68 J. Simpson and F. Dahan, *Mortgages in Transition Economies: Secured Transactions Reform and Access to Credit* (EBRD, 2008), p. 195.

69 Recommendation 57. *See also* Akseli, International ST Law, pp. 195–8.

70 Guide, chapter IV, paras. 10–14.

recommendation or a document registration approach discussed in the commentary.

With regard to the amount of information required in a notice, the Guide balances the rights and interests of searchers and secured creditors.[71] In an effort to ensure the confidentiality of the transaction and avoid use of the registry by lenders to obtain information about the clients of competitors, the Guide recommends that a search be made possible only by the identifier (e.g. name and any identification number) of the grantor, and not by the identifier of the secured creditor.[72] In a further effort to ensure confidentiality, the Guide recommends that the secured creditor may choose not to identify itself on the notice, but give the identifier and address of a representative.[73] The possibility to identify a representative also facilitates secured transactions that involve multiple lenders that appoint one of them to be their representative for the purpose of registration.

The flexible approach followed in the Guide is evident also in the requirements for the sufficient description of encumbered assets in a notice. The description may be generic or specific, depending on what is a reasonable identification in each case.[74] Whether the notice should describe the encumbered assets by stating their serial numbers, if any, is left to each practice. For example, description of the encumbered assets by serial number should be possible in the case of high-value mobile equipment, such as ships or aircraft, and intellectual property rights, such as patents or trade marks, while such description would be impractical in the case of inventory. With respect to indexing and searching, the Guide recommends that reference should be made only to the grantor identifier. The reason is that grantor indexing and searching greatly simplifies the registration process, to the extent that a single registration can cover a changing pool of assets and future assets.

[71] For a comparison of the registry systems under UCC Article 9, the Canadian PPSAs, the OAS Model Law on Secured Transactions and the OAS Registry Regulations, on the one hand, and the Guide, on the other, *see* M. Dubovec, 'UCC article 9 Registration System for Latin America' 28(1) *Arizona Journal of International & Comparative Law* 117 (2011).

[72] Recommendations 54, subpara. (h) and 58–60. The commentary explains that this approach is intended to prevent lenders from using the registry in order to identify the clients of their competitors. The commentary also explains that this approach does not prevent a State from designing a registry so as to permit search by secured creditor identifier for internal purposes of the registry, such as, for example, for making a global amendment of notices at the request of the secured creditor to whom the notices relate (*see* Guide, chapter IV, paras. 29 and 30). *See also* DCFR, Book IX (3:318).

[73] Recommendation 57, subpara. (a).

[74] Recommendation 63.

At the same time, the Guide discusses in the commentary, but does not recommend, indexing and searching by serial number.[75] Thus, a legislator may determine whether to adopt grantor indexing, asset indexing, or both. This is the flexibility that is inherent in a guide. Each recommendation is a final suggestion that follows a balanced analysis, which includes several possibilities, as long as several possibilities are workable. A State may adopt the recommendation or another approach discussed in the commentary.

Going even further in providing sufficient flexibility, the Guide leaves it to the national legislator to determine whether the amount for which the security right may be enforced should be mentioned in the notice in order to facilitate subordinate lending.[76] The commentary discusses the arguments both in support and against one or the other approach.[77]

Another example of the flexible approach of the Guide is that it recommends electronic registration 'if possible'.[78] This means that access to the registry need not be electronic, that is, paper notices may be registered. However, such an approach would require that the information in a notice be entered into the registry database by the registry staff, which would create time, cost error and liability issues (all of which can be addressed, but at some cost).

A further example of this flexibility of the Guide is that . . . it is a guide(!) and thus leaves it to each national legislator to determine whether there will be any registration and searching fees. At the same time, the Guide draws a line to avoid undermining the registry system by excessive registration fees and recommends that any fees should be set at a level no higher than necessary to recover the costs of establishing and operating the registry.[79]

Yet another example of the flexibility of the Guide is the recommendation on the impact of a transfer of the encumbered assets on the effectiveness of registration.[80] The Guide leaves the matter to the national legislator, without even making a recommendation. However, the commentary provides guidance, by discussing the advantages and disadvantages of the various approaches that range from requiring the registration of an amendment notice within a certain period of time after the transfer

[75] Guide, chapter IV, paras. 31–36. [76] Recommendation 57, subpara. (d).

[77] Guide, chapter IV, paras. 92–97.

[78] Recommendation 54, subpara. (j) and chapter IV, paras. 21–24 of the Guide.

[79] Recommendation 54, subpara. (i) and chapter IV, para. 37 of the Guide.

[80] Recommendation 62.

or only after the secured creditor learns of the transfer, to requiring no amendment at all.[81]

Following the same royal middle road, the Guide enhances certainty and efficiency by recommending that registration should be possible even before a security agreement is entered into or a security right is created.[82] At the same time, to protect grantors, the Guide recommends that no registration be effective without proper grantor authorization,[83] and that the grantor be able to seek to clean the record through an expedited judicial or administrative proceeding if authorization has not been given or does not cover the transaction as described in the notice, or the debt has been paid and no further commitment to extend credit exists.[84] The Guide discusses and leaves to other law further protection of grantors from unauthorized registrations.[85]

In this context, it is worth noting that, at its 46th session in July 2013, UNCITRAL adopted the UNCITRAL Guide on the Implementation of a Security Rights Registry (the 'Registry Guide').[86] The Registry Guide intends to deal with all the practical issues associated with the establishment and operation of a security rights registry in line with the recommendations of the Guide.[87] For example, the Registry Guide deals with duties of the registry, registration of notices (e.g., identification of grantor and secured creditor information, as well as description of encumbered assets, in a registered notice), and registry searches.

VI. Certainty and predictability combined: priority and enforcement

1. Priority

An area in which most traditional secured transactions systems are out of tune with modern financing transactions is the area of the priority among conflicting claims of several creditors in the same encumbered

[81] Guide, chapter IV, paras. 78–80.

[82] Recommendation 67. Advance registration in this respect somehow follows the system of pre-notation of mortgages.

[83] Recommendation 71. [84] Recommendation 72.

[85] Guide, chapter IV, para. 20.

[86] The draft of the Registry Guide considered by the Commission is contained in documents A/CN.9/WG.VI/WP.54 and Add. 1–4, *see* www.uncitral.org/uncitral/en/commission/working_groups/6Security_Interests.html, as well as documents A/CN.9/781 and Add. 1 and 2 (last accessed 10 August 2013).

[87] H.C. Sigman, 'Some thoughts about registration with respect to security rights in movables' 15 *Uniform Law Review* 507 (2010).

assets. Being out of tune is relatively the best scenario. The worst scenario is where there are no priority rules or no comprehensive priority rules, or priority rules that conflict with each other. Here is an example. In some legal systems, even in countries with developed economies (which, of course, does not mean that they are developed in all respects), the main non-possessory security devices are title devices in which, in principle, the grantor has to transfer ownership of its assets and the secured creditor has a sort of monopoly even if the amount of credit extended is far below the value of the assets. Then, in these legal systems, lawyers and courts have to earn their pay by crafting all sorts of ingenious theories to solve the riddle that the inactivity of the legislator has created, and allow a grantor to use the full value of its assets to obtain credit.[88]

These valiant efforts of judges and practitioners should be applauded. The Guide, though, starts from another premise, that is, that the legislator should do its duty and provide certainty and predictability and not rely on . . . the heroism or the ingenuity of judges and practitioners (that is necessary for a good law to be interpreted correctly and applied well, anyway)! After all, while it is extremely difficult to determine the cost benefits of any law, a secured transactions law is bound to affect the availability and the cost of credit, and with that, the competitiveness of a business or even of a whole economy.[89] The Guide does not suggest, however, that any law may have automatic effect. Quite the contrary, it accepts that such effect will depend heavily on harmonization with existing law, the legislative methods and drafting techniques, post-enactment acculturation and, like every human endeavour in the area of law, the quality of the courts, the lawyers, the judicial and other enforcement infrastructure, the market conditions and other factors.[90]

So, in effect, the Guide recommends what every rational law should, that is, a set of rules dealing in as clear and comprehensive a way as possible with priority conflicts. The goal of the Guide is not to make every risk disappear (this is neither possible nor desirable, as it would lead to a paternalistic approach to law). The goal of the Guide instead is to enhance certainty and *ex ante* predictability so as to make it easier for the parties to determine the risk and price a transaction.

[88] U. Drobnig, 'Basic Issues of European Rules on Security in Movables', in *The Reform of UK Property Law: Comparative Perspectives*, J. De Lacy (ed.) (London, New York: Routledge-Cavendish, 2010), p. 444.

[89] Guide, Introduction, paras. 1–14.

[90] Ibid., paras. 73–9.

Apart from the registration-based priority recommendations of the Guide that may be new to many legal systems, the priority recommendations generally reflect approaches followed in most legal systems.[91] A good example of such an approach is the rule that provides that a transferee of an encumbered asset takes the asset subject to the security right, with the exception of situations that have to do with the good faith acquisition of an encumbered asset or its acquisition in the normal course of business of the transferee.[92]

Another example is the rule that, if a State establishes any statutory preferential claims (the Guide takes no position in this respect) prevail, these claims should be limited both in type and amount.[93] The reason for this approach is that preferential claims serve important policy goals of a State and thus should be left to each State; to the extent a State provides for such preferential claims, that prevail over security rights, it typically considers their potential effects on the availability and cost of credit.[94] This recommendation reflects a similar recommendation in the insolvency part of the Guide,[95] which is based on a recommendation of the UNCITRAL Insolvency Guide.[96] This recommendation follows the general trend in the world to limit preferential claims to the greatest extent possible and, in any case, state them in a transparent way in the law so that parties are able to take them into account in pricing their transactions. The same approach is followed, for example, by English law, according to which the preference in favour of the Crown for taxes was abolished (but not the preference for employee claims) and counter-balanced by a clearly stated carve-out from floating charges of a percentage of assets of the estate up to a limited amount for the satisfaction of secured claims.[97]

Yet another example is the recommendation that provides that an unsecured creditor has priority over a security right if the unsecured creditor has obtained a judgment and taken the steps necessary to have it enforced before the security right became effective against third parties.[98]

[91] Akseli, International ST Law, at pp. 207 and 208. [92] Recommendations 79–82.

[93] Recommendation 83. [94] Guide, chapter V, paras. 90–93.

[95] Recommendation 239. [96] Recommendation 188.

[97] Section 176A of the English Insolvency Act 1986 (Prescribed Part) Order 2003, and analysis by R. Goode, *Principles of Corporate Insolvency Law* (London: Sweet & Maxwell, 4th edn., 2011), pp. 6–38 and 8–20. *See also*, www.purnells.co.uk/limited-company/the-prescribed-part/the-definition-of-the-prescribed-part.html (last accessed 10 January 2013).

[98] Recommendation 84.

Similar examples may be found in the rules regarding the priority of a service provider's or a supplier's claim,[99] and the priority of a security right in a negotiable instrument or document (made effective against third parties by possession) that is intended to preserve the negotiability of instruments and documents, and the priority of a security right in a bank account, money or letter of credit (made effective by control) that is intended to serve purposes of law other than secured transactions law.[100]

Worth mentioning are also the recommendations of the Guide with respect to the irrelevance of knowledge of the existence of a security right, subordination, the impact of continuity in third-party effectiveness on priority, the priority of security rights securing existing and future obligations, the extent of priority, the priority of security rights in future assets and proceeds. The Guide recommends that whether a third-party creditor knew or ought to have known that a security right existed be treated as irrelevant for the purpose of determining priority. Establishing what a person knew at any particular time is not an easy task, and relying on what a person ought to know is equally arbitrary; it may even be costly, because if a person ought to know that a security right would exist in any case, credit would become more expensive, even in cases in which a security right did not exist at all or was limited to a smaller amount than thought. This approach is not encouraging bad faith or fraud. It simply avoids allowing bad faith or situations of fraud to become the main example that would dictate the commercial law rule, which, in any case, is inadequate in addressing bad faith or fraud. For such circumstances, sanctions of contract, tort, civil procedure or even criminal law are necessary. This approach does not disregard bad faith either. If a person knew that by acquiring encumbered assets he, she, or it violated the rights of a secured creditor, that person would not acquire the encumbered assets free of the security right.[101]

As to subordination, the Guide recommends that competing claimants may agree to change their respective order of priority by agreement, as long as they do not affect the rights of third parties.[102] This is a typical example of flexibility intended to accommodate party autonomy but at no cost to third parties. With respect to continuity in third-party effectiveness, the Guide recommends that it result in continuity in priority, even if

[99] Recommendations 85 and 86. [100] Recommendations 101–109.
[101] Recommendation 81. [102] Recommendation 94.

third-party effectiveness is based on different methods (e.g. first registration and then possession).[103] This approach allows the secured creditor to determine which method of third-party effectiveness best fits its needs in each particular case.

As to the scope of the priority of a security right, the Guide recommends that it extend to all secured obligations, irrespective of the time they were incurred, except if they were incurred after a judgment creditor took the steps necessary to have the judgment enforced, or they exceed the maximum amount for which the security right may be enforced, if any.[104] The Guide also recommends that the priority of a security right extend to all encumbered assets, irrespective of whether they are acquired or come into existence after the time of registration.[105] This permits grantors to obtain higher amounts of credit and at better terms. To the extent, however, that this is not permitted under consumer protection or other law, the Guide recommends that consumer protection or that other law prevail.[106]

Finally, the Guide recommends that the priority of the security right extend to the encumbered assets and their proceeds.[107] This approach facilitates lending on the basis of non-possessory security rights. Except in certain situations, the secured creditor will retain its security right in the encumbered assets and also acquire a right in their proceeds, while, of course, the secured creditor cannot be paid more than it is actually owed.

2. Enforcement

At the outset, the Guide recognizes that an enforcement regime that results in delays or excessive costs is bound to affect the availability and the cost of credit.[108] At the same time, the Guide recognizes the need for an enforcement mechanism that could be adapted to each national legal system.[109] Thus, the Guide strikes a balance between judicial enforcement, which it treats neither as a problem nor as a perfect solution, and extra-judicial enforcement, which it treats neither as a panacea nor as a threat, if properly regulated. The Guide recommends that judicial enforcement, which is left to the national civil procedure regime, must also include expedited proceedings,[110] and extra-judicial enforcement, which is subject to the

[103] Recommendations 95 and 96. [104] Recommendations 97 and 98.
[105] Recommendation 99. [106] Recommendation 99, subpara. (b).
[107] Recommendation 100. [108] Guide, chapter VIII, para. 6.
[109] Ibid., para. 1. [110] Recommendations 137 and 138.

Guide, must include protections for the grantor and any third party with interests in the encumbered assets.[111]

In any case, the enforcing secured creditor must act in good faith and in a commercially reasonable manner (e.g. avoid selling the encumbered assets at a price below their actual market price);[112] and, in the case of any violation of these principles that results in damage to the grantor, the enforcing secured creditor is liable.[113] To protect the grantor from undue pressure on the part of the secured creditor, the Guide recommends that the grantor may not waive the general standard of conduct recommended in it.[114] Other rights existing under the enforcement recommendations of the Guide may be waived, but only after default, not at the time of the negotiation of the security agreement, to avoid putting the grantor in the position of having to give up its rights to obtain a concession from the secured creditor.[115]

It is worth examining the way in which the Guide balances the rights of the enforcing secured creditor with the rights of the grantor and third parties with rights in the encumbered assets, in particular, in the case of extra-judicial enforcement. The first step is made with the secured creditor obtaining possession of the encumbered assets (assuming that the grantor is in possession). Three conditions must be met. First, the grantor must have consented in the security agreement to the secured creditor obtaining possession of the encumbered assets out of court. Second, the secured creditor must have given the grantor and any person in possession of the encumbered assets notice of default and extra-judicial repossession. And third, the grantor and any person in possession of the encumbered asset must not object to extra-judicial repossession at the time it takes place.[116] In this way, the grantor should be able to obtain better credit terms at the time the security agreement is entered into. In addition, the grantor and any person in possession are sufficiently and in a timely manner informed, so as to take any step necessary to avoid extra-judicial repossession of the assets by the secured creditor. Moreover, in any case, the grantor and persons in possession may avoid extra-judicial repossession by objecting at the time the secured creditor attempts to obtain the assets. This approach essentially means that extra-judicial repossession will only take place when all parties involved agree because they are convinced that extra-judicial enforcement is in their

[111] Recommendations 147–149, 152, 153, 156 and 161. [112] Recommendation 131.
[113] Recommendation 136. [114] Recommendation 132.
[115] *See* Recommendation 133. [116] Recommendation 147.

interests as it is likely to produce a higher value, higher satisfaction of the secured obligation and thus, higher debt release.

At the stage of out-of-court disposition of the encumbered assets, the Guide recommends that the secured creditor may select the method, manner, time, place and other aspects of the disposition, but must always meet the standard of good faith and commercial reasonableness or face a claim for damages. Of course, what good faith and commercial reasonableness mean is subject to local standards and ultimately to interpretation by national courts.[117] A further protection for the grantor and third parties with interests in the encumbered assets is achieved through an elaborate notice system according to which notice of the secured creditor's intention to dispose of the encumbered assets out of court must be given well in advance to all those parties.[118] Similar safeguards for the grantor and other parties with interests in the encumbered assets are foreseen in the case of a proposal by the secured creditor to acquire the encumbered assets in satisfaction of the secured obligation.[119]

At the stage of the distribution of proceeds from the extra-judicial disposition of encumbered assets, the Guide recommends that the enforcing secured creditor must apply the net proceeds (after deducting the costs of enforcement) to the secured obligation; if there is a shortfall, the grantor remains liable, but the secured creditor then has the position of an unsecured creditor; and any surplus remaining must be turned over to the grantor or to other creditors announced during the enforcement proceedings, or, in the case of doubt, be deposited with a competent judicial or other authority.[120]

To ensure finality of the rights acquired pursuant to an out-of-court disposition, the Guide recommends that the transferee (lessee or licensee) acquire the encumbered assets free of any security rights that are subordinate to the security right of the enforcing secured creditor, but subject to any security rights with priority over the security right of the enforcing secured creditor.[121] This is extra-judicial enforcement under the Guide, neither a panacea, nor a threat, and is dealt with in a practical, not an ideological, way.

[117] Recommendation 148.

[118] Recommendations 149–151. For a very similar approach, *see* DCFR, IX (7:208–7:210).

[119] Recommendations 156–159. Very similar is DCFR, IX (7:216).

[120] Recommendations 152, 153 and 155.

[121] Recommendation 161.

VII. Efficiency and flexibility enhanced: acquisition financing

It must be clear by now that a secured transactions law that does not, at least to some extent, include interests created to secure credit obtained to acquire an asset (acquisition financing) is problematic.[122] The reason is simple. If a lender can obtain a credit monopoly with a title device, there is no reason it would be satisfied with a security device. And if a lender cannot obtain a title device, but is prepared to lend, it will lend at a higher cost either to obtain an assignment of the obligation secured with the title device or to cover the risk that the retention-of-title seller will be paid first. What is worse is that, as retention-of-title sales are hidden security rights, the lender will always have to assume that there might be a retention of title and lend at a higher cost, whether there is actually a retention of title or not, and, as a result, the cost of credit will be higher for all.[123]

In line with this analysis, the Guide deals with the so-called 'acquisition financing' devices, that is, retention-of-title sales, financial leases and other acquisition-financing transactions. This approach does not negatively affect any of these devices. On the contrary, it recognizes them within the appropriate context. This result is achieved in several respects. First, this approach does not mean that title devices need to be re-characterized. They maintain their character as title devices, sales or leases for purposes of property law, sales, leasing, tax or other law. The same applies even to outright transfers of receivables, which are also covered, as re-characterization would negatively affect useful receivables-financing transactions, such as factoring or securitization of receivables, which are based on a sale of receivables.[124]

Second, this approach does not mean that the conclusion of an acquisition financing transaction need be made more difficult. The Guide recommends that it be created by agreement between the buyer and the seller.[125] The agreement must reflect the intent of the parties, identify the buyer and the seller, and describe the credited price and the goods in a manner that reasonably allows their identification.[126] The agreement need not be in writing, as it is accompanied by the delivery of the goods to the buyer.[127]

[122] Drobnig, 'Basic Issues of European Rules', p. 453. [123] Ibid.
[124] Recommendation 3. [125] Recommendation 13.
[126] Recommendation 14. [127] Recommendation 15.

Third, this approach means that a notice needs to be registered in the general security rights registry within a certain period of time after delivery of the goods, except if it relates to consumer goods, in which case no registration is required.[128] This is a necessary change to the regime existing in many countries. The reason has already been explained. Allowing hidden security devices has a cost to the economy as a whole, while there is no concrete benefit from keeping them secret as long as registration is easy, quick and inexpensive. The Guide recommends such a registration regime. A notice may be registered easily, quickly and at a nominal cost;[129] it may cover multiple transactions between the same parties over a long period of time selected by the parties in the notice or set out in the law;[130] and registration need not delay delivery of the goods, as it is enough if it is effected within a short period of time *after* delivery of the goods.[131]

Fourth, this approach does not mean that the current priority status of acquisition financing transactions need be changed. If a State wishes to encourage supplier credit and give it priority over bank credit, this result may be achieved by the secured transactions law through the appropriate priority rules. The Guide recommends such rules. Thus, an acquisition security right has priority even over a prior registered security right as long as it is registered within a short period of time after delivery of the goods.[132] This priority extends to certain proceeds.[133]

Fifth, in a unique demonstration of flexibility, the Guide offers options to States with respect to acquisition financing devices. One option is the unitary approach, in which all such devices are categorized under the notion of acquisition security right.[134] The other option is the non-unitary approach, in which a terminological distinction is drawn between retention-of-title and financial lease interests (supplier credit), on the one hand, and acquisition security rights (bank credit), on the other.[135] Within each of these options, further alternatives are offered in the context of the priority rules. One distinguishes between inventory and goods other than inventory.[136] Another, simpler alternative makes no such

[128] Recommendations 179 and 180. [129] Recommendation 54.

[130] Recommendations 68 and 69. [131] Recommendation 180.

[132] Ibid. Compare DCFR, IX (4:102(1)). [133] Recommendation 185, alternative A.

[134] Recommendations 178–186. This approach was adopted to ensure that not even nominal re-characterization of title devices would be necessary (*see* A. Garro, 'Creation of a Security Right and its Extension to Acquisition Financing Devices' 15 *Uniform Law Review* 375, 388 (2010)).

[135] Recommendations 187–202.

[136] Recommendations 180, alternative A, and 192, alternative A.

distinction.[137] Further alternatives are offered with respect to the priority of acquisition security rights in proceeds.[138]

Sixth, if a State chooses to adopt the unitary approach, the enforcement of an acquisition security right follows the rules applicable to the enforcement of any security right. However, if a State chooses to adopt the non-unitary approach, the enforcement of a retention-of-title or financial lease right follows the rules applicable to the enforcement of any security right 'except to the extent necessary to preserve the coherence of the regime applicable to sale and lease'.[139]

Needless to say, this balanced result was achieved by consensus after long and difficult discussions during which approaches followed in various legal systems had to be combined in a balanced and workable way to satisfy the need to facilitate supplier credit and give it priority over bank credit, while placing matters in the proper context for all legal systems.[140]

VIII. A guide within the Guide: applicable law[141]

1. General

The Guide is based on the premise that conflict-of-laws rules are useful for several reasons.[142] First, as worldwide unification of the substantive secured transactions law is an impossible task, it is useful to facilitate the movement and the financing of goods across national borders with a regime that would allow the cross-border recognition of national security rights. Second, in the case of an international secured financing transaction, conflict-of-laws rules are useful in determining the place of registration, but also the scope of the applicable secured transactions law. Thus, the conflict-of-laws recommendations of the Guide deal in a comprehensive way with the law applicable to the creation, third-party effectiveness, priority and enforcement of a security right in a movable asset, as well as with the law applicable to the mutual rights and obligations of the

[137] Recommendations 180, alternative B, and 192, alternative B.

[138] Recommendations 185 and 199. [139] Recommendation 200.

[140] For a discussion of acquisition financing under the Guide, *see* S.V. Bazinas, 'Acquisition Financing under the UNCITRAL Legislative Guide on Secured Transactions' 16 *Uniform Law Review* 483 (2011).

[141] This section of the chapter is based on an article by the author published in the *Banking & Financial Services Policy Report*, Vol. 30, No. 6, June 2011.

[142] DCFR, Book IX does not contain conflict-of-laws rules, except with respect to the recognition and adaptation of security rights in assets imported from non-European countries.

grantor and the secured creditor. There are general recommendations in the Guide that deal with the law applicable to tangible and intangible assets. In addition, there are asset-specific recommendations that deal with the law applicable to certain types of tangible asset (such as mobile goods) or intangible asset (such as rights to payment of funds credited to a bank account). The Guide reflects the consensus achieved by States in UNCITRAL after discussions that took more than six years. It is important to note that the conflict-of-laws recommendations were prepared by UNCITRAL in close cooperation with the Permanent Bureau of the Hague Conference on Private International Law.[143]

2. *Characterization or qualification*

While the Guide explains the term 'security right' for the benefit of the reader,[144] it does not include definitions as a part of its recommendations. The commentary of the Guide explains that the characterization of a right as a security right will normally reflect the substantive secured transactions law in a State.[145] Thus, the Guide is based on the assumption that, in principle, a court or other authority will use its own law whenever it is required to characterize an issue for the purpose of selecting the appropriate conflict-of-laws rule.

The commentary of the Guide also explains that the fact that the substantive secured transactions law of a State might not apply to transactions that are functionally similar to secured transactions should not preclude the State from applying to those transactions the conflict-of-laws rules applicable to security rights. The Guide recommends this approach to a State that adopts the non-unitary approach to acquisition financing, where retention-of-title sales remain subject to the sales provisions of the civil code, but the secured transactions law applies to certain secured transactions law issues, such as registration of a notice in a public registry, and priority.[146]

Similarly, the commentary of the Guide explains that the fact that the substantive law of a State might not apply to outright assignments of receivables should not preclude a State from applying to all types of assignment the conflict-of-laws rules applicable to security rights in

[143] For a discussion of English, French and German conflicts rules, *see* R. Stevens, B. Jäkel, M. Bridge and U. Drobnig in *Cross-Border Security and Insolvency*, M. Bridge and R. Stevens (eds.) (Oxford University Press, 2001).

[144] Guide, Introduction, B. Terminology and Interpretation.

[145] Guide, chapter X, para. 10.

[146] Recommendation 202 and Guide.

receivables. An example is found in the Receivables Convention, which, in both its substantive and conflict-of-laws rules, applies to outright transfers of, as well as to security rights in, receivables.[147] This policy choice is motivated, notably, by the necessity of referring to a single law all priority conflicts between competing claimants with a right in the same receivable. The Guide recommends the same policy.[148] Otherwise, in the event of a priority dispute between a purchaser of a receivable and a creditor with a security right in the same receivable, it would be more difficult (and sometimes impossible) to determine who is entitled to priority if the priority of the purchaser were governed by the law of State A, but the priority of the secured creditor by the law of State B.

As already mentioned, the substantive law recommendations of the Guide draw a clear distinction between 'creation' (effectiveness between the parties) and 'third-party effectiveness' of a security right. To the extent the forum does not recognize such a distinction and does not adopt the substantive law recommendations of the Guide, it would not be in a position to implement the conflict-of-laws recommendations that refer creation to one law and third-party effectiveness to another law. However, there are very few instances in the conflict-of-laws recommendations of the Guide where creation and third-party effectiveness are subject to different laws.[149]

Similarly, as the substantive law recommendations of the Guide draw clear lines in distinguishing 'priority' from 'enforcement' of a security right, if the forum characterizes issues differently, a different law may be applicable simply because of the characterization of a priority issue under the Guide as an enforcement issue under the *lex fori*, and vice versa. However, this would be the case, though only with respect to the law applicable to security rights in tangible assets, because the Guide recommends that the law applicable to the enforcement of security rights in intangible assets be the law applicable to priority.[150]

3. *Law applicable*

With respect to the law applicable to the creation, third-party effectiveness and priority of a security right in a tangible asset, the Guide suggests a

147 Article 2, para. (a) of the Convention.

148 Recommendation 208 and chapter X, para. 11 of the Guide.

149 For example, recommendation 215 on the law applicable to a security right in proceeds (*see* section VIII.6 below).

150 Recommendation 218.

codification of existing law by recommending the application of the law of the State in which the encumbered assets are located. In addition, the Guide provides some guidance with respect to mobile goods (the law of the State in which the grantor is located), goods subject to registration (the law of the State under whose authority the registry is maintained), goods in respect of which a negotiable document has been issued (if third-party effectiveness is achieved by possession of the document, priority is subject to the law of the State in which the document is located) and goods in transit (the law of the State of origin or destination).[151] Following generally applicable rules, enforcement of a security right in a tangible asset is referred to the law of the State in which enforcement takes place.[152]

With respect to the law applicable to security rights in an intangible asset (with the exception of receivables related to immovable property, bank accounts, assets subject to registration, letters of credit, proceeds and intellectual property, that are subject to special rules),[153] the Guide reflects the principles embodied in the Receivables Convention. Under these principles, the law applicable to the creation, third-party effectiveness, priority and enforcement of a security right in an intangible asset is the law of the grantor's location.[154]

In both the Guide and the Convention, location of the grantor is defined by reference to its place of business and, in the case of places of business in more than one State, by reference to the place where the grantor has its central administration.[155] The rationale of this rule is that it is the rule that: (a) is most likely to lead to the application of the law of one State; (b) can reasonably be determined in most cases; and (c) is the law of the State in which the main insolvency proceeding with respect to the grantor will most likely be commenced. This last reason is most important, since the litmus test as to the certainty of rights of secured creditors and other third-party creditors of the grantor is certainty of substantive rights and certainty as to the applicable law in the case of the grantor's insolvency. Any other rule cannot produce the same degree of certainty to the extent it may be set aside as contrary to the public policy or the internationally mandatory rules of the law of the forum.[156]

[151] Recommendations 203–207. [152] Recommendation 218, subpara. (a).

[153] Rcommendations 209–215 and 248. [154] Recommendation 208.

[155] Recommendation 219 of the Guide and article 5, subpara. (h) of the Convention.

[156] For an analysis of these recommendations, *see* U. Drobnig, 'Die Kollisionsnormen des Legislative Guide on Secured Transactions von UNCITRAL (2007)' in *Die richtige Ordnung: Festschrift für Jan Kropholler zum 70. Geburtstag*, D. Baetge et al. (eds.) (Tübingen: Mohr Siebeck, 2008), pp. 533–51.

4. *Legal certainty and flexibility*

The conflict-of-laws chapter of the Guide does not contain: (a) escape clauses authorizing courts to deviate from the conflict-of-laws rules in appropriate circumstances; (b) composite or 'soft' connecting factors, such as the 'closest connection' or 'strongest connection'; (c) malleable 'approaches' or similar formulae that do not directly designate the applicable law but, rather, provide a list of factors that the court must consider in choosing that law; or (d) other similar devices, granting courts discretion in deciding individual cases. The reason is that such devices could reduce the certainty intended to be achieved by the recommendations of the Guide with respect to the law applicable to security rights in movable assets. This is a key objective of the Guide and should be a key objective of every secured transaction law codification, whether at the substantive or the conflict-of-laws level, as legal certainty is likely to have a positive impact on the availability and the cost of credit.[157]

However, there is potentially one exception. The law applicable to the mutual rights and obligations of the parties to the security agreement, arising from the agreement, is the law chosen by them and, in the absence of a choice of law, the law governing the security agreement.[158] The commentary refers to various conflict-of-laws rules applicable to contractual obligations, such as the Rome Convention on the Law Applicable to Contractual Obligations (which includes the close-connection test in article 4, para. 1).

5. *Issue-by-issue choice and* dépeçage

There is an effort made in the conflict-of-laws chapter of the Guide for reasons of certainty and predictability of the law applicable to recommend, conflict-of-laws rules that refer the property law aspects of a security agreement (that is, the creation, third-party effectiveness, priority and enforcement of a security right) to a single law. There are cases where this is not achieved. The reason is that approaches are preferred that are likely to best achieve the main objective of the Guide, that is, to facilitate secured financing, even if not all of those issues are referred to a single law.

Referring at least the creation and third-party effectiveness of a security right to the same law is of particular importance for States that treat these

[157] Recommendation 1. [158] Recommendation 216.

two issues as one (effectiveness of a security right *erga omnes*) and wish to adopt the conflict-of-laws recommendations of the Guide without the substantive law recommendations. As already mentioned, for these States it would be very difficult to apply a rule that would refer these two issues to different laws. This problem is addressed to a large extent with respect to the law applicable to a security right in an intangible asset. Here all property law issues, that is, the creation, third-party effectiveness priority and enforcement of a security right, are referred to a single law, that is, the law of the State in which the grantor is located.[159]

In this context, it should also be noted that, with respect to the law applicable to a security right in the case of insolvency, the Guide contains an important recommendation aimed at establishing a balance between the law applicable to secured transactions and the law applicable to insolvency proceedings. The Guide recommends that the commencement of insolvency should not displace the conflict-of-laws provisions that determine the law applicable to the property law aspects of a security right. However, this recommendation is subject to the application of the insolvency law of the State in which insolvency proceedings are commenced (*lex fori concursus*), to issues such as avoidance, treatment of secured creditors, ranking of claims or distribution of proceeds.[160]

An instance where not all issues are referred to a single law relates to the law applicable to a security right in a tangible asset. While the creation, third-party effectiveness and priority of a security right in a tangible asset is generally referred to a single law,[161] enforcement is referred to a different law.[162] More concretely, with respect to the law applicable to a security right in a tangible asset, the Guide recommends a single applicable law (the law of the State in which the asset is located) for the creation, third-party effectiveness and priority of the security right.[163] The issue of enforcement, however, is dealt with in a separate recommendation, which refers enforcement of a security right in a tangible asset to the law of the place where enforcement takes place (*lex fori*).[164] In view of the fact that procedural enforcement issues are normally subject to the *lex fori*, and in view of the difficulty of crafting a recommendation in such a guide that would distinguish between procedural and substantive law

159 Recommendations 208 and 218, subpara. (b).

160 Recommendation 223.

161 The main exception is the law applicable to security rights in proceeds (recommendation 215).

162 Recommendations 203 and 218, subpara. (a).

163 Recommendation 203.

164 Recommendation 218, subpara. (a).

enforcement issues (such as the nature and extent of the remedies of a secured creditor), this result was unavoidable.

Another similar instance refers to the law applicable to the proceeds of a security right. To meet the reasonable commercial expectations of the parties, the Guide recommends one law for the creation of the security right in the proceeds (that is, the law applicable to the security right in the original encumbered asset from which the proceeds arose); and, to protect the interests of third parties, the Guide recommends potentially a different law for the third-party effectiveness and priority of the security right in the proceeds (that is, the law applicable to the third-party effectiveness and priority of a security right in the same kind of asset as the proceeds).[165] As a result, for example, if the original encumbered asset is inventory, the inventory is sold and the proceeds generated from the sale are in the form of receivables, the creation of the security right in the receivables is referred to the law of the State in which the inventory is located at the time of the putative creation of the security right.[166] However, in this same example, the third-party effectiveness and priority of the security right in the receivables is referred to the law of the State in which the grantor is located at the time the issue arises.[167]

As already mentioned, contractual matters are also referred to a different law. As the application of the principle of party autonomy is generally acceptable and makes commercial sense with respect to the mutual rights and obligations of the parties to a security agreement, these issues are referred to the law chosen by the parties and, in the absence of a choice of law, to the law governing the security agreement.[168] The conflict-of-laws chapter of the Guide does not attempt to provide a conflict-of-laws recommendation as to the law governing the security agreement as this is not, strictly speaking, a secured transactions law issue and is dealt with in codifications dealing with the law applicable to contractual obligations.[169]

6. *Public order and mandatory rules*

Under the recommendations of the Guide, the public policy exception is to be applied only defensively, at least with respect to the third-party effectiveness and priority of a security right, in the sense that it would not

[165] *See* recommendation 215.
[166] Recommendation 220, subpara. (a) deals with the relevant time for determining location.
[167] Ibid. [168] *See* recommendation 216.
[169] The commentary refers to other texts, such as the Rome Convention (Guide, chapter X, para. 61).

permit the application of all the rules of the law of the forum State to these issues in a situation where the conflict-of-laws rule points to another law (rules of the applicable law other than the one the application of which was found to be offensive should apply).[170] The rationale for this approach is that setting aside the third-party effectiveness and priority rules of the applicable law would create uncertainty as to the law applicable to these matters, and such uncertainty would be likely to have a negative impact on the availability and the cost of credit.

This rule also applies with respect to enforcement, as a result of the combined application of recommendations 222 and 218. With respect to the law applicable to the enforcement of a security right in a tangible asset, the law of the forum State and the law of the State in which enforcement takes place will be the law of the same State. With respect to the law applicable to the enforcement of a security right in an intangible asset, as the law applicable to enforcement is the law governing priority, the law applicable to enforcement cannot be the law of the forum State (unless the law of the forum State governs priority). However, with respect to creation issues, the public policy exception may be applied even offensively, and thus result in the application of the creation rules of the forum State.[171] It appears that the rationale mentioned above is less applicable to creation issues.

The Guide recognizes both the concept of internationally mandatory rules and the public policy exception.[172] The concept of internationally mandatory rules includes only rules of the forum State. The application of the internationally mandatory rules of the forum may result in the application of the rules of the forum State to creation issues, but not to third-party effectiveness or priority issues.[173]

IX. A unique balancing act: interests in insolvency

The Guide recognizes that the function of a security right is to cover the risk of default, and that default is unavoidable in the case of insolvency. Thus, it recommends that an efficient secured transactions law needs to be coordinated with an efficient insolvency law.[174] Chapter XII of the Guide provides guidance to States as to how this coordination could be

[170] *See* recommendation 222, subpara. (c). [171] Ibid.

[172] Recommendation 222, subparas. (a) and (b).

[173] Recommendation 222, subpara. (c).

[174] The DCFR, Book IX, chapter 7 contains rules on enforcement of security rights that may also apply in the case of insolvency. However, it does not address insolvency as such.

organized, in the sense that it deals with the enforcement of a security right in line with insolvency law, and in particular, the UNCITRAL Insolvency Guide.[175]

This result is achieved in several steps. First, encumbered assets are part of the insolvency estate and subject to a stay, while the secured creditor may seek relief and protection of the value of the encumbered asset.[176] Second, the effectiveness of a security right is preserved in the case of insolvency of the grantor, but is subject to avoidance.[177] Third, the priority of a security right is preserved in the case of the grantor's insolvency, but is subject to preferences established by insolvency law.[178]

Fourth, secured creditors may participate in reorganization proceedings and their rights are not affected unless they have an opportunity to vote on a reorganization plan.[179] A reorganization plan may be confirmed by the insolvency court, provided that: (a) the approval process was properly conducted and the necessary approvals were obtained; (b) creditors will receive as much as they would have received in liquidation, unless they accepted to receive less; (c) the plan is not contrary to law; (d) administrative claims and expenses have been paid in full, unless otherwise agreed by the holders of the claims; and (e) unless otherwise agreed by affected classes, the class is given full recognition of its ranking.[180] Where confirmation by a court is not required and a reorganization plan is binding upon approval by creditors, affected persons, including secured creditors, may challenge it.[181]

Finally, a security right granted after commencement of the insolvency proceedings has no priority unless granted by the insolvency court after hearing the existing secured creditor, the debtor proves that it cannot obtain finance in any other way and the interests of existing secured creditors are protected.[182]

The insolvency chapter of the Guide makes it unique in another way, namely, that it achieves the coordination between modern international standards in the areas of secured transactions and insolvency law. This

175 *See* www.uncitral.org/uncitral/en/uncitral_texts/insolvency/2004Guide.html (last accessed 10 August 2013).

176 Recommendations 35, 50 and 51 of the UNCITRAL Insolvency Guide.

177 Recommendations 238 of the Guide and 87 of the UNCITRAL Insolvency Guide.

178 Recommendations 239 of the Guide and 188 of the UNCITRAL Insolvency Guide.

179 Recommendations 126 and 146 of the UNCITRAL Insolvency Guide.

180 Recommendation 152 of the UNCITRAL Insolvency Guide.

181 Recommendation 153 of the UNCITRAL Insolvency Guide.

182 Recommendation 67 of the UNCITRAL Insolvency Guide.

is much more than is done in many national legal systems in which the lack of any or sufficient coordination between secured transactions and insolvency law continues to create friction and inconsistencies.

X. Teaching a gorilla to play a Stradivarius:[183] the Supplement on security rights in intellectual property

Balancing of interests becomes the trade mark of the Guide, in particular after the preparation of the Supplement.[184] The overall objective of the Supplement is to make credit more available and at a lower cost to intellectual property right holders, thus enhancing the value of intellectual property rights as security for credit. At the same time, the Supplement seeks to achieve this objective without interfering with fundamental policies of intellectual property law.[185]

This balance is the foundation of the Supplement and it was established by a principle that became famous as the principle of recommendation 4, subparagraph (b).[186] According to this principle, the Guide and the Supplement give way to intellectual property law (defined in a broad way to include national law and international treaties) if an issue is addressed in that law in an asset-specific and different way from how it is addressed in the Guide. This principle became the key to the consensus reached in the Supplement between the secured financing and the intellectual property world, because it made it easier for intellectual property law experts to

[183] The title of this section makes reference to a very interesting comment by Professor Jeremy Philips at a conference on intellectual property financing, that 'We cannot give an intellectual property right as collateral to a gorilla (lender). He can only destroy it!' At the end of this project, Jeremy Philips posted the following comment on his blog: 'The blog and UNCITRAL have both grown through the experience which, initially filled with friction, suspicion and misunderstanding, has brought a good deal of benefit to both the IP and the finance communities. Thank you, Spiros and UNCITRAL, for taking our comments, and our commitment, so seriously', *see* http://ipfinance.blogspot.co.at/search?q=IP±Supplement (last accessed 10 January 2013). The author would also like to thank Prof. Philips and the world intellectual property community for their invaluable contribution to this almost impossible task of . . . teaching a gorilla to play a Stradivarius!

[184] *See* www.uncitral.org/uncitral/en/uncitral_texts/payments/ip-supplement.html (last accessed 10 January 2013). For a discussion of the Supplement, *see* S.V. Bazinas, 'Intellectual Property Financing under the UNCITRAL Guide' 43 *UCC Law Journal* (April 2011).

[185] A. Tosato, 'Security Interests over Intellectual Property' 6(2) *Journal of Intellectual Property Law & Practice* 93 (2011).

[186] Referred to in the discussions as the principle or Hamletian dilemma '*to be or not to be?*'!

accept some of the fundamental principles of modern secured transactions laws and the Guide.

At the same time, this principle was accepted by secured transactions law experts as the primacy of intellectual property law was generally recognized and as long as the intellectual property law rule to which secured transactions law would defer would be asset-specific and thus apply specifically to intellectual property law rights (otherwise, old secured transactions law displaced with respect to other types of asset after law reform would remain applicable with respect to intellectual property rights). Deference to intellectual property-specific rules dealing with security rights in intellectual property rights is certainly a limitation of the Supplement and its harmonization effect, but was a necessary one in view of the need to facilitate the extension of credit to intellectual property owners and other right holders without interfering with the fundamental policies of intellectual property law.

The realization of the exact scope of the potential overlap and conflict between secured transactions and intellectual property law was one of the benefits drawn from the discussion of this principle. The Supplement deals with the creation, third-party effectiveness, priority and enforcement of a security right in an intellectual property right. It does not deal with the creation, effectiveness, priority and protection of an intellectual property right. These are exclusively matters of intellectual property law. To the extent better coordination between secured transactions and intellectual property law would be served by a revision of intellectual property law (for example, with respect to registration of a security right in the relevant intellectual property right registry), the Supplement deals with that matter by way of mild suggestions in the commentary as to how States enacting the Guide and the Supplement might better coordinate their intellectual property law with that enactment.

The Supplement breaks new ground with respect to acquisition financing, the law applicable to security rights in intellectual property and the treatment of licence rights in insolvency.[187] While the idea of a special regime of acquisition financing for intellectual property is not unknown, its application has been rather limited. By establishing such a regime, the Supplement breaks new ground to facilitate acquisition financing in an intellectual property context.[188] The basic idea is that, as a

[187] For a discussion of security interests in intellectual property licences, *see* G. Koziol, *Lizenzen als Kreditsicherheiten* (Tübingen: Mohr-Siebeck, 2011).

[188] Recommendation 247.

retention-of-title seller of goods or a lender financing the acquisition of goods by the grantor deserves a special priority status, since without that acquisition money the grantor could not acquire the goods, a financier financing the acquisition of an intellectual property right or a licence by a grantor deserves to be treated in the same way. In essence, the Supplement implements in an intellectual property context the super-priority recommended in the Guide for a retention-of-title seller, financial lessor or other acquisition secured creditor. This means, *inter alia*, that the super-priority does not extend to cash proceeds of intellectual property held by the grantor for sale or licence (quasi-inventory).[189]

The Guide and the Supplement do not deal with the law applicable to ownership rights with respect to intellectual property rights. They do, however, deal with the law applicable to the creation, third-party effectiveness, priority and enforcement of a security interest in an intellectual property right. As there is no generally acceptable applicable law rule with respect to security interests in intellectual property rights, UNCITRAL took the time to discuss this issue at length and in depth. Various alternatives were considered and their comparative advantages and disadvantages were discussed. The outcome, which was considered to be a significant success, in particular, as it was agreed upon after a long and well-informed discussion by consensus, may be briefly described as follows.

The Supplement discusses in the commentary various options with their comparative advantages and disadvantages.[190] The recommended approach refers to the law of the grantor's location on some issues and to the law of the State in which the intellectual property right is protected on others.[191] The main argument for this approach is that it maximizes the advantages of both options and minimizes their disadvantages. More concretely, this approach allows parties to choose either the law of the protecting State or the law of the grantor's location as the law applicable to creation (effectiveness between the parties, not affecting third parties). It refers third-party effectiveness and priority to the law of the protecting State, giving appropriate recognition to the principle of territoriality and the need to refer security interests in registrable intellectual property rights to the law of the State of registration. It also permits third-party effectiveness as against judgment creditors and insolvency administrators to be achieved under a single law (the law of the State of the grantor's

[189] Supplement, chapter IX, paras. 254–283.
[190] Supplement, chapter X, paras. 301–337.
[191] Recommendation 248 and Supplement, chapter X, paras. 290–300.

location). Furthermore, this option refers enforcement to a single law (the law of the grantor's location), subject to the principle of the application of the *lex fori* to procedural matters and the *lex fori concursus* to certain insolvency-related matters (avoidance, ranking of claims and distribution of proceeds). Contractual matters are referred to the law chosen by the parties and, in the absence of such a choice by the parties, the applicable law will be the law governing the security agreement as determined by the conflict-of-laws provisions generally applicable to contractual obligations.[192] The result achieved in the Guide is, to a large extent, consistent with the result achieved in the Principles on Conflict of Laws in Intellectual Property ('CLIP').[193]

With respect to licence rights and security rights in licence rights in the licensor's or licensee's insolvency, the Supplement discusses various ways in which licence rights as encumbered assets could be protected against the risk of rejection of a licence agreement by the licensor's or licensee's insolvency administrator. For example, it refers to the possibility of a secured creditor obtaining an interest not in licence rights, but in the intellectual property right itself and being treated as a secured creditor in the licensor's or licensee's insolvency. The Supplement also refers to licence agreements that may be treated as fully performed, or transactions creating property rights (e.g., an exclusive licence agreement) or that may be registered, and thus not subject to rejection. The Supplement refers to approaches taken in different legal systems in order to protect licence rights, including registration of a licence agreement.[194]

XI. The Guide under sniper fire proves to be fire-proof: a rebuttal[195]

The Guide is pretty good and probably much better as an international standard than any existing national legislation, in the sense that no national law can provide the guidance that the extensive commentary

192 For a discussion of the various options, *see* S. Bariatti, 'The Law Applicable to Security Interests in Intellectual Property Rights' 6(2) *Journal of Private International Law* 395 (2010).

193 www.cl-ip.eu/en/pub/home.cfm (last accessed 10 January 2013).

194 Supplement, chapter IX, paras. 345–367, and Koziol, *Lizenzen*, p. 115.

195 The title of this section comes from the article by G. Herrmann and J. Sekolec, 'UNCITRAL Arbitration Rules under sniper fire prove to be fire-proof: rebuttal to R. Coulson', *World Arbitration & Mediation Report* (NY: Irvington-on-Hudson) 4:4:93–96, April 1993. It is unfortunate, but this is not the first time a UNCITRAL text has come under sniper fire.

of the Guide provides or the flexibility inherent in a guide. Certainly, no national law is the result of a recent international consensus among States that achieves a unique amount of coordination among modern international standards on secured financing prepared by various organizations, as well as between international standards on secured financing and insolvency. Still, like every human endeavour, the Guide is not perfect, so any criticism of one or the other approach discussed or recommended in the Guide is, of course, both legitimate and useful, to the extent that it advances the discussion. What is neither legitimate nor useful is to use incomplete or inaccurate statements so as to discredit the Guide as an enactment of 'American neo-liberalism'. This section explains why.

1. The Guide, ideologies and legal transplants

It is a commonly known fact that UNCITRAL texts in general do not reflect any particular ideology.[196] This is evident in the range of countries that adopt them.[197] This applies also to the Guide, which has been or is being implemented by countries ranging from Australia to China, Ghana and Malawi, and has influenced texts such as the DCFR, Boox IX.[198] Thus, the conclusion that 'This closeness in approach [of the Guide] to article 9 is likely to militate against the prospects of the Guide gaining widespread international acceptance'[199] is simply factually inaccurate.

In addition, the argument that the Guide 'is an instrument of American economic power',[200] and statements such as those implying that the Guide was intended to be a 'magical elixir' or the 'Holy Grail' belong to the realm of political science fiction.[201] Moreover, the argument that the Guide attempts to reform the law worldwide along 'neo-liberal American lines'[202] contains several inaccuracies. The Guide does not attempt to

196 McCormack, Chapter 2 above, p. 31.

197 See, for example, the status of CISG, www.uncitral.org/uncitral/en/uncitral_texts/sale_goods/1974Convention_status.html (last accessed 10 January 2013).

198 For example, China has adopted a new receivables financing registry that has been heavily influenced by the registry recommended in the Guide, as has Ghana, Malawi and many other countries (*see* Secured Transactions and Collateral Registries, IFC Advisory Services/Access to Finance, 2, in www1.ifc.org/wps/wcm/connect/793e79804ac10fff9ea69e4220e715ad/Secured±Transactions±and±Collateral±Registries±Brochure-English.pdf?MOD=AJPERES (last accessed 10 January 2013).

199 G. McCormack, 'American Private Law Writ Large? The UNCITRAL Secured Transactions Guide' 60 *ICLQ* 597 (2011).

200 *See* McCormack, Chapter 2 above, p. 51.

201 *See* ibid., p. 58.

202 *See* ibid., p. 33.

reform secured transactions law worldwide, as it is not a convention, or even a model law (which is more flexible than a convention but less flexible than a guide). It simply discusses all policy issues that need to be addressed in a secured transactions law, suggests various workable approaches with comparative advantages and disadvantages, and makes flexible recommendations to the national legislator, at times with several options for States to choose from.

One may have wished for a higher level of flexibility. That is legitimate. But one cannot reasonably argue that the Guide does not offer any flexibility as if it was a law and, in particular, a certain law like the Uniform Commercial Code (UCC) Article 9. Moreover, even if the Guide were a copy of UCC Article 9, it is a logical jump that UCC Article 9 is the result of national ideology, and in particular one that appeared decades after its initial enactment and several years after its latest revision. In addition, the argument about any national law reflecting a single ideology is a very dangerous one and has been used in the past in very unfortunate ways. As indicated in this chapter, the Guide does not ignore the regulatory and cultural plurality of the various countries. Quite the contrary, it is in the nature of soft law like a guide to take this plurality into account and to offer multiple options, as it does.

Furthermore, the discussion about legal transplants[203] can have no or very little relevance to soft law like a guide, which by definition is flexible, and the enactment of any of which is subject to the sovereign decision of each State. In this context, it is worth noting that the Guide discusses in a clear and transparent way issues of harmonization between a law enacting its recommendations and existing law, issues of legislative method and drafting technique, as well as issues of post-enactment acculturation.[204] Most importantly, the Guide discusses in detail issues of transition from the existing to a new secured transactions law and includes a series of recommendations dealing with all relevant issues.[205] In any case, the discussion of legal transplants appears to be incomplete, at least to the extent that it fails to mention, for example, the value of comparative, uniform or harmonized law, as well as the role of Roman law, or even English common law as successful examples of legal transplants. Legal transplants cannot be bad only if they do not originate from English common law!

[203] Ibid., p. 51. [204] Guide, Introduction, paras. 76–89.
[205] Guide, chapter XI.

2. *The Guide and UCC Article 9*

It is true that the Guide has been influenced by approaches followed in UCC Article 9, for example, to the extent that the Guide recommends a functional approach, notice-based registration and extra-judicial enforcement. However, these approaches are, to one extent or another, common to almost all modern secured transactions regimes, on which the Guide was based,[206] including the recommendations of the English Law Reform Commission, which to a large extent are similar to the recommendations of the Guide, or texts which the Guide has influenced, including the new PPSA of Australia[207] and Draft Commission Frame of Reference (DCFR), Book IX.[208] The reason is simple. There is no viable alternative to the functional approach as a way of addressing the gaps and inconsistencies of legal systems that do not have a comprehensive and rational code on secured transactions; nor is there a viable alternative to the notice-based registration system as explained in this chapter; nor is there a viable alternative to the Guide as a flexible and comprehensive international standard which discusses all workable approaches and makes recommendations that national legislators are free to implement, as they are or revised, or reject, having been convinced by the informative commentary to take another approach.

In addition, for a number of reasons, no guide is or can be identical to any national law. First, a guide (non-binding, soft law with commentaries and recommendations) cannot be a copy of any law. As already mentioned, the Guide includes a discussion of all workable approaches to the various policy issues and leaves matters to the national legislator. Even the recommendations of the Guide do not form a model law and they provide numerous options for States to choose from, as explained in this chapter. No law does or can provide so many options, and certainly not UCC Article 9. Second, with respect to acquisition financing, no law does or can include two options (unitary and non-unitary) for States to choose from. Third, no law includes such a detailed set of recommendations on the law applicable to security rights. Fourth, and most importantly, no secured transactions law does or can include the guidance that the Guide provides on insolvency issues. Fifth, no law includes detailed rules on security rights in intellectual property and foresees acquisition financing devices in intellectual property, the law applicable to security rights in

[206] Guide, Introduction, para. 12. [207] Section II of this chapter *ad finem*.
[208] Drobnig, 'Basic Issues of European Rules', 455.

intellectual property, or such a treatment of licence rights in the case of insolvency. If the Guide is an inexact copy of UCC Article 9, what about the insolvency chapter of the Guide? Is it, too, an inexact copy of the US bankruptcy code? No one has ever dared suggest that. The same applies to the applicable law, acquisition financing and intellectual property parts of the Guide, which are key parts of it, not peripheral.

The statements that the approach of the Guide with respect to the treatment of title transactions that serve security purposes 'conforms with the approach evidenced in the US Article 9 but is one that is at variance with the English common law' and that 'in the details of the filing system suggested for security rights, the UNCITRAL Guide maps on to the American rather than the English system'[209] may be revealing, but are not fully accurate. As already mentioned, the acquisition financing chapter of the Guide has been influenced by the approaches followed in UCC Article 9 and other legal systems. Similarly, the Guide maps on all the secured transactions laws that have introduced a modern security rights registry in the last twenty years, as well as on the PPSAs of common law countries, such as Australia,[210] Canada[211] and New Zealand,[212] and the recommendations of the Law Reform Commission of England,[213] all of which to a large extent are consistent with the recommendations of the Guide. It is true that the Guide is and will be at variance with English common law, at least until the recommendations of the English Law Reform Commission are enacted into law.

3. The Guide and the EBRD Model Law

Comparing the Guide with the EBRD Model Law and suggesting that the Guide ignores the distinction between common law and civil law shows a remarkable lack understanding of what the Guide does and what the international legislative process, at least in the context of UNCITRAL, is

209 *See* McCormack, Chapter 2 above, p. 39.

210 *See* Fischer, 'Personal Property Security Law Reform in Australia', 366.

211 For a comparison of the PPSAs of Australia and Canada, *see* J.G.H. Stumbles, 'Personal Property Security Law in Australia and Canada: a Comparison' 51 *Canadian Business Law Journal* 425 (2011).

212 *See* D. Brown, 'The New Zealand Personal Property Securities Act 1999', in *The Reform of UK Property Law: Comparative Perspectives*, J. De Lacy (ed.) (London New York: Routledge-Cavendish, 2010), p. 328.

213 *See* http://lawcommission.justice.gov.uk/areas/company-security-interests.htm (last accessed 10 January 2013).

supposed to do.[214] The Guide cannot go much further than the EBRD Model Law or any other model law, because it is not a model law.[215] And certainly the legal world in UNCITRAL cannot be divided between civil law and common law, because there are other legal traditions, and one civil law or common law tradition differs widely from another (at times, in a very uncivil, or even in too common a way).

In addition, the suggestion that, unlike the EBRD Model Law, the Guide 'is firmly in the common law mould'[216] is inconsistent with the argument that the Guide is heavily influenced by UCC Article 9, to the extent UCC Article 9 constitutes a codification that departs from the common law tradition and that comes very close to the civil law tradition.[217] Of course, the argument is accurate if 'common law' means English common law. But in that case the argument is very weak, as in the area of secured transactions law English common law is very different from the law in other common law countries, such as the US, Canada, Australia, India and New Zealand.

4. *The discussion of UNCITRAL's working methods*

It is true that UNCITRAL engaged recently in a discussion of its working methods. However, this discussion had nothing to do with the impact of a neo-liberal American agenda on UNCITRAL texts.[218] The relevant background documents[219] make it clear that the discussion was about the lack of a *written set of rules of procedure* for UNCITRAL, the role of non-governmental organizations (NGOs), the languages used in informal meetings and the decision-making process at UNCITRAL.[220] At its forty-third session in 2010, the Commission considered those matters and confirmed its *long-standing unwritten rules of procedure*, namely, the

214 *See* McCormack, Chapter 2 above, p. 38.

215 For a more objective comparison of the EBRD Model Law and the Guide, *see* Röver, 15 *Uniform Law Review* 50 (2010).

216 *See* McCormack, Chapter 2 above, ibid.

217 Although the view is also expressed in a joking manner that UCC is neither uniform (as it is a model law enacted differently by each state in the US), nor commercial (as it deals with civil law matters, such as sales and leases), nor a code (as its articles appear to be casuistic rather than generally to state a rule of law)!

218 *See* McCormack, Chapter 2 above, p. 33.

219 *See* A/CN.9/635, A/CN.9/638 and Add. 1–6, and A/CN.9/639, A/CN.9/653, A/CN.9/676 and Add. 1–9, and A/CN.9/680 and A/CN.9/697, and their discussion by the Commission A/63/17, paras. 373–381, A/64/17, paras. 379–397 and A/65/17, paras. 299–306 and Annex III.

220 *See* A/CN.9/635.

decision-making process (consensus, but without veto powers), the status of NGOs (participation in the discussions, but not in the decisions) and the working methods of the Secretariat (statements by members of the UNCITRAL secretariat during meetings and recourse to assistance by experts).[221] To refer generally to this discussion without the necessary explanations, thus creating a negative implication about the work of UNCITRAL, without offering any explanation, is sniper fire at its best![222]

5. *The concept of 'security right' and self-help remedies under the Guide*

The fact that, in the case of default, there is tension between the debtor, the grantor (if the grantor is a third party), and the secured creditor is clear. However, what is often overlooked[223] is the common interest of the borrower and the lender in a secured financing transaction. The borrower wants to borrow at the best possible terms to develop its business and repay the loan out of the profits. The lender wants to have some security that it will be paid its capital with some profit. As a result of the security, the borrower can borrow and the lender can lend at terms that are typically far better than the terms of unsecured credit.

In addition, to suggest that there are constitutional problems with self-help remedies without some elaboration is not accurate or helpful.[224] There are no constitutional problems with self-help remedies as long as they are subject to public policy restrictions of the kind included in the Guide.[225]

6. *Assets that can be used as security and characterization of title transactions under the Guide*

The Guide does not eliminate restrictions on the taking of security; nor does it increase the range of assets that can be used as security.[226] According to recommendation 18 of the Guide, the law 'does not override provisions of any other law to the extent that they limit the creation or enforcement of a security right in, or the transferability of, specific types of asset'.

In addition, the Guide does not suggest that title transactions should be re-characterized. It simply suggests that some transactions that are title

[221] *See* A/65/17, paras. 299–306 and Annex III.
[222] *See* McCormack, Chapter 2 above, p. 33.
[223] Ibid. [224] Ibid., p. 34.
[225] Section VI.2 of this chapter on enforcement.
[226] *See* McCormack, Chapter 2 above, p. 35.

transactions only in name but actually serve security purposes, should be subject to secured transactions rules, without re-characterizing those transactions that remain subject to other law (whether insolvency law re-characterizes these transactions is a separate issue).[227] It should be noted here that even though the Guide applies to outright transfers of receivables, it does not re-characterize them as secured transactions, as this would undermine useful receivables financing transactions that are based on the notion of a sale, such as factoring and securitization.[228]

7. Preferential claims under the Guide

Security rights are false exceptions to the pari passu principle, as preferential claims are the only true exceptions.[229] This is a matter of insolvency law, with respect to which the (secured transactions) simply follows the approach recommended in the UNCITRAL Insolvency Guide. The Guide does not reject the idea of a carve-out for unsecured creditors. It discusses the advantages and disadvantages of carve-outs and makes balanced recommendations that apply to preferential claims within or outside insolvency.[230] This approach is in line with the trend all over the world to limit preferences (including carve-outs for unsecured creditors) to the greatest extent possible, and otherwise, to state them clearly in the law.[231] In taking this approach, the draftsmen of the Guide considered and adopted the English law approach, according to which preferences are limited, and the remaining preferences are clearly stated in the law.[232] Thus, suggesting that the Guide recommends *the 'full' priority of security rights'*[233] shows a total disregard of recommendations 83 and 239 of the Guide.

8. Notice filing under the Guide

It is true that the Guide recommends a notice-based registration system for the reasons already mentioned.[234] However, as also already mentioned, a

[227] Guide, chapter IX, paras. 60–84.

[228] Recommendation 3 and Guide, chapter I, paras. 25–31.

[229] McCormack's view, Chapter 2 above, p. 49 is countered by Goode, *Principles of Corporate Insolvency Law*, paras. 8–16 and 8–17.

[230] Recommendations 83 and 239.

[231] Recommendation 83 and Guide, chapter V, paras. 90–93. For preferences in the case of insolvency, *see* recommendation 239 and chapter XII, paras. 59–63.

[232] Guide, chapter V, para. 97.

[233] *See* McCormack, Chapter 2 above, p. 5.

[234] Section V.2. above.

guide cannot follow any law and the Guide does not simply follow a UCC Article 9 approach.[235] It follows an approach adopted in almost every modern secured transactions law enacted in the last twenty years, which may have been influenced by UCC Article 9 to one extent or another, but is neither a copy of it, nor a foreign transplant, to the extent it has become a workable part of national law. In other words, the origin of this approach was UCC Article 9, but its most modern enactments are in the PPSAs of Australia, Canada, India and New Zealand, in the Convention on International Interests in Mobile Equipment and its Protocols, in DCFR, Book IX, and in the recommendations of the Law Commission of England.[236] So the criticism is addressed against all modern legislation, and, to the extent that legislation is successful, it is a theoretical criticism proven to be wrong by reality. It is essentially an appeal for England not to adopt notice filing. Everyone is entitled to his or her opinion, and some of the arguments mentioned have some merit. However, the problems referred to have solutions, and the Guide recommends these solutions.[237]

First, if one wants to have a registration system that is quick, easy and inexpensive and one that would preserve the confidentiality of a transaction, notice registration is the only way. One may have a document registration system, and if a registrant may enter the document directly into the registry record without any intervention by registry staff, such registration may be quick, easy and inexpensive, assuming that electronic registration is possible, which is something that the Guide recommends but does not assume in all cases.[238] However, unless someone checked the transaction document and confirmed its accuracy, a document registration would be unnecessary, since a third-party searcher would not be able to rely on it fully, and would have to seek and find information off the registry record. If, on the other hand, the registrar had to check every transaction document, the registration would be neither quick nor inexpensive. Furthermore, even in that case some important information would still not be available on record, since the registrar may check the accuracy and legality of the information but may be unable to determine whether the transaction was indeed completed or whether the documentation is genuine.

235 McCormack, Chapter 2 above, p. 39.

236 For a critical discussion of the English Law Commission's recommendations, *see* R. Calnan, 'What is Wrong with the English Law of Security?' in *The Reform of UK Property Law: Comparative Perspectives*, J. De Lacy (ed.) (London-New York: Routledge-Cavendish, 2010), p. 162.

237 *See* section V.2. above.

238 Recommendation 54, subpara. (j) recommends an electronic registry '*if possible*'.

This result would be unnecessary if the legal consequence of registration was simply to make a security right effective against third parties. Of course, if registration was supposed to create the security right, a notice would not suffice, and the transaction document would have to be registered. This approach would have several unintended or negative effects. First, it would make registration as cumbersome and costly as registration of a mortgage. Second, it would unnecessarily complicate the creation of a security right. Third, it would make it impossible for the law to be comprehensive and cover acquisition financing devices, such as retention-of-title sales and financial leases, which are form-free transactions and should not be subjected to form requirements and thus be made more difficult. Fourth, it would complicate the searcher's job of having to parse through voluminous documentation on record to find the information he or she needs. Even when the searcher finds the registration he or she is looking for, he or she would have to interpret the security agreement on record and determine whether or not a security right with respect to some assets had in fact been created.

Finally, notice filing works, as a searcher may use the registry as a warning and an encouragement to seek and find information off record, which would not be possible without the registry. A potential lender may not lend if the potential borrower does not provide complete information on previous secured transactions. And a potential borrower may seek to clean inaccurate registrations from the record through an expedited judicial or administrative proceeding. For all of these reasons, as already mentioned, notice-based registration has been adopted even in the context of specialized (asset-based) registries with respect to the types of high-value mobile equipment covered by the Cape Town Convention and its Protocols, intellectual property rights such as patents and trade marks registries, and is being advocated even for the registration of mortgages in immovable property registries.[239] One may agree or disagree with these views, but I would suggest that they have more to do with common sense than anything else. There is nothing exclusively American, or neo-liberal, in common sense – or in practical thinking, for that matter!

XII. Conclusions

The Guide, which builds on UCC Article 9 and all modern national and international secured transactions regimes of the last twenty years, is by

239 *See* section V.2. above.

definition a non-binding, soft law instrument, which is intended to assist States in their law reform efforts in the area of secured transactions law. It is the result of an international consensus reached by States (and not NGOs) after several years of hard negotiations and achieves its goal of providing guidance to States through commentary and recommendations. The commentary provides the necessary flexibility by discussing various workable approaches with their comparative advantages and disadvantages. It also gives the necessary certainty with recommendations, which provide a number of options for the legislator to consider.

The balanced combination of flexibility and certainty is the main characteristic reflected in all chapters of the Guide that include general and asset-specific commentary and recommendations for States to choose the parts they may wish to consult and perhaps implement. It is also reflected in all the chapters of the Guide dealing with the various issues that need to be addressed in an efficient and effective secured transactions law.

With respect to the creation (effectiveness between the parties) of a security right, this balance is reflected in several ways, including that: (a) a security right may be created by simple agreement that need not be in writing if accompanied by delivery of the encumbered assets to the secured creditor; (b) where the security agreement must be in writing, an electronic record and an electronic signature are sufficient; (c) the written agreement need only be signed by the grantor and may reflect the grantor's intent by itself or in conjunction with the course of conduct between the parties; (d) the encumbered assets may be described in the security agreement in a manner that reasonably allows their identification (namely, specifically or generally); (e) States may choose to require that the maximum amount for which the security right may be enforced must be indicated in the security agreement; and (f) the recommendations of the Guide do not override limitations in other law to the creation or enforcement of a security right, or the transferability of specific types of asset (with the exception of limitations to the transferability of future receivables as such and the effects of contractual clauses limiting the transferability of receivables).[240]

With respect to the third-party effectiveness of a security right, this balance between flexibility and certainty is reflected in several respects, including that: (a) the main method for achieving third-party effectiveness (but not effectiveness between the parties) of a security right is

[240] Recommendations 13–18.

registration of a notice in a general security rights registry; and (b) various other methods (possession, control or registration of a document or notice in a specialized registry) apply either generally to all types of asset, or to specific types of asset.[241]

With respect to registration, the above-mentioned balance is achieved by way of commentary and recommendations on various issues, including: (a) at the discretion of States, a registry may be electronic or not;[242] (b) at the discretion of States, a notice may include a statement of the maximum amount for which a security right may be enforced; (c) the description of the encumbered assets in the notice may be specific or generic, depending on what is considered a reasonable description in each particular practice; (d) at the discretion of States, the transfer of an encumbered asset on the effectiveness of registration may require the registration of a new notice stating the name of the transferee or not; (e) authorization by the grantor is required for an effective registration, although the authorization need not be part of the registry record; and (f) a grantor may utilize an expedited judicial or administrative proceeding to clean the registry record whenever, in his or her view, the record does not reflect the agreement of the parties.[243]

With respect to priority, the balance between flexibility and certainty is reflected in various commentaries and recommendations on issues such as that: (a) priority is based on the time of registration of a notice in the general security rights registration, but registration of a document or notice in a specialized registry beats registration of a notice in the general security rights registry; (b) while the introduction of preferential claims is left to the discretion of each State, the Guide simply recommends that they be limited and clearly stated in the law; (c) the priority of unsecured creditors such as judgment creditors, service providers and suppliers of goods is preserved, as long as certain acts take place before registration of a notice with respect to a security right; and (d) with respect to certain types of asset, control or possession beats registration.[244]

With respect to the enforcement of a security right, the balanced combination of flexibility and certainty is expressed in several ways, including: (a) a person must exercise its rights and perform its obligations with

[241] Recommendations 32–38.

[242] If not possible, access to the registry need not be electronic, but, to the extent possible, the internal processes and storage of data should be electronic (recommendation 54, subpara. (j)) and chapter IV, paras. 21–24 of the Guide).

[243] Recommendations 54, subpara. (j), 57, subpara. (d), 62, 63 and 72.

[244] Recommendations 77, 78, 83–86 and 101–109.

respect to enforcement in good faith and in a commercially reasonable manner; (b) this standard of conduct may not be waived by agreement of the parties; (c), any other right may be waived, but only after default; (d) judicial enforcement is referred to national civil procedure law; and (e) self-help remedies are limited in several ways so as to ensure that they may not be used if the grantor or any other person in possession of the encumbered assets objects at the time of the conclusion of the security agreement or at the time of enforcement.[245]

With respect to acquisition financing, this balance is reflected in several respects, including: (a) States may choose between a unitary and a non-unitary approach; (b) several options are offered within the unitary and the non-unitary approach for States to choose; (c) according to one approach, it is sufficient for a retention-of-title seller to register one notice with respect to several transactions between the same parties over a number of years within a short period of time after delivery of the goods; (d) such registration ensures that a retention-of-title right has priority even over a prior registered security right; (e) such priority may extend to certain types of proceeds; and (f) the rules applicable to the enforcement of a security right should apply to the enforcement of a retention-of-title right, except to the extent necessary to preserve the coherence of the regime applicable to sales.[246]

With respect to conflict of laws, the balance between flexibility and certainty is reflected in: (a) the extent to which the recommendations are based on generally accepted notions of conflict-of-laws rules (e.g., the *lex rei sitae* is the law applicable to security rights in tangible assets); (b) the certainty achieved with regard to a number of issues (e.g., the impact of commencement of insolvency on the law applicable); (c) the options provided with respect to certain issues (e.g., law applicable to security rights in bank accounts); and (d) the adoption of certain innovative rules (e.g. the law applicable to security rights in intellectual property).[247]

With respect to insolvency, the balance between flexibility and certainty is reflected in the balance achieved in the UNCITRAL Insolvency Guide, in particular with respect to the following issues: (a) encumbered assets are part of the insolvency estate and subject to stays, while a secured creditor may seek relief; (b) the effectiveness of a security right is respected in the case of insolvency, subject to any avoidance actions; (c) the priority of a security right is also respected in insolvency, subject to any preferential

[245] Recommendations 131–133, 147–151. [246] Recommendations 178–202.

[247] For example, recommendation 203, 210 and 223.

claims, which should be limited and clearly stated in the law; (d) secured creditors may participate in reorganization proceedings and, in certain cases, bound against their consent pursuant to a decision of the insolvency court; and (e) post-commencement finance does not have priority over pre-commencement finance, except if the insolvency court determines otherwise.[248]

With respect to security rights in intellectual property, the balance between flexibility is reflected in various ways, and most notably in: (a) the deference to intellectual property law; (b) the priority of security rights, document or notice of which is registered in an intellectual property registry; (c) the introduction of acquisition financing in the area of intellectual property; and (d) the combination between the law of the State in which the intellectual property is protected with the law of the State of the grantor's location to form the law applicable to security rights in intellectual property.[249]

The Guide as a soft law instrument has already influenced a number of laws, such the new PPSA of Australia, and is being implemented, to one extent or another, in countries from different legal traditions and different levels of economic development, from China to Ghana and from Malawi to Mexico. Like any other text, the Guide is not perfect, but a soft-law international standard cannot be compared with any national secured transactions regime. Most importantly, it is part of a series of international secured transactions texts, which were prepared by Unidroit, the Hague Conference and UNCITRAL, and which States may adopt to establish a comprehensive, internally consistent, balanced and efficient security rights regime for both domestic and cross-border transactions.[250]

248 Recommendations of chapter XII of the Guide.

249 Recommendations 2, subpara. (b), 77, 78, 247 and 248.

250 *See* n. 27 above, 39.

9

The utility and efficacy of the UN Convention on the Assignment of Receivables and the Facilitation of Credit

N. ORKUN AKSELI*

I. Introduction

Assignment of receivables is at the core of commercial law. Raising finance through assignment of receivables is a vital financing technique for small businesses and routinely used by companies in financing their businesses.[1] Receivables financing also has a significant role in economic growth. As one commentator pointed out, raising finance through assignment of receivables 'is simply bigger business than the financing of mobile goods'.[2] Receivables financing has seen considerable growth as 'receivables are self-liquidating and . . . an excellent short-term source of cash'.[3] Divergence in the regulation of the law of assignment in national systems causes uncertainty and increases the cost of credit in cross-border assignment of receivables contracts, hence the need to have a modern and sophisticated international instrument. Businesses, particularly in developing economies, have difficulty in gaining access to finance, mainly because intangibles are not widely accepted as collateral.[4] The majority of world

* The author would like to thank Mr. Spiros Bazinas for his comments on an earlier draft of this chapter. Usual disclaimers apply.

1 Law Commission, *Report on Company Security Interests* No. 296 (2005), para. 4.1 ('Law Commission Report').

2 N.B. Cohen, 'Harmonizing the Law Governing Secured Credit: The Next Frontier' 33 *Texas International Law Journal* 173, 185 (1998).

3 S. Schwarcz, 'Towards a Centralized Perfection System for Cross-Border Receivables Financing' 20 *University of Pennsylvania Journal of International Economic Law* 455, 456 (1999). For the significance of receivables financing *see also* F. Oditah, *Legal Aspects of Receivables Financing* (London: Sweet and Maxwell, 1991), at p. 2.

4 *See e.g.*, M. Safavian, 'Firm-Level Evidence on Collateral and Access to Finance', in F. Dahan and J. Simpson (eds.), *Secured Transactions Reform and Access to Credit* (Cheltenham: Edward Elgar, 2008), pp. 110, 113 *et seq.*

trade relies on credit supplied by banks and other financial institutions to SMEs that comprise 90 per cent of businesses and 50 per cent of employment globally.[5] Movable and intangible assets and their use as collateral may have positive impact on production and growth.[6] Lack of modern enforceability mechanisms to deal with security based on intangibles and receivables, or unclear nature of the law, may be cited as particular issues that hinder businesses from accessing credit. With the continuous effects of the credit crisis, the access to credit for businesses has become a significant problem in both developed and developing economies.[7]

The United Nations Commission on International Trade Law (UNCITRAL) has prepared the United Nations Convention on the Assignment of Receivables in International Trade (the Receivables Convention, the Convention) after almost a decade of careful work.[8] It was adopted in 2001.[9] The Receivables Convention promotes a sophisticated model for the modernization of domestic assignment laws, as well as overall harmonization of the law of assignment of receivables in international trade. It can, arguably, be considered as a substantive step towards the facilitation of cross-border flow of credit and access to low-cost credit. The widespread application of the Receivables Convention may lead to greater predictability and certainty in cross-border assignment of receivables. It covers outright and security transfers of receivables. The Receivables Convention removes legal obstacles to certain international financing practices, including securitization, factoring and project financing, by validating the assignment of future receivables and bulk assignments and assignments made notwithstanding anti-assignment agreements. It also introduces rules that unify the effectiveness of an assignment as between

5 www1.ifc.org/wps/wcm/connect/277d1680486a831abec2fff995bd23db/SM12_IFCIssueBrief_SMEs.pdf?MOD=AJPERES (last accessed 8 June 2013).

6 H. Fleisig, 'The Economics of Collateral and of Collateral Reform', in Dahan and Simpson (eds.), *Secured Transactions Reform*, pp. 81, 89 *et seq.*

7 According to Federation of Small and Medium Sized Businesses statistics, small businesses in the UK have serious problems in access to credit; *see* www.fsb.org.uk/ *Report on Number Crunching the Credit Crunch* (last accessed May 2012).

8 For the background to the project and its inception point, *see* Report of the Secretary General: *Study on Security Interests* (A/CN.9/131 and Annex). Previous attempts are a uniform conditional sales act enacted by Norway, Sweden and Denmark between 1915 and 1917; Unidroit Draft provisions of 1939 and 1951 concerning the impact of reservation of title in the sale of certain goods; provisions regarding the effect of bankruptcy of reservation of title in the sale of goods in the draft EEC Bankruptcy Convention of 1970; and model reservation of title clauses contained in several General Conditions elaborated by the UN Economic Commission for Europe: H.S. Burman, 'The Commercial Challenge in Modernizing Secured Transactions Law' *Uniform Law Review* 347, 348–9 (2003).

9 A/RES/56/81.

the assignor and the assignee, and as against the debtor. Legal predictability is also enhanced in the facilitation of credit by setting the law applicable to priorities between competing claims.[10] The Receivables Convention has adopted a mixture of rules on the formal validity of assignments and priority of the assignee's right in the assigned receivable against other competing claimants. In addition to a conflict-of-laws approach, there is an optional annex that serves as a model for substantive priority rules. The Convention also offers a model for the registration of security interests for the purposes of obtaining priority.[11]

This chapter will discuss the general principles of the Convention in facilitating the availability of and lowering the cost of credit. In particular, the chapter will seek to identify the utility and efficacy of the Receivables Convention in the availability of credit in the face of financial crisis. The recurrent theme is that modern rules that efficiently endorse receivables financing are critical in the reduction of the cost of credit and have the potential to increase cash flow and further investment in the face of financial crisis.

II. Availability of credit and the need for a predictable regime

Ability to access credit for businesses is essential for a number of reasons. Firstly, the ability to obtain credit is said to enable businesses to expand their operations and help create economic growth.[12] If the law provides favourable rules for the lender to be able to take security, credit may be

[10] On these issues *see, e.g.*, S. Bazinas, 'Key Policy Issues of the United Nations Convention on the Assignment of Receivables in International Trade' 11 *Tulane Journal of International and Comparative Law* 275 (2003); S. Bazinas, 'UNCITRAL's Work in the Field of Secured Transactions' 36 *Law Journal* 67 (2004); S. Bazinas, 'An International Legal Regime For Receivables Financing: UNCITRAL's Contribution' 8 *Duke Journal of International and Comparative Law* 315 (1998); S. Bazinas, 'Lowering the Cost of Credit: the Promise in the Future UNCITRAL Convention on Assignment of Receivables in International Trade' 9 *Tulane Journal of International and Comparative Law* 259 (2001); S. Bazinas, 'UNCITRAL's Contribution to the Unification of Receivables Financing Law: The United Nations Convention on the Assignment of Receivables in International Trade' *Uniform Law Review* 49 (2002); F. Ferrari, 'The UNCITRAL Draft Convention on Assignment in Receivables Financing: Applicability, General Provisions and the Conflict of Conventions' 1 *Melbourne Journal of International Law* 1 (2001); F. Ferrari, 'The UNCITRAL Draft Convention on Assignment in Receivables Financing: Critical Remarks on Some Specific Issues', in J. Basedow, I. Meier, A.K. Schnyder, T. Einhorn and D. Girsberger (eds.), *Private Law in the International Arena: Liber Amicorum Kurt Siehr* (The Hague: T.M.C. Asser Press, 2000), p. 179; M. Deschamps, 'The Priority Rules of the United Nations Receivables Convention' 12 *Duke Journal of International and Comparative Law* 389 (2002).

[11] Article 42(4).

[12] *See generally*, R. Levine, 'Finance and Growth: Theory and Evidence' *National Bureau of Economic Research, Working Paper 10766*, 85 (2004).

extended at lower cost. Thus, secured credit leads to economic activity and increases the opportunities for lending, while decreasing the risk of default.[13] Security is a necessary tool to prevent default of the debtor. This is because with the ability to take security, the risk of non-payment of credit will be reduced, as the lender will have a right of recourse to the collateral.[14] The debtor in the course of ordinary business may not take a decision that puts the collateral at risk.[15] The existence of the collateral and the lender's control over it may facilitate the access to credit. Secondly, the availability of credit may be a possibility if the lender has a priority position. This may be possible if there is security. The lender bargains for a priority position. If the law provides clear rules for lenders to obtain priority, access to credit is likely to be facilitated.[16] Thirdly, the existence of the collateral and the lender's control over it, as well as the responsiveness of the law to the needs of the financial community may act as catalysts in the businesses' access to credit. These factors may arguably lead to the lender's reduction of interest rates whereby the risk premium, which acts as a buffer for the lender in case of default,[17] may not be included in the interest rate, or the lender may agree to lend with long-term maturities.[18]

[13] *See* U. Drobnig 'Secured Credit in International Insolvency Proceedings' (33) *Commercial Law Journal* 53, at 54 (1998).

[14] Ibid.

[15] *See generally*, A. Schwartz, 'Priority Contracts and Priority in Bankruptcy' 82 *Cornell Law Review* 1396 (1997); R.J. Mann, 'Explaining the Pattern of Secured Credit' 110 *Harvard Law Review* 625, 683 (1997), where Mann concludes that secured credit '... [enhances] the borrower's ability to give a credible commitment to refrain from excessive future borrowing and by limiting the borrower's ability to engage in conduct that lessens the likelihood of payment'.

[16] However, there are different views on this matter. *See e.g.*, E. Warren, 'Making Policy with Imperfect Information: The Article 9 Full Priority Debates' 82 *Cornell Law Review* 1373 (1997); L.A. Bebchuk and J.M. Fried, 'The Uneasy Case for the Priority of Secured Claims in Bankruptcy' 105 *Yale Law Journal* 857 (1996); J. McDonnell, 'Is Revised Article 9 a Little Greedy?' 104 *Commercial Law Journal* 241, 262 (1999). In England, by virtue of the Enterprise Act 2002, a certain proportion of floating charge realizations has to be set aside for unsecured creditors (s. 252 and s. 176A of the Insolvency Act 1976).

[17] Banks in developing markets charge higher interest rates and fees in order to protect their interests against non-performing debtors. On this point, *see* T. Beck, A. Demirguc-Kunt and M.S. Martinez Peria, 'Bank Financing for SMEs around the World' *Policy Research Working Paper 4785* (2008).

[18] There has been a debate in the US on the correlation between 'long term loans' and 'security'. On this *see, e.g.*, T. Jackson and A. Kronman, 'Secured Financing and Priorities Among Creditors' 88 *Yale Law Journal* 1143, 1159 (1979); F.H. Buckley, 'The Bankruptcy Priority Puzzle' 72 *Virginia Law Review* 1393, 1444 (1986); S.L. Harris and C.W. Mooney, Jr, 'A Property Based Theory of Security Interests: Taking Debtors' Choices Seriously' 80 *Virginia Law Review* 2021, 2028 (1994); A. Schwartz, 'Security Interests and Bankruptcy Priorities: A Review of Current Theories' 10 *Journal of Legal Studies* 1, 13–14 (1981).

Empirical studies draw a correlation between long-term economic growth and that functioning of financial system.[19] Similar studies also established that legal and financial factors among others constrain a firm's growth, and that affected firms are consistently small ones.[20] The UNCITRAL Guide states that:

> [s]tudies have shown as the risk of non-payment is reduced, the availability of credit increases and the cost of credit fall. Studies have also shown that States where lenders perceive the risks associated with transactions to be high, the cost of credit increases as lenders require increased compensation to evaluate and assume the increased risk.[21]

There is a correlation between the borrower's financial strength and the attraction to secured credit. In that context, Professor Mann pointed out that 'borrowers exhibit an increasing tendency toward unsecured debt as their financial strength increases'.[22] Professor Wood similarly notes that public companies usually borrow on an unsecured basis, as they have sufficient credit strength and need to spread their sources of finance, and prefer to use negative pledge clauses in their contracts.[23] The Law Commission observed this preference and reported that 'well-established public companies are able to borrow readily on an unsecured basis, but for many smaller enterprises credit can be obtained on significantly better terms... if the borrower is able to offer security to the lender'.[24] This is also supported by empirical studies, which suggest that security is mainly used by small businesses that carry risk.[25] It is also clear that small businesses are mainly able to offer receivables owed to them as the only meaningful collateral in order to access credit. It is, therefore, important to modernize secured credit laws, or at least certain aspects

19 *See generally*, Levine, 'Finance and Growth'.

20 T. Beck, A. Demirguc-Kunt and V. Maksimovic 'Financial and Legal Constraints to Firm Growth: Does Size Matter?' 60 *Journal of Finance* 137 (2005).

21 A/CN.9/WG.6/WP.2 at para. 2.

22 Mann, 'Explaining the Pattern of Secured Credit', 674.

23 P. Wood, *Law and Practice of International Finance* (London: Sweet and Maxwell, 2008), p. 253. Fleisig empirically provides that in the US one-third of credit is unsecured and about two-thirds is secured: Fleisig, 'The Economics of Collateral and of Collateral Reform' 88.

24 Law Commission Report No. 296 (2005), para. 1.2.

25 J. Armour, 'The Law and Economics Debate About Secured Lending: Lessons For European Lawmaking?', in H. Eidenmüller and E.M. Kieninger (eds.), *The Future of Secured Credit in Europe, ECFR* special, vol. 2 (Munich: De Gruyter Recht, 2008), p. 3, at p. 9; M.A. Lasfer, 'Debt Structure, Agency Costs and Firm's Size: An Empirical Investigation' *Working Paper* Cass Business School, at 18 (2000). Lasfer concludes that small firms hold more secured and less unsecured debt than larger companies.

of them, to promote the availability of capital and credit at affordable rates.[26]

In terms of receivables financing and the use of receivables as collateral, restrictions over assignment of receivables adversely affect small businesses' access to credit. It was this aspect that led UNCITRAL to remove obstacles before receivables financing and modernize domestic systems[27] and thus 'unlock the dead capital'.[28] It has been argued that intangible property acts as the most valuable collateral and has advantages over tangible property.[29] Without an adequate system on security interests, States may be deprived of the opportunity to access low-cost credit. Collateral has clear significance in the private sector's access to low-cost credit.[30] The use of intangibles and movables in some developed countries is more attractive. However, financiers in economically less developed countries rather prefer the use of immovables as collateral.[31] It has been observed that 'in most countries *intangible capital* is the largest share of total wealth'.[32] Between 2001 and 2005, the World Bank Enterprise Surveys, conducted in sixty low- and middle-income countries, established that 22 per cent of company assets are land and buildings, 34 per cent accounts receivables and 44 per cent machinery. Nevertheless, as collateral only 9 per cent accounts receivables, 18 per cent machinery and 73 per cent lands and buildings are accepted.[33] The figures provide the evidence that in unreformed regimes there is strong confidence in

[26] *See e.g.*, Preamble to the Receivables Convention '*Being of the opinion* that the adoption of uniform rules governing the assignment of receivables would promote the availability of capital and credit at more affordable rates . . . '.

[27] A/CN.9/378/Add.3; A/48/17, paras. 297–301.

[28] M. Safavian, H. Fleisig and J. Steinbuks, 'Unlocking the Dead Capital', *View Point* Note Number 307 (March 2006).

[29] L. Gullifer (ed.), *Goode on Legal Problems of Credit and Security* (London: Sweet & Maxwell, 4th edn., 2009), pp. 2–3 and 95; H.L. Buxbaum, 'Unification of the Law Governing Secured Transactions: Progress and Prospects for Reform' (1/2) *Uniform Law Review* 322, at 324 (2003).

[30] H. Fleisig, M. Safavian and N. De la Pena, *Reforming Collateral Laws to Expand Access to Finance* (Washington DC: The World Bank, 2006), p. 1 *et seq.*

[31] *See generally, e.g.*, Safavian, 'Firm Level Evidence on Collateral and Access to Finance'; S. Simavi, 'Making Finance Work for Africa: The Collateral Debate', *World Bank PDP Forum*; 'Vietnam Increasing Access to Credit through Collateral (Secured Transactions) Reform' (IFC/MPDF, 2007); 'Reforming Collateral Laws and Registries: International Best Practices and the Case of China' (FIAS/IFC PEP China, March 2007).

[32] *Where is the Wealth of Nations? Measuring Capital For the 21st Century* (2006), 87 (emphasis added) available at http://siteresources.worldbank.org/INTEEI/214578-1110886258964/20748034/All.pdf (last accessed 10 May 2012).

[33] Safavian, Fleisig and Steinbuks 'Unlocking Dead Capital', at 2 and Figure 3.

tangible and immovable assets. However, in terms of modern financing this may be regarded as an inadequate system that fails to promote secured credit and recognize the value of receivables.[34] The economic impracticality of pledge of movables has been observed by UNCITRAL[35] and economists.[36] Complementing this finding, other empirical studies demonstrate the need to introduce non-possessory security in order to facilitate the availability of credit.[37] If the scope of security is expanded by modernizing the law, unlimited ability to use any types of assets as collateral, better creditor and predictable priority rights, SMEs in developing economies may have facilitated access to finance, as this will stimulate lending practices of banks.[38] Limitation on the ability to provide receivables or inventory as collateral has been illustrated in the World Bank studies.[39] Similar studies have also illustrated that the legal origin has an impact upon the availability of credit and creditor protection, and that common law jurisdictions have more tendency to lending and creditor protection than civil law jurisdictions.[40] Evidence gathered from these data established that facilitation of credit and access to credit are necessary in emerging markets. A similar line of argument applies equally for developed economies, where shortcomings of the law need to be eliminated in order to create a modern set of rules responsive to the needs of businesses.

The rationale of harmonization of rules governing receivables financing can, generally, be summarized as the facilitation of credit, increasing

34 For the key objectives of an effective and efficient secured transactions regime, *see* A/CN.9/631 recommendation 1.

35 UNCITRAL *Legislative Guide on Secured Transactions*, Chapter I, paras. 57 and 62, at 44 and 46.

36 Fleisig, 'The Economics of Collateral and of Collateral Reform' at p. 90, arguing that movable assets cannot effectively serve as collateral in unreformed economies; *see also* H. Fleisig, 'The Proposed Unidroit Convention on Mobile Equipment: Economic Consequences and Issues' *Uniform Law Review* 253, 256 (1999).

37 Armour, 'The Law and Economics Debate', 14–19.

38 *See generally*, R. Haselmann, K. Pistor and V. Vig, 'How Law Affects Lending' *Columbia Law and Economics Working Paper No. 285* (2006); M. Safavian and S. Sharma, 'When do Creditor Rights Work?' *Policy Research Working Paper No. 4296* (2007).

39 For further information, *see generally*, World Bank, 'Doing Business in 2004: Understanding Regulation' (Washington DC: Oxford University Press for the WB and IFC, 2004).

40 *See generally*, T. Beck, A. Demirguc-Kunt and R. Levine, 'Law and Firms' Access to Finance' *Policy Research Working Paper No. 3194* (2004); T. Beck, A. Demirguc-Kunt and R. Levine, 'Law and Finance: Why Does Legal Origin Matter?' *Policy Research Working Paper No. 2904* (Washington DC: World Bank, 2002).

cross-border trade and enabling small- and medium-sized businesses in developing markets to obtain access to low-cost credit. The law should be able to provide certain features in order to meet the needs of businesses effectively and that credit can be made available at low cost. From this perspective an efficient and effective secured credit law must contain certain characteristics and have objectives.[41] Similar arguments apply equally to the assignment of receivables. Receivables financing by its nature involves transfer of a continuous stream of receivables from the assignor to the assignee. This stream may involve both present and future receivables. However, not every legal system permits the assignment of future receivables. Assignment of future receivables is the backbone of many receivables financing transactions such as securitization. Some jurisdictions have special legislation to allow the assignment of future receivables for securitization practices.[42] Other jurisdictions do not recognize the assignment of future receivables on the basis of the specificity doctrine, according to which all receivables must be specifically indicated in the assignment contract at the time of the assignment and by virtue of a rather more interesting rule which already has many exceptions – the *nemo dat* rule. Further restrictions on the assignment of receivables in bulk, such as the requirement of specificity and notification of debtors as a condition of validity even as between the assignor and the assignee are significant impediments on receivables financing. Assignment of receivables in bulk is also used in factoring practices, in the context of which particularly the requirement of notification makes it an unworkable method of raising finance. Notification requirement for the effectiveness of an assignment is also a significant impediment before securitization practices, hence the

[41] These are clearly set out in the UNCITRAL *Legislative Guide on Secured Transactions* and include the promotion of secured credit, allowing utilization of the full value broad range of assets to support credit in the widest possible array of secured transactions, obtaining security rights in a simple and efficient manner, providing for equal treatment of diverse sources of credit and of diverse forms of secured transactions, validating security rights in assets that remain in the possession of the grantor, enhancing predictability and transparency with respect to rights serving security purposes by providing for registration of a notice in a general security rights registry, establishing clear and predictable priority rules, facilitation enforcement of creditors' rights in a predictable and efficient manner, balancing the interests of affected persons, recognizing party autonomy and harmonizing secured transactions laws, including conflict-of-laws rules. *See* Guide, Recommendation 1.

[42] A. Flessner and H. Verhagen, *Assignment in European Private International Law Claims as Property and the European Commission's 'Rome I Proposal'* (Munich: Sellier, 2006), pp. 6–7.

need for modernized harmonization of the law of assignment of receivables.

The assignor should be able to use all of the suitable assets as collateral to secure any obligation. However, in some legal systems receivables or intangibles are not regarded as acceptable types of collateral. The law should also be able to permit security to be taken over both future and existing assets of the assignor. It should protect the debtors while facilitating credit and promoting assignment practices by making law more transparent and modern. The law should also be able to ensure that third parties can be informed about the legal status of the assignor's property (whether it is subject to a security interest or whether it is sold) and that third-party effectiveness is achieved in a transparent way. Furthermore, the law should establish clear rules of priority for assignees.

III. Background of the Receivables Convention

Harmonization in the area of receivables financing is necessary for the facilitation of credit at lower costs, which is particularly beneficial for emerging markets, and reduces legal conflicts and costs in cross-border transactions. Appropriate legal reforms may achieve modernization and lead to economic growth. Divergence in the way national legal systems regulate taking security over or sale of receivables, which are matters deeply rooted in the cultural, legal and historical traditions of nations, increases the cost of credit in the global markets, and affects the competitiveness of businesses. Divergence in the way legal systems treat creation, third-party effectiveness, priority and enforcement of a security right affects the fundamental aspects of secured transactions laws,[43] and in the comparative perspective these differences arise out of the proprietary effects of security.[44] Particularly the role of possession in some civil law jurisdictions as the significant element in proprietary rights[45] is

[43] Report of the Secretary General: *Study on Security Interests* (A/CN.9/131 and Annex), reprinted in: 8 *Yearbook of the United Nations Commission on International Trade Law* 180 *et seq.* (1977). For a similar view, *see also generally* Buxbaum, 'Unification of the Law Governing Secured Transactions: Progress and Prospects for Reform' *Uniform Law Review* 322.

[44] For a comparative analysis of cross-border receivables financing, *see e.g.*, H.C. Sigman and E.M. Kieninger, *Cross-Border Security over Receivables* (Munich: Sellier, 2009).

[45] *See generally*, R. Goode, 'Reflections of the Harmonization of Commercial Law', in R. Cranston and R. Goode (eds.), *Commercial and Consumer Law: National and International Dimensions* (Oxford: Clarendon Press, 1993), vol. III, p. 12. For example, receivables are

considered to be an obstacle to the development of receivables financing and its harmonization.

The differences among national secured credit legislations were established by a report prepared by Professor Ulrich Drobnig.[46] This report suggested that the harmonization of secured transactions laws was at that time not possible due to their great divergence. It also reflected that the divergence of national laws was experienced in the fundamental aspects of security interests, including formality needed to create them, the limited recognition of non-possessory security, unitary security over all assets of the debtor, publicity and registration. The report also suggested three methods of harmonization of secured credit laws.[47] Following the Drobnig Report, UNCITRAL considered two further reports,[48] and a study on the feasibility of uniform rules on security interests was prepared.[49] Due to reasons such as a wide range of difference which are closely connected to insolvency laws and the obvious difficulties then existing in the harmonization work, the study on security interests was postponed until the 1990s.[50]

However, since the 1970s and 'with the accelerating pace of market interdependency [and the recognition of] . . . the importance of a sound legal regime for security interests in personal property, both for domestic and cross-border transactions',[51] there has been a movement towards the harmonization of secured transactions laws at both regional and international levels. This movement has resulted in the preparation of a number of important international instruments.[52] Following the UNCITRAL

intangible assets which cannot be transferred using traditional methods of transfer or security.

46 Report of the Secretary General: *Study on Security Interests* (A/CN.9/131 and Annex), reprinted in: 8 *Yearbook of the United Nations Commission on International Trade Law* 171 (1977); for a recent general report prepared by Professor Drobnig *see also* U. Drobnig, 'Present and Future of Real and Personal Security' 5 *European Review of Private Law* 623 (2003).

47 Recommendations, model law and conventions. See *Yearbook* at 218.

48 A/CN.9/130 and A/CN.9/132. These reports relate to the national systems' security interest laws and the other was related to the UCC Article 9.

49 UNCITRAL Report on its Tenth Session (1977) A/32/17, para. 37.

50 UNCITRAL Report on its Thirteenth Session (1980) A/35/17, paras. 26–28.

51 *See* R. Goode 'Harmonised Modernisation of the Law Governing Secured Transactions', Outline, in *Worldwide Harmonisation of Private Law and Regional Economic Integration*, Congress for the Celebration of the 75th Anniversary of Unidroit, Rome (2002) 7.

52 UN Convention on the Assignment of Receivables in International Trade (2001); Unidroit Convention on International Interests in Mobile Equipment (2001); OAS Model Inter-American Law on Secured Transactions (2002) and UNCITRAL *Legislative Guide on Secured Transactions.*

Congress in 1992,[53] UNCITRAL prepared three reports that elaborate the possibilities of the work on the assignment of receivables.[54] It identified certain legal problems in receivables financing. The reports concluded that it would be both desirable and feasible to develop a set of uniform rules in order to remove obstacles to international receivables financing.[55] UNCITRAL observed that:

> the diversity of national laws and the lack of standard transnational rules creates significant additional expenditure, delays and uncertainty [in] many international business transactions . . . [and] parties may be dissuaded from using receivables financing at all and are then forced to rely on . . . more expensive arrangements, such as overdraft facilities, letters of credit or export guarantees.[56]

Although the Receivables Convention has been signed by three countries and ratified by one,[57] feasibility studies as to the possibility of its adoption have been underway in North American jurisdictions.[58] It is believed that other countries will follow suit soon.[59]

IV. General principles of the Receivables Convention

The Convention validates assignments of future receivables and receivables assigned in bulk, and by partially invalidating contractual

[53] Uniform Commercial Law in the Twenty-First Century: Proceedings of the Congress of the United Nations Commission on International Trade Law. A/CN.9/378 Proposals for possible future work made at the UNCITRAL Congress: Note by the Secretariat, *Yearbook of the United Nations Commission on International Trade Law* vol. XXIV at 227 *et seq.* 1993.

[54] A/CN.9/378/Add.3; A/CN.9/397; A/CN.9/412.

[55] *See* A/CN.9/412 reprinted in *Yearbook of the United Nations Commission on International Trade Law* vol. XXVI at 228, para. 83 1995.

[56] 'UN investigates receivables financing' *International Trade Finance*, 3 June 1994; 213 ABI/INFORM Global at 4 *et seq.*

[57] www.uncitral.org/uncitral/en/uncitral_texts/payments/2001Convention_receivables_status.html (last accessed 10 May 2012).

[58] For calls urging the US to adopt the Receivables Convention, *see e.g.*, R.M. Kohn, 'Convention to bolster exports and jobs U.N. Pact would increase business loans based on receivables' *The Washington Times*, 6 March 2012. *See e.g.*, Uniform Law Conference of Canada, www.ulcc.ca/en/us/Assignment_Receivables_International_Trade_En.pdf (last accessed 10 May 2012); National Conference of Commissioners on Uniform State Laws (NCCUSL) www.law.upenn.edu/bll/archives/ulc/aor/2007june_amreport.htm (last accessed 10 May 2012). Particularly in the United States the self-execution method of implementation may be chosen. *See* www.uncitral.org/pdf/english/colloquia/3rdSecTrans/Ed_Smith_Implementation.pdf (last accessed 10 May 2012).

[59] *See generally*, S. Bazinas, R.M. Kohn and L.F. del Duca, 'Facilitating a Cost-Free Path to Economic Recovery-Implementing a Global Uniform International Receivables Financing Law' 44 *UCC Law Journal* 277 (2012).

limitations to the assignment of receivables. Certainty is achieved with respect to the rights of the assignor and assignee, as well as with respect to the effectiveness of the assignment as against the debtor. The Convention also establishes a much debated conflict-of-laws provision on priority of competing claims. It also provides a substantive law regime as an optional annex governing priority between competing claims.

1. Applicability

1.1 Scope of application as to substance

The scope of application of the Receivables Convention is based on the scope of the terms '*assignment*' and '*receivables*'. These two terms have been defined together with the terms 'debtor', 'assignor' and 'assignee' in article 2(a). The term 'assignment' encompasses assignments by way of sale and for security purposes, contractual subrogation and possessory security interests (pledge), thus the Convention adopts a functional approach to receivables financing.[60] It excludes unilateral assignments and transfers by operation of law, such as statutory subrogation.[61] It does not deal with the nature of a transfer as an assignment by way of sale or security. The matter has been left to the law applicable outside the Convention.[62] This may be a cause for concern from a harmonization perspective, as an assignment by way of sale and by way of security are distinct, and not all jurisdictions treat them in a unitary manner.[63]

[60] For further discussion, *see e.g.*, C. Walsh, 'Security Interests in Receivables', in Eidenmüller and Kieninger (eds.), *The Future of Secured Credit in Europe*, pp. 321, 322 *et seq.*

[61] S. Bazinas, 'UNCITRAL's Contribution to the Unification of Receivables Financing Law: the United Nations Convention on the Assignment of Receivables in International Trade' *Uniform Law Review* 49, at 51 (2002). It should be noted, however, that not all forms of subrogation will necessarily be by operation of law, and that it depends on intention; *see generally*, C. Mitchell, *Subrogation: Law and Practice* (Oxford University Press, 2007).

[62] *See* Explanatory Note of the UNCITRAL Secretariat on the United Nations Convention on the Assignment of Receivables in International Trade (New York: United Nations Publications, 2004), at 29.

[63] *E.g.* Under English law assignment by way of sale and security are treated distinctly. Under s. 136 Law of Property Act 1925 the assignment must be absolute and not by way of charge. While the assignment by way of security is registered as a charge under CA 2006, sale of receivables is not registered. The Law Commission Report supported the registration of outright sales to create certainty and transparency and to reduce the cost of credit. *See* paras 1.12 and 2.34–2.39. Whilst an assignment by way of security may be set aside for grounds related to the Insolvency Act 1986 (*e.g.* defrauding creditors, transactions at an undervalue), assignment by way of sale cannot be set aside except where the discount is extortionate. An assignment by way of security may be prohibited, whereas an outright sale

The term 'receivable' in general indicates a present or future right to payment deriving from contracts of sale or services. Receivables may arise from either commercial or consumer contracts. Receivables arising out of the rights of parties under a negotiable instrument, consumer transactions or real estate transactions, such as rents, fall within the scope of the Convention. These types of receivables constitute significant income revenues. However, under article 4(3)–(5), the Receivables Convention cannot affect the rights of certain parties to the assignment of such receivables. This is particularly important since for public policy reasons the Convention takes the position that consumer protection legislation should not be adversely affected. Similarly, it takes the position that State sovereignty over the immovable property should not be adversely affected. Disputes between the assignee and a person with a right over the property related to receivables arising out of immovable property are referred to the law of the State where the immovable property is located.[64] The Receivables Convention limits its scope under article 4(1) and (2), by excluding assignments of certain types of receivables and certain types of assignments. The rationale for excluding the latter being 'lack of market'.[65] These excluded assignments are made to individuals for personal, family or household use and as part of the sale or change in the ownership or legal status of the business out of which the assigned receivables arose. Thus, it is arguable that the Receivables Convention aims to include those assignments that are related to the continuous flow of receivables.

cannot. *See* L.S. Sealy and R.J.A. Hooley, *Commercial Law: Text, Cases and Materials* (London: Butterworths, 3rd edn., 2003), p. 983. In the outright sales or factoring of receivables, the financier is concerned with the value of the receivable as opposed to the creditworthiness of the SME. *See generally*, L. Klapper, 'The Role of Factoring for Financing Small and Medium Enterprises' *World Bank Policy Research Working Paper 3593* (2005). *See also, Siebe Gorman & Co Ltd* v. *Barclays Bank Ltd.* [1979] 2 Lloyd's Law Reports 142; *Re Kent and Sussex Sawmills Ltd.* [1947] Ch. 177; *Lloyds & Scottish Finance* v. *Cyril Lord Carpet Sales* [1992] BCLC 609. On the other hand, UCC Article 9 treats assignments by way of security and by way of sale more or less the same for purposes of perfection and priorities, but differently for enforcement purposes. Filing an assignment by way of sale under UCC Article 9 does not convert this transaction into a secured transaction.

64 *See* S. Bazinas, 'Multi-Jurisdictional Receivables Financing: UNCITRAL's Impact on Securitization and Cross-Border Perfection' 12 *Duke Journal of Comparative and International Law* 365, n. 14 (2002); *but cf.* H. Sigman and E. Smith, 'Toward Facilitating Cross Border Secured Financing and Securitization: An Analysis of the United Nations Convention on the Assignment of Receivables in International Trade' 57 *Business Lawyer* 727, at 735–6 (2002).

65 Explanatory Note of the UNCITRAL Secretariat, para. 11, at 30.

Receivables arising out of financial contracts governed by netting agreements, foreign exchange transactions, deposit accounts, letters of credit or independent guarantees, inter-bank payments, receivables arising under securities[66] and transactions on a regulated exchange are excluded. These receivables are sufficiently regulated[67] and it would be futile to create an overlapping regulation.[68]

1.2 Territorial scope of application

The Receivables Convention applies to international assignment of domestic receivables (international assignment connection) and to domestic assignment of international receivables (international receivable connection).[69] The Convention applies when there is an international assignment or an international receivable. Exceptionally, it also applies to some extent to the domestic assignment of domestic receivables.[70] The connecting factor is location of the assignor.

Internationality is based on the time of the original contract out of which the receivables arise and the time of the contract of assignment (article 3). The Receivables Convention applies to assignments that are international at the time of the conclusion of the contract of assignment or to receivables that are international at the time of the original contract. The international criterion is met when the receivables are assigned internationally or the assignment relates to international receivables. The applicability is expanded by fixing internationality on both the assignment, and the receivable. An '*international assignment*' is an assignment where the assignor and the assignee are located in different States, as it relates to the contract of assignment, and an '*international receivable*' is a receivable where the assignor and the debtor are located in different States, as it relates to the original contract.

66 The Convention especially by virtue of article 4(2)(e), excludes transactions involving the assignment of receivables from securities or other financial assets or instruments held by an intermediary. For more information *see* The Report of the UNCITRAL 34th session, U.N. G.A.O.R. 56th session, Suppl. No. 17, P135, UN Doc. A/56/17 (2001).

67 Such as letters of credit and independent guarantees that have been regulated in the international arena with the 1995 United Nations Convention on Independent Guarantees and Stand-by Letters of Credit.

68 *See e.g.*, Bazinas, 'Lowering the Cost of Credit: The Promise in the Future UNCITRAL Convention on Assignment of Receivables in International Trade' 268; Bazinas, Kohn and Del Duca, 'Facilitating a Cost-Free Path' at 286 noting that assignments to a consumer under article 4(1)(a) do not occur often in practice.

69 Article 1(1)(a).

70 Article 1(1)(a) and (b).

A fictional location has traditionally been attributed to intangible property; however, this is far from satisfactory.[71] The location under the Receivables Convention is the real location of the assignor where the insolvency proceedings will be commenced. The determination of the time of location under article 22 is the time of the conclusion of the contract of assignment.[72] Ascertaining the location under the Convention will assist parties to determine the law applicable to priority, and priority has no relevance to the question of who the debtor should pay. This latter aspect is related to the discharge of debt, and under both the Rome I Regulation article 14(2) and the Receivables Convention it is adequately protected.

The definition of the term '*location*' under article 5(h) affects both the scope of application of the Convention and the priority rule envisaged under article 22. It is defined as the place of business of a person (in the case of several places of business, the central administration)[73] or, in the event there is no place of business, the habitual residence of a person. In the case of multiple places of business of the debtor, the Convention's approach is different. Location in that regard refers to the place which has the closest relationship to the relevant transaction.[74] As a result, if the assignor's central administration is located in a Contracting State, the Convention applies even to assignments made through branch offices.[75]

The Convention, in principle, does not apply to domestic assignments of domestic receivables. However, there are two exceptions. The first arises when there is a subsequent assignment under article 1(1)(b). The Receivables Convention '. . . applies to such subsequent assignments irrespective of whether the subsequent assignments are international or relate to international receivables, provided that any prior assignment in the chain of subsequent assignments is governed by the Convention'.[76] Therefore the

[71] For discussion and criticism of attributing a *situs see e.g.*, P. Rogerson, 'The Situs of Debts in the Conflict of Laws – Illogical, Unnecessary and Misleading' 49 *CLJ* 441, 453 *et seq.* (1990).

[72] A/CN.9/455, paras. 19 and 21.

[73] *See also* E.M. Kieninger and H. Sigman, 'The Rome I Proposed Regulation and the Assignment of Receivables', *The European Legal Forum*, 1–2006, 3.

[74] Explanatory Note of the UNCITRAL Secretariat, para. 19, at 32. The Note suggests that the place of central administration can also be understood '(in other words, the principal place of business or the main centre of interests)'.

[75] For further information *see* ibid., at 32–33, para. 20.

[76] Ibid., at 31, para. 15.

Convention is applicable to that domestic receivable.[77] This regulation on subsequent assignments broadens the applicability of the Convention. The second exception arises where the Convention covers all priority issues by being applicable to the conflicts between the domestic assignee of a domestic receivable and a foreign assignee of the same domestic receivable, by virtue of articles 5(m)(i) and 22. In the application of priority provisions, the law of the assignor's State shall apply and govern the priority of the right of the assignee in the above alternatives.

2. Contractual and statutory limitations and the effectiveness of an assignment

The Receivables Convention removes certain contractual and statutory restrictions to assignment of receivables. Anti-assignment clauses in underlying contracts and restrictions on the assignment of future receivables and receivables assigned in bulk are significant obstacles to modern financing transactions.

2.1 Statutory restrictions

Article 8 aims to facilitate the flow of credit by eliminating statutory limitations in national laws. In this context, the Convention especially facilitates financing practices such as securitization, project financing and asset-based financing by recognizing the effectiveness of the assignment of future receivables and receivables not identified individually. Certain legal systems restrict the assignment of future receivables and receivables assigned in bulk in order to protect the assignor from over-charging its assets.[78] The cost of credit is increased by describing each receivable upon its creation and notifying the debtor of every receivable, and this difficulty is multiplied by the administrative work to ensure an effective transfer. Administrative costs arise when the assignor and the assignee create new agreements each time a receivable comes into existence.

There are particular reasons for restricting these types of assignments. One of the main reasons States restrict assignment of future and bulk receivables is to protect 'the assignor from excessive limitations on its

[77] A/CN.9/489, para. 38 and also paras. 19–20. ('[I]f a receivable is domestic, its assignment may come within the ambit of the . . . Convention if it is international or it is part of a chain of assignments that includes an earlier international assignment.')

[78] For a similar assertion, *see* Bazinas, 'Lowering the Cost of Credit: The Promise in the Future UNCITRAL Convention on Assignment of Receivables in International Trade' *Tulane Journal of International and Comparative Law* 265.

economic activity, addressed by requirements for a specific description of the assigned receivable'.[79] The reasoning behind the concerns over assignments of bulk and future receivables is that these types of financing practices may have impact 'on the economic freedom of the assignor or related specificity concerns'.[80] The restriction of security over future receivables arises out of 'the desire to restrict security and . . . the desire to prevent future property being caught up as a security for pre-existing debt'.[81] Also, in some legal systems statutory prohibitions on bulk assignments have been justified with the 'concerns about the advantage gained by [large] financing institutions, obtaining a bulk assignment . . . and future receivables from their borrowers, over small suppliers, who are often protected by retention of title arrangements'.[82]

Due to specificity and publicity requirements, the assignability of future receivables is recognized in most jurisdictions with the exception of traditional Napoleonic legal systems.[83] Specificity and publicity doctrines may not be compatible with the requirements of modern finance. The doctrine of specificity[84] may be defined as identification, specification and separation of the asset from the transferor's assets in order to be assigned.[85] This separation may be either in the form of specification of the debtor or the information on the receivable. The rationale of specification is that the owner of assets needs to be known in order for it to be transferred. Publicity and specificity are intertwined and the former depends on the latter, because publicity may require some form of creditor's control or possession over the assets and, for this, assets need to be specifically

[79] Ibid. [80] Bazinas, 'Multi-Jurisdictional Receivables Financing' 371.

[81] P. Wood, *Comparative Law of Security and Guarantees* (London: Sweet & Maxwell, 1995), p. 41.

[82] Bazinas, 'Multi-Jurisdictional Receivables Financing' 372.

[83] K. Zweigert and H. Kötz, *An Introduction to Comparative Law* (Oxford: Clarendon Press, 3rd edn., 1998), p. 445 *et seq.*; *see also* P. Wood, 'World-Wide Security – Classification of Legal Jurisdictions', in J. Norton and M. Andenas (eds.), *Emerging Financial Markets and Secured Transactions* (London: Kluwer, 1998), pp. 39, 40 *et seq.*

[84] This doctrine was abolished in England by *Tailby* v. *Official Receiver* (1888) LR 13 App. Cas. 523 and *Holroyd* v. *Marshall* (1861) 10 HLC 191, [1861–1873] All ER Rep 414. The doctrine has three bases. Firstly, one cannot transfer an asset unless the asset is identified. Secondly, if a security is created at the present time over a future asset to cover an existing debt, then this is actually a creation of security for a pre-existing debt when the asset comes into existence and is treated as a potentially voidable preference. Thirdly, there may be a prejudice against debtors granting security over all of their future receivables, and thereby either destroying their means of income or weakening the cushion available to unsecured creditors, *see* Wood, *Comparative Law of Security and Guarantees*, p. 40 *et seq.*

[85] P. Wood, *Maps of World Financial Law* (London: Allen & Overy LLP, 2005), p. 83.

identified otherwise the transfer cannot be publicized.[86] Under the publicity requirement, if an assignment requires notification of the debtor whose identity may not be known at the time of the contract of assignment, that may be considered as an obstacle to the assignment of future receivables. The critical problem with notification to underlying obligors is that it provides no means of constituting a present pledge of the future accounts of a business, since there is no debtor to notify until the right to payment arises.[87]

These systems require the assignor to specify each receivable before assigning it. The Receivables Convention article 8(1) recognizes the effectiveness of an assignment of future receivables and receivables that are not identified individually. An assignment cannot be deemed as ineffective as against the assignor, the assignee, and the debtor or a third party just because it is an assignment of future receivables or a receivable that is not individually identified at the time of the assignment. The only condition that the Convention sets in article 8(1)(a) and (b) is that these receivables should be identified as receivables to which the assignment relates. It does not require a specific description of the receivables, and the description can even be general, so long as the receivables may be identified in the contract of assignment. If the parties provide general descriptions in an assignment, this will be effective as long as receivables are described in such a manner that they can be identified as receivables to which the assignment relates, which means that the debtor and the amount owed should be identifiable in order for the assignments made in bulk to be valid.

Article 8(1)(b) provides that assignments of future receivables are to be given effect provided that the receivables can, at the time of the conclusion of the original contract, be identified as receivables to which the assignment relates. Further, in relation to bulk assignments, they should

86 Wood, *Law and Practice of International Finance*, p. 258.

87 *See* R. Serick, *Securities in Movables in German Law: An Outline* (Deventer: Kluwer, 1990), pp. 81–2 (where he argues that this sort of limitation as to future accounts, rather than a desire to maintain secrecy, is the main reason why pledges of intangibles are not generally used in German financing practice); *see also* J. Rakob, 'Germany', in Sigman and Kieninger, *Cross-Border Security over Tangibles*, p. 63, arguing:

> . . . the creation of a pledge over receivables requires that notice of the pledge be sent to the third party debtor. This . . . made pledges unpopular – loss of possession deprives the pledgor of the chance to work with the collateral, notice to third party debtors of receivables may damage the reputation and credit of the pledgor or may confuse the debtor about who to pay to.

be identifiable at the time of the assignment, if they cannot be identified individually by virtue of article 8(1)(a). Once again, identification of the exact moment at which the transfer becomes effective would clarify doubts in those legal systems where bulk assignments and assignments of future receivables are not recognized due to different problems. Effectuating the assignment of future receivables as of the time of the conclusion of the original contract 'would not compromise the rights of the assignee, since in practice credit was extended at the time when an actual transaction from which receivables might flow was concluded'.[88] It is a correct approach to give effectiveness to the assignment of future receivables as of the time of the original contract as opposed to the time of the assignment, since the assignor might assign the same receivable to another person; therefore the Convention protects the interests of the assignee and takes a step towards the facilitation of credit.[89]

Under article 8(2), there is no need of a new contract of assignment to be executed when there is an assignment of future receivables and the future receivable thereafter arises or is created naturally, and can be identified in the contract of assignment. The rationale is that future receivables arise after the contract of assignment, therefore there is no need to have a new assignment document covering that receivable. Article 10(1) supplements the position and provides that a personal or property right securing payment of the assigned receivable is transferred to the assignee without a new act of transfer.

2.2 Contractual restrictions

The Receivables Convention under article 9(1) recognizes the effectiveness of an assignment made notwithstanding an anti-assignment

[88] *See* A/CN.9/434, para. 118.

[89] *See generally*, B. Markell, 'UNCITRAL's Receivables Convention: The First Step, But not the Last', 12 *Duke Journal of Comparative and International Law* 401 (2002). *See also* A/CN.9/445, para. 224, where it was noted that:

> [t]here was general support for the principle that a future receivable should be deemed as having been transferred at the time of the contract of assignment. It was observed that, in view of the risk that, after the conclusion of the contract of assignment, the assignor might assign the same receivables to another assignee or become insolvent, it was essential to set the time of the transfer of the assigned receivables at the time of the conclusion of the contract of assignment... in practice, the assignee would acquire rights in future receivables only when they arose, but in legal terms the time of transfer would be deemed to be the time of the contract of assignment.

clause.[90] The assignment made in those circumstances will be effective as against the debtor and third parties such as the creditors of the assignor and his trustee in bankruptcy. Effectiveness of an assignment in violation of an anti-assignment clause would not adversely affect small debtors, as 'they do not have the bargaining power to insert anti-assignment clauses in their contracts and . . . would continue paying the same bank account or post office box'.[91] This approach would not affect large debtors, as they have sufficient bargaining power.[92] The Receivables Convention protects the assignee under article 9(2) by providing that the breach of an anti-assignment clause by the assignor is not in itself a sufficient reason for the avoidance of the original contract by the debtor. The liability of the assignor for breach of the anti-assignment clause is preserved under the Receivables Convention; however, the debtor may not terminate the agreement on the grounds of breach of an anti-assignment clause (articles 9(2) and 10(3)). This approach prevents the debtor avoiding the contract and strengthening his bargaining power.[93] It is argued that the assignee is given some confidence in the outcome of the transaction. The assignor may be held liable for breach of contract as a result of anti-assignment, but the right to compensatory damages that the debtor may have under the applicable law has been left outside the Receivables Convention.[94] Article 9(2) expressly protects a person who is not party to an agreement between the assignor and the debtor on the sole ground that he had knowledge of the agreement. In general, the knowledge of the assignee of the anti-assignment clause is irrelevant and he cannot be held liable on the sole ground of his knowledge of it; there must be additional grounds to knowledge in order for the assignee to be held liable as the third party. However, knowledge may be relevant in the case of tortious liability of the assignee, such as for malicious interference with

[90] For a more detailed treatment of anti-assignment clauses under the Receivables Convention, *see e.g.*, O. Akseli, 'Contractual Prohibitions on Assignment of Receivables: An English and UN Perspective' *JBL* 650 [2009]. In the US under the UCC Article 9 regime, UCC §9–406(d) provides free alienability of rights to payment and that any agreement between an account debtor (*debtor*) and an assignor is ineffective.

[91] A/CN.9/WG.II/WP.105, para. 83; *see also* A/CN.9/489, para. 103.

[92] A/CN.9/WG.II/WP.105, para. 83. The Addendum to the Legislative Guide on Secured Transactions para. 230 clearly indicates that a debtor such as a consumer may protect itself through statutory prohibitions, A/CN.9/631/Add.1.

[93] Bazinas, 'Key Policy Issues of the United Nations Convention on the Assignment of Receivables in International Trade' 287.

[94] A/CN.9/489, para. 99.

advantageous relations.[95] Article 18(3) of the Receivables Convention does not allow the debtor to make a claim for breach of an anti-assignment clause against the assignee by way of set-off so as to defeat the assignee's demand for payment. The Contracting States are not permitted to make a declaration to override the effectiveness of the provision of free assignability. Under article 40, a Contracting State is permitted to declare whether an assignment of a receivable owed by a governmental debtor in that State will be excluded from the Convention rules that override contractual anti-assignment terms. Although the Convention overrides the effectiveness of anti-assignment clauses by virtue of article 9, this provision will have no effect on a sovereign debtor who is located in a Contracting State if that State makes a declaration by virtue of article 40 and article 9 does not apply to restrictions arising by statute or other rule of law. It could have been a better and more consolidated approach had the Receivables Convention treated sovereign debtors and ordinary debtors on an equal basis and granted effectiveness to assignments made notwithstanding an anti-assignment clause between assignors and sovereign debtors.[96]

3. *Priority of competing claimants*

The Receivables Convention regulates priority disputes through carefully designed conflict-of-laws rules and an optional annex containing substantive rules. While the conflict-of-laws rule of the Receivables Convention has received both support and criticism,[97] it is a sophisticated and potentially far-reaching rule.

The significance of having clear rules on priority disputes is that an assignee needs to know its priority position or, at least, what law will determine its priority position, before extending credit. Unclear priority rules carry the risk of increasing the cost of credit. The Convention defines *priority* under article 5(g) and *competing claimant* under article 5(m). *Priority* is defined in a way that includes both the concept of perfection and

95 A/CN.9/470, para. 102; *see also* A/CN.9/WG.II/WP.105, para. 85.

96 *Cf.* A/CN.9/466, paras. 107–115.

97 *See e.g.*, L. Steffens, 'The New Rule on the Assignment of rights in Rome I – The Solution to All our Proprietary Problems?: Determination of the Conflict of Laws rule in respect of the Proprietary Aspects of Assignment' 4 *European Review of Private Law* 543 (2006); Flessner and Verhagen, *Assignment in European Private International Law*; R. Verhagen, 'Assignment in the Commission's "Rome I Proposal"' *LMCLQ* 270 (2006); Financial Markets Law Committee, Issue 121 – European Commission Final Proposal for a Regulation on the Law Applicable to Contractual Obligations (Rome I) October 2006 and April 2006.

priority of UCC Article 9.[98] In this connection, priority includes whether the claimant has a proprietary or a personal right. Whether an assignment is an outright assignment or an assignment by way of security and whether the necessary requirements to render the right effective against a competing claimant have been satisfied are not treated distinct from priority. Thus, priority may mean validity. The definition of a *competing claimant* covers all potential priority conflicts.[99] The formal validity of the assignment as a condition of priority is subject to the law of the assignor's location (articles 22 and 5(g)).

In many jurisdictions priority issues with respect to security rights in tangible assets are normally decided according to the *lex situs*. However, attribution of a fictional location to receivables is not feasible.[100] One of the main reasons for this is that the traditional *lex situs* rule is regarded as inefficient and outdated, particularly in the assignment of future receivables and bulk assignments.[101] *Lex situs* does not provide clear results because at the time of the contract of assignment when the debt has not yet come into existence (as in the case of assignment of future receivables), location cannot be ascertainable. In the case of bulk assignment the *lex situs* rule will lead to the complex results according to which the assignee will be required to execute extensive due diligence to ascertain the applicable law in each case. Furthermore, 'there is no universal agreement on where a receivable is located'.[102] Especially in international receivables financing transactions or in bulk assignments and assignments of future receivables, parties will have to face the difficulty of determining the location of receivables in order to find the applicable substantive law and it will create unworkable results if the law governing the receivable or the law chosen by the parties apply. The law of the receivable also 'exposes retrospective assignees to the burden of having to determine the notional *situs* of each receivable separately'.[103] The law of the assigned receivable may create acceptable results in the assignment of single receivables or financial contracts, receivables arising from securities, swap agreements, claims arising from bank accounts and foreign

[98] *See* Sigman and Smith, 'Toward Facilitating Cross Border Secured Financing' 747. UCC Article 9 §9–308(a).

[99] A/CN.9/489, para. 77.

[100] For a criticism of attributing a *situs* to book debts, *see* Rogerson, 'The Situs of Debts' 453 *et seq.*

[101] For a similar view, *see* M. Moshinsky, 'The Assignment of Debts in the Conflict of Laws' 108 *LQR* 591, at 610 (1992).

[102] A/CN.9/489/Add.1, para. 30.

[103] Ibid.

exchange transactions;[104] in the assignment of bulk receivables it proves to be burdensome for the assignee to check each document to ascertain whether the receivable is assignable.[105] Further, as all receivables cannot have the same *situs*, the assignee will be forced to execute due diligence for each receivable. Application of divergent laws to priority and formal validity issues causes inconvenience for the assignee. Finally, allowing party autonomy for property aspects of an assignment and to govern priority of competing assignees cannot provide correct results. This has the risk of increasing the cost of credit for assignors despite the possibility that assignees may subject credit to the selection of favourable law. The law of the assignment contract does not take into consideration third party rights and may lead to divergent laws applicable to two competing rights. Parties with strong bargaining powers generally impose laws favourable to their interests. Thus, the law of the assignor presents workable results, particularly in international trade. However, there are different views in relation to the utility and efficacy of the law of the assignor location.[106]

An assignee under the Convention's priority rule needs to comply with the priority rules of the law of the assignor's State for the purposes of perfection and priority. This causes concern in some States that require a public filing system as a condition precedent to the third-party effectiveness of an assignment.[107] The reason for this is that some States where the assignor is located may not have a developed priority system or a public disclosure system. Once the conflict-of-laws rule leads the assignee and third parties to the law of the assignor's State, the substantive priority rules contained in the annex become crucial. One can argue that this two-step priority solution may lead to harmonization. This is because third parties and the assignee will, at least, have the certainty that the law of the assignor's State will apply, and this law, on the substantive basis,

[104] The Receivables Convention article 4(2) excludes these transactions and receivables from their scope.

[105] For some suggestions and a brief overview *see* Walsh, 'Security Interests in Receivables', p. 321.

[106] For a treatment of different conflict-of-laws rules and the Rome I Regulation, *see* T.C. Hartley, 'Choice of Law Regarding the Voluntary Assignment of Contractual Obligations under the Rome I Regulation' 60 *ICLQ* 29 (2011).

[107] *See e.g.*, Report of the Committee on Foreign and Comparative Law of the Association of the Bar of the City of New York (December 21, 2001), at 10 (where it was stated. 'Although . . . a choice of law rule, is by no means a negligible accomplishment, it is something of a disappointment for those legal practitioners and business people who operate in States which have filing systems and who were hoping to see such a system established worldwide').

will be either of these substantive law priority rules in the optional annex if they opted in, or another one, i.e. the substantive law of the assignor's State. The merit of the optional annex has been explained as follows: 'One of the purposes of the Annex is to provide a framework for future development of such a worldwide system, [p]erhaps if a few States create an international filing system, others will be able to observe its merits in action.'[108]

'Location' under the Convention 'was considered as being the real location of the [assignor] and . . . it leads to the law of the State in which the main insolvency proceedings [against the assignor] would most likely be opened'.[109] Professor Walsh focuses on two possible methods to define location. These are the assignor's actual centre of administration or the legal centre of the assignor's business, which may be either the place under whose laws it is constituted or where it is registered.[110] The time for the determination of location under article 22, for predictability purposes, is the time of conclusion of the contract of assignment.[111] The law of the assignor's State where the assignor has more than one place of business will be determined at the time of the assignment, and is the place where the central administration of the assignor is exercised. The location of the assignor 'would result in the application of the law of the jurisdiction in which any main insolvency proceeding with regard to the assignor would be most likely to commence'.[112]

The key advantage of article 22 is that, in the event of insolvency of the assignor, the law governing the priority and the law governing the insolvency of the assignor will be the same (i.e. the law of the assignor's State). Thus, the applicable law will not be set aside because its application may be manifestly contrary to the public policy or mandatory rules of the forum. This article is subject to articles 23 and 24 (mandatory law and public policy exceptions and special law on priority in proceeds). Under article 23, mandatory rules of the forum or the applicable law cannot override the law of the location of the assignor. However, in an insolvency

[108] Ibid.

[109] Article 5(h); UNCITRAL *Legislative Guide on Secured Transactions*, para. 21, at 395.

[110] C. Walsh, 'Receivables Financing and the Conflict of Laws: The UNCITRAL Draft Convention on the Assignment of Receivables in International Trade' 106 *Dickinson Law Review* 159, 175 (2001).

[111] Receivables Convention article 1(1)(a) '. . . if, at the time of conclusion of the contract of assignment, the assignor is located in a Contracting State, . . .'. For a similar determination of time formula, *see* Rome I Regulation, article 19(3).

[112] A/CN.9/489/Add.1, para. 32.

proceeding commenced in a State other than the assignor's State, any preferential right that arises and is given priority over the rights of the assignee in insolvency proceedings may be given priority notwithstanding the application of the law of the location of the assignor.

The optional annex comprises substantive law priority rules, which the Contracting States may opt into if they 'wish to modernize or to adjust their laws to accommodate assignments under the Convention'.[113] The rules are based on UCC Article 9 (first registration in time), English law (*Dearle* v. *Hall*) and the civil law system (first assignment in time). As prescribed in article 42(4), even if a State applies its own priority rules, they can still utilize the registration system in order to benefit from the main objectives of the Convention and to create certainty in receivables financing. One of the main reasons the Commission has prepared this optional annex is that some States may have no national priority rules, or the rules that they have may be outdated or not fully adequate for addressing all relevant problems.[114]

3.1 Priority rules based on registration

Sections I and II of the optional annex deal with registration and aim to provide notice to potential financiers that certain receivables may have been assigned, and it establishes priority. The rule on priority among several assignees, under Section I article 1 of the optional annex, is that the assignee that registers the data about the assignment first gains priority. If no such data are registered, priority will be determined by the order of conclusion of the respective contracts of assignment. The rationale underlying such registration is 'not to create or constitute evidence of property rights, but to protect third parties by putting them on notice about assignments made and to provide a basis for settling conflicts of priority between competing claims'.[115] Section I article 2 regulates the priority between the assignee and the insolvency administrator or creditors of the assignor. The main point in article 2 is that, if registration takes place and the receivable is assigned before the commencement of insolvency proceedings in relation to the assets and affairs of the assignor, the assignee will have priority. Section II article 3 sets out the details of establishment of a registration system. This is an especially important guide for Contracting States that do not have a registration system. The registry

[113] Bazinas, 'Multi-Jurisdictional Receivables Financing' 380 *et seq.*

[114] A/CN.9/489/Add.1, para. 72. [115] Ibid., para. 74.

is open to any person to search the records according to identification of the assignor, and a search in writing can be obtained. The written search result issued by the registry is admissible as evidence and is proof of the registration of the data to which the search relates. The registration is proposed to be simple and inexpensive and requires a limited amount of data by virtue of article 4, which establishes the basic characteristics for an efficient system, and, therefore, an assignee and an assignor would not be required to register information that is too detailed. These basic characteristics are 'the public character of the registry, the type of data that need to be registered, the ways in which the registration-related needs of modern financing practices may be accommodated and the time of effectiveness of registration'.[116]

3.2 Priority rules based on the time of the contract of assignment

Article 6 deals with priority among several assignees based on the order of the conclusion of the respective contracts of assignment. Article 7 is concerned with priority between the assignee and the insolvency administrator or creditors of the assignor. The right of the assignee has priority over the right of an insolvency administrator and creditors, provided that the receivable is assigned before the commencement of insolvency proceedings. The time of the assignment may be established by any method of proof under article 8.

The time of the assignment determines priority, although under the *nemo dat* rule, after the first assignment, the assignor cannot assign the same receivable to another assignee, because he has no right to assign. The disadvantage of this approach is that third-party creditors may be unable to determine whether certain receivables have been assigned, as there is no registration system that they can check. This may have a negative impact on the availability and the cost of credit, because third-party creditors would need to cover themselves against the risk of a previous assignment having taken place. On the other hand, 'in a closed market, banks can still rely on borrowers' representations and gain knowledge about their clients' financial transactions [and] and the penalty for double financing of receivables in these markets outweighs the potential benefits'.[117]

[116] Ibid., para. 78.
[117] Bazinas, 'Multi-Jurisdictional Receivables Financing' 284.

3.3 Priority rules based on the time of notification of assignment

Priority is determined by the order in which the debtor receives notifications of the respective assignments. However, the knowledge of a prior assignment by an assignee makes it impossible for that assignee to obtain priority over that prior assignment, even if the subsequent assignee notified the debtor first. With respect to priority between the assignee and the insolvency administrator or creditors of the assignor, article 10 introduces a similar approach to that followed in other articles in the Annex. According to article 10, the assignee has priority over the right of an insolvency administrator if the receivable was assigned and notification was received by the debtor before the commencement of such insolvency proceedings. It is arguable that in this system potential assignees may inquire from the debtor, whose accurate and immediate response is vital, whether prior to them certain receivables have been assigned. Also, in the assignments of bulk and future receivables the system may not respond to the needs of potential assignees, as the identity of the debtor will be unknown, or there will simply be multiple debtors. Therefore, it may be very costly for assignees to find out whether certain receivables have been assigned.[118]

For instance, in England there is fragmentation of the law in this area. An assignment made by a company will only be registrable if it is an assignment by way of security over book debts.[119] If it is an assignment by way of sale, it is not registrable. On the other hand, all types of assignments (outright or for security purposes) by an individual are registrable.[120] The Law Commission in its report recommended that sale of receivables by companies should also be registered.[121] The issue has wider implications. As, functionally, sale of receivables is similar to charge over receivables, it seems perfectly reasonable to make the sale of receivables registrable. Lack of registration causes problems such as that subsequent creditors or assignees have to rely on the representations of the assignor and may not be informed of the existence of a functional equivalent of charge over receivables.[122] What is more striking is that the rule in *Dearle* v. *Hall*,[123] which regulates priority over receivables, is outdated. It is not suitable for

[118] For the criticism of the rule in *Dearle* v. *Hall see e.g.*, J. de Lacy, 'The Priority Rule of Dearle v. Hall Restated' 63 *Conveyancer* 311 (1999).

[119] CA 2006, s. 860(7)(f). [120] Insolvency Act 1986, s. 344.

[121] Law Commission Report No. 296, para. 4.7 *et seq.* [122] Ibid.

[123] (1828) 3 Russ I.

modern financing techniques. Take as an example of assignment of bulk receivables: it seems almost impossible to notify each debtor, to fulfil the requirements of *Dearle* v. *Hall*.[124] Failure to notify debtors will result in the loss of priority status in subsequent assignment under *Dearle* v. *Hall* and in civil law jurisdictions the assignment becomes void in the insolvency of the assignor.[125] It is arguable that this is because formal validity and publicity requirements are considered as a condition of priority, and they have not been met. Professor Oditah succinctly explains the danger of application of this outdated rule to assignment of bulk receivables as follows:

> ... bulk assignees of receivables, especially lenders as opposed to invoice discounters generally do not give notice of their bulk assignments until the assignor defaults and it is necessary for the assignee to collect the assigned receivables itself.[126]

In the assignment of future receivables the rule does not produce any logical results. It is not possible to notify debtors who are unknown at the time of conclusion of the contract of assignment. However, even when the identities of future debtors are known ('all my future rights of payment from XYZ Ltd. arising from the sale of aluminium wheels') and notice is given prior to the coming into existence of the receivables, this may not be sufficient to secure priority, because a notice given to the debtor after the receivables have come into existence will have priority.[127]

The risk that the rule in *Dearle* v. *Hall* offers in both assignments of bulk and future receivables is self-explanatory. The cost of credit will obviously increase, and for small businesses, factoring or other types of financing will become increasingly difficult. Thus, registration of sale of receivables to give notice to other assignees, particularly in the assignment of future and bulk receivables, seems to be necessary. Registration will prevent later assignees giving notice under *Dearle* v. *Hall*[128] and obtaining priority. This may, arguably, lift difficulties before the assignment of bulk receivables.

[124] Nevertheless, the rule also applies to assignment of bulk receivables: *Compaq Computer Ltd.* v. *Abercorn Group Ltd.* [1993] BCLC 602.

[125] For a similar assertion, *see* F. Oditah, 'Recurrent Issues in Receivables Financing', in J. Armour and J. Payne (eds.), *Rationality in Company Law: Essays in Honour of DD Prentice* (Oxford: Hart, 2009), p. 321, at p. 351.

[126] Ibid. [127] *Re Dallas* [1904] 2 Ch. 385.

[128] The second limb of the rule under *Dearle* v. *Hall* requires that the subsequent assignee have no information of the existence of an earlier assignee and gives notice.

3.4 Independent conflict-of-laws rules

The Convention also contains independent conflict-of-laws rules for priorities in addition to the normal conflict-of-laws rules for priorities prescribed in article 22. Article 30 prescribes the independent conflict-of-laws rules for priorities based on the law of the assignor's location, and it applies to transactions to which article 22 does not apply due to absence of territorial connection.[129] Although the law applicable to priority is governed by the conflict-of-laws rule under article 22, the significance of article 30 is that it enables the application of the Convention to transactions which may not normally fall within its ambit due to lack of territorial connection. The assignor does not have to be located in a Contracting State for the application of the Convention. This, arguably, enables assignors to enjoy the value of the Convention in those States that prefer not to adopt the Convention.

The scope of application of article 30 is reiterated in article 1(4), according to which the provisions of Chapter V, where article 30 is located, apply to assignments of international receivables and to international assignments of receivables independently of paragraphs 1 and 2. Article 1(1) and (2) set out the applicability of the Convention, and according to these paragraphs the Convention applies to assignments of international receivables and to international assignments of receivables if, at the time of the conclusion of the contract of assignment, the assignor is located in a Contracting State and subsequent assignments are governed by the Convention. Since article 30 regulates the priority issues even if the assignor's State is not a Contracting State, the applicability of the priority issues is enlarged. However, in the second sentence of article 1(4) it is noted that those provisions do not apply if a State makes a declaration under article 39. Therefore, if a State declares that it will not be bound by the provisions of Chapter V, then the law of the assignor's State shall not govern priority issues if the State of the assignor is not a Contracting State. The same goal is confirmed in article 26(a).

V. Conclusions

The Receivables Convention is a substantive step forward in the direction of the harmonization of receivables financing laws. By virtue of its

[129] Some writers define this type of application of priority rules contained in article 30 as 'indirect application through the conflicts of laws provisions of the Convention', Bruce A. Markell and Richard F. Broude, 'A Short Introduction to the Priority Provisions of the UNCITRAL Convention on the Assignment of Receivables in International Trade' 16 *Insolvency International* 1, at 2 (2003).

sophisticated, flexible and far-reaching solutions on many issues, it will be a production model for future work in the area of receivables financing and generally an acceptable text in commercial and financial life.

While the Convention has not yet been widely implemented, many of its principles have been implemented in national laws.[130] This has been done in two ways. First, States have directly implemented principles of the Convention in their domestic law; and second, States that have implemented a secured transactions law that is consistent with the recommendations of the UNCITRAL *Legislative Guide on Secured Transactions* have essentially implemented the principles of the Convention in their domestic law.[131]

Reforming the law in line with the Receivables Convention will assist small firms to be able to access credit.[132] The solution provided by the Convention on priority issues through offering an optional substantive annex and a conflict-of-laws rule creates a predictable and workable solution in cross-border assignment transactions. The Convention's rules on priorities will create certainty and predictability, particularly for the financiers who make lending decisions based on how the law efficiently protects their interests in the case of debtor default and whether they can ascertain this fact in advance of their credit agreements. Recognizing the effectiveness of the assignment of bulk and future receivables through the Convention's rules will enable small firms to be able to utilize the value of their expectant assets.

Arguably, the Receivables Convention, among many of its modern features, has certain aspects that will help reduce the cost of and facilitate access to credit. This is particularly important for financiers, as the Convention, while aiming to achieve the confidence of financiers in the market, establishes predictability in the law. Firstly, it sets aside statutory restrictions that limit small businesses' access to credit. Requirements that make assignability impossible in future and bulk receivables are set aside. Priority status of an assignee may not be adversely affected just because an assignment of future receivables is made. Furthermore, notification requirement to the debtor is irrelevant, and is also not a requirement under the Convention. Specificity requirements in certain jurisdictions restrict the assignability of bulk and future receivables. As long as the receivable is identifiable and relates to the assignment, this

130 *See generally e.g.*, Sigman and Kieninger, *Cross-Border Security over Receivables.*

131 For the general principles and efficacy of the UNCITRAL *Legislative Guide on Secured Transactions see* Chapter 8 above by Bazinas.

132 For the availability of credit and problems with money and debt, *see* Chapter 1 above.

will be sufficient. Secondly, priority of competing claimants is subject to a single and predictable conflict-of-laws rule. The law of the assignor's location achieves consistency and predictability in assignment of receivables transactions. Some commentators argue that this conflict-of-laws rule may not be conveniently applicable in securitization transactions,[133] as the assignor's change of location may cause change of priority rules, and thus the debtor may not receive a good discharge. However, when critically reviewed, a debtor's discharge seems irrelevant in the context of the applicability of the law of the assignor's State to priority disputes. The argument does not concern priority but, rather, the debtor's discharge.

Finally, article 42(4) of the Convention suggests the creation of a registration system. As the Convention covers both assignment by way of sale and by way of security, this corresponds to the recommendations made by the Law Commission in its report. Registration of the sale of receivables will enable predictability. Furthermore, this argument may be complemented by the recently adopted UNCITRAL Guide on the Implementation of a Security Registry.[134] This is a timely decision, as the Law Commission's past experience may be extremely helpful.

133 J. Perkins, 'A Question of Priorities: Choice of Law and Proprietary Aspects of the Assignment of Debts' 2 *Law and Financial Markets Review* 238, at 240 (2008).

134 A/CN.9/WG.VI/WP.50, Add.1 and Add. 2.

10

Commentary on the availability of credit and the utility and efficacy of UNCITRAL's legislative efforts in secured transactions

HENRY DEEB GABRIEL

The United National Commission on International Trade Law's (UNCITRAL)[1] activities in the area of security rights law fits squarely within the broad mandates of the Commission: harmonization and modernization of the law, legal predictability, and the encouragement of economic growth. In their respective chapters included in this volume, Dr. Orkun Akseli and Mr. Spiros Bazinas analyse the two major projects that UNICTRAL has undertaken in the area of security rights law: the United Nations Convention on Assignment of Receivables and the UNCITRAL *Legislative Guide on Secured Transactions.* These projects, in addition to the Convention on International Interests in Mobile Equipment, and its attendant protocols,[2] undertaken by the International Institute for the Unification of Private Law (Unidroit),[3] constitute some of the most important work in private international commercial law in the last two decades.

1 The United Nations Commission on International Trade Law (UNCITRAL) is a subsidiary body of the General Assembly of the United Nations. UNCITRAL was established in 1966. The Commission has a general mandate to harmonize and unify the law of international trade. Since its founding, UNCITRAL has prepared a wide range of conventions, model laws and other instruments that deal with the substantive law that governs trade transactions or other aspects of business law which have an impact on international trade. UNCITRAL is made up of sixty member states from five regional groups. Members of the Commission are elected for terms of six years. The terms of half the members expire every three years.

2 The Cape Town Convention on International Interests in Mobile Equipment and the relevant Protocols, www.unidroit.org/english/conventions/mobile-equipment/main.htm (last accessed 10 January 2013).

3 The International Institute for the Unification of Private Law (Unidroit) is an independent intergovernmental organization with its seat in Rome. The purpose of Unidroit is to study the needs of and the methods for modernizing and harmonizing private law, particularly commercial law, at the international level. There are presently sixty-three Member States.

To appreciate the importance of this work, one must understand the significance and centrality of secured finance in modern commercial transactions. Quite simply, without external finance, the vast majority of large transactions in goods and services, both domestic and international, would not take place. Thus, UNCITRAL's work in the area of secured finance is focused specifically on the creation of credit that will result in economic growth.

At the heart of UNICTRAL's work in the area of secured transactions are two assumptions. First, that capital is global, and second, that the reduction of risks in financing will increase credit and thereby the availability of goods and services. Both of these assumptions are axiomatic and central to the work of UNCITRAL in secured finance.

The work undertaken by UNICTRAL in the area of security rights has coincided with domestic and other international legal developments worldwide in security right that further suggests the importance and timeliness of this work.[4] Thus, we have seen in recent years such major projects in security rights as the Cape Town Convention and its protocols, as well as the modernization of domestic security rights laws[5] to conform to modern commercial practices. Importantly, the Legislative Guide and the United Nations Convention on the Assignment of Receivables conform to the general emerging international standards for security rights, and therefore add to the probability that in a few years there will be general uniform global law for security rights.

I. The UNCITRAL *Legislative Guide on Secured Transactions*

As noted in Chapter 5 above, Spyridon Bazinas emphasizes the advantages of a soft law instrument over binding positive law. Early in its work on secured transactions, UNICITRAL decided to create a legislative guide instead of a convention.[6] Largely, this was inevitable, as it was clear that the problems in creating a globally applicable convention were probably

[4] For an overview of this harmonization process and the various international legal instruments, *see* N.O. Akseli, *International Secured Transactions Law* (London, New York: Routledge, 2011).

[5] For example, in the US, major revisions in the domestic law were made in 2000, with substantial amendments in 2010. Australia and New Zealand have both recently substantially revised their respective laws of security rights in personal property.

[6] *See* Official Records of the General Assembly, Fifty-Sixth Session, Supplement No. 17 (A/56/17), paras. 351, 358 and 359, www.uncitral.org/uncitral/en/commission/sessions/34th.html (last accessed 10 January 2013).

insurmountable. I suggest this fallback position, though, is likely to have created a more useful instrument[7] than a convention in the area, due to some of the specific benefits that soft law instruments have over treaties and conventions.[8]

First, soft law instruments, such as the Legislative Guide, are not subject to the same pressure to be harmonized with existing domestic laws as are treaties and conventions and other forms of hard law. In the case of a treaty or convention, there is the strong desire by adopting jurisdictions to make the treaty or convention consistent with the domestic law of the jurisdiction. Yet the ability to harmonize a new treaty or convention with existing domestic or international law is subject to a variety of difficulties. This is particularly the case with the law of secured transactions that goes to the heart of a jurisdiction's law of property and creditor rights.

Moreover, as discussed above, although the Legislative Guide is for the most part consistent with recent legislative enactments of security rights law, it is not wholly consistent with any other existing law. Because of its non-binding nature, there was less pressure to harmonize the Legislative Guide with any particular national law,[9] and the working group was able to pick provisions selectively from another law, or craft wholly new provisions to fit specific needs.[10]

[7] The Legislative Guide is often referred to as a 'soft law instrument'. '[S]oft law' is understood as referring in general to instruments of normative nature with no legally binding force and which are applied only through voluntary acceptance. M. Bonell, 'Soft Law and Party Autonomy: The Case of the Unidroit Principles' 51 *Loyola Law Review* 234 (2005). These are generally established legal rules that are not positive law and are therefore not judicially binding. The various soft law instruments in international commercial law include model laws, a codification of custom and usage promulgated by an international non-governmental organization, the promulgation of international trade terms, model forms, contracts, restatements by leading scholars and experts, and of course, legislative guides. Although soft law principles do not begin as positive law, as I will discuss below, they can become positive law both by adoption by courts or tribunals, in the agreements of transactional parties, or as the basis for domestic legislation.

[8] The promulgation of successful soft law instruments is quite common among the international organizations. Two of the most successful include the Unidroit Principles on International Contracts and the UNCITRAL Arbitration Rules. Tribunals have extensively used both of these for guidance. Other private organizations, such as the International Chamber of Commerce, have a long history of drafting very successful soft law documents. In the case of the ICC, this would include the highly influential INCOTERMS (shipping terms) and the Uniform Customs and Practice for Documentary Credits (letters of credit).

[9] There clearly was some pressure to conform the Legislative Guide to a particular existing model, particularly the American Uniform Commercial Code, Article 9.

[10] This selective borrowing also lends itself to borrowing from various sources. For the Legislative Guide, for the most part this process of picking and choosing lends itself to systematic reflection on what should be the best result, and not simply a possible result. It

The Legislative Guide, unlike treaties and conventions, also has the advantage of not needing to be ratified, and therefore is not subject to the often lengthy process of ratification that can hold up enforcement for years.[11] It has been suggested that 'soft law' instruments have been successful 'precisely because they are not binding, have not been influenced by governments and do not pose any threat to national legal systems. Like the UNCITRAL Model Law on Arbitration, the Legislative Guide is designed to be a unifying influence and a resource, but it is left to legislatures, courts and arbitral tribunals to decide to what extent it can be of use.[12]

The Legislative Guide is specifically intended to be the basis for legislative adoption, either as drafted or with minor revisions, but it may also be used as a source for new legal rules and principles within the context of existing law, as well as gap fillers when the otherwise

is often the case with binding legal instruments that the need to accommodate specific legal traditions locks the actors into a straitjacket of limited possibilities that often prevents the examination for the best solution. This is often politically driven. The late Professor Allan Farnsworth, for example, describes what distinguished the work leading to the United Nations Convention on Contracts for the Sale of Goods, in which he was an American delegate, and that which brought about the non-binding Unidroit Principles of International Commercial Contracts, in which he was a member of the working group: 'While the atmosphere in UNCITRAL was political (because delegates represented governments, which were grouped in regional blocs), that in UNIDROIT was apolitical (because participants appeared in their private capacity).' E.A. Farnsworth, 'The American Provenance of the UNIDROIT Principles' 72 *Tulane Law Review* 1985–94, 1989 (1998).

11 For example, one of the most successful international conventions in recent times, the United Nations Convention on the Recognition and Enforcement of Foreign Arbitral Awards (New York Convention), was completed in 1958, but not ratified by the US until 1970. Moreover, although the New York Convention has been very successful, this has not been the case with many recent international commercial law conventions. In fact, the recent history of private international law treaties has been unsuccessful in general. The 1964 Convention relating to a Uniform Law on the International Sale of Goods (ULIS) has only been ratified by 8 countries. The 1970 International Convention on Travel Contracts has had only 3 ratifications. The 1973 Convention providing a Uniform Law on the Form of an International Will has been ratified by only 3 countries. The 1983 Convention on Agency in the International Sale of Goods has been ratified by only 2 countries. The 1988 Unidroit Convention on International Financial Leasing has been ratified by only 4 countries. The 1988 Unidroit Convention on International Factoring has been ratified by only 4 countries. The 1995 Unidroit Convention on Stolen or Illegally Exported Cultural Objects has been ratified by 11 countries.

12 R. Goode, 'Communication on European Contract Law', cited in S. Gopalan, 'New Trends in the Making of International Commercial Law' *Journal of Law and Commerce* 117–68 2004.

applicable international or domestic law does not address the specific question.[13]

There is, of course, a drawback to the Legislative Guide as a soft law instrument, in that it does not create certainty in the law and transactions in and of itself. In other words, to be effective, it has to be adopted as legislation. However, having been formulated as a non-binding instrument, one hopes that it will be the model, in some form, for future legislation.

In some areas of commercial law, certainty of the law and the enforcement of the specific rules is a necessity. Because international conventions are binding, once they are ratified they have the advantage of instant uniformity and enforceability. It is useful to compare the Legislative Guide with the Unidroit Cape Town Convention. The Cape Town Convention and its protocols govern security interests in large value international mobile goods. In these transactions, financiers need a large degree of certainty in the law and the ability to know that security interests will be enforceable. Without these guarantees, it is unlikely that the transactions covered by the Convention would ever be consummated.

Conversely, the Legislative Guide is specifically designed as a model for future development of security rights law where it does not previously exist, and it is intended as a model for domestic law where it is presently absent. Thus, its greatest utility is as a template for adoption, and therefore it meets the needs for which it was designed.

II. The United Nations Convention on the Assignment of Receivables

As Akseli correctly points out in Chapter 9, the assignment of receivables is a significant part of commercial finance. It is interesting to note that, given the tremendous value of receivables and its potential for being the substantial part of the assets that a debtor may have as the basis of secured credit, in many jurisdictions the use of receivables as collateral has only recently been recognized. UNCITRAL, in promulgating the Convention,

[13] Whether this guidance is always useful may be questioned because, with the convenience of having existing rules in place, there is some reported tendency of tribunals to follow soft law principles blindly without any analysis of why the rules are appropriate or whether the rules are better suited for the issue than competing rules. However, to the extent that the principles were drafted carefully and thoughtfully, this concern should be minimal. The tribunals, in effect, are likely to stumble upon the best rule.

hoped to increase the use of accounts as collateral and thus unlock this source for credit.

Unlike the Legislative Guide, the Receivables Convention is not intended as a model for future legislation, but instead, to be ratified as is. Moreover, unlike the Legislative Guide, the Convention applies primarily to international transactions.[14] As with the Legislative Guide, the Receivables Convention is largely consistent with the emerging universal standards of security rights law. The Convention, however, has not been successful to date. With only three signatures[15] and one ratification,[16] it is a long way from coming into force. The reason for this lack of acceptance appears implicit in Akseli's chapter, and this is the point I would like to concentrate on in my comments.

As Akseli accurately points out, the Convention achieves the three major goals one seeks in an international commercial law convention: it lowers the costs of transactions, it adds greater certainty to transactions, and it reduces legal obstacles. Specifically, the Convention seeks to lower the cost of and increase the availability of credit by providing for a source of collateral that may not otherwise be available to debtors who seek credit.[17]

Moreover, as noted in Akseli's chapter, the greater the financial strength of a borrower, the more likely the borrower will be able to obtain unsecured credit. Thus, the Convention, by providing for a source of secured credit, should favour smaller borrowers in less developed economies. Most importantly, by opening up new potential markets for capital, and thereby creating a wider number of potential borrowers in a greater number of jurisdictions, the Convention should serve the larger goal of providing a vehicle for capital to move toward its most efficient use by finding borrowers who can best use the resources.

Thus, the question arises why the Convention has not been more successful. There appear to be several factors that explain this. First, there is the reluctance of a country to adopt laws different from its basic legal principles of that country. In this regard, the Convention provides two possible changes to domestic laws that may fundamentally differ from that domestic law. First, the domestic law may not provide for secured financing of accounts at all. Second, in those jurisdictions where accounts

[14] United National Convention on the Assignment of Receivables, art. 1(1)(a).

[15] Luxembourg, Madagascar, and the US. [16] Liberia.

[17] As Akseli notes, in low- and middle-income countries, receivables may constitute up to 34 per cent of a company's assets.

can be used as collateral, there may be some restriction on accounts being secured in bulk.[18] Also, as noted by Akseli, 'the role of possession in some civil law jurisdictions as the significant element in proprietary rights is considered to be an obstacle to the development of receivables financing and its harmonization'.[19] Moreover, because the Convention is primarily concerned only with international transactions, it sets up the problem of having two sets of legal rules for secured finance: one for domestic transactions and one for international transactions.

There is also the issue of familiarity within the financial community. Even if the law might provide for accounts receivables financing, if the financial community is not familiar or comfortable with financing these assets, they will not support the Convention. This lack of industry support will inevitably inhibit the desire of a country to adopt the Convention.[20]

It may be that the Convention is implicitly attempting to do more than its stated goal. The Convention explicitly provides for the secured financing of accounts receivables in international transactions. As with the Legislative Guide, it adopts modern rules of secured financing; rules well known and developed in many countries. As such, the Convention is implicitly serving as a catalyst for the adoption of these rules in the domestic laws of those countries that have not previously adopted this model. The very reasons discussed above as to why the Legislative Guide may be more effective as a soft law instrument that does not require ratification, and therefore wholesale revision of existing domestic law, are the reasons the Convention has run into resistance in ratification.

The future success of the Receivables Convention may have to wait until the domestic laws of the various countries begin to be in accord with the principles of secured finance promulgated in it. If the Legislative Guide becomes an effective harmonizer of the law of secured transactions, this may happen. At that point, the Convention may be ripe for widespread ratification.

18 The Convention provides for a single security interest in 'all account'. In this way, the security interest is created in all new accounts as they are created, and ends when the accounts are no longer in existence.

19 *See* Akseli, Chapter 9, above, at pp. 193–4, , *citing* R. Goode 'Reflections of the Harmonization of Commercial Law', in R. Cranston and R. Goode (eds.), *Commercial and Consumer Law National and International Dimensions* (Oxford: Clarendon Press, 1993), p. 3, at p. 12.

20 It is important to note that international lenders in some developing economies do not look to secured credit as a significant aspect in assessing a loan. Instead, the lenders rely on the cash flow of the borrower. Here, it is not just a lack of interest in accounts as a basis of collateral, but a disregard for secured credit as a whole.

PART IV

Availability of credit and secured transactions law reform

11

How may international standards assist law reform in England?

ANJANETTE H. RAYMOND

I. Introduction

It is no longer a matter of debate that the current law of England as it relates to security over personal property is cumbersome, confusing and difficult to manoeuvre.[1] Yet, previous reform efforts have failed in England, and current reform efforts are still too new to have major impacts upon the confusing system. Consequently, England stands in a somewhat precarious position, a financial leader with a confusing secured transactions regime. Meanwhile, harmonization efforts in other domestic and regional systems are pushing ahead, often reforming through the use of a set of international secured transactions standards. England's rejection of the reform efforts may seem daft, but the rejection is most likely a signal of the next big issue for the supporters of secured transactions reform: what is to be done when a robust finance system fails to match other major players in the field? In terms of the English reform efforts, one has to ask: what is the next step for England in terms of its law of security over personal property?

This chapter seeks to engage the reader in both of these debates. First, the chapter will explore the existence of international standards of secured

[1] As highlighted by the Secured Transactions Law Reform Project, 'in comparison to that in many leading economies around the world, [the English system] is out-of-date and cumbersome'. The Secured Transactions Law Reform Project, *Secured Transactions Law: The Case for Reform* (2011) available at http://securedtransactionsproject.files.wordpress.com/2010/12/case-for-reform.pdf (last accessed 10 January 2013) (hereinafter: Law Reform Project, Case for Reform).

transactions. Second, it will briefly identify the key areas of divergence between the identified international standards and the law as it currently exists in England. Third, it will briefly describe the prior English reform efforts as well as discussing the current reform efforts. Fourth, the chapter will consider the problems in terms of international harmonization and will then explore in limited detail the problems specific to England. And finally, the chapter will consider the long-term solutions to both of these systems.

II. Key international characteristics in secured transactions

The last twenty years has seen a surge of interest in the harmonization of the law governing secured transactions.[2] Yet, this surge of interest has not resulted in a definitive legal instrument that sets the standard for secured transactions law. Instead, based on many years of trial and error, harmonization advocates have realized that it simply may not be possible to have a single definitive text. In the place of a single text stand numerous texts, crafted by various agencies, each covering different areas – or the whole area – of secured transactions. Despite this lack of unity, one thing is true, however; all of the agencies that draft secured transactions legal text start with a basic premise in mind – a level of harmonization within the area of the law of secured transaction is needed to remove barriers to access to finance. Interestingly, despite the wide divergence in promulgation institutions and approaches to the problem of harmonization of secured transactions, there seems to be an emerging set of international concepts that guide the drafting of the various texts. And many of these texts are having an influence on domestic and regional secured transactions reform efforts.[3]

International organizations, such as the World Bank,[4] have been a catalyst in encouraging nations to reform domestic law so that it is more

[2] For an excellent discussion in terms of harmonization and the various international legal instruments, *see* N.O. Akseli, *International Secured Transactions Law: Facilitation of Credit and International Conventions and Instruments* (London: Routledge, 2011), especially Chapter 2.

[3] Such as the European Bank for Reconstructions and Development, Model Law on Secured Transactions, available at www.ebrd.com/.

[4] For further information, *see* http://web.worldbank.org/WBSITE/EXTERNAL/TOPICS/LAWANDJUSTICE/GILD/0,,contentMDK:20196839~menuPK:146205~pagePK:64065425~piPK:162156~theSitePK:215006,00.html (last accessed 10 January 2013).

harmonized with other regional and domestic regimes, while regional organizations such as the European Bank for Reconstruction and Development,[5] Organization of American States[6] and the Asian Development Bank[7] have all promulgated model laws on secured transactions. International organizations have also developed legislative guides[8] and model laws[9] designed specifically to shape reform considerations, while the same international organizations have promulgated international hard law,[10] such as the United Nations Convention on the Assignment of Receivables in International Trade[11] and the Unidroit Convention on International Interests in Mobile Equipment (Cape Town Convention).[12] One could certainly argue that the proliferation of texts covering secured transactions has led to a set of international standards.

However, my argument depends upon several important assumptions in terms of harmonization of secured transactions law, the main assumption being that harmonization of this area of law is something that we should be seeking to achieve. One should note:

> States all over the world have had to recognize that a diversity of national laws is no longer adequate to meet the needs of the market place, and that long standing legal traditions, concepts and techniques, however laudable in their objectives, must now be modified so as to be responsive to the

[5] For further information, *see* www.ebrd.com/ (last accessed 10 January 2013).

[6] The model law was adopted on 8 February 2002, by the Sixth Inter-American Specialized Conference on Private International Law, CIDIP-VI, Final Act3(f),OEA/Ser.K/XXI.6/ CIDIPVI/doc.24/02 rev.3 (5 March 2002).

[7] For more information visit the Asian Development Bank website at www.adb.org/ (last accessed 10 January 2013).

[8] *See* the UNCITRAL *Legislative Guide on Secured Transactions*, available at www.uncitral.org/ (last accessed 10 January 2013).

[9] European Bank for Reconstructions and Development, Model Law on Secured Transactions.

[10] On the regional level, for example is the Financial Collateral Directive, (Directive 2002/47, OJ L168, 27.06.2002, pp. 43–50). The main point of the Collateral Directive is that it prohibits EU Member States from requiring the performance of any formal act for the creation, validity, perfection, enforceability or admissibility in evidence of a financial collateral arrangement or the provision of financial collateral under such an arrangement. *See* Article 3 of the Directive.

[11] United Nations Convention on the Assignment of Receivables in International Trade, available at www.uncitral.org/ (last accessed 10 January 2013).

[12] Unidroit in the Convention on International Interests in Mobile Equipment (Cape Town, 2001) available at www.unidroit.org/ (last accessed 10 January 2013).

> needs of commerce and finance, which requires above all the minimum degree to formality and the maximum degree of flexibility.[13]

Numerous studies have supported the link between successful commercial and financial businesses to a modern secured transactions regime.[14] And while one could temper the enthusiasm toward these studies by arguing that the impacts tend to be the greatest in nations without already entrenched security in personal property laws, the truth is nations with long-standing secured transactions laws are also reforming with success. For example, Canada[15] and New Zealand[16] underwent reform to great success, while Australia is in the final implementation stages.[17] Each of these systems had existing secured transactions laws and each of these systems stand to benefit from their arduous work toward harmonization. Consequently, the debate has passed; the international community should be seeking to harmonize the law of secured transactions, as even nations with long-standing secured transactions laws have been able to overhaul systems to large success.

The second assumption within this chapter is that we can identify a set of secured transaction concepts that are in widespread use, so much so that the concepts have risen to the level of an international standard. I would argue this assumption can also be supported. For a considerable time now, many international institutions, domestic systems and regional legislative bodies, as well as academic commentators from around the world, have used the following set of key characteristics familiar to those within the field to guide both modernization and reform efforts.

13 Goode roundtable 343.

14 *See*, among others, Heywood Fleisig, Mehnaz Safavian and Nuria de la Peña, *Reforming Collateral Laws to Expand Access to Finance: The World Bank* (Washington DC, 2006); F. Dahan and J. Simpson (eds.), *Secured Transactions Reform and Access to Credit*, Elgar Financial Law Series (Cheltenham: Edward Elgar, 2009); Akseli, *International Secured Transactions Law*.

15 *See also*, R.C.C. Cuming, *An Overview of a Canadian Personal Property Security System*, National Law Center for Inter American Free Trade, available at www.natlaw.com/pubs/overview.htm (last accessed 10 January 2013).

16 Personal Property Securities Act 1999 (NZ) available at www.legislation.govt.nz/act/public/1999/0126/latest/DLM45900.html (last accessed 10 January 2013). For a greater discussion, *see* Mike Gedye, 'The Development of New Zealand's Secured Transactions Jurisprudence', 34(2) *University of New South Wales Law Journal* 696–733 (Oct 2011).

17 Discussion and updates available at The Australian Government Initiative, PPS Reform, www.ppsr.gov.au/About_PPS/PPSReform/Pages/Personal_property_securities_reform.aspx (last accessed 10 January 2013).

(A) The system should be based on the use of a 'universal security interest'[18] with the ability to use any suitable asset to secure an obligation.

(B) The system should use a definition of a 'secured transaction'[19] that includes both present and future interests,[20] and quasi-security interests,[21] the nature of which is characterized and identified by substance rather than form.[22]

(C) The security agreements should be subject to a small set of requirements, intended to establish little more than intent, identity, and a brief description of the assets or category of assets.[23]

(D) The system of registration should be based on a notice-filing approach[24] used for the majority of secured transactions, the alternative method of notice being provided by either: (1) taking possession[25] or (2) control of the collateral.[26]

(E) The system should make use of a central registry,[27] intended to cover all types of secured transactions.[28] Of course, possessory and quasi-possessory securities would not need to be filed.[29]

18 *See* for example, UNCITRAL Legislative Guide, page 13.

19 The use of this term has proven to be one of the many debates. For example, EBRD Model Law uses the term 'charge' (*see* EBRD Model Law, Notes on Terminology), while the Legislative Guide uses 'Secured Transactions' (Legislative Guide, Introduction, page 12). I would argue the preferred terminology is secured transaction, unless, of course, you are speaking of a particular secured transactions device, such as the Receivables Convention which uses the terms 'receivable' and security right (Receivables Convention Arts. 2 and 10).

20 *See*, for example, Legislative Guide, Terminology, page 4, para. 2(a); page 10, para. 16; page 25, para. (a); EBRD Model Law, page 2, para. 5; Art. 4.1, comment, Art. 4.3.4.; OAS Model Law, Art. 31.

21 See, for example, Legislative Guide, Discussion, pages 57–9; EBRD Model Law, Art. 9 (retention of title, known as unpaid vendors charges).

22 *See*, for example, Legislative Guide, page 56, para. 103 (basic approaches); EBRD Model Law, Art. 8.4.

23 *See*, for example, EBRD, Art. 7 (charging instrument) and Legislative Guide, Section II (creation of security right); OAS Model Law, Art. 7.

24 UNCITRAL Receivables Convention, para. 52; OAS Model Law, Art. 10.

25 With regard to negotiable instruments: Legislative Guide, Terminology, paras. 101, 102, 109; EBRD Model Law, Art. 6.1; OAS Model Law, Art. 27.

26 *See*, for example, Legislative Guide, Terminology, para. 174; EBRD, Art. 10 (Possessory Charge); OAS Model Law, Art. 37.

27 *See*, for example, Legislative Guide, Terminology, para. 1(f), §3, para. (b); UNCITRAL Receivables Convention, Art. 4; EBRD Model Law, part 5; OAS Model Law, Art. 44.

28 *See*, for example, Legislative Guide, Operational Framework of the Registry, page 150, para. 8.

29 *See*, for example, Legislative Guide, Section III, page 114; EBRD, Art. 10.

(F) The actual information filed should include limited information, that which is necessary to inform of the interest without requiring a high level of specificity or description.[30]

(G) The registration system should be established on-line,[31] with a minimal filing fee[32] and an easy to use search directory.[33]

(H) The instrument should contain a clear priority structure.[34]

(I) Priority should be determined on the date of filing[35] or the date of effective control/possession.[36]

(J) Pre-filing of the security interest, such as a financing statement, should be allowed.[37]

(K) Priority should extend to the proceeds of the sale of the collateral.[38]

(L) In situations where registration is required, failure to file would mean that the security interest is ineffective against other secured creditors[39] and/or insolvency trustees.[40]

(M) Special priority would be given to Purchase Money Security Interests (PMST)[41] with the PMSI ranking ahead of a general security interest over after-acquired property that might have been granted at an earlier date.[42]

(N) The sale of goods in the ordinary course of business would take priority over a security interest in the goods unless the purchaser had express knowledge of the existing security interest.[43]

30 Model Law, Arts. 7, 8 and Schedule 1; Legislative Guide, Section III, pages 103–4; OAS Model Law, Art. 38.

31 *See* the International Registry of Mobile Assets which operates under the legal framework of the Cape Town Convention and the Aircraft Protocol. Available at www.internationalregistry.aero/irWeb/Controller.jpf (last accessed 10 January 2013). UNCITRAL Legislative Guide, Centralized and Consolidated Registry, page 154, para. 21.

32 *See* ibid., page 158, para. 37.

33 *See*, for example, ibid., pages 155–8, discussing public access and indexing; EBRD Model Law, Art. 34.1.2; OAS Model Law, Arts. 44 and 45.

34 *See*, for example, EBRD Model Law, Art. 17; Legislative Guide, section 3.

35 *See*, for example, ibid., page 196 paras. 46 and 48, recommendation 76(a); EBRD Model Law, Art. 17.2; OAS Model Law, Art. 35.

36 *See*, for example, Legislative Guide, page 196 paras. 46 and 48, recommendation 76(b); EBRD Model Law, Art. 17.4.

37 *See*, for example, UCC §9–502(d).

38 *See*, for example, Legislative Guide, 34(b), 35, 39.

39 *See*, for example, OAS Model Law, Art. 47.

40 This, of course, arises in bankruptcy/insolvency law.

41 *See*, for example, Legislative Guide page 214, para. 114. Possibly an outdated term – for example, the Legislative Guide uses the term 'acquisition' with a caveat that it has specifically rejected the use of PMSI. *See* Legislative Guide, page 29.

42 *See*, for example, ibid., Section IX; OAS Model Law, Art. 51 (Acquisition Purchase).

43 *See*, for example, Legislative Guide, page 131, para. 114; OAS Model Law Art. 49.

(O) Filing would be valid for a specified period of time,[44] with continuation possible by mere filing.[45]

(P) Moving collateral into another jurisdiction would not defeat the security interest, but instead would allow continued perfection for a specified period of time.[46]

(Q) Enforcement should occur through a dual mechanism[47] of self-help[48] and/or judicial involvement.[49]

(R) In situations where self-help is allowed, the enforcing party should be held to standards of good faith and commercial reasonableness.[50]

(S) In situations of judicial involvement, the enforcement mechanism must be easy to set in motion, and predictable.[51]

(T) Enforcement delays should be held to a minimum, with few limitations or additional hurdles placed in the way of the enforcing party.[52]

(U) The secured transactions law would need to be compatible and supported by the appropriate insolvency and bankruptcy laws.[53]

(V) The system should anticipate cross-border transactions and the likelihood of the asset relocation.[54]

As can be seen from the above list and corresponding footnotes, there is a growing body of secured transactions characteristics that appear across numerous legislative texts. And while variations of the means of accomplishing these key characteristics certainly exist, the similarities far outweigh the differences. One could argue that the widespread use of these characteristics has, in fact, set an international standard, and that harmonization of secured transactions is slowly creeping toward a reality.

[44] *See*, for example, Legislative Guide, page 182, para. 69; OAS Model Law, Art. 39.

[45] *See*, for example, Legislative Guide, page 182, para. 69.

[46] *See*, for example, ibid., page 132, para. 118.

[47] *See*, for example, ibid., section 8; EBRD Model Law, Art. 22.

[48] *See*, for example, Legislative Guide, page 278, para. 12 (through seizure of the encumbered asset); EBRD Model Law, Art. 24.1; OAS Model Law, Art. 56.

[49] *See*, for example, Legislative Guide, page 280, para. 18; EBRD Model Law, Art. 22.2.

[50] EBRD Model Law, Features, para. 7; Legislative Guide, page 278 para. 15; OAS Model Law, Art. 59.

[51] *See*, for example, Legislative Guide, page 310, Recommendation 131, Purpose; EBRD Model Law, Art. 29.

[52] *See*, for example, Legislative Guide, page 311, para. 138.

[53] The importance of this cannot be over-emphasized, *see* Legislative Guide, Introduction, page iii.

[54] *See*, for example, ibid., page 401 (discussion of connecting factors) paras. 73–8; EBRD Model Law, Art. 31; OAS Model Law, Arts. 69 and 70.

III. What are the major issues within the English law of security over personal property when compared to the international standards?

In contrast to the systems reformed with the international standards,[55] England has no comprehensive code or statute for its secured transactions law. Instead, England embodies its secured transactions law within a multitude of sources, including case law. And while this may seem straightforward, one of the criticisms of an 'outsider looking in' is often the wide range of various legal sources that cover the various issues within the secured transactions regime. For example, case law defines a security interest, while property law defines the kind of security right that may be created.[56] And while one can assume those within the system appreciate this nuanced approach to secured transactions law, the reality of the situation is that the system is very confusing to those attempting to understand it.

A secured transaction within the English system is a 'right over property to ensure the payment of money or performance of some other obligation'.[57] While this definition is compatible with the international standards, difficulties arise when attempting to characterize the type of secured transaction created. English property law defines the type of instruments as: mortgage, charge, pledge, and liens.[58] Despite what appears to be a streamlined process, in fact the four categories actually contain a litany of different forms.[59] And the form that the security takes is a key component in determining many issues, especially the issues surrounding priority and enforcement. Issues of form are especially confused in three areas: fixed and floating charges, quasi-security interests and financial collateral. First, in terms of the characterization of fixed and floating charges, these two categories remain within the system as a historical relic of the insolvency regime.[60] These concepts have long

[55] Canada, New Zealand and Australia have all used the international standards as a guidepost for reform, *see* Section VIII. While the US has led the way in its use of the standards, *see* Section VIII.

[56] G. McCormack, *Secured Credit and the Harmonization of Law: The UNCITRAL Experience* (Cheltenham: Edward Elgar, 2011), p. 56 (hereinafter: McCormack, The UNCITRAL Experience).

[57] Ibid., p. 92 fn. 57, citing *Paramount Airways.*

[58] *See* H. Beale, M. Bridge, L. Gullifer and E. Lomnicka, *The Law of Personal Property Security* (Oxford University Press, 1st edn., 2007), para. 1.16 (hereinafter Beale et al., Law of PPS).

[59] For example, a lien has at least two forms. *See* McCormack, The UNCITRAL Experience, p. 93.

[60] *See* Law Reform Project, Case for Reform, s. 3.

been captured within other asset categories, such as receivables,[61] and the remaining division between the two causes a high amount of uncertainty in terms of priority. In terms of the quasi-security interest, quasi-security interests are the functional equivalent of a security interest, yet they are not classified as security interests for the purposes of the regime.[62] The classification of these devices as distinct from traditional security interests creates great confusion, as quasi-security interests are covered by different rules in terms of priority and enforcement. In terms of financial collateral,[63] while the characterization of financial collateral seems relatively straightforward, the classification of this type of asset causes difficulties in terms of enforcement, as several key issues fail to match the current English law in relation to other asset types.[64] Based on this brief introduction, one can quickly appreciate that the classification of the form of the security interest has a lasting impact on the priority and enforcement of the security interest.

In terms of registration, England has a system in place with key determination made based on the party taking the security interest. Under the English secured transactions regime, the Companies Act defines the particulars of registration when a company executes the security agreement,[65] but the Bills of Sale Act specifies the requirements of registration of a security agreements executed by individuals.[66] Unsurprisingly, these two Acts are fundamentally different in terms of approach and execution of the registration of the interests that are covered within them. In terms of the registration of those interests covered within the Companies Act, the system of registration is fraught with difficulties, as the information within the register is incomplete and inaccurate in providing necessary information for lenders making important decisions in terms of priority. The company creating a charge over an asset is responsible for filing the registration, with a specific timeframe to register that quickly begins to

[61] *See* Beale et al., Law of PPS, at para. 21.126. Of course, as pointed out in Ch. 21, there are differences between the international standards and the fixed/floating charge regime, one of the main issues being the date used for establishing priority. *See* ibid.

[62] *See* ibid., at para. 1.20.

[63] At its most basic, financial collateral is financial instruments, cash held in a bank or other accounts, and 'similar claim for the repayment of money'. *See* ibid., at para. 10.02.

[64] Because of the Directive on Financial Collateral Arrangements. For a complete description and discussion, see Beale et al., Law of PPS at Ch. 10.

[65] See, Companies Act 2006, Chapter 25.

[66] Bills of Sale Act. According to Gerard McCormack, 'the requirements [of the Bills of Sale Act] are so cumbersome and difficult to comply with that the Bills of Sale Acts are effectively bypassed in practice'. The UNCITRAL Experience, p. 95.

expire after the creation of the charge (unless an extension is granted by the court). In addition, the registration system lacks the ability to register an interest. Moreover, unincorporated businesses are left in an uncertain position, as registration is overly technical and fraught with difficulties, if it can be accomplished at all in these situations.

In terms of priority amongst competing secured creditors, two fundamental issues must be understood; the law recognizes the right of parties to craft priorities amongst secured creditors[67] and the failure to register a security interest, that was otherwise registrable, results in the security interest being void in liquidation or bankruptcy.[68] Of course, the second fundamental issue is not a true priority issue, but unsurprisingly, the result of a void interest has a devastating impact on the presumed priority of a creditor. Priority between competing security interests is a mix of numerous factors, all of which are determined within the complex system of various laws and definitions described briefly above. If parties have not created their own priority structure amongst competing interests, the priority structure is determined by a jumble of security interest types, order of creation and notice.[69]

Finally, while insolvency is not a focus of this chapter, its impact upon secured transactions is great. It is frequently cited in reform literature that the main reason for the continued use of fixed and floating charges is the importance of these two terms within the insolvency law. And of course, similar to other key areas in relation to secured transactions, adding to a confusing structure are the various European Regulations that seek to harmonize insolvency law.[70]

Based on this incredibly brief description of the English regime, one can highlight the main areas of wide divergence between the English system and the international standards. The English system creates narrow categories of security types that are classified not by the function they

[67] *See* Beale et al., Law of PPS, at para. 6.94. [68] *See* ibid., at para. 8.01.

[69] *See* McCormack, The UNCITRAL Experience, p. 96. For an in-depth discussion, *see* Beale et al., Law of PPS, at Chs. 12–15.

[70] Financial Markets and Insolvency Regulations 1996 and Financial Markets and Insolvency Regulations 1999 (SI 1999/2979). 'These Regulations change the insolvency regime that applies to any exchange which is a "recognised investment exchange" (RIE) and any central counterparty clearing house which is a "recognised clearing house" (RCH) within the meaning of the Financial Services and Markets Act 2000 (c. 8) (see Part 18 of that Act). They do so by amending Part 7 of the Companies Act 1989 (c. 40) (Part 7); the Financial Markets and Insolvency Regulations 1991 (SI 1991/880) (the 1991 Regulations) and the Financial Services and Markets Act 2000 (Recognition Requirements for Investment Exchanges and Clearing Houses) Regulations 2001 (SI 2001/995) (the 2001 Regulations).'

serve, but instead by the semi-narrow categories of security rights based in property law. Companies are the primary grantors, as the regime covering individuals and consumers are trapped within an even more cumbersome and confusing system. The registration system is out of date, as it does not contain all of the necessary information and is difficult to correct. The priority structure is a confusing array of rules based upon the type of security created, while the enforcement mechanism is equally confusing, as the type of security can and does change the rules in relation to enforcement. And most importantly, functionally equivalent charges are not covered by this regime. Within this regime, businesses are confused and uncertain that priority and enforcement will occur in relation to the security interests: a situation that is wholly unacceptable in a system that should be seeking to be a leader in security over personal property. It is unsurprising that the Secured Transactions Law Reform Project provides: 'in comparison to that in many leading economies around the world, [the English system] is out-of-date and cumbersome'.[71] Something must be done.

IV. A brief description of England's reform efforts prior to 2010

England has in the past and continues to work on the reform of the law of security over personal property.[72] Within this section, focus will be placed upon the publication of the Law Commission's Consultation Paper, *Registration of Security Interest: Company Charges and Property Other Than Land* (2002),[73] which has been heralded as a major shift in the English approach to secured transactions. It was this publication that

[71] Law Reform Project, Case for Reform, at page 1.

[72] *See* Report of the Committee on Consumer Credit (1971) (the Crowther Report), The Halliday Report 1986 and A. L. Diamond, *A Review of Security Interests in Property* (1989) (the Diamond Report). *See also*, Company Law Review: Proposals for Reform of Part XII of the Companies Act 198, Law Commission, Registration of Security Interests: Company Charges and Property other than Land (2002) Consultation Paper No. 164 and Company Security Interests, a consultative report, Consultation Paper No. 176 (2004), Company Security Interests, The Law Commission Final Report (Law Com. No. 296, 2005) – Company Security Interests, Department for Business Innovation and Skills Consultation Paper (2010) – Registration of Charges Created by Companies and Limited Liability Partnerships, Proposals to amend the current scheme and relating to specialist registers.

[73] Law Commission, Consultation Paper 164, *Registration of Security Interest: Company Charges and Property Other Than Land* (July 2002) (hereinafter Consultation Paper 164).

marked one of the Law Commission's most ambitious attempts to reform the law of secured transactions in England. At the time of its drafting, many believed the reform efforts would result in a fundamental switch toward the use of international secured transaction standards.

For the most part, the reform efforts focused on several broad areas of necessary reform: (1) shifting to a notice system of filing and hence registration, (2) the inclusion of quasi-security devices, (3) overseas companies, and (4) unincorporated businesses and individuals.[74] In practice, each of these broad categories contains numerous areas of reform. For example, a notice system would allow for an easier to use system,[75] affording greater certainty in priority with fairer rules of priority.[76] Moreover, the Law Commission advances that the move toward a more reliable notice filing system would also allow for priority to be determined, generally, by a 'first to file rule',[77] and that the system should be extended to include quasi-security devices.[78] The Law Commission also proposes that the same types of charge and quasi-security interests should be capable of registration, even when created by unincorporated businesses, and the rules of priority should also be the same.[79]

With the 2002 Consultation Paper, the Law Commission hoped to begin amending the law of personal property within the United Kingdom, and to move toward a level of international harmonization. The vast majority of the proposals seemed to follow the previously identified international standard approaches to secured transactions law, and many of the proposals matched portions of the previously discussed international legal texts. Unfortunately, the 2002 Consultation Paper was beset by delays and problems and, as such, the Law Commission was forced to publish a second Consultative Paper in 2004.[80] In many ways, the 2004 paper tracked the 2002 recommendations, with a few new approaches and proposals.

74 *See* ibid., Summary of the Consultation Paper (2002) (hereinafter Consultation Paper, Summary).

75 *See* ibid., para. 35. For example, by proposing the filing of a financial statement and the removal of the criminal sanction for failure to file. See, Consultation Paper 164, 12.5–12.7, 12.20, 12.24, 12.29–12.30, 12.68 and for sanctions *see* ibid., 12.12–12.13.

76 *See* Consultation Paper, Summary, para. 38.

77 *See* Consultation Paper 164, 12.36–12.37.

78 Also known as hire-purchase agreements, conditional sales and retention of title clauses. *See* ibid., 12.76–12.78.

79 *See* ibid., 12.92–12.96.

80 *See* Law Commission, Paper No. 176, *Company Security Interest: A Consultative Report* (2004).

The second Consultation Report was more successful, resulting in a Final Report being issued in 2005.[81]

The Final Report did advance some of the key areas of reform, but other key areas were conspicuously absent. For example, the Law Commission retained the recommendation for notice filing,[82] and included a more specific method of filing which included the use of an electronic registry.[83] The 2005 paper also retained the 'first to file' as a priority measurement,[84] with a simple method of filing with limited information required,[85] recommended the removal of criminal sanctions for the failure to file and removed the 21-day timeframe for filing.[86] It removed the dual registration that can sometimes be required in the case of intellectual property, and other collateral covered by two registries,[87] and pulled within the scheme sales of receivables.[88] The Final Report, however, retained the distinction between fixed and floating charges[89] and rejected the previous recommendation to extend the scheme to cover quasi-security devices.[90] The Commission agreed, in principle, with the extension to unincorporated business, but left the delineation of the final scheme for further discussion.[91]

As John de Lacy, Consultant to the English Law Commission on the *Registration of Security Interests: Company Charges and Property Other Than Land* project wrote: 'by the time the Law Commission published its Final Report in 2005, the promising ideals of reforming this area, . . . had gone and a more limited scheme based on pragmatic reality of getting City practitioners to agree to reform was produced'.[92] As de Lacy points out, practitioners were fearful of the major changes proposed. Consequently, as previously mentioned, the Final Report retains the division between fixed and floating charges and rejects the recommendation to include quasi-security devices, both reform measures that most would

[81] *See* Law Commission, Report 296, *Company Security Interests* (2005) (hereinafter Report 296).

[82] *See*, ibid., para. 1.9. [83] *See*, ibid., paras. 3.69–3.71.

[84] *See*, ibid., paras. 3.149–3.155.

[85] *See*, ibid., para. 5, including merely general terms.

[86] *See*, ibid., paras. 3.149–3.155. [87] *See*, ibid., paras. 3.35–3.41.

[88] *See*, ibid., paras. 4.19–4.25. [89] *See*, ibid., para. 11.

[90] *See*, ibid., para. 1.14, but recommends further study. [91] *See*, ibid., para. 1.14.

[92] J. de Lacy (ed.), *The Reform of UK Personal Property Security Law: Comparative Perspectives* (London: Routledge Cavendish, 2010) at p. 1 (hereinafter de Lacy, PPSL, Comparative Perspectives).

consider essential in the harmonization of the law of security over personal property.

Unfortunately, even the limited reform scheme would ultimately be rejected in the Companies Act 2006, leaving the UK without harmonization of many of the key areas within its law of security over personal property. For example, the Companies Act 2006 retains the 21-day filing rule,[93] does not include provisions for electronic filing,[94] and retains the historic certificate of registration system.[95] Moreover, it does nothing to substantially alter the divisions between fixed and floating charges,[96] remains tied to the exclusion of quasi-security interests from the registration scheme[97] and does not give the much needed clarity in relation to priority contests.[98] The Companies Act 2006 does contain sections to eliminate the need for dual registration, such as those registered in special registers,[99] and does give powers to the Secretary of State to amend the scheme in the future.[100] Overall, these revisions are small in comparison to the amount of time and effort undertaken in considering the reform. As de Lacy points out, '. . . we are now left, following the most extensive law reform review ever undertaken, with essentially the same law on company charges as we had before'.[101] Unsurprisingly, he later goes on to label the new company charge provisions as a disappointment.[102]

V. The new reform efforts

Recently the Department for Business, Innovation and Skills (BIS)[103] has taken up the reform debate in relation to security over personal property by asking for comments on the Revised Scheme for Registration of

93 *See* Companies Act 2006, s. 870(1). 94 *See* ibid., s. 860(1).

95 *See* ibid., s. 869(6)(a). 96 *See* ibid., s. 860(7)(g).

97 By retaining a 'registrable charge list' (ibid., s. 860(7)) and not including *quasi*-security devices.

98 Part 25 of the Companies Act 2006 contains no rules of priority. For a further discussion, *see* Beale et al., The Law of PPS, Chapter 11.

99 *See* Companies Act 2006, s. 893. 100 *See* ibid., s. 894.

101 de Lacy, PPSL, Comparative Perspectives, p. 2.

102 Ibid., p. 3.

103 More information can be found at www.bis.gov.uk/ (last accessed 10 January 2013). In terms of the consultation, further information can be found at http://webarchive.nationalarchives.gov.uk/±interactive.bis.gov.uk/companycharges/ (last accessed 10 January 2013).

Charges Created by Companies and Limited Liability Partnerships.[104] The newest version[105] of the proposal explains:

> The main intention of the changes is to provide for a single scheme that applies to charges created by UK companies and LLPs regardless of either the location of the charged assets or the law used to create the charge. Key elements of the revised scheme include: the possibility of filing electronically; the charge instrument being placed on the public record; If there is a charge instrument, then the brief particulars being only: the registered name and number of the chargor; the date of creation of the charge, and tickboxes to show whether the charge is the subject of a court order for registration more than 21 days after the date of its creation; the instrument has been redacted along with confirmation that only permitted material has been redacted; and it is a floating charge and, if so, whether it has a negative pledge.[106]

It should be noted that the proposal eliminates some of the key areas of criticism, such as limiting the amount of information contained within the registration,[107] creating an online system of registration,[108] and eliminating the differences between Scotland, England and Wales over the list of what constitutes a 'registrable' charge.[109] In addition, the proposal tackles some previously contentious issues, such as allowing either the chargee or chargor (or someone on their behalf, such as a lawyer) to register the charge,[110] the removal of criminal penalties for failure to file,[111] creation of a clear 'date of creation' for the purposes of the time limit for registration of a charge[112] and for registration to serve as constructive notice of the charge.[113] One of the more interesting proposals involves the filing of information in relation to charges created without an instrument. Since English law allows charges to be created orally,[114] the filing of 'information that would otherwise have to be visible in the

[104] BIS, *Proposed Revision of Part 25, Companies Act 2006* (August 2011), www.bis.gov.uk/assets/biscore/business-law/docs/r/11-1108-revised-scheme-registration-of-charges-part-25.pdf (last accessed 10 January 2013) (hereinafter Proposed Revision, Part 25, (2011)).

[105] With comments closed on 30 September 2011, the BIS hope to produce a draft regulation in early 2012.

[106] Proposed Revision, Part 25, (2011), at para. 4.

[107] *See* Proposed Revision, Part 25, (2011), 860A.

[108] *See* ibid., Procedures for registration of charge, para. 2.

[109] *See* ibid., Registrable charges, option 2.

[110] *See* ibid., 860(2), Commentary.

[111] *See* ibid., 860A, Commentary.

[112] *See* ibid., 863A.

[113] *See* ibid., 863A.

[114] *See* ibid., Effect on third parties, para. 37.

filed instrument'.[115] And as a matter of future interest, the proposals do not include any provision which allows a charge registered in a specialist register to be treated as if it had been registered with Companies House.[116]

It is important to note that the proposal addresses and attempts to eliminate several other areas at issue in terms of registration: updating the list of those charges that are registrable,[117] allowing for more charges to be registered (via a mandatory and a voluntary[118] registration scheme),[119] eliminating the registration of those charges that fall within the Financial Collateral Directive,[120] and altering the effect of non-registration.[121] In addition, the clarification that a registration of an interest within a specialist register cannot satisfy the registration requirements of a charge[122] is an important and timely proposal in terms of charges secured over intellectual property, as the argument had previously been advanced in some jurisdiction that registration in the special intellectual property registry (such as copyright registration) should be treated as satisfying the registration requirements.

Of course, issues still remain that have not been addressed in the proposal, but the majority of issues are outside the remit of the particular proposal or the agency hosting the reform of the registration system. For example, the proposal retains the use of both fixed and floating charges within its text. As explained by the Law Reform Project[123] the distinction between the two does nothing but add to the confusion within the area and

115 BIS, *Registration of Company Charges, Issues to be resolved before preparation of draft regulations*, 20 (April 2011), available at www.bis.gov.uk/assets/biscore/business-law/docs/r/11-862-registration-of-company-charges-issues.pdf (last accessed 10 January 2013).

116 BIS, *Government Response, Consultation on Registration of Charges created by Companies and Limited Liability Partnerships* (Dec 2010). Foreshadowing of IP issues to come, one would assume.

117 *See* Proposed Revision, Part 25, (2011), Registrable charges, option 2.

118 Such as in the case on assignments and/or negative pledges, BIS, *Government Response*, para. 21.

119 Ibid. 120 *See* Proposed Revision, Part 25, (2011), 860(B). 121 *See* ibid., 874.

122 The revised proposals do not include any provision that a charge registered in a specialist register should be treated as if it had been registered with Companies House. BIS, *Government Response*, para. 27. 'Several respondents looked forward to the registers sharing information. However, unless and until it is possible for information filed at an asset registry to be readily available for searching at Companies House, all considered that the importance of cheap and easy searching outweighs the (relatively minor) disadvantage of a chargee sometimes having to register a charge in an asset registry as well as at Companies House.' BIS, *Summary of Responses*, Consultation on Registration of Charges created by companies and limited liability partnerships 22 (Oct 2010).

123 *See* Law Reform Project, Case for Reform.

really serves no commercial purpose. However, the distinction is required within the existing insolvency legislation.[124] The matter, therefore, can only be handled within the remit of insolvency reform.

Also not included within the proposal is a means to reduce or eliminate the confusing array of rules, case law and complicated classifications that underlie the determination of priority among competing security interests. Although the rules of priority are often thought of as distinct from the rules of registration, in some key ways there is potential overlap. First, in terms of constructive notice, and the searchable registry, these can both be important in light of priority determinations. For example, these two proposals may impact both the bona fide purchaser for value and the rule in *Dearle* v. *Hall.*[125] Both of these instances place a high amount of value on the use of notice and the existence of an easily searchable registry. The Government's response to the proposal clearly establishes '[a]ny person taking a charge over the company's property will be deemed to have notice of any previously registered charge.'[126] Of course, this most likely signals the end of the long-hated rule in *Dearle* v. *Hall*, which should be loudly applauded.

Also at issue in terms of registration reform was the potential movement away from a system of 'transaction filing'[127] toward a system of 'notice filing.'[128] After the initial consultation, the use of a notice filing system

[124] Ibid.

[125] *Dearle* v. *Hall*; *Loveridge* v. *Cooper* (1828) 3 Russ. 1. For a detailed description, *see* R. Calnan, 'What is Wrong with the Law of Security?' in de Lacy, PPSL, Comparative Perspectives, p. 175. The rule broadly provides that where the equitable owner of an asset purports to dispose of his equitable interest on two or more occasions, and the equities are equal between claimants, the claimant who first notifies the trustee or legal owner of the asset shall have a first priority claim. Subsequently the rule was turned from an example of the principle that the first in time rule will not apply if the equities are not equal into an absolute rule that the first to give notice will take priority unless the later assignee was a volunteer (*Re General Horticultural Company* (1886) 32 Ch D 512) or was aware of the earlier assignment at the time he obtained his assignment (*Re Holmes* (1885) 29 Ch D 786). The rule applies even if the later assignee made no enquiries of the trustees (*Foster* v. *Cockerell* (1835) 3 Cl & Fin 456) and even if the first assignee was not negligent in failing to give notice, for instance because he was not aware of it (*Re Lake* [1903] 1 KB 151) or because there was no one to whom notice could be given. Although the original decisions related to interests under a trust, most modern applications of the rule relate to the factoring of receivables or multiple grants of equitable security interests.

[126] UK Government Response at para. 17.

[127] Originally recommended by the CLR Report, Chapter 12 and The Law Commission's Report, but rejected in the Final Report.

[128] Used in the US, Canada and New Zealand.

was rejected for inclusion within the proposal.[129] Thus, it will remain the case that the requirement to register a charge arises after its creation,[130] with sanctions for failure to register.[131] This omission, in my opinion, is a strange one, as it is but a small step as compared to some of the other proposals being considered within the text. The absence of this provision means the law will remain without the recognition of a 'provisional' or 'pre-filing' system of registration of a security agreement. While one can appreciate the extra work that may be required of a company to confirm the final execution of the charge, the benefit of protecting one's interest and providing notice to others that may be considering extending credit with the same property as collateral seems to outweigh the additional work involved.[132] However, as the BIS explained, reform in this area would require primary legislation to replace the current scheme with one based on 'notice-filing'.[133] Therefore this option has not been considered in any real detail within the current reform efforts. However, this is certainly an issue that should be considered in the future, as there are practical issues in relation to the time lag that arise under the current system. Moreover, the issue highlights one of the main areas that has yet to be dealt with: the lack of a clear priority structure. A point that one would hope is taken up with an eye to reforming the insolvency law at the same time.

[129] Recommended in both the Crowther and Diamond Reports, see *supra* n. 72.

[130] *See* discussion *supra* at p. 235. [131] *See* discussion *supra* at p. 236.

[132] The Companies Ordinance of Hong Kong has been based on English law. Several years ago, Hong Kong underwent a reform of its Companies Ordinance, Explanatory Memorandum, www.cr.gov.hk/en/companiesbill/docs/explanatory_memorandum-e.pdf (last accessed 10 January 2013). The outcome of this reform was to continue to follow the English position on key provisions and reject the use of the Article 9-type system. Within the consultation, Hong Kong also considered and ultimately rejected the use of a system of registration that allowed for the early registration of a charge. *See* Hong Kong Companies Ordinance, Part 8, Div. 2, Clause 333, www.cr.gov.hk/en/companiesbill/docs/part8-e.pdf (last accessed 10 January 2013). Specific to the rejection, *see* Possible Changes to the Registration Regime of Charges That Have Been Considered But Rejected, Appendix V, www.cr.gov.hk/en/publications/docs/042008_app5-e.pdf (last accessed 10 January 2013).

[133] Impact Assessment, para. 21, www.bis.gov.uk/assets/biscore/business-law/docs/i/10-1336-impact-assessment-registration-of-charges.pdf (last accessed 10 January 2013). *See also*, BIS, *Proposals to amend the current scheme and relating to specialist registers*, (March 2010) emphasizing: 'Law Commission's proposals, . . . provides the Secretary of State with a power to alter, add or repeal the provisions relating to registration of charges. The Department's view is that this does not provide the power to determine the relative priority of registered charges. Therefore it is not possible to use this power to introduce a notice-filing system or otherwise provide for priority rules'. Ibid. at para. 7, www.bis.gov.uk/assets/biscore/business-law/docs/10-697-registration-of-charges-created-by-companies-proposals.pdf (last accessed 10 January 2013).

Finally, two issues remain – the system of charges created under the Bills of Sale Act and the inclusion of quasi-security devices within the entire system. Turning to the first issue, it has long been understood that the Bills of Sale Act is ill-suited for consumer lending as it has evolved in the past twenty years.[134] In December 2009, the predecessor to the BIS published a consultation on the proposal to ban the use of bills of sale for consumer lending.[135] This initiative was considered of great importance, and as such the initiative has been followed up on and continued to be advanced by the BIS. In January 2011, the BIS issued the Government Response to the consultation.[136] While it was decided that the Bills of Sale Act would continue to apply to consumer lending,[137] several provisions were to be advanced to better protect consumers in these transactions.[138] This chapter will not take up this initiative any further, as the predominance of the issues raised are more akin to consumer protection than secured lending. Moreover, this is a heavily regulated portion of the European Union framework with a new Directive in February of 2011.[139] However, this is yet a further example of the complex system of secured lending that exists in England. It is, however, unsurprising that consumers and individuals, for that matter, have been handled within a different reform structure. The majority of international legal texts and some domestic systems have found it difficult to reconcile consumer protections within a larger secured transactions regime.

In terms of the inclusion of quasi-security interests within the list of registrable charges, one must assume at this point that the debate is closed within the English reform efforts.[140] While the updated and expanded list clarifies that '[a]ll charges are registrable unless specifically

134 *See* Beale et al., Law of PPS, at para. 21.73.

135 *See* BIS, *Consultation on proposal to ban the use of bills of sale for consumer lending* (Dec 2009), www.bis.gov.uk/assets/biscore/corporate/docs/migrated-consultations/a%20better%20deal%20for%20consumers%20consultation%20on%20proposals%20to%20ban%20the%20use%20of%20bills%20of%20sale%20for%20consumer%20lending.pdf (last accessed 10 January 2013).

136 *See* Government Response To The Consultation On Proposals To Ban The Use Of Bills Of Sale For Consumer Lending www.bis.gov.uk/assets/biscore/consumer-issues/docs/g/11-516-government-response-proposal-ban-bills-of-sale (last accessed 10 January 2013).

137 Ibid. at para. 37.

138 Ibid.

139 The Consumer Credit Directive came into force in February 2011.

140 BIS, Summary of Responses, Consultation on Registration of Charges created by companies and limited liability partnerships (Oct 2010). www.bis.gov.uk/assets/biscore/business-law/docs/s/10-1230-summary-responses-consultation-registration-of-charges (last accessed 10 January 2013).

exempted'[141] several key features, such as quasi-security devices, have been omitted. Interestingly, within the Financial Collateral Arrangements Directive,[142] the European Union has come to a different conclusion upon the inclusion of financial collateral quasi-security devices. The Financial Collateral Arrangements Directive applies to financial collateral arrangements made between two persons (other than individuals).[143] Within the Directive, the term 'financial collateral' means cash or financial instruments (e.g. shares, bonds, securities).[144] While the Directive does not include forms of security over book debts (receivables)[145] or rent payments,[146] it does cover title transfers where ownership of the collateral passes to the collateral taker, on terms that it or equivalent assets will be transferred back when the obligations are discharged.[147] Moreover, the Directive covers security arrangements where the collateral taker obtains a security interest in the collateral, coupled with physical possession or control, but does not become the owner.[148] Consequently, within the context of the Directive quasi-security device involving financial collateral, such as a repurchase agreement, fall within the scheme.[149] While financial instruments are clearly a specialist type of secured transactions, it is nonetheless yet another area of law that has created the need for specific carve-out rules in both the Companies Act and the Insolvency Act.[150]

[141] BIS, Revised Scheme For Registration of Charges Created by Companies and Limited Liability Partnerships Proposed Revision of Part 25, Companies Act 2006 (Aug. 2011).

[142] Directive 2002/47/EC of the European Parliament and of the Council on Financial Collateral Arrangements [2002] OJ L168/43 (hereinafter the Collateral Directive), implementing The Financial Collateral Arrangements (No. 2) Regulations 2003 (No. 3226 (2003)); The Financial Collateral Arrangements (No. 2) Regulations 2003 (Amendment) Regulations 2009; The Financial Markets and Insolvency (Settlement Finality and Financial Collateral Arrangements) (Amendment) Regulations 2010, www.legislation.gov.uk/all?title=The%20Financial%20Collateral%20Arrangements (last accessed 10 January 2013).

[143] *See* Regulation 3. [144] *See* Directive, Art. 2. [145] Ibid. [146] Ibid.

[147] Ibid. [148] Ibid. [149] Ibid.

[150] The implementing legislation in the United Kingdom is the Financial Collateral Arrangements (No. 2) Regulations 2003 (FCAR) which came into force on 26 December 2003, as amended by the Financial Collateral Arrangements (No. 2) Regulations 2003 (Amendment) Regulations 2009 to reflect the Companies Act 2006 and by the Financial Markets and Insolvency (Settlement Finality and Financial Collateral Arrangements) (Amendment) Regulations 2010 (2010 Regulations) to give effect to the amendments required by Directive 2009/44/EC. Note that the 2010 Regulations, made on 15 December 2010, only came into force on 6 April 2011. Unsurprisingly, this has caused issues in England, *See* Look Chan Ho, 'The Financial Collateral Directive's Practice in England' *Journal of International Banking Law and Regulation* 151 [2001].

VI. Issues in the harmonization of secured transactions

One of the more perplexing problems in terms of harmonization is the means of achieving it. While one can appreciate that harmonization via a single convention would be the easiest to accomplish for the international community, this approach is very short-sighted in terms of secured transactions. The concept of placing a personal item in the possession of another to secure the performance of an obligation is a concept rooted in cultural and legal history.[151] This concept exists in most, if not all legal cultures, and is recorded in everything from the New Testament[152] to Roman law.[153] It is clear that civilizations such as the early Greek, Indian and Turkish regimes recognized the concept.[154] In fact, some of these civilizations had an advanced pledge law that included the use of a non-possessory security interest.[155] Clearly, the concept of an obligation being secured by an item is well rooted in historical legal culture. Unsurprisingly, the concept of a security interest thrives today and in many ways looks similar to the instruments of old. Consequently, systems seeking to reform the law of secured transactions are often asked to amend well-rooted legal concepts.

The well-rooted nature of pledge law creates several difficulties for the overall harmonization efforts. First, legal systems by their very nature are local. Defined by mores, cultural quirks and regional bias, law reflects both the origins of the system from which it was created and the present variations and permeation of a culture that develops the law over time. Secured transactions law captures within its broad category some of the most local law in the world – property law. Failing to recognize the local nature of property law overlooks one of the largest hurdles in terms of the harmonization of secured transaction law. Property law is embedded in almost every other area of law, thus a small change can create ripples in ways often unconsidered within the drafting of a secured transactions regime. Thus, even the smallest of tweaks to already existing law can create serious periods of uncertainty, as other parts of the legal system will also need to be reformed or updated as part of the overall harmonization process.

Second, the well-rooted nature of personal property security interest, especially in domestic systems that view its secured transactions law as

151 *See* A.J.M. Steven, 'Rights in Security over Moveables', in *A History of Private Law in Scotland: Introduction and Property*, K.G.C. Reid and R. Zimmermann (eds.) (Oxford University Press, 2000), p. 334.

152 Ibid., citing Genesis 38:18. 153 Ibid. 154 Ibid. 155 Ibid.

positive, flourishing, and/or based on years of tradition, leaves legislative bodies and the draftsmen empowered by them with an uphill battle to convince government, business and other stakeholders that the effort will be worth the cost and time. That is, of course, unless something, such as world financial crises tied to the interlinking of the financial system, draws the minds of lawmakers into the harmonization arena. In these instances, legislative bodies and the draftsmen empowered by them face a difficult decision: facilitate a complete overhaul of the entire system or tackle those issues identified as the most pressing to the overall system. Unsurprisingly in a time of financial crisis, those issues that present the greatest concern to the overall system tend to garner the greatest resources and attention because there can be no real argument against the immediate need for reform for the betterment of the entire system. For example, the European Commission on its website proclaims:

> The aim of the Collateral Directive (2002/47/EC) is to create a uniform EU legal framework to limit credit risk in financial transactions through the provision of securities and cash as collateral.[156]

Based on what was at the time viewed as an immediate need, one can quickly see that the Collateral Directive (warts and all) simply had to be pushed through, as everyone appreciated the need to address the limiting of credit risk. Yet this has put the domestic systems within the region in a difficult situation, as the Directive is substantially different from much of the existing domestic law.

The position of the English security over personal property reform efforts as it relates to the EU Directive gives us the perfect example. The already existing Company Law, the Insolvency Law, as well as the registration proposal, needed to accommodate the Directive provisions in relation to financial collateral.[157] Of course, the push to implement the Collateral Directive required an immediate allocation of time and resources to be focused on its implementation. But, for the most part, the focus was placed on the implementation of the Directive and not

[156] European Commission, *Financial Markets Infrastructure, Collateral*, Introduction page, available at http://ec.europa.eu/internal_market/financial-markets/collateral/index_en.htm (last accessed 10 January 2013).

[157] The entire implementation of the Directive required numerous changes to existing law. To review the text, see The Financial Collateral Arrangements (No. 2) Regulations 2003, available at www.legislation.gov.uk/uksi/2003/3226/contents/made (last accessed 10 January 2013).

focused on the need to consider reforming the entire system; time was too precious and the implementation could not wait. As such, the reaction to an immediate regional need takes precedence over the domestic need for a long-term plan in terms of reform. The result is not surprising: domestic legal systems are under large stress as regional concepts fail to match existing domestic law. For example, the Directive does not envisage the tracing of proceeds in the same manner as the majority of domestic or international texts. Under the Directive, the collateral taker does not have an interest in proceeds,[158] or even an interest in an equivalent asset, instead the collateral taker is left with a contractual claim for the transfer of an equivalent asset.[159] The approach taken by the Directive is a fundamentally different one than the recovery available under English law.[160] One can quickly appreciate why domestic systems seeking the possibility of reform will look cautiously at harmonization efforts that are undertaken in this manner, as the time of instability created by piecemeal harmonization will undoubtedly seem never-ending to the system.

How can this difficult situation be overcome? Actually, it should be simple: use a set of key characteristics, such as those discussed above, to guide all legislative initiates. But even this has proven incredibly difficult. First, while harmonization is a goal of many formulating agencies, there is certainly a level of competition between the agencies themselves. Professor Loukas Mistelis, from the Centre for Commercial Law Studies, highlighted the difficulties in the competition between the organizations:

> Inevitably there are at least two competing strategies in the harmonisation of international commercial law on a world-wide basis: the competition is between the 'global' conventions proposed by international organisations and the regional agreements drafted by regional organisations.[161]

And while the tension between regional and international organizations can be concerning, more at issue for the domestic systems is the fact that

[158] *See* Regulation 16 and Directive, Art. 5(3). [159] Ibid.

[160] This determination is one that is covered within the distinct concepts of fixed and floating charges. Floating charges allow a business to dispose of assets within the ordinary course of business. *See* Beale et al., Law of PPS, at para. 4.81. In the case of a fixed charge, proceeds would be considered as part of the charged asset, as traceable proceeds. *See* ibid., at para. 4.97.

[161] L. Mistelis, 'Is Harmonisation a Necessary Evil? The Future of Harmonisation and New Sources of International Trade Law', in *Foundations and Perspectives of International Trade Law*, I. Fletcher, L. Mistelis and M. Cremona (eds.) (London: Sweet & Maxwell, 2001), pp. 19–20.

these competing systems produce texts covering the same subject area, as Professor Mistelis explains:

> The goals of such regional conventions often derive from quite different motivations, but often produce agreements that concern the same subject matter as the global conventions.[162]

However, the texts are often drafted in a manner that does not consider or find concern with the potential conflicts between the competing texts. These conflicts can be found in even the most recent of secured transactions texts, even those drafted within the same organization, as Professor Gerard McCormack highlights:

> In general, UNCITRAL [in the Insolvency Guide] declined to tread on sensitive national toes by skipping over imperative recommendations on matters likely to lead to stalemate or polarization such as creditor priorities and the treatment of preferential claims.[163]

In contract, in the Secured Transactions Guide the draftsmen headed full bore into these contentious issues. Within the Guide, there are:

> no carve outs for unsecured creditors, recharacterisation of quasi-security interests, notice filing and the first-to-file priority principles with an exception for purchase money security interests.[164]

The divergence between these texts and numerous others often arise for well-founded reasons; however, the divergences are concerning for domestic systems considering reform. Concepts have to match across legislative texts and tough issues have to be resolved prior to the rolling out of the text. Legislative texts that exclude or intentionally ignore key issues within the area of secured transactions grant implicit permission for domestic systems to remain unchanged in areas of law that are the greatest hindrance to secured transactions harmonization. In the text of legislation we need as much sameness as possible if harmonization is to be supported; the incorporation of these texts into domestic systems will introduce enough variance in interpretation to cause issues for the overall system. Issues cannot remain unresolved at the creation level.

Another key issue within harmonization is the determination of the use of influential legal texts and systems. In this area, secured transaction harmonization efforts have become a serious and growing issue, as there is a strengthening voice of resistance toward the use of American

[162] Ibid.

[163] *See* McCormack, The UNCITRAL Experience, p. 181.

[164] Ibid.

law as the transplanting device. This resistance is particularly strong in relation to instruments that follow the American style of secured transactions. Professor McCormack goes into detail in making his arguments for and against this attitude.[165] In his arguments, Professor McCormack highlights a Frederick Schauer quote:

> factors other than the receiving nation's own evaluation of the legal ideas, and other than objective assessment of the worth of legal ideas, are significant determinates of the patterns of legal transplantation and legal globalization.[166]

Professor McCormack goes on to note that:

> copying US law has a bad smell in numerous parts of the world, or in some political quarters at least, and therefore avoiding American influence, just because it is American, often appears to be the driving force.[167]

And while Professor McCormack does not agree with the use of the source of law as a single determinative evaluative tool,[168] his highlighting of this growing dislike of American-style law is one that must be considered in terms of harmonization. Ultimately, much of this attitude arises from two key facts: (1) in terms of systems that need modernization, American law seems to be more widely used at least in part because of economic forces behind the drafting and eventual implementation;[169] (2) in terms of harmonization, the simple fact is that the American law of secured transactions is, for the most part, contained in a single instrument with a crowd of supporters that are willing to travel the world and sing its praises.

In terms of the first issue, while the full scope of it is beyond the coverage of this chapter,[170] one should note that this position is not surprising in the current financial situation. People, lenders and financial institutions like things that look familiar to them. There is nothing shocking about this,

165 Ibid. Some commentators argue the resistance to a US-style of secured transactions system is one reason that the Legislative Guide is not gaining wide support.

166 McCormack, The UNCITRAL Experience, p. 194, citing F. Schauer, 'The Politics of Incentive of Legal Transplantation' (2000) Centre for International Development at Harvard Working Paper Series No. 44 at 24.

167 Ibid., paraphrasing Schauer. 168 Ibid.

169 *See* McCormack, The UNCITRAL Experience, p. 72. For a further, detailed discussion of the use of the identified international standards in emerging financial systems, *see* J. Norton and M. Andenas (eds.), *Emerging Financial Markets and Secured Transactions* (Deventer: Kluwer Law, 1998).

170 For more on the topic, *see* McCormack, The UNCITRAL Experience, Ch. 3.

we gravitate toward the known. When it comes to secured transactions, if you want an American lender to be comfortable lending in a faraway place, it is easiest to convince them to lend if they have assurances that they will recover in the event of default. These assurances are bolstered by a system that looks familiar to the lenders and investors, i.e. has adopted the American approach to secured transactions. However, if we consider lenders from outside the American influence, one has to concede that some areas of the world are not at all impressed with the American way of doing business or American-influenced secured transactions law.

Moreover, some domestic and regional systems are not appreciative of the American way of drafting, influencing and selling law. The former Secretary General of Unidroit, Herbert Kronke, speaks to the difficulties created when countries with a level of economic interest and influence employ policy think tank members to draft laws:

> we must convince our Member States [of Unidroit] that private and commercial law ought to be discussed and drafted in these organizations where the expertise is, rather than through economic policy think tanks which in turn employ Norwegian, German or Wall Street practitioners who, at Wall Street rates, design Norwegian insolvency law, German company law and U.S. secured transactions law for the same client government.[171]

As Kronke points out, hired gunmen often produce laws that look remarkably similar to the laws with which they are familiar. While this approach can produce a workable domestic law, it does not produce the best long-term solutions, as the resultant law is often a patchwork of legal concepts, stitched together without an eye to the overall harmonization needs of the larger global, regional or even domestic, financial and legal system. The mention of the US within the area of secured transactions legal reform is not an accident, as Americans tend to push the use of US law in terms of secured transactions. Moreover, the hired gunman approach overlooks and often excludes the participation of those within the system seeking reform. The absence of participation of transplanting nations and the high level of participation by key economic nations is a growing concern for many nations. Unfortunately, these approaches employed by Americans are increasing the anti-American legal bias. The result is an uphill climb for the drafters of international texts when implementation is being undertaken, as the first battle in terms of reform is often a debate about

[171] *See* H. Kronke, 'The UN Sales Convention, The UNIDROIT Contract Principles And The Way Beyond' 25 *Journal of Law and Commerce* 451, at 459 (2005–6).

the use of an American-influenced and styled law, and not a debate about the usefulness of the legal concepts and text itself.

VII. Some of the immediate considerations for the English reform community

England is in a difficult position in terms of deciding if it should push ahead with its reform efforts in relation to security over personal property. This is because the reform efforts seem to be stuck at a precarious point, needing to decide: (1) if reform is needed, (2) if so, when to reform, (3) in what manner to reform, and (4) what text to use, if any, as the influencing text. Each of these determinations is greatly intertwined.

First, in terms of the need to reform, there is little argument that can be made for England not to undertake at least some reform of its security over personal property. As was explained in Section V, the BIS has put forward some interesting proposals for the amendment of the registration scheme for company charges. While one hopes this is just the beginning, it is a clear signal of two things: the reform of English law in relation to security over personal property will move ahead, and move ahead in a two-stage process – amendments to a portion of the existing system, hopefully followed by a full review of the entire system.

In terms of the text, as has been previously discussed, a set of international standards have been developed that are being used with increasing frequency around the world. However, the international standards have not been widely adopted within the region in which England sits. In fact, Europe seems to have a great distaste for the international standards of secured transactions, as these seem to be heavily influenced by the US. This situation should not dissuade the use of the international standards within England. England should seek to remain the leader within the region in terms of its law of security over personal property. Although the English law is confusing and cumbersome, in many ways it is one of the most flexible and encompassing in terms of the company's use of its assets. However, the law is also restricted in terms of the entities that can benefit from the protections within the law, contains a strange and sometimes incomplete registration system, has a highly technical and unclear set of rules in relation to priority, and has widely different rules in relation to enforcement. Each and every one of these issues can be amended with the relevant international standards. These changes would push the English law into the realm of the not so confusing.

In terms of the timing and the manner of reform, these two issues are being pushed by actions of the EU. The EU has stepped in and created several asset/transaction-specific directives and regulations in relation to security over personal property. While these EU initiatives have not been met with high praise within the region, the initiatives have forced England to undergo reform that reflects these directives and regulations. Unfortunately, this has prompted two immediate consequences: England has been forced to begin the reform process without full consideration of the entire system, and the reform is occurring in a piecemeal fashion. At this point, there seems little that can be done about this. More concerning might be the impact that these EU efforts have on the overall reform efforts in England. One has to wonder if the activity of the EU in relation to some of the big ticket and prominent areas of secured transactions will reduce the likelihood of harmonization of the entirety of the laws of security over personal property.

There remains one key issue to consider: what should be done in the future to reform the English law of security over personal property? It seems that in this area, the Secured Transactions Law Reform Project[172] may be best suited to address this issue. One hopes that the Reform Project moves expediently in examining the English law relating to secured transactions and to consider the need for and shape of future reform.

VIII. My humble suggestions: an argument to reform the entire system

As has been pointed out numerous times, many jurisdictions have undergone the process of reform, even some that started from a legal culture and text that is similar or the same as the law of England. One has only to look at the most recent experience of Australia.

The Australian Personal Property Securities Act (PPSA) (2009) amended by the Personal Property Securities Amendment (Registration Commencement) Act 2011[173] is the most recent example of a domestic system that has reformed with the use of the international standards. In many ways, Australia is a good system for comparison, as it shares a set of hurdles similar to those faced by England. Prior to reform, Australia had in excess of seventy pieces of legislation at both the state and

172 Information available at http://securedtransactionsproject.wordpress.com/ (last accessed 10 January 2013).

173 Personal Property Securities Amendment (Registration Commencement) Act 2011.

Commonwealth level that govern the registration of securities, with numerous registers across Australia, at either state or Commonwealth level.[174] '[R]egistration and search varied according to jurisdiction, the nature of the collateral, the kind of security interest or whether the debtor is a natural person or a company.'[175] Moreover, some interests were required to be registered on more than one register to gain protection, some interests could not be registered at all[176] and the majority of registries were stand alone.[177] Consequently, it is easy to see why the Australian personal property securities law was criticized in a similar manner to the law of England as being hindered by levels of 'inefficient complexities'.[178]

Also in a similar vein as the English law reform efforts, the Australian reform efforts suffered from slow progress and loss of momentum:

> There can be no single cause of such slow progress, but a list of factors would arguably include the lack of business and government enthusiasm, ignorance of what the reform would mean, and the loss of momentum in favor of other projects, such as tax and consumer credit reform.[179]

Despite these issues, Australia has now moved into the fellowship of nations that have reformed domestic law based upon the harmonized secured transactions standards.[180] The influence of the international

[174] *See* Australian Government Initiative, Personal Property Securities Register, PPS Roadshow 2011 (transcript, part 1), available at www.ppsr.gov.au/NewsRoom/News/Road_Show_2011/Pages/Road_Show_2011.aspx (last accessed 10 January 2013).

[175] Australian Attorney-General's Department, Office of Legal Services Coordination, *Discussion Paper, Review of Registration and Search Issues, the Law of Personal Property Securities*, (Nov. 2006) para. 5, available at www.ppsr.gov.au/Information_resource/Documents/PPS-DiscussionPaper1.pdf (last accessed 10 January 2013).

[176] *See* ibid. [177] *See* ibid. (transcript, part 1).

[178] P. Quirk, 'Whether Australian Secured Transactions Laws Will Transition From The English System To The Personal Property Securities Act? 31 *Thomas Jefferson Law Review* 2 (2009).

[179] Quirk, ibid., 226, citing R. Goode, 'The Codification of Commercial Law', 14 *Monash University Law Review* 135, 138–9 (1988).

[180] I do think it is incredibly important to note that Australia literally poured money into the reform efforts. 'The Australian federal budget of May 2007 allocates $113.3 million to the Australian Federal Attorney-General to implement proposals for a new scheme of personal property securities law over the following five years.' Quirk, Australian PPSA, 232, citing Media Release, Australian Attorney-General's Department, Personal Property Securities Reform (8 May 2007) (on file with author), available at www.ag.gov.au/www/agd/agd.nsf/Page/PublicationsBudgetsBudget_2007 (last accessed 10 January 2013) (click on the link for 'Media Releases'; follow hyperlink to 'Personal Property Securities Reform').

texts and other reformed domestic systems is both obvious and stated in numerous reform consultation/discussion texts:

> New Zealand revised its personal property security arrangements in 2002, and it is proposed that Australia should adopt the New Zealand model as a basis for reform except where good cause can be shown for departing from the approach taken in New Zealand. One substantial benefit of this approach is that it would more closely harmonise the arrangement in Australia and New Zealand, consistent with the goal of achieving closer economic relations between the two countries.[181]

The final text of the Australian PPSA does, in fact, substantially follow both the concepts and text of the New Zealand Personal Property Securities Act 1999,[182] as well as the work by the United Nations Commission on International Trade Law and the International Institute for the Unification of Private Law. In fact, the New Zealand Law Commission's Advisory Committee acknowledged the influence of the Canadian and American models in the creation of its Act. As important to note is the Commission's stated intent to 'adopt standardised procedures between Australia and New Zealand'[183] while 'playing a significant role in harmonisation between Australasian jurisdictions and their major trading partners in Canada, the United States and the United Kingdom'.[184] The influence of the texts of both international institutions and harmonized domestic systems is clear at this point, at least within common law jurisdictions.

However, one must appreciate two key points in relation to the reform; none of the reforming common law nations cited sit within the same geographic or political region as England, and all of the reforming nations

[181] Australian Attorney-General's Department, Office of Legal Services Coordination, Discussion Paper, para. 50.

[182] The various discussion papers, text and the roll out of the process to the community that Australia has undertaken can be found at the Personal Property Securities Register, hosted by the Australian Government at www.ppsr.gov.au/Pages/ppsr.aspx (last accessed 10 January 2013). The text of the New Zealand PPSA 1999 can be found at www.legislation.govt.nz/act/public/1999/0126/latest/DLM45900.html (last accessed 10 January 2013). The New Zealand PPSA underwent amendment (primarily in relation to financing change statements) in 2011. Personal Property Securities Amendment Act 2011, available at www.legislation.govt.nz/act/public/2011/0042/latest/whole.html#dlm3558101 (last accessed 10 January 2013).

[183] D. Brown, 'The New Zealand Personal Property Securities Act 1999', in de Lacy, PPSL, Comparative Perspectives at p. 328, citing, *A Personal Properties Securities Act for New Zealand*, NZLC R8 (Wellington: Law Commission 989), pp. 8–9.

[184] Ibid.

frequently cited had several political and economic reasons to adopt the American style of secured transactions.

In terms of location, England is not the odd-man-out in terms of its law in relation to security over personal property when compared to the laws of its neighbours within its geographic region. In fact, the entire region has widely divergent laws and approaches to security over personal property. The reform of the English law in relation to security over personal property will not change this fact. Moreover, Australia did not have to navigate, anticipate and react to regional institutions such as the EU. The reform of security over personal property must be done with careful planning and understanding of the forces that drive directives within the EU. Australia was free to design its law as it saw fit, with the hope of moving toward harmonization within a region that had already begun to use the American style of law. England is not in the same position, as its reform efforts will be first within the region to adopt the international standards. These two points are fundamental and must be taken into account when comparison is made between the common law jurisdictions. However, these points must be considered, not something that should be used to justify stopping the use of international standards or the reform of the entire system.

IX. The plan for the reform of English law of security over personal property

The English reform efforts must stay focused on three key areas: (1) move forward to amend the scheme of registration for company charges, (2) design a system of secured transactions based on the international standards, and (3) convince industry that a comprehensive reform of the system is worth the effort. Of course, as everything in this chapter, the successful completion of these three elements is based in an intertwined series of issues.

England has already done the vast majority of the hard work in considering, suggesting, evaluating and drafting the text of a reformed personal property security act.[185] The Law Commission, prior to its final report, encapsulated the vast majority of the concepts considered essential in the establishment of a modern secured transactions law,[186] some of which mirror or arise from giving greater deference to the international

[185] *See supra* n. 103 and corresponding text at pp. 240–1. [186] Ibid.

legal texts.[187] These recommendations should be the starting point of the reform efforts; to argue anything else would, in this author's opinion, be foolish.

As previously highlighted, the Law Commission focused on four broad areas in need of reform: (1) shifting to a notice system of filing and hence registration, (2) the inclusion of *quasi*-security devices, (3) overseas companies, and (4) unincorporated businesses and individuals.[188] The BIS has taken the lead in the more recent reform efforts, specifically in terms of registration.[189] Within its suggestions to amend the registration scheme are numerous advances that seek to simplify and streamline the registration process as it relates to company charges.[190] However, as described in Section III, the secured transactions system needs reform from top to bottom. It is within the areas outside the registration scheme that the Secured Transactions Law Reform Project can be the most beneficial. The Project has been set up to 'examine the English law relating to secured transactions and to consider the need and shape of future reform',[191] laudable goals under the circumstances.

Probably most impressive, in terms of the Project, is its intent to attempt to involve industry to a greater extent than any other prior reform effort. As previously discussed, one of the major issues for the reform of English security over personal property law is the apathy of business, government and the academic community. The various international and domestic reform efforts have discovered one universal truism – government and industry support is essential to successful reform of secured transaction law.[192] One only has to look to the Cape Town Convention as an example of 'practice driven drafting'[193] that has garnered both industry and government support. While industry was, to a limited extent, behind the previous attempts to amend the personal property security reform in

[187] *See* discussion at p. 228. [188] Law Commission, Consultation Paper 164.

[189] One should note that while one could argue that the use of a filing system does not necessarily improve the access to credit in developing nations, few could argue against the usefulness of a robust filing system in the context of an interconnected Europe with a large variety of truly movable assets.

[190] *See* discussion, Section V at p. 240.

[191] *See* Law Reform Project, Case for Reform, website, information available at *supra* n. 1.

[192] *See* Section II at p. 228.

[193] Kronke, 'The UN Sales Convention', citing Unidroit, Protocol to the Convention on International Interests in Mobile Equipment on Matters Specific to Aircraft Equipment, 16 Nov. 2001 (Cape Town, South Africa).

England, the government failed to invest time and resources.[194] And when the tide turned and it became clear that a full reform, one encompassing all areas of law impacted by the reform of personal property security law, failed, industry lost its patience and its willingness to enter into the unknown. At least for a period of time, England had lost the will,[195] the investment and the belief in its ability to reform security over personal property.

The overall loss of will is captured in the Government Response (2010) to the Consultation on Registration of Charges created by Companies and Limited Liability Partnerships.[196] The response explains the wide consultation that was desired; however, this seems not to have materialized. The consultation document was placed on the BIS website and links to it were sent to 144 individual organizations. In addition, 800 others who have been asked to be on the BIS circulation list for matters relating to corporate law and governance were alerted to its publication. Yet the BIS received only thirty-three responses: four from legal professional associations, six from law firms, seven from individual lawyers, academic or practising, three from accounting bodies, six from bodies primarily representing those who use the information on the public record, one each from the British Bankers Association, Lloyd's and the Confederation of British Industry, as well as responses from the Registers of Scotland, the Land Registry, the Financial Markets Law Committee and the Financial Services Authority.[197] While one can appreciate that several

[194] *See* Law Reform Project, Case for Reform.

[195] In the more recent Consultation on Registration of Charges created by companies and limited liability partnerships, the Summary Of Responses of Oct. 2010 notes that the Consultation Document had an attempted wide solicitation of responses. The Consultation Document was placed on the departmental website, links to it were sent to 144 individuals and organizations, and 800 others were notified based on their participation in the department's circulation list for matters relating to corporate law and governance, and who were all alerted to its publication. Even an internet discussion forum was set up with threads for each of the main policy areas. Yet just 33 responses were received. See BIS, Consultation Summary of Responses, para. 9, www.bis.gov.uk/assets/biscore/business-law/docs/s/10–1230-summary-responses-consultation-registration-of-charges.pdf (last accessed 10 January 2013).

[196] BIS, Government Response, Consultation on Registration of Charges created by companies and limited liability partnerships (2010), www.bis.gov.uk/assets/biscore/business-law/docs/g/10–1319-government-response-consultation-registration-of-charges.pdf (last accessed 10 January 2013).

[197] BIS, Summary of Responses, Consultation on Registration of Charges created by companies and limited liability partnerships (Oct 2010) www.bis.gov.uk/assets/biscore/

of these responses were coordinated across large professional bodies, the lack of response is concerning. The Project is attempting to overcome some of this apathy by engaging industry at a greater level by organizing seminars with industry, practitioners, judges and academics designed to elicit group identification of the problems within the already existing law, evaluate prior reform proposal and to consider the path forward for the reform efforts.[198] Reading the aims of the Reform Project, one can quickly ascertain that this approach will take considerable time and investment. It is often the first refuge of the pessimists to argue that the effort is too great, the cost is too high and the time is either not right, or not available to make the harmonization of secured transactions law a priority. However, these reasons are not enough to justify the continued lack of harmonization efforts. Canada underwent reform to great success[199] New Zealand has a new personal property security law,[200] as does Singapore,[201] Hong Kong,[202] and Australia.[203] Important to consider in terms of the influencing laws, these countries have not all adopted wholesale the US style of secured transactions. Instead, each system weighed its options and undertook the harmonization efforts it thought were essential to its global future in secured transactions, most with great effort, cost and invested time sunk into the harmonizing efforts.

In this same vein, the pessimists would argue, are the cost, time and difficulties associated with the fact that secured transactions laws must be reformed in conjunction with insolvency laws.[204] The secured transactions system must be considered as part and parcel of a larger system of lending and finance. And of course, any secured transactions reform must work in conjunction with insolvency updates and/or reform.

business-law/docs/s/10–1230-summary-responses-consultation-registration-of-charges (last accessed 10 January 2013).

198 The first of which took place in December 2011. The Secured Transactions Law Reform Project, *Secured Transactions Law: the Case for Reform* (2011), available at http://securedtransactionsproject.files.wordpress.com/2010/12/case-for-reform.pdf (last accessed 10 January 2013).

199 *See also*, Cuming, *An Overview of a Canadian Personal Property Security System* available at www.natlaw.com/pubs/overview.htm (last accessed 10 January 2013).

200 *See* discussion at p. 23. 201 *See* n. 132.

202 *See* n. 132. 203 *See* discussion at p. 230.

204 For just one example, *see* Office of the General Counsel, Asian Development Bank, *Technical Assistance Completion Report*, (2005) (stating 'the important issues and concerns relating to secured transactions law reform necessitated a parallel examination of the issues involving insolvency, and how these intersect with each other') available at www.adb.org/Documents/TACRs/REG/31389-REG-TCR.pdf (last accessed 10 January 2013).

There is little doubt that the insolvency laws must be reflective of and responsive to the changes in the secured transactions law. Without this interaction the best secured transactions law will be destined to fail. Although the need to reform two interrelated, yet separate, laws is a daunting task, it is not a problem that has not been overcome on numerous other occasions.[205] Instead, the presence of the concern strongly suggests that reform efforts must be highly coordinated or reform will fail.

Consequently, the reform advocates must redouble their efforts in terms of convincing industry that the work will be worth investment. To undertake this project, England should consider the drafting and reform efforts surrounding the Cape Town Convention.[206] Leaving aside the shear breadth of the Convention itself,[207] the drafting and eventual success of the Convention[208] can be tied to several factors which English drafters should take on board. Of note should be: (1) interest groups should serve as active, committed, long-term participants – not merely after the fact consultants and critics, and (2) a wide, progressive, long-term structured and organized plan of progression must be established to tackle the very large task ahead. Without success in these factors the English reform efforts in relation to security over personal property will continue to be unsuccessful.

X. Conclusion

The current law of England as it relates to security over personal property is cumbersome, confusing and unclear. And while reform efforts have previously been undertaken, those efforts stalled at the implementation stage. However, new efforts are underway that would amend the law in relation to the registration of company charges, but more needs to be done. The entirety of the law in relation to secured transactions should be reformed to reflect international standards. England should undertake four key aspects of reform: (1) seek to engage interest groups and other stakeholders as active, long-term participants of the reform efforts,

[205] *See* discussion at p. 23.

[206] For a more detailed history of the drafting process, *see* www.unidroit.org/.

[207] The Convention on International Interests in Mobile Equipment (Cape Town, 2001). One of the key features of the Convention is its two-instrument structure: the Convention, which covers aircrafts, railway rolling stock and space property; and the Controlling Protocol.

[208] To date there are 35 contracting States, including the UK, the US and the European Union. For further information, *see* www.unidroit.org/ (last accessed 10 January 2013).

(2) begin a plan of publication and engagement with the community designed to convince the community that comprehensive reform is worth the long-term investment, (3) create a progressive, long-term structured and organized plan of progression that will allow the entire law of secured transactions to be reformed, and (4) design a law of security over personal property that is influenced by and developed in line with international standards.

12

Commentary on the international standards and the reform of English personal property securities law

NOEL McGRATH

I. Introduction

In the opening sentence of a chapter of a book published in 2010, de Lacy observed that, at governmental levels at least, '[t]he passage... of the company charge provisions of the Companies Act 2006 has, for the time being... signalled the end of serious debate about the reform of English personal property security law'.[1] Ironically, the ink of that chapter could scarcely have been dry before the Department of Business, Innovation and Skills (BIS) commenced yet another round of consultation on the reform of the company charge register.[2] That consultation process, begun in March 2010, has generated a number of proposed changes to the registration of company charges, which were expected to be implemented by regulations in 2012. Even at official level, the debate about the reform of English personal property security law is still, it would seem, some way from its final conclusion.[3]

The secured transactions debate requires the English legal community to choose between three options: (a) preserve the status quo; (b) enact comprehensive reform – probably based on one or more of the Canadian

[1] J. de Lacy, 'The Evolution and Regulation of Security Interest over Personal Property in English Law', in *The Reform of UK Personal Property Security Law*, J. de Lacy (ed.) (London: Routledge, 2010), p. 1.

[2] Department of Business, Innovation and Skills, *Registration of Charges Created by Companies and Limited Liability Partnerships: Proposals to Amend the Current Scheme and relating to Specialist Registers* (2010).

[3] The Secured Transactions Law Reform Project website also reports that BIS officials have indicated that the implantation of the proposed company charge register reforms 'is not intended to prejudice a thorough-going review of the law'. *See* http://securedtransactionsproject.wordpress.com/about/ (last accessed 31 March 2012).

or New Zealand Personal Property Security Acts suitably modified for local conditions; (c) enact limited reforming legislation aimed at ameliorating the worst of the current problems while maintaining the essential structures of the existing law. As the history of failed reform efforts over the last thirty years demonstrates, building a consensus around a particular choice is by no means easy. The very need for major change is strongly disputed by some well-known commentators.[4] In the absence of a loud clamour for change from those who routinely utilize English security law, the positive case for the benefits of reform must be clearly articulated if it is to be accepted. Once this has been done, reformers must then steer a difficult course between the Scylla of overly ambitious proposals which will be difficult to sell to practitioners and other stakeholders, and the Charybdis of a limited package of technical changes which may exhaust the political energy for law reform without achieving real progress on important issues.

Thus far, the English legal community has proven resistant to the charms of radical reform proposals, but if that resistance should weaken in the future, law reformers will be faced with the further dilemma of whether to adopt one of the existing international models (and if so, which one), or to attempt to develop a bespoke secured transactions system. Only when these strategic questions have been answered can the choice of working out the details of a reform package begin.

Recent decades have witnessed an unprecedented interest in the reform of secured credit regimes, with national, regional and international bodies publishing reports,[5] model laws,[6] legislative guides[7] and harmonizing instruments[8] in great number. As Raymond has rightly pointed out, many

[4] *See* R. Calnan, 'The Reform of Company Security Interests' *JIBFL* 25 [2005]; R. Calnan, 'Reforming Commercial Law' *JIBFL* 335 [2005]; R. Calnan, 'What is Wrong with the Law of Security?', in de Lacy (ed.), *The Reform of UK Personal Property Security Law*, pp. 175–80; I. Chiu, 'Replacing the Default Priority Rule for Secured Creditors: Some Reservations' *JBL* 644 [2006].

[5] The most important of the national level initiatives is the Australian adoption of the Personal Property Security Act, 2009 (Cth.); for details of this project, *see* www.ag.gov.au/PPS/Pages/HistoryofPPS.aspx (last accessed 10 April 2012).

[6] Including the Model Laws adopted by the European Bank for Reconstruction and Development, the Organization of American States and Asian Development Bank.

[7] *See* the UNCITRAL *Legislative Guide on Secured Transactions.*

[8] Including the Cape Town Convention on International Interests in Mobile Equipment and its several protocols, the UNDROIT Convention on International Factoring, and the UNCITRAL Convention on the Assignment of Receivables in International Trade.

of these documents have common features.[9] It is tempting to conclude, therefore that the job of the English law reformer has, to large extent, already been done. The models for establishing a modern secured transactions regime already exist. All that remains is for England to pick the most convenient model from the shelf, tweak it to accommodate local drafting conventions and enact it as soon as possible. This chapter will argue that the international standards identified by Raymond, though significant, may have a limited impact on the ultimate reform of English law. It further suggests that English law reformers may be better off focusing attention on limited adjustments which would enable the law to achieve the objectives of modern secured transactions code.

II. The emerging international standards in perspective

Raymond identifies twenty-two characteristics which are commonly found in international discussions of secured transactions laws. These characteristics encompass all aspects of a secured credit regime, but can be summarized briefly as follows:

(A) The law should recognize a single universal security interest which would subsume the existing security devices as well quasi-security interests such as retention of title.
(B) Security interests should be publicized in a single central registry, organized on notice-filing principles with non-registration resulting in the invalidity of the security interest concerned.
(C) Priority between competing security interests should be determined by the order of registration, subject to exceptions for purchase money security interests (PMSIs).
(D) Security interests should be enforceable through a mix of self-help and court-provided remedies.

The characteristics identified above are most clearly identifiable in the UNCITRAL *Legislative Guide on Secured Transactions*,[10] which in turn was heavily influenced by Article 9 of the Uniform Commercial Code.[11] As is

[9] Raymond, Chapter 11 above.
[10] *See* www.uncitral.org/pdf/english/texts/security-lg/e/09–82670_Ebook-Guide_09–04–10English.pdf (last accessed 8 April 2012) (hereinafter 'the Legislative Guide').
[11] *See* G. McCormack, *Secured Credit and the Harmonisation of Law: The UNCITRAL Experience* (Cheltenham: Edward Elgar, 2011), pp. 152–3 (hereinafter 'Secured Credit and the Harmonisation of Law').

well known, the impact of Article 9 is not simply confined to international instruments – it served as a model for domestic reform processes in the various Canadian provinces which were subsequently adopted as models for reform in New Zealand and Australia.

Raymond's list of internationally accepted characteristics represent what McCormack might term a 'straight-down-the-line prescription of Article 9'.[12] The main features of that system – the universal security device, the prominent role of a notice filing registration system in determining priority, the recognition of PMSIs, are to be found in the list. At one level, therefore, one might read Raymond's list as embodying two implicit claims. First, that the international legal community has adopted Article 9 as its preferred model for law reform.[13] Second, that English lawyers, by using the list of characteristics 'to guide all legislative initiatives', should do likewise.[14]

The first of these claims is not uncontroversial; indeed, Raymond acknowledges that the international texts contain 'variations of the means of accomplishing these key characteristics'. It is not the case that all international harmonization efforts have simply re-expressed the core ideas of Article 9 in a different form. In some instruments, leading characteristics of the Article 9 approach, such as the recognition of a single, all-embracing security device, are either entirely absent or substantially different in detail. For instance, the EBRD Model Law does not attempt to regulate consumer lending and confines its scope to business transactions alone.[15] It also conceptualizes perfection and priority in significantly different terms to Article 9 systems,[16] recognizes a separate retention of title-type security device[17] and omits the PMSI concept entirely. Important divergences are also to be found in other instruments. The UNIDROIT Factoring Convention does not address priority questions at all,[18] and it has been suggested that the Model Law produced by the Organization of American States, although it closely mirrors many features of Article 9, may not be sufficiently clearly drafted to warrant the recharacterization of retention of title clauses and finance leases as security

[12] Ibid., p. 153. [13] Raymond, Chapter 11 above.

[14] Ibid. [15] Article 2, EBRD. [16] Article 6.5 and Article 17.

[17] Referred to as an 'unpaid vendor's charge' in EBRD parlance, *see* Article 9.

[18] Akseli has suggested that this omission may be among the reasons why the Convention has not been widely adopted, *see* N.O. Akseli, *International Secured Transactions Law: Facilitation of Credit and International Conventions and Instruments* (London, New York: Routledge, 2011), p. 209.

interests.[19] The very structure of the Cape Town Convention implicitly recognizes that a one-size-fits-all model is not always appropriate. By according legislative primacy to its various asset-specific protocols,[20] the Convention enshrines tolerance for divergent rules for different asset classes, particularly with respect to remedies and enforcement. The international picture has retained a significant level of diversity and the core prescriptions of Article 9 have not been followed in all cases.

When attention is turned to the national level, a picture of even greater diversity emerges. The progressive successes in introducing Article 9-based systems in Canada, New Zealand and Australia has perhaps given the impression that all modernizations of security law (at least, in the common law world) will inevitably follow a similar path. Is England, as Goode provocatively puts it, 'to ignore the experience of no fewer than 60 common law jurisdictions?'[21]

In answer to this question, it should be noted that the jurisdictions which have implemented Article 9-based systems have not all adopted identical laws. To take but one well-known example, in New Zealand the Personal Property Security Act (PPSA) does not render an unperfected security interest invalid, but relies on the prospect of a loss of priority to encourage secured creditors to perfect their interests. Article 9 itself, the Candian PPSAs and Raymond's list of characteristics suggest that an unperfected security interest should be void in the debtor's insolvency. This comment is not the appropriate place to debate the merits or otherwise of the contrasting provisions,[22] for the present it suffices to note that on some points at least the reformed jurisdictions have differing lessons to teach.

Second, it is worth noting that in declining to follow the recent trend towards Article 9, English law does not stand alone among the common law jurisdictions. Hong Kong, Singapore and Ireland have all examined aspects of their secured credit regimes in recent years and have opted to continue with regimes which are organized on English lines. In Hong Kong, the Companies Ordinance Rewrite Group was unconvinced of the

[19] Secured Credit and the Harmonisation of Law, p. 124.

[20] Article 6(2) Cape Town Convention.

[21] R. Goode, 'Removing the Obstacles to Commercial Law Reform' 123 *LQR* 601, 604 (2007).

[22] For a detailed discussion of the merits of this position, *see* D. Dugdale, 'The Proposed PPSA' *New Zealand Law Journal* 268 [1998] and J. Ziegel, 'Canadian Perspectives on the New Zealand Chattel Securities Act' 7 *New Zealand Business Law Quarterly* 118 (2001).

necessity to adopt various aspects of the Article 9 system.[23] Ultimately the Group recommended the enactment of a limited series of reforms to the company charge register, including the abandonment of the conclusive certificate of registration.[24] In Singapore, the Public Consultation on the Review of the Companies Act recommended even more modest reforms to the existing position, with the Steering Committee apparently taking the view that a comprehensive reform of priorities was beyond its terms of reference.[25] The Irish Company Law Review Group proved more adventurous and adopted significant changes to the company charge register,[26] though they stopped significantly short of the introduction of an Article 9-type regime. A version of the English system of company charge registration also remains in force in India.[27]

Third, as Raymond notes, the international standards which she proposes have not been adopted by the United Kingdom's primary trading partners on the European continent. In a short chapter such as this, it is not possible even to scratch the surface of the various continental systems;[28] however, it is worth noting that the civilian systems have developed a wide variety of different credit and security laws and that so far, at least, the Article 9 model has had little impact on the continent. Indeed, a PPSA-style reform was considered and rejected by a French governmental expert group in 2005.[29]

This necessarily brief examination of the international context establishes that there is a wide diversity of solutions to the problems posed

[23] *See*, in particular, Appendix V, Second Consultation on Companies Ordinance Rewrite, (2005) available at www.fstb.gov.hk/fsb/co_rewrite/eng/pub-press/doc/2ndPCCOR_Appendix_V_e.pdf (last accessed 10 April 2012).

[24] *See* Part 8, Draft Companies Bill (2011), available at www.fstb.gov.hk/fsb/co_rewrite/eng/pub-press/doc/2nd_Consolidated.Explantory.Notes.Part8_e.pdf (last accessed 10 April 2012).

[25] *See* Chapter 6, Public Consultation on the Review of the Companies Act and the Regulatory Framework for Foreign Entities, available at http://app.mof.gov.sg/data/cmsresource/public%20consultation/2011/Review%20of%20Companies%20Act%20and%20Foreign%20Entities%20Act/SC%20Report%20Chpt%206%20Registration%20of%20Charges.pdf (last accessed 10 April 2012).

[26] *See* Chapter 8, Second Report of the Company Law Reform Group (2004) available at www.clrg.org/cuuploads/editor/file/SecondReportFinalDraft.pdf (last accessed 20 April 2012).

[27] *See* Part V, Companies Act 1956.

[28] For a useful survey, *see* E. Kieninger (ed.), *Security Rights in Movable Property in European Private Law* (Cambridge University Press, 2004).

[29] *See* the Report of the Grimaldi Group cited by J. Leavy, 'France', in H. Sigman and E. Kieninger (eds.), *Cross-Border Security over Intangibles* (Munich: Sellier, 2007).

by secured lending within both the existing body of international instruments and the existing national laws. In this context, Röver has written of a 'competition of international proposals'[30] in which Article 9-based solutions are but one contender among many in a marketplace populated by a growing number of reform offerings.

It is submitted that the characteristics suggested by Raymond are overly detailed and fail to capture the variety of international opinions and experiences. Adoption of such a list as a guide to what reform should look like and achieve is premature and would run the risk of cutting off valuable insights and options for the ongoing English debate. That is not to say that English lawyers have nothing to learn from international experience of law reform. An alternative set of characteristics, expressed at a much higher level of generality, was published in the form of the EBRD's Core Principles for a Secured Transactions Law in 1997.[31] The Core Principles seek to 'form a basis for assessing a country's secured transactions law . . . [and] to indicate the result that should be achieved'. Ironically, as McCormack has noted,[32] at least when measured in relation to companies, existing English law comes out reasonably well if tested against the Core Principles. There are two exceptions: (a) English law does not provide methods for the provision of security between all types of person (principle 7); and (b) the mechanism for publicizing the existence of security rights is far from effective (principle 8). The prospects for a more limited reform, which might address some of these shortcomings, are addressed in the next section.

III. Achieving domestic law reform: a case for incrementalism?

It is now over forty years since the Crowther Committee recommended changes to the law of secured credit in England.[33] In the intervening period, change has proven elusive and identifying reasons for the failure of the several efforts at reform is far from easy. The fact that, in spite of the manifest deficiencies of the present law, it remains possible for English lenders to take effective security over a broad range of assets

[30] J.H. Röver, *Secured Lending in Eastern Europe: Comparative Law of Secured Transactions and the EBRD Model Law* (Oxford University Press, 2007), p. 314.

[31] Available at www.ebrd.com/pages/sector/legal/secured/core/coreprinciples.shtml (last accessed 12 April 2012).

[32] G. McCormack, *Secured Credit under English and American Law* (Cambridge University Press, 2004), p. 67 (hereinafter 'Secured Credit').

[33] *The Report of the Committee on Consumer Credit* (Cmnd. 4596, HMSO, 1971).

must form a part of the puzzle.[34] A second explanation may lie in the fact that the adoption of an Article 9 system, and with it the effective abolition of the floating charge, would have important implications for the position of preferential creditors and the unsecured creditor's fund. The Law Commission has proposed a modified version of New Zealand's law, which the Commission believes would be 'broadly insolvency neutral';[35] however, it is difficult to be certain of how these proposals would work out in practice.

A third explanation may be political. McCormack has noted that 'writing a new legislative blueprint risks reopening old controversies'.[36] In circumstances where the existing corpus of English law is broadly favourable to secured creditors, it is easy to see how banks, in particular, might take the view that the risks of change outweigh the benefits of a rationalized and streamlined system. The final piece of the jigsaw is likely to be simple inertia. In order to make an informed judgment about a complete reform of English credit and security law, it is necessary to gather a substantial amount of information about how the details of the new system would work before comparing the proposed reform with existing practice. While Article 9's provisions may be more rational and coherent than their existing English counterparts, they cannot, however far one stretches one's imagination, be described as simple. It is no surprise, therefore, if some people, working under the pressures of day-to-day practice, prefer the devil they know to the new one over the horizon. It should also be borne in mind that the costs of transitioning to a radically new system will be significant. In addition to technical barriers such as the adjustment of standard documentation and the creation of appropriate information technology systems for the new regime, those using the system will have to bear a substantial burden in retraining staff and developing new expertise and work practices as part of the reform process. It is easy to dismiss such costs as a 'one-off' burden which can be overcome, but the costs of transition may be a real barrier to building a consensus for change,

34 This, of course, is in sharp contrast to the pre-Article 9 position in the US where the decision of the Supreme Court in *Benedict* v. *Ratner* 268 US 353 (1925) retarded the development of an American equivalent of the all-assets floating charge. For a full history of the development of pre-Article 9 American law after *Ratner, see* G. Gilmore, *Security Interests in Personal Property*, vol. 1 (Little, Brown & Co, 1965), Chapter 8.

35 Law Commission, *Company Security Interests* (Cm 6654, 2005) [3.165]–[3.170].

36 McCormack, Secured Credit, p. 69, citing M. Bridge, 'Form, Substance and Innovation in Personal Property Security Law' *JBL* 1 [1992].

especially where there is a perception that things are working reasonably well at the moment.

In light of the above, it may be that those interested in reform in England should consider advocating incremental changes rather than seeking a 'big-bang' alteration. As noted above, English law scores well when measured against the EBRD's Core Principles. A limited set of changes, focused on remedying the most serious deficiencies, but without a fundamental alteration of the existing structure, might not encounter the pattern of resistance and failure which has been the lot of attempts to secure an English PPSA.

The current BIS proposals are based on the power, taken in section 894 of the Companies Act 2006, to amend the legislative provisions concerning the registration of company charges. The scope of the power is narrower than was originally proposed,[37] but a literal reading of the legislation seems to suggest that the entirety of Part 25 of the Act may be open for amendment without the need for recourse to primary legislation. For political and parliamentary reasons, it seems that the scope for change is narrower still. In the course of the House of Lords debate on the section, Lord Sainsbury, speaking for the Government, indicated that the power would be used only to 'make changes within the confines of the present system'.[38] In particular, he mentioned the requirement for the delivery of the original instrument to the Registrar of Companies and the list of registrable charges as possible targets for future regulations.[39]

At the time of writing, BIS has published a detailed description of the proposed changes together with a 'mock-up' of what a revised Part 25 would look like after the introduction of new regulations.[40] These proposals address some of the more egregious problems with the existing scheme, including: the extension of the obligation to register so as to cover all charges not specifically exempted from the scheme,[41] the provision of

[37] *See* Part 31, Company Law Reform Bill 2005, which made provision for 'company law reform orders' to be made by the Secretary of State. This proposal was withdrawn following objections on constitutional grounds, *see* G. Morse et al. *Palmer's Company Law: Annotated Guide to the Companies Act 2006* (London: Thomson Sweet & Maxwell, 2007), p. 668.

[38] *See* Hansard, HL Deb., 2 November 2006, vol. 686, cols 480–481. [39] Ibid.

[40] Department of Business, Innovation and Skills (BIS), *Registration of Charges Created by Companies and Limited Liability Partnerships: Registration of Company Charges – Issues to be Resolved before Preparation of Draft Regulations* (2011) (hereinafter 'BIS Proposed Revision').

[41] Proposed s. 860B, BIS Proposed Revision.

a definition for the date on which a charge is created,[42] restrictions on the conclusive effect of the certificate of registration,[43] and a mechanism for placing redacted copies of charge documents on the register.[44] These proposals are to be welcomed. Given that the Government had indicated that the use of the section 894 power would be very limited, proposals of this nature are probably about all that can be expected with secondary legislation. However, important issues have been left unaddressed.

The first of these is priority. The company charge register has no priority effect beyond the sanction of invalidity where a charge is not registered in time. It is long past the time for English company law to accord priority to competing charges in order of registration, and it should be noted that such an approach is not an import from America or anywhere else. Time of registration was first used as a priority point in English law in 1663.[45] Its use as such continues in the much-maligned Bills of Sale Acts,[46] and its omission from the Companies Act is perhaps the single greatest failure of the company charge registration system. Once a first to file priority rule is established, it will then become possible to dispense with both the 21-day requirement and the unnecessarily cumbersome checking function which, though criticized by the Company Law Steering Group,[47] Companies House will retain (albeit in a simplified form) under the BIS proposed revision.

Another issue which could be fairly easily addressed is the extension of the company charge system to assignments of receivables. As priorities between such assignments are governed by the rule in *Dearle* v. *Hall*,[48] which Raymond has accurately described as 'long hated'[49] and which another leading English scholar has described as a lottery,[50] the extension of a reformed company charge register (at least for priority purposes)

42 Proposed s. 863A, ibid.

43 Proposed s. 869(3), ibid. Under this proposal the certificate will be conclusive evidence of the delivery of the particulars only and not, as is the case currently, conclusive evidence that the particulars of registration were correctly delivered.

44 Proposed s. 860A(3) in combination with s. 1080 of the existing legislation, BIS Proposed Revision.

45 Bedford Levels Act 1663, s. 8. For a discussion of the operation of the principle in the context of conveyances of unregistered land, *see* J. Howell, 'Deeds Registration in England: A Complete Failure?' 58 *Cambridge Law Journal* 366 (1999).

46 Bills of Sale Act 1878, s. 10.

47 Company Law Review Steering Group, *Registration of Company Charges* (DTI 2000), [3.18] and [3.20].

48 (1828) 3 Russ. 1. 49 Raymond, Chapter 11 above.

50 F. Oditah, *Legal Aspects of Receivables Financing* (London: Sweet & Maxwell, 1991), p. 141.

so as to eliminate the rule in *Dearle* v. *Hall* would be a fairly modest proposal which would simplify priorities without imposing a substantial additional burden on those engaged in receivables finance. Once these issues are resolved, others, including the shift to a system of notice filing and the introduction of a capacity to register a transaction in advance of the creation of a charge, might seem more appealing.

Once the problems with the company charge register are resolved, attention can be turned to the Bills of Sale Acts. Here the problems are more difficult to resolve, but reform of the bills of sale legislation is important because it continues to restrict access to secured credit by sole traders. Significant change here will almost certainly require the outright repeal of the existing legislation and its replacement with a statute which is focused on the needs of sole traders and partnerships, with the consumer protection elements of the existing legislation removed. Since the United Kingdom has no system of registration for sole traders, it will be difficult to design a registration system which can easily and accurately capture the unique identity of each potential debtor. A combination of identifiers, including name, place of business, and perhaps VAT numbers will be required, but if this question can be resolved, the design of the remainder of the system should require no more than a transplantation of the provisions of the reformed company system.

The above programme of reform could be achieved with two pieces of primary legislation. Upon enactment, there would still be significant problems – these suggestions omit any reference to retention of title and quasi-security interests other than assignment; however, the operation of the law would be simplified, and English law would satisfy almost all of the EBRD's Core Principles. While it is true that an English PPSA would provide a more comprehensive and ultimately neater solution to the problems of secured credit in the twenty-first century, it is also true that many other well-developed economies continue to survive and thrive without an all-embracing credit and security statute. Perhaps, after forty years of failure, the time has come to forego the perfect in favour of the possible.

13

The UNCITRAL *Legislative Guide on Secured Transactions* as a model for law reform: some conclusions

HUGH BEALE

The principal aim of the conference papers which form the core of this volume was to assess the suitability of the UNCITRAL *Legislative Guide on Secured Transactions* ('the Guide') for use in jurisdictions around the world, including the UK. In this short concluding chapter it seems better not to repeat what has been said in favour of the Guide itself[1] or its 'twin', the United Nations Convention on the Assignment of Receivables in International Trade,[2] but to consider to what extent the principal criticisms of it made in the earlier chapters are justified.

On the face of it, the Guide is a major achievement of which both UNCITRAL and the many experts who took part in its production should be proud. It was drawn up with the help of representatives of sixty States.[3] It is the product of a form of consensus. It is a guide, not a cast-iron model that States must adopt. By and large, the recommendations reflect the provisions of the most advanced schemes for security interests known to the world. What could be wrong with that?

Indeed, most of the chapters in the volume that deal with the Guide itself, as opposed to the wider role of banks and other credit institutions in the world's economies, support the Guide (and the Convention).[4] But two chapters give grounds for pause for thought.

[1] *See*, in particular, Bazinas, Chapter 8 above and Raymond, Chapter 11 above.
[2] *See* Akseli, Chapter 9 above. [3] Guide, Preface, iii.
[4] *See* not only Bazinas, Chapter 8, above, but also Raymond, Chapter 11 above. Note McGrath's comment, Chapter 12 above, at p. 265.

Halliday's chapter[5] makes us consider the motivation for any attempt to produce international or regional instruments or standards, whether they be guides, restatements, conventions or model laws. I suspect anyone who has been involved in any such process[6] will recognize some or all of the factors that Halliday mentions as likely to motivate it. Certainly, idealism is an important factor, but so is professionalization – 'legalization', and with it inter-professional competition, must play a role. So, too, does the struggle for autonomy between competing international organizations. And it would be naive to claim that what Halliday calls 'realism' plays no part. Those of us who witnessed what happened after the emergence of the new democracies in Central Europe can have no doubt. Teams of experts arrived very quickly, proposing law reform along lines that would coincide closely to their national models, whether these were North American or Western European.[7] There can be little doubt that in part this was motivated by a desire to make it easier for companies from the experts' home State to do business in the new economies, by persuading the governments of the latter to adopt legal institutions that would be familiar to the experts' States' companies.

Halliday claims that many delegates believed that UNCITRAL's work on the Guide was dominated by the delegations from the US and Canada and two US organizations.[8] I have no way of assessing the perceptions of the participants.[9] However, supposing that this is how the process appeared to some of the participants, does this mean the Guide should be rejected? Perception is not necessarily reality. Halliday has a useful list of suggestions of how the process of producing international norms can be managed to avoid such criticisms and to give the resulting instrument the best possible chance of being adopted and implemented. It would be useful to know how far the process of producing the UNCITRAL Guide did or did not conform to the recommendations. I am not in a position to say. I can only judge the published products – the Guide and the accompanying Commentary.

[5] Chapter 4 above.

[6] I have had the privilege to be involved in the various international projects, e.g. *Principles of European Contract Law, Parts I and II* (O. Lando and H. Beale, eds.) (The Hague: Kluwer, 2000) and *Principles, Definitions and Model Rules of European Private Law: Draft Common Frame of Reference* (Outline Edition) (Munich: Sellier, 2009).

[7] *Cf* Raymond's quotation of Kronke, Chapter 11 above, at p. 252.

[8] Above, at p. 7.

[9] I was present only at one session. On the day in question the US and Canadian delegations were very vocal, but so, too, was the German delegation.

McCormack makes the much stronger claim that the Guide is the product of US hegemony and imperialism:[10]

> In the sphere of secured credit, the UNCITRAL Guide can be considered as an instrument by which the norms set out in Article 9 of the American Commercial Code are writ large across the globe.[11]

It is certainly true that the Guide's recommendations resemble closely the provisions found in Article 9 and the schemes derived from it. But that itself does not prove hegemony or imperialism. It may be that the solutions proposed were chosen because technically they are the best solutions. In other words, even if Halliday's claim about the perceptions of the participants or McCormack's stronger claims of hegemony and imperialism were true, an outsider to the process like myself can judge the Guide only by the final outcome. And this is surely how it should be assessed – not so much by the means by which it was arrived at, but by what it proposes. If the solutions are indeed the best solutions, then they should be adopted. If they are not, or if they are superior only in certain circumstances that do not pertain in every jurisdiction, then they should be adopted only as and where appropriate.

However, we may also consider how the recommendations are presented. Proposals for change are more likely to be understood and accepted if they set out fully the assumptions on which they have been drafted and how far those assumptions are likely to hold true in any one country; and if they explain fully the possible alternatives and the reasons for the choices made. A document which simply sets out a scheme – particularly a scheme that for many lawyers is very different to their traditions and which seems to mirror the law of a few, powerful States – is likely to be misinterpreted.

The argument that the Guide is only a guide, not a prescriptive model law or a convention that has to be adopted in full,[12] takes us only so far. The Guide is likely to be highly persuasive. It is well known that international monetary institutions prefer to see strong legal institutions in countries to which they are considering directing finance; and a good system of security rights is certainly considered important. Bazinas is, of course,

[10] *See* also McCormack, *Secured Transactions and the Harmonisation of Law: the UNICTRAL Experience* (Cheltenham: Edward Elgar, 2011), pp. 28 and 76.

[11] Ibid., at p. 76.

[12] A point particularly emphasized by Bazinas, Chapter 8 above, at p. 135 and Gabriel, Chapter 10 above.

correct that the Guide need not be implemented in full and that States need implement only those parts necessary.[13] However, Recommendation 2 is likely to be read as a very firm call for States to ensure that their law should reflect the scheme in full. Governments hoping to attract international finance but whose laws do not provide a reasonably full scheme of security rights will no doubt think long and hard before concluding that parts of the Guide can safely be ignored. This impression can only be reinforced when, Bazinas writes, the World Bank is aligning its requirements to the recommendations of the Guide.[14]

So it seems appropriate to consider the criticisms made in this volume of the substance of the Guide and the accompanying commentary, and to ask: are the Guide's recommendations indeed the best ones? And, does the Commentary, long and detailed though it is, give enough consideration to differing conditions, alternative solutions and the reasons for the choices made?

What are the details of the complaints? Some of the points made by McCormack relate to the Guide only distantly, if at all. For example, it would be hard to contest his assertion that privatization has not been universally effective,[15] but what is the link between this and the recommendations of the Guide? A State that wants to preserve or develop a command economy, or which still favours that model for major parts of its economy, will find the Guide less useful that one contemplating a full market economy. That hardly needs to be stated in the Guide. It may also be that reluctant States will get less help from players such as the World Bank than *States* that allow a greater role to the free market. Neither point is a valid criticism of the Guide. What matters is whether it is useful for those who do wish to attract international finance to a significant sector, or to encourage financing by domestic institutions. As McCormack himself writes:

> [T]he merits of secured credit reform should be disaggregated from wider notions about the alleged efficiency of market-based decision making and the implementation of a privatisation agenda.[16]

Precisely

It is also correct that the importance of security rights, and indeed, of property rights in general, to developing economies can be overstated. McCormack is correct to point out that major economic growth can take

[13] Bazinas, Chapter 8 above, at p. 137. [14] Ibid., at p. 138.
[15] McCormack, Chapter 2 above, at p. 50. [16] Ibid., at p. 51.

place without a secure system of property rights, as seems to be happening with real estate in China. If the rewards (judged in comparison to the actor's current situation) are perceived to be great enough, people will take what to other eyes seem to be enormous risks. It is hard to know what weight to give to the argument that economies can flourish without a particular institution, however. This is because we will never know what would have happened if the institution had existed – it might have been that the development would have been even faster or more secure. Moreover, if it is argued that the people concerned are not aware of the risks they are taking, because they assume (incorrectly) that the property rights they are acquiring will be protected, then social justice demands that the rights be protected. It is also undoubtedly true that many businesses, particularly well-established ones, do not have to give security when they borrow.[17] But that does not diminish the usefulness of security, or the value of the Guide to those who cannot borrow, or can only obtain limited credit, on an unsecured basis.

So again, the argument that security rights are not a *sine qua non* to economic success is not an argument against recommending a developed system of security rights. The best evidence so far available suggests that secured credit is 'a good thing'.[18]

It is plausible to argue that a country's adoption of an effective system of security rights along the North American model may make it easier for North American industry to do business there.[19] But this point needs careful explanation. Making it easier for the foreign business should result in benefits for both sides of any subsequent transaction. It is not just the creditor who stands to benefit from more effective security; the debtor should also get the benefit of more extensive or cheaper credit. It would be a concern if the scheme proposed would permanently benefit some exporting countries, ones that are used to such provisions, over other exporting countries that are not. At first the scheme may be new and hard to understand, but is that more than a temporary phenomenon? And is there an alternative scheme that could have been put forward?[20] So while we should certainly not assume that 'what is good for the United States is

[17] Ibid., at p. 48. *See also*, Law Commission, *Company Security Interests: a consultative report* (CP No. 176, 2004), para. 1.8.

[18] *See* J. Armour, 'The Law and Economics Debate About Secured Lending', in H. Eidenmüller and E.-M. Kieninger (eds.), *The Future of Secured Credit in Europe* (European Company and Financial Law Review, Special Volume 2, 2008), pp. 3, 4–13.

[19] *Cf.* McCormack, Chapter 2 above, at p. 37.

[20] *Cf.* Bazinas, Chapter 8 above, at p. 174.

good for the world',[21] a proper critique must identify what is wrong with the recommendations or with the way in which they are explained.

We must also take into account the limited nature of the Guide. Clearly, it cannot simply be adopted by any country regardless of its legal or economic development in other respects. This is one of many valuable points made in Dahan's chapter.[22]

McCormack is not against security rights in general. It is the particular model put forward by the Guide that he criticizes. He seems to identify four particular aspects of the recommended scheme as questionable: (1) the removal of all restrictions over the kinds of asset that can be used as security; (2) the possibility of taking security over all a debtor's assets;[23] (3) full priority of security rights in the debtor's insolvency;[24] and (4) notice filing.[25] He also refers to the re-characterization of retention of title and other devices.[26] So what might be questionable about these recommendations, and what alternatives might have been put forward?

If we consider the potential effects of the recommendations as to the types of assets over which security may be taken, and particularly the 'all assets' security, there seem to be three possible problems. (A) The debtor may at the end of the day be left with nothing. (B) A secured creditor may gain excessive control over the debtor or its business. (C) Other creditors may be excluded or their rights unduly demoted.

Many laws provide that even if an individual debtor is insolvent, not all their assets should be taken by creditors. That would leave the debtor destitute and would often prevent them making a living. The Guide recognizes this, but only in an apparently limited way, in the closing words of Recommendation 17:

> 17. The law should provide that a security right may encumber any type of asset, including parts of assets and undivided rights in assets. A security right may encumber assets that, at the time the security agreement is concluded, may not yet exist or that the grantor may not yet own or have the power to encumber. It may also encumber all assets of a grantor. Any exceptions to these rules should be limited and described in the law in a clear and specific way.

[21] McCormack, Chapter 2 above, at p. 56.
[22] Dahan, Chapter 6 above, at pp. 106–7.
[23] McCormack, Chapter 2 above, at p. 35.
[24] Ibid., at p. 38.
[25] Ibid., at p. 39 ('a degree of scepticism about notice filing seems appropriate').
[26] Ibid.

This may give the impression that exceptions are undesirable, and the impression is reinforced by the Commentary:

> 56. In some legal systems, special laws for specific types of security right introduce limitations as to the types of asset that may serve as security or as to the part of the value of assets that may be encumbered. An example of a limitation justified for public policy reasons would be one preventing the creation of a security right in employment benefits (for example, wages and pensions) under a certain minimum amount. In other legal systems, limitations are placed on the purposes for which certain classes of grantors may create a security right in their assets. . . .
>
> 57. All of these limitations, which are usually intended to protect grantors, also have the unintended result of preventing grantors from utilizing the full value of their assets to obtain credit.

Though the paragraph continues,

> Therefore, the positive and negative impacts of such limitations need to be carefully weighed,

a casual reader might well get the impression that exclusions are not important, or should even be discouraged.

However, as the Guide to Secured Transactions makes clear, it needs to be read alongside the UNCITRAL *Legislative Guide on Insolvency Law*, parts of which are reproduced in the Guide on Secured Transactions.[27] The recommendations of the Guide on Insolvency Law also state merely that insolvency law should specify the assets, if any, that are to be excluded from the debtor's estate where the debtor is a natural person.[28] But study of the Commentary to the Guide on Insolvency Law reveals that it is actually suggested that there may be an exclusion for 'assets that are necessary for the debtor to earn a living and personal and household assets such as furniture . . . necessary to satisfy the basic domestic needs of the debtor and his family';[29] and:

> A further consideration may be the economic effects of exclusions; some research suggests that the full or substantial exemption of personal assets from insolvency proceedings may have a positive effect on entrepreneurship and risk-taking.[30]

So, taken together, the Guides do not in fact recommend that all of an individual debtor's assets should be subject to seizure by secured creditors.

[27] *See* Chapter XII. [28] Insolvency Guide (IG) Recommendation 38.
[29] IG para. 18. [30] IG para. 19.

But it takes some effort to work this out; and we may wonder whether the presentation of the point is as clear and as helpful to potential legislators as it might have been. If exceptions to the scheme are not only perfectly sensible but positively desirable, it would be better to spell them out wherever relevant.

Many systems try to ensure that secured creditors may not take everything even from a corporate debtor, so as to leave something for other creditors. This may be done by preventing any creditor taking security over the whole of the debtor's assets or by requiring that certain unsecured creditors be paid ahead of some secured creditors, for example, over a creditor with an 'all assets' security, and some fund may be ring-fenced to pay unsecured creditors.[31] The two methods are to some extent functionally equivalent. Again the Guide recognizes that either may be done, but the casual reader may get the impression that any such restrictions or carve-outs are strongly discouraged. This is partly because the two methods are discussed separately, without any cross-reference between them. Thus, the first reference is in the middle of a discussion of whether it should be possible to create security rights that allow the debtor also to dispose of its assets in the ordinary course of business:[32]

> 61. As mentioned above, some legal systems do not permit grantors to create a security right in assets that are described in general terms. By contrast, many other legal systems do. Nonetheless, even in some legal systems that permit the general identification of categories of encumbered assets and even permit a general identification of categories of present and future assets, grantors are often not permitted to create a security right in all of their assets (that is by means of a super-general description such as 'all present and future assets'). In other legal systems, grantors are permitted to create a security right in all of their assets, but only up to a certain percentage of their total value. Such limitations, which are intended to provide some protection for grantors and unsecured creditors, usually end up limiting the credit available to debtors and increasing its cost.
>
> 62. By contrast, some legal systems impose no limitations on the scope of a security right. Grantors are permitted to create a non-possessory security right in all of their assets, including tangible and intangible assets,

[31] In the UK, 'preferred' creditors are unpaid employees (or, if the employees are compensated by the State, the State in respect of the amount due to the employees); a former preference in favour of the State for unpaid taxes was replaced in 2003 by a ring-fenced fund for unsecured creditors. For the complex legislative provisions *see* H. Beale, M. Bridge, L. Gullifer and E. Lomnicka, *The Law of Security and Title-based Finance* (Oxford University Press, 2nd edn., 2012), paras. 20.21 *et seq.*

[32] *See* Chapter II of the Guide.

> movable assets and immovable property (although different rules may apply to security in immovable property) and present and future assets.

There is no discussion here of alternative approaches. There is a discussion of possible justifications for 'carve-outs' in insolvency, but it is much further on, in Chapter V.

> 90. In many States, as a means of achieving general social goals, certain unsecured claims are re-characterized as preferential claims and given priority within or even outside insolvency proceedings over other unsecured claims . . .
>
> 91. The advantage of establishing these preferential claims is that a social goal may be furthered. The possible disadvantage . . . .
>
> 92. To avoid discouraging secured credit, many States have recently cut back on the number of preferential claims that are given priority over existing security rights. The trend in modern legislation is to establish such claims only when there is no other effective means of satisfying the underlying social objective. For example, in some jurisdictions tax revenue is protected through incentives for company directors to address financial problems quickly or face personal liability, while wage claims are protected through a public fund. In addition, many States have also sought to limit the impact of preferential claims on the availability of secured credit by imposing a cap either on the amount that may be paid to the preferred claimant or on the percentage of the amount realized upon enforcement that may be used to pay them.
>
> 93. If preferential claims are permitted to exist, the laws establishing them should be sufficiently clear and transparent so that a creditor is able to calculate the potential amount of the preferential claims in advance and to protect itself . . .

All of this is perfectly sound advice, but it can be read as implying that carve-outs are seldom, if ever, justified. No doubt the Guide is correct that we do not need to worry about the State, which should be able to find other means to limit its exposure to the risk of the insolvency of a taxpayer or debtor which holds tax payments collected from others – efficient and prompter tax gathering, for example. Nor need we worry unduly about unsecured creditors who are alive to the risk of default by the debtor and able to levy interest or other charges appropriately. As McCormack points out,[33] the real concern is with those unsecured creditors who are either unable to adjust (such as tort victims, who have figured very prominently

[33] McCormack, Chapter 2 above, at p. 49.

in academic discussion of the issue in the US[34]) or who are poor at doing so. A legislator in a country with an under-developed economy might want to think how many of its small businesses are likely to be sufficiently sophisticated to adjust their interest charges to credit risks. Would it not have been helpful to have put more discussion and explanation into the Commentary, pointing the legislator to the relevant questions, even if, at the end of the day, the drafters of the Guide thought that on balance carve-outs are not a good idea?

The third question is whether the recommendations of the Guide will give secured creditors excessive control. This is a difficult issue. A system of security rights which does not enable the secured creditor to enforce its security will be pointless; but enforcement may have the result that the debtor cannot carry on its business. That is obviously so if the security is over all the debtor's assets, but it applies even if the security is over only a specific item, if that item is essential for the business. Should the debtor be protected in some way, and if so, how?

In many systems the traditional answer was that non-possessory security could be enforced only by or after a court order.[35] Even in systems in which this was traditional, it now seems to be acknowledged that the delay and cost that often result make the security so much less valuable that when the enforcement takes place outside insolvency, these forms of controls are being abandoned.[36] A court is not the appropriate place for dealing with these issues unless it is a tribunal that is specialist and which can act very quickly. So the Guide should not be criticized for recommending that the creditor should normally have the right to enforce its security without a court order.[37]

Enforcement when the debtor is insolvent is more important in practice; a creditor is unlikely to seek to enforce its security if it thinks that the debtor can in fact pull through. Again I think everyone agrees that enforcement should be as fast as possible; if the debtor's problems are not resolvable, delay merely prolongs the agony and normally means that the collateral falls in value, helping no one. But the debtor or other creditors may not agree that the case is hopeless, and the public interest in preserving jobs may suggest that the defaulting company should not be

[34] *E.g.* the articles cited by Armour, 'The Law and Economics Debate' at 9, n. 24 (and compare the empirical study referred to by Armour, ibid., at 11).

[35] Compare McCormack's remarks about self-help, Chapter 2 above, at pp. 34–35.

[36] *See* E. Dirix, 'Remedies of Secured Creditors outside Insolvency', in Eidenmüller and Kieninger (eds.), *The Future of Secured Credit in Europe*, p. 223.

[37] *See* Bazinas, Chapter 8 above, at p. 154.

forced into immediate insolvency. Rather, if there is a prospect of rescuing a corporate debtor, it seems more appropriate to impose a moratorium on enforcement, with or without a change of management. What matters is that whoever is in charge is not likely to act in the interests only of the creditor which appointed them. Increasingly modern systems in both the common and civil law countries are adopting procedures to restrain individual creditors from enforcing their rights, either by centralizing the powers to realize the assets with an administrator or by imposing a moratorium.[38]

On this, the Guide says:

> 65. An interesting feature of some forms of enterprise mortgage is that, upon enforcement by the secured creditor or another creditor, an administrator can be appointed for the enterprise. This may assist in avoiding liquidation and in facilitating reorganization of the enterprise with beneficial effects for creditors, the workforce and the economy in general. Sometimes, however, administrators appointed by the secured creditor may favour the secured creditor. This problem may be mitigated to some extent if the administrator is appointed and supervised by a court or other authority. This enforcement feature of an enterprise mortgage might usefully be expanded to all-asset security rights. In other words, a secured transactions law might provide for the appointment of an administrator either by agreement of the grantor and the secured creditor or by the court. The administrator would then be responsible for enforcing the security right outside insolvency and, subject to insolvency law, even in the case of insolvency.

However, it is not only a question of creditor control on or just before insolvency. Economists have argued that the system should encourage monitoring by creditors; and that the most plausible way of encouraging this is to allow a creditor to have an interest in the business as a whole – in other words, a creditor with an all assets security is more likely to monitor the debtor's situation carefully, and to give advice when needed, than one whose interest is limited to a particular asset or assets.[39] This seems to be another argument in favour of allowing 'all assets' securities, though I did not see it mentioned in the Guide.

McCormack's last doubt seems to be over notice filing. There are two issues. The most basic one is whether publicity should be required at all. There are systems, like those in Germany and the Netherlands, in which there is no register, or at least no register that is accessible to

[38] Dirix, 'Remedies of Secured Creditors', 225.

[39] *See* Armour, 'The Law and Economics Debate', at 16–17.

third persons, from which it may be discovered whether or not a debtor has created non-possessory security over its assets. In these systems it seems to be assumed that potential creditors who want to get information about a debtor's affairs must either ask the debtor and trust it to give full and accurate information; or must ask all potential lenders. Such a system perhaps works conveniently among a small group of possible lenders who are prepared to give information to each other, but it seems reasonable to suspect that it may result in restricting competition from financiers outside the group. The Guide is surely right to say that allowing grantors to create 'secret' non-possessory security interests in property which remains in the grantor's possession may negatively impact on access to and the cost of secured credit.[40]

More probably, McCormack's concern is over the Guide's recommendation that the registration system be one of notice filing, which is a key feature of the US and Canadian legislation. This certainly differs from some legal traditions. In some, such as Scots Law, registration is seen as an essential step in the creation of the security right.[41] In others, such as in the law of England and Wales, registration is a perfection requirement rather than one of creation, but it is possible only after the security has been created.

Notice filing seems to have some advantages over either system. In particular, when combined with a system in which the priority of competing security interests is primarily based on the date of registration, it enables a creditor which is considering making a secured loan to secure its priority in advance, and thus not to have to worry that another competing interest might rank ahead of its own. But again we may ask whether the Guide and the Commentary explain the issues as fully as they might.

The reasons given for a scheme which separates the questions of effectiveness between the parties and effectiveness as against third parties, as opposed to a scheme in which the security interest is created by registering, are that:

> most legal systems impose fewer formalities for the effectiveness of contractual obligations between the parties than they do when property rights are being created . . . [and] there is no need to subject effectiveness as between the parties to notification or registration, which could create an

[40] Chapter III, para. 20.

[41] *See* Scottish Law Commission, *Discussion Paper on Moveable Transactions* (DP No. 151, 2011), paras. 5.9 and 20.16.

> obstacle to transactions that serve security purposes but are based on informal sale or lease techniques (such as retention-of-title sales and financial leases).[42]

Notice filing, as opposed to registration of an actual transaction (possibly including placing the security document on the register) is justified quite briefly:

> 13. Notice registration has many advantages. It greatly simplifies the registration process and minimizes the administrative and archival burden on the registry system. In addition, registrants are relieved of the delay and cost of having to provide proof of the underlying security documentation. Moreover, the registry is relieved of the need to provide storage facilities for that documentation and to employ staff to scrutinize it. The risk of error and consequent liability of the registry is also greatly reduced. Furthermore, because the notice need contain only basic details, it is much easier to establish an electronic entry to record this data, rather than having to file the notice in a less time- and cost-efficient paper system. Finally, registration of a notice rather than a document is sufficient in view of the legal consequences of registration, that is, thirdparty effectiveness rather than creation of a security right . . .[43]

However, that begs a big question: what is meant by a security interest? The statement seems to be predicated on the assumption that, as in Article 9 and the PPSAs, retention of title devices and/or outright sales of receivables should be registrable. This is not the case in many jurisdictions that have highly developed systems of finance. Thus, in the UK, a charge created by a company over its 'book debts' (which will encompass many, but not all receivables) is registrable,[44] but an outright assignment of book debts is not.[45] Nor are title-retention devices.[46]

Title retention was a topic on which it was hard to find consensus, and in the end a compromise was reached which is based on the solution found in the Quebec Civil Code. The Guide recommends that in respect

[42] Chapter II, para. 3. *See* also Bazinas, Chapter 8 above, at p. 136.

[43] Chapter IV, para. 13.

[44] Companies Act 2006, s. 860(7)(b)(vii).

[45] A general assignment of book debts by an unincorporated trader is registrable as a bill of sale: Insolvency Act 1986, s. 344.

[46] However, a clause retaining title to inventory and claiming that the supplier is entitled to either new products made from the inventory supplied or to the proceeds of sale is almost certain to amount to a registrable charge over those forms of proceeds: *see, e.g.*, *Clough Mill Ltd* v. *Martin* [1985] 1 WLR 111, *Re Andrabell* [1984] 3 All ER 407 and other cases cited in Beale, Bridge, Gullifer and Lomnicka, *The Law of Security*, para. 7.19.

of such devices when they are used to provide acquisition finance, States may adopt one of two approaches:

> States may adopt what is characterized, for the specific case of acquisition financing, either a unitary or a non-unitary approach... Under a unitary approach, the same basic principles... would apply to all acquisition financing transactions... Under a non-unitary approach, States would retain separately denominated acquisition financing devices... the ownership rights of a retention-of-title seller and a financial lessor would be maintained, but the specific rules governing each transaction would be adjusted so as to produce outcomes that are functionally equivalent to those produced by an acquisition security right...[47]

In fact, this is a very limited concession to the traditions of States that do not treat retention of title devices as security for any purpose. Even under the non-unitary approach, registration is still recommended for purposes of priority and perfection. On enforcement, it appears that should the creditor realize more than the secured obligation, a non-unitary scheme *may* provide that the surplus may be kept by the supplier,[48] but the Guide strongly suggests that there should be rules applicable to retention devices that would in effect require any surplus to be paid over to the debtor or junior creditors,[49] as would be done under the unitary approach.

There is not space here to discuss in full the Guide's approach to either title-retention devices or to outright sales of receivables. In respect of each, a good case can be made for requiring registration, at least for the purposes of perfection and priority, even if, as I have argued elsewhere, nether case is as strong as it is with traditional security rights.[50] The point I wish to make here is much simpler. It is that the possibility of filing once for a series of transactions, which is often said to be one of the great advantages of a notice-filing scheme, is really only necessary if it is contemplated that parties will enter into many small, repeated transactions. That is likely to happen if clauses retaining title to inventory supplied are to be made registrable, or if outright sales of receivables are to be made registrable and

[47] Guide, Chapter I, para. 111.

[48] *See* Recommendation 200(a) ('Rules... should deal with... (iii) Whether the seller or lessor may retain any surplus; ....').

[49] Chapter IX, para. 194. The fact that the parties may deliberately have chosen a different structure with the intention that the creditor should retain any surplus seems to be ignored.

[50] *See* H. Beale, 'The Exportability of North American Chattel Security Regimes: the Fate of the English Law Commission's Proposals' 43 *Canadian Business Law Journal* 177 (2006).

the sales are likely to occur in small blocks, each one being a separate sale of receivables.[51] In contrast, if only traditional non-possessory securities such as charges are to be registered, transactions are likely to be much less frequent and filing to create the interest or as post-creation perfection requirement can work perfectly well – particularly if potential secured creditors are provided with the facility to register a priority notice that will secure priority in respect of any security interest actually taken within, say, three weeks after the registration. Indeed, such a system might have advantages, as there would be less of a potential problem of 'empty filings', notices that were filed by creditors who never in fact entered a security agreement. A short-lived priority notice can simply lapse after the period of guaranteed priority has ended without an actual security interest being registered.

Further, if 'transaction filing' were adopted, and at least if the registry were electronic, it would be possible to require the creditor to put the charge document on the register. The Guide's warnings about 'the administrative and archival burden' seem to reflect concerns that are outdated with modern information technology. The UK Department of Business brought in just such a system in 2013.[52] There are arguments for and against. On the one hand, simply registering the document is a good deal easier for the secured creditor, as there is no risk that the particulars might omit an item of collateral; and the register will provide searchers with much more information than is available under a notice-filing scheme. That will save making so many enquiries of the secured creditor. On the other hand, having the full document rather than a shortlist of collateral may make it harder for searchers to see quickly what is or is not covered by the security interest;[53] and in any event, potential second secured creditors may still have to ask the first, registered secured creditor for information that will not be shown, such as the amount currently secured.

Lastly, if small (and probably informal) agreements such as retention of title for inventory and outright sales of receivables are not to be covered, so

[51] *See* Law Commission, *Company Security Interests* (Law Com No. 296, 2005), paras. 3.86–3.91.

[52] *See* Raymond, Chapter 11 above, at pp. 24–4 and McGrath, Chapter 12 above, at p. 271. The proposals are explained in some detail in Beale, Bridge, Gullifer and Lomnicka, *The Law of Security*, Ch 10. The changes were introduced in April 2013 (SI 2013/600).

[53] This seems to be behind the new requirement that the charge must also give limited and brief particulars of the property charged. It is wholly unclear what the position is to be if the particulars accidentally omit to mention an item of collateral that is listed in the charge document itself.

that post-agreement 'transaction filing' would be adequate, the argument for dividing creation from third party effectiveness is weakened. It will be very rare that a secured creditor will want to enforce its right against the debtor before it has registered it to ensure its effectiveness against other parties. Thus there seems little force in the argument that creation and effectiveness should be kept separate. The Scottish Law Commission's *Discussion Paper on Moveable Transactions* has provisionally proposed that registration should be a necessary step to create a non-possessory security, as this is consonant with the Scottish tradition.[54] It is not obviously unworkable.

This is not the place to debate the arguments in full. I am personally in favour of requiring the registration of outright sales of receivables at least;[55] and if that is to be done, notice filing would be an advantage. My point is quite different. It is that the Guide comes out strongly in favour of a scheme that in most respects models Article 9 and the PPSAs very closely, but it does not always explain the contingent nature of its more controversial recommendations or, indeed, the full reasoning behind the choices that have been made. It is this, I suggest, that can lead a reader who knows the law in the US and Canada, but who does not know what discussions took place or how decisions were reached, into thinking that the delegations from those jurisdictions may have had a dominating influence. Halliday says:

> One-size-fits-all norms, a lack of alternative ways of conforming to high level norms, the attempted imposition of bright-line rules on all countries – all these increase the probability of avoidance or rejection by nations or their interest groups.[56]

I do not argue or believe that the Guide is an attempt to impose a rigid system or that the drafters thought that only one system is acceptable. Nor do I want to suggest that the drafters of the Commentary have not tried hard to give clear explanations. I am quite ready to assume that the Commentary reflects the discussion. It is possible that some of the issues I have raised were not discussed, since if one group had a ready-made solution that appeared convincing, others may not have taken every point that, with the benefit of hindsight, we might think could have been argued. However, my impression of the Guide and Commentary is that there is not

[54] *See* Beale, Bridge, Gullifer and Lomnicka, *The Law of Security*, p. 41.

[55] For the reasons set out in Law Commission, *Company Security Interests* (LC No. 296, 2005), Part 4.

[56] Halliday, Chapter 4 above, at p. 81.

always as much explanation, such a full exploration of alternatives good and not-so-good, as we might want and need in order to convince those who are unfamiliar with such a complex scheme and may be sceptical of it.

Fortunately, it is not too late to make the arguments and thereby to correct any false impressions. No doubt much more will be written about the Guide and many presentations will be made by its supporters. They can take the opportunity to explain and justify its recommendations more fully, and to show why they are thought to be technically better than any of the alternatives. I hope they will do so. I believe that the Guide is a valuable tool and that legislators who follow it, or at least its general principles, and also provide the other institutions that must go along with its recommendations, will help their economies in a very significant way.

In countries like the UK that already have a developed system of security rights but along substantially different lines from the model recommended by the Guide, it seems unlikely that the finance industry, the legal profession or the Government will wish to adopt wholesale reform without a clear demonstration that the current system is not working. That case simply cannot be made at present. The most that can be said is that the system could be made to work more efficiently. The changes effected by BIS[57] introduce some improvements; and certainly there are others that are long overdue. For example, it would be good to replace the system of registration within 21 days, with the concomitant that a great deal of money is wasted each year on applying to the court to register out of time, with a system where priority depends on the date of registration.[58] But though there are those who argue for a more-or-less complete 'Article 9'-type scheme based on the provisional proposals in the Law Commission's Consultative Report of 2004,[59] McGrath[60] is probably right to suggest that incremental changes are more likely to be fruitful. There are signs that this may happen. In late 2012, the City of London Law Society, which was seriously opposed to many aspects of the Law Commission's scheme, produced a discussion document which contains

57 Beale, Bridge, Gullifer and Lomnicka, *The Law of Security*, p. 53.

58 *See* also Raymond, Chapter 11 above, at pp. 243–4.

59 *See* the Secured Transactions Law Reform Project led by Professor Sir Roy Goode, referred to by Raymond, Chapter 11 above, at p. 254. Details may be found at http://securedtransactionsproject.wordpress.com (last accessed 26 December 2012).

60 Above, at p. 269.

quite radical proposals on traditional security, including replacement of the current multiplicity of types of mortgage and charge by a single security interest.[61] If the debate over fundamental reform of security interests in the UK develops, the UNCITRAL Guide to Secured Transactions will be very helpful and influential, even if its more far-reaching proposals, such as re-characterizing quasi-security devices,[62] are very unlikely to be adopted in the foreseeable future.

[61] *See* www.citysolicitors.org.uk/FileServer.aspx?oID=1290/1ID=0 (last accessed 26 December 2012).

[62] *Cf* Raymond, Chapter 11 above, at p. 245 ('at this point debate [on this issue] is closed').

INDEX

Lightning Source UK Ltd.
Milton Keynes UK
UKHW011323011218
333162UK00019B/859/P

9 781107 027442